The Jews of Medieval Western Chr

Between the years 1000 and 1500, western Christendom absorbed by conquest and attracted through immigration a growing number of Jews. This community was to make a valuable contribution to rapidly developing European civilization but was also to suffer some terrible setbacks, culminating in a series of expulsions from the more advanced westerly areas of Europe. At the same time, vigorous new branches of world Jewry emerged and a rich new Jewish cultural legacy was created. In this important new historical synthesis, Robert Chazan discusses the Jewish experience over a 500-year period across the entire continent of Europe. As well as being the story of medieval Jewry, the book simultaneously illuminates important aspects of majority life in Europe during this period. This book is essential reading for all students of medieval Jewish history and an important reference for any scholar of medieval Europe.

ROBERT CHAZAN is S. H. and Helen R. Scheuer Professor of Hebrew and Judaic Studies in the Skirball Department of Hebrew and Judaic Studies, New York University. His numerous books and articles on medieval Jewish history include *Fashioning Jewish Identity in Medieval Western Christendom* (Cambridge, 2004).

Cambridge Medieval Textbooks

This is a series of introductions to important topics in medieval history aimed primarily at advanced students and faculty, and is designed to complement the monograph series Cambridge Studies in Medieval Life and Thought. It includes both chronological and thematic approaches and addresses both British and European topics.

For a list of titles in the series, see end of book.

THE JEWS OF MEDIEVAL WESTERN CHRISTENDOM,
1000–1500

ROBERT CHAZAN

CAMBRIDGE
UNIVERSITY PRESS

CAMBRIDGE UNIVERSITY PRESS
Cambridge, New York, Melbourne, Madrid, Cape Town, Singapore, São Paulo

Cambridge University Press
The Edinburgh Building, Cambridge CB2 2RU, UK

Published in the United States of America by Cambridge University Press,
New York

www.cambridge.org
Information on this title: www.cambridge.org/9780521616645

First published 2006

Printed in the United Kingdom at the University Press, Cambridge

A catalogue record for this publication is available from the British Library

ISBN-13 978-0-521-84666-0 hardback
ISBN-10 0-521-84666-8 hardback

ISBN-13 978-0-521-61664-5 paperback
ISBN-10 0-521-61664-6 paperback

For
Jonah and Adam
Gabriel and Nathan
Arlo and Eve

CONTENTS

——————— • ———————

List of maps	*page* ix	
Preface	xi	
Introduction	1	
1	Prior legacies	23
	The Muslim legacy	24
	The Christian legacy	27
	The Jewish legacy	30
2	The pan-European Roman Catholic Church	43
	Theological doctrine	44
	Ecclesiastical policies	51
	Imagery of Judaism and the Jews	66
	Cultural and spiritual creativity: danger, challenge, stimulus	70
	Looking ahead	75
3	The older Jewries of the south	77
	Southern France	78
	Christian Spain	90
	Italy and Sicily	115
4	The newer Jewries of the north: northern France and England	129
	Northern France	131
	England	154

5 The newer Jewries of the north: Germany and
   Eastern Europe   169
   Germany   170
   Eastern Europe   198

6 Material challenges, successes, and failures   209
   Obstacles and attractions   210
   The governing authorities   219
   Successes   231
   The dynamics of deterioration   239

7 Spiritual challenges, successes, and failures   243
   Proselytizing, conversion, and resistance   247
   Strengthening traditional lines of Jewish cultural creativity   257
   Innovative lines of cultural creativity   267
   New and creative Jewish cultures   282

   Epilogue   285

   Notes   289
   Bibliography   313
   Index   321

MAPS

————————— • —————————

1   Europe, circa 1000   *page* xvi

2   Europe, circa 1250   4

3   Europe, 1490   8

PREFACE

———— • ————

This book began with an invitation extended by Cambridge University Press to write a one-volume history of the Jews of medieval western Christendom for its Cambridge Medieval Textbooks series, a series I have long used and admired. The desire of Cambridge University Press to include a volume on the Jews in its distinguished series seemed to me to reflect a sea change in perceptions of the place of the Jews on the medieval scene. Fifty years ago, such an invitation would have been unthinkable, for the broad academic community exhibited little interest in Jewish life in medieval Latin Christendom.[1] Over the past half century, however, scholarly – and even popular – perceptions of the Middle Ages have changed considerably, with the prior sense of a homogeneous and static period giving way to accelerating interest in the diversity and evolution of medieval society, the fracture lines that afflicted it, and its variegated minority communities.

These changes in the study of medieval history have in fact been characteristic of the recent study of Western history in all its periods. Augmented interest in the history of minority communities in a variety of settings and epochs has resulted in the opening of academic portals *inter alia* to historians of the Jews. Jewish history has become an accepted specialty in universities, and academic presses regularly publish scholarship on the Jews of the ancient, medieval, and modern periods. As a result of this new openness, research into the Jewish experience in general and the medieval Jewish experience in particular has proliferated. Scholars in North America, Israel, and Europe have investigated increasingly diverse aspects of medieval Jewish life, resulting in an impressive corpus of new books and articles on the Jews of medieval western Christendom. Innovative questions and perspectives have surfaced regularly, and knowledge of medieval Jewish life has increased exponentially.[2]

The importance of the Cambridge Medieval Textbooks series and the challenge of presenting the new scholarship on medieval Jewry in western Christendom warranted a positive reply on my part to the Press's generous invitation. I very much agreed with the sense that a one-volume history of the Jews in medieval Latin Christendom would be most useful at this point in time. While the Jewish experience in medieval Europe has been treated in the context of overall histories of the Jews and while two one-volume histories of medieval Jewry have recently appeared, the time seems ripe for a new introduction to the Jews of medieval western Christendom.[3]

More personal factors as well influenced my decision to proceed with this project. The first has to do with my prior books. They have all involved carefully delimited topics and manageable bodies of source material. At the same time, I believe – or at least hope – that they have addressed issues of critical significance to the medieval Jewish experience, for example Christian and Jewish imageries of one another, Christian pressures physical and spiritual and Jewish reactions, neglected aspects of medieval Jewish intellectual and spiritual creativity. The challenge of absorbing these earlier studies into a comprehensive treatment of the medieval Jewish experience was appealing. Readers familiar with my prior work will see these earlier investigations reflected throughout this book.

Over and above my writing, my teaching played a critical role in moving me to undertake this book. I have been teaching medieval Jewish history at university level for over forty years now and have taken this teaching responsibility very seriously. I have experimented with a range of organizational schemes for presenting medieval Jewish history and have tinkered with a variety of topical approaches. These teaching efforts have left me with a full appreciation of the difficulties associated with conveying the medieval Jewish experience and with a number of ideas as to how to do so effectively. More than imparting satisfaction with conveying medieval Jewish history, my teaching experience has inspired me to attempt a more focused effort at "getting it right" at last. A voice deep inside assures me that the effort is worthwhile; to be sure, the same voice also suggests that, when this project is finished, I shall still remain somewhat dissatisfied.

I undertook this project fully aware that it would constitute a new experience, in fact a very challenging new experience. I committed myself, for the first time, to writing an extended synthetic history. All my prior books have addressed carefully defined aspects of medieval Jewish history. I have regularly set manageable parameters for these studies and have felt capable of examining all relevant sources in investigating these focused issues. Essentially, I have gathered extensive data, have analyzed them, and have then followed them where they led me. While I have aspired to present important developments on the medieval Jewish scene, my studies have all been limited to specific times and spaces.

The present project differs markedly in its spatial and temporal scope. I propose to discuss Jewish experience stretching across almost the entirety of Europe and spanning five centuries. There is more even than simply vast territory and a lengthy time period. Neither the territory nor the time period is homogeneous. There were, as we shall see rather fully, enormous differences among the various Jewish communities of medieval western Christendom and wide-ranging changes through the centuries. Encompassing these differences and changes constitutes a profound challenge to the historian attempting to make sense of the diversified Jewish experiences in medieval western Christendom. Indeed, to complicate matters yet further, I intend to discuss major developments on both the material and spiritual planes. This study will begin with demographic, economic, and political realities and changes, but will include issues of Jewish identity and Jewish intellectual and spiritual creativity as well.

The vastness of the topic and the richness of the literature have necessitated painful decisions as to coverage or – more precisely – as to inclusion and omission. This book was not intended by the Press or by me to be excessive in length and exhaustive in coverage; it was intended, rather, to provide an overview of the diverse Jewish communities of medieval western Christendom and their material and spiritual experience and to offer analysis of the broad evolutionary patterns of Jewish life in medieval Europe and the key factors influencing those evolutionary patterns. None of the Jewish communities depicted and none of the developments tracked could be treated fully.[4] Decisions as to inclusion and exclusion and the fullness in depiction of those topics covered have been extremely difficult.[5]

Ultimately, these difficult decisions have been made on the basis of an over-arching view of the medieval Jewish experience in medieval western Christendom, a view that will be articulated and will surely give rise to criticism on the part of respected colleagues. It is out of such articulation and criticism that historical knowledge progresses.

The conceptual framework underlying this work proposes that medieval western Christendom was highly ambivalent in its attitude to the growing Jewish minority in its midst, with some elements in Christian society accepting this minority, some rejecting it, and yet others accepting it with reservations and limitations. In response, the Jews themselves viewed the Christian environment with parallel ambivalence, acknowledging Christendom's dynamism and achievements while at the same time fearing it and denigrating it. On the spiritual plane, the same ambivalences are manifest. The Christian majority – heir to a rich set of views of Judaism and the Jews – despised Judaism and the Jews, respected both, and feared both. In turn, the Jews – heirs to a far less developed tradition with respect to Christianity and Christians – forged a new sense of the two, again made up of repulsion, attraction, and fear.

The divergences of the medieval Jewish experience in space and the changes in this experience over time flowed from the working out of the inherent ambivalences on the part of Christian majority and Jewish minority, conditioned by differing circumstances of place and time. Beyond these divergences, however, there is an overriding commonality: both the Christian majority and the Jewish minority were deeply affected by the mutual engagement that took place between 1000 and 1500 CE. Both sides emerged with altered perceptions of one another, for good and ill. Inevitably, minorities are more deeply affected by such interactions than majorities, and our case is no exception. Between 1000 and 1500, the Jewish world was radically transformed in both material and spiritual terms by its encounter with medieval western Christendom. A new constellation of Jewish life was created, and new forms of Judaism emerged.

At times, writing this book has felt like flying over the panorama of medieval Jewish history at 35,000 feet, perceiving and sketching the broadest of outlines, knowing that the fields and towns were filled with living human beings, but failing inevitably to discern and portray them in their full reality. Such of course is the nature of a survey. I have attempted to compensate a bit by introducing into this account of the Jews of medieval western Christendom an occasional reconstruction of specific events and personalities and – perhaps more important – by citing recurrently the sources from our period. All this is done in order to recover somewhat the elusive sense of particularity that a survey risks losing. In general, readers would be well served by keeping at their side one or another collection of translated medieval sources, into which they might periodically dip.[6]

Like all volumes in the Cambridge Medieval Textbooks series, this one also is intended for an audience of literate and interested readers. Some of these readers will be university undergraduate and graduate students; some will be scholars of a variety of periods of the Jewish past or of medieval history; some will be interested lay readers. I hope that all these disparate groups of readers will find an account that is comprehensible, stimulating, and satisfying, albeit by no means exhaustive. The experience of medieval Jewry in western Christendom has taken on great symbolic significance in subsequent Christian and Jewish thinking. This symbolic significance has often led to gross over-simplification and distortion. I hope the present overview will contribute in some measure to a more balanced sense of the Jews as a vital element on the medieval scene and of western Christendom during the Middle Ages as a formative period in the evolution of subsequent Jewish life.

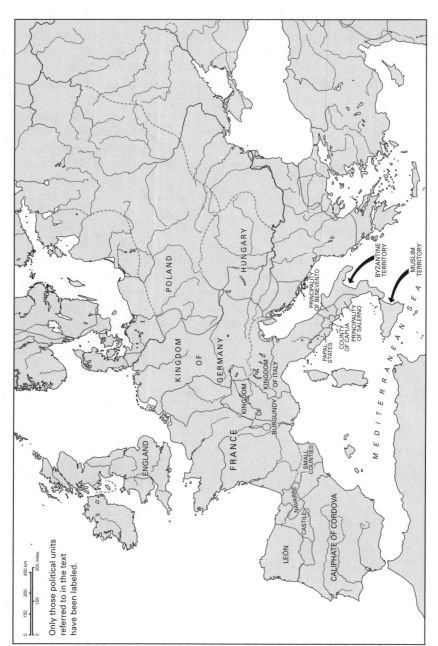

Map 1 Europe, circa 1000

Only those political units
referred to in the text
have been labeled.

ENGLAND

POLAND

HUNGARY

KINGDOM
OF
GERMANY

KINGDOM
OF
BURGUNDY

KINGDOM
OF
FRANCE

KINGDOM
OF ITALY

PRINCIPALITY
OF BENEVENTO

PAPAL
STATES

COUNTY
OF CAPUA

PRINCIPALITY
OF SALERNO

BYZANTINE
TERRITORY

MUSLIM
TERRITORY

M E D I T E R R A N E A N   S E A

LEÓN

CASTILE

NAVARRE

SMALL
COUNTIES

CALIPHATE OF CORDOVA

0   150   300   450 km
0   150   300 miles

INTRODUCTION

——————— • ———————

An observer viewing world Jewry in the year 1000 would have readily discerned an obvious Jewish demographic distribution and an equally obvious configuration of Jewish creativity. The oldest, largest, and most creative Jewish communities were located in the Muslim sphere, stretching from Mesopotamia westward through the eastern littoral of the Mediterranean Sea, across North Africa, and over onto the Iberian peninsula. Somewhat smaller, but still sizeable and venerable were the Jewish communities of the Byzantine Empire. Our putative observer might have noted, as an afterthought, the small Jewish settlements in western Christendom, huddled along the northern shores of the Mediterranean Sea, in Italy, southern France, and northern Spain; he might have – reasonably enough – not even bothered to mention them, for they would hardly have seemed worthy of serious attention.

Our observer would almost certainly have known that this pattern of Jewish demography and creativity had been established more than a thousand years earlier, long before the rise of Islam to its position of power during the seventh century. He would have been aware that, subsequent to the exile of the Jews from their homeland in the sixth pre-Christian century, two major centers of Jewish life had emerged, one as the result of Jewish resettlement in Palestine and the other as a result of the decision of Jews to secure for themselves a permanent place in Mesopotamia. He would have known that the great religious–political leaders of world Jewry had been the patriarchs of Palestinian Jewry and the exilarchs of Mesopotamian Jewry;

that the classical texts of post-biblical Judaism were the (Palestinian) Mishnah, the Jerusalem (Palestinian) Talmud, and the Babylonian (Mesopotamian) Talmud; that the distinguished rabbis whose teachings were enshrined in the Mishnah and the two Talmuds were all residents of either the Holy Land or the Mesopotamian territory that Jews anachronistically called Babylonia.

Our hypothetical observer would also have recalled that Palestinian Jews had, from a fairly early date, made their way westward, creating new centers of Jewish life all along the Mediterranean shorelines. He would have been aware that the centers in what are today Syria and Egypt were the oldest and largest of these western communities. Newer and smaller settlements stretched out all along the southern and northern coastlines of the Mediterranean Sea – across North Africa, through Asia Minor, and into what is today Italy, southern France, and Spain.

With the rise of Islam during the seventh century and its remarkable conquests, the overwhelming majority of world Jewry fell under the rule of the new religion and the empire built upon it. The only Jewries left outside the realm of Islam were the Jewish communities of the shrunken Byzantine Empire, along the northeastern shores of the Mediterranean Sea, and those of the relatively backward western Christian states in Italy, southern France, and northern Spain, along the northwestern shores of that same sea.

While we do not have the kind of observations just now suggested from the year 1000, we do possess the writings of a European Jew who traveled from west to east during the middle decades of the twelfth century. This Jew, Benjamin of Tudela, did not attempt the kind of assessments just now suggested. However, his travelogue – generally rather dry and boring – does provide a first-hand sense of the various areas of Jewish settlement he encountered.[1]

Benjamin made his way down the Ebro River from his home town, reached the Mediterranean, visited some major Spanish port cities, traversed much of southern France, and crossed over into Italy and down the peninsula. Throughout this portion of his journey, he encountered a variety of Jewish communities. The largest of these numbered a few hundred souls or males or households.[2] When Benjamin reached the Byzantine Empire, he encountered much greater urban enclaves and much larger Jewish communities. In Constantinople, he found a city far exceeding in size, wealth, and culture anything he had seen further west. The Jewish community numbered some three thousand. Again, it is not clear whether this means souls, males, or households. In any case, the Jewish community of Constantinople was many times larger than any Benjamin had encountered in the Roman Catholic sphere of southern Europe.

When Benjamin entered the realm of Islam, he was overwhelmed by what he found. The city of Baghdad, then arguably the greatest city in the Western world, captivated him. His description of the size and splendor of the city reveals an utterly enthralled visitor. The Jewish communities of the Islamic realm in general far surpassed in size and strength those of the Roman Catholic world from which he came. In Damascus, Benjamin found three thousand Jews; in Alexandria, seven thousand Jews; in Baghdad, the staggering number of forty thousand Jews.[3] In Baghdad, according to Benjamin, there were twenty-eight synagogues and a Jewish officialdom that enjoyed remarkable prestige and respect in the caliph's court. While Benjamin limits himself to fairly specific and often pedestrian observations, his travelogue indicates clearly an Islamic realm far superior to Byzantium and Roman Catholic Europe, and Jewish communities that reflect the same ordering of size, strength, and creativity. Even though Benjamin traveled at a time when the balance of power had already begun to shift, he still found that the Jewries under Muslim domination were larger and more fully developed than those under Christian control.

Pressed to predict what the future might hold, our hypothetical observer in the year 1000 would have assumed that the known configuration of Jewish life would surely last into the indeterminate future. In general, of course, most of us have great difficulty in imagining radically altered circumstances. Such a lack of imagination would have hardly been the only factor influencing our observer, however. For there was nothing in the year 1000 to suggest that radical change was in the offing. The constellation of world power appeared remarkably stable. Islam's domination seemed to be challenged seriously by no one, neither the Greek Christians of the eastern sectors of the Mediterranean nor the Latin Christians of the western sectors of Europe. Our observer of the year 1000 would surely have concluded that the contemporary power structure was unlikely to shift and that Jewish life would thus continue along the lines currently discernible.

Benjamin, traveling and writing in the middle of the twelfth century, had the benefit of a century and a half of change. By time he made his journey, western Christian forces had driven the Muslims

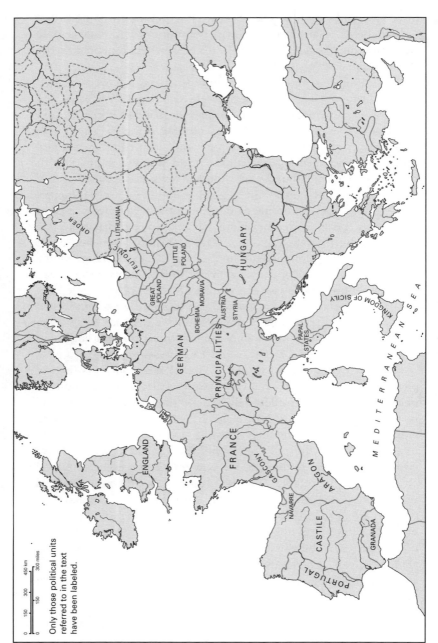

Map 2 Europe, circa 1250

Only those political units referred to in the text have been labeled.

0   150   300   450 km
0   150   300 miles

ENGLAND

FRANCE

GASCONY

NAVARRE

ARAGON

CASTILE

PORTUGAL

GRANADA

GERMAN PRINCIPALITIES

BOHEMIA

MORAVIA

AUSTRIA

STYRIA

GREAT POLAND

LITTLE POLAND

LITHUANIA

TEUTONIC ORDER

HUNGARY

ITALY

PAPAL STATES

KINGDOM OF SICILY

MEDITERRANEAN SEA

out of their Italian strongholds and had begun to push the Muslims southward on the Iberian peninsula. Western Christian armies had even managed to journey eastward and conquer portions of the Holy Land, including the symbolically important city of Jerusalem. Yet it is unlikely that even Benjamin could have envisioned the further changes in the offing.

Were our hypothetical observer of the year 1000 in a position to view world Jewry in the year 1250, halfway through our period, and again in the year 1500, he would have been stunned by the changes. While the Jewries of the Muslim world remained in place in the years 1250 and 1500, they were well on their way to losing their position of demographic and creative eminence. They were in the process of being supplanted in their physical and cultural primacy by the diverse Jewish communities of western Christendom. The rise of Latin Christendom to its central role in the Western world, achieved from the eleventh through the thirteenth centuries, brought in its wake – not surprisingly – a parallel ascendancy of the Jewish communities it harbored and attracted.

Periodically – but not all that often – new powers have erupted from fringe areas and radically altered the power structure of the Western world. Such an unanticipated eruption and restructuring took place during the seventh century, when the forces of Islam exploded unexpectedly out of the Arabian peninsula and over-whelmed both the Neo-Persian and Byzantine empires. A more recent example of this restructuring has involved the rise of the United States to its central position in the West, in the process usurping the hegemony long associated with such European powers as England, France, Germany, and Spain. It was between the eleventh and the thirteenth centuries that these European powers – especially England, France, and (Christian) Spain – emerged from their rel-atively backward state and began to dominate the Western world. The rapid and unexpected emergence of Roman Catholic western Christendom transformed the West and, in the process, realigned the pattern of world Jewish population, authority, and creativity that had remained relatively static for almost a millennium and a half. As a result of this seismic shift in the world power structure, the Jews became and have remained a European and eventually North Atlantic people.[4]

Herein lies the enormous significance of the period we shall study for Jewish history. This era of roughly five hundred years – approximately 1000 to 1500 – established an entirely new pattern of Jewish settlement and civilization. The geographic lexicon of the Jewish people had heretofore been almost entirely Near Eastern; Jerusalem, Tiberias, Antioch, Damascus, Sura, Baghdad, Alexandria, Cairo were dominant and resonant names. Now, new names came to the fore – Mainz, Cologne, Paris, London, Toledo, Madrid, Cracow, Warsaw, Vilna, and eventually New York, Chicago, and Los Angeles as well. The earlier Semitic languages of the Jewish people – Hebrew, Aramaic, Arabic – declined, to be replaced by the languages of the West – German, French, Spanish, and English. Political ideas and ideals underwent radical alteration, as did cultural and religious norms and aspirations. It is impossible to exaggerate the importance of these changes.

The relocation of the center of Jewish gravity from the Middle East and North Africa to Europe involved, above all else, a new religious and cultural ambiance. During the period under consideration, the Jews established themselves firmly within the Christian orbit. To be sure, the history of Christian–Jewish relations did not begin in the year 1000. Christianity was, after all, born in the Jewish community of Palestine. Fairly quickly, however, the religious vision centered around the figure of Jesus of Nazareth won adherents beyond Palestinian Jewry. The original leadership of the Jesus movement had been entirely Jewish; as that movement evolved into Christianity, new and gentile leadership came to the fore. The rapid spread of Christianity took place outside of Palestine, across the length and breadth of the Roman Empire, and involved a largely gentile population. Despite its Jewish roots, Christianity established itself as a separate religious faith, the patrimony of a set of non-Jewish peoples.

So long as the vast majority of Jews lived outside the orbit of Christian power, the Jewish issue was muted for the Christian authorities. Church leaders, it is true, produced an extensive anti-Jewish literature during the first Christian millennium. Much of that literature, however, was theoretical, focused on buttressing convictions as to the rejection of Old Israel (the Jews) and the election of a New Israel (the Christians). Genuine engagement with real Jews was, however, limited. From the Jewish side, the lack of engagement with Christianity is yet more marked. Up until the year 1000 and well beyond, we possess not one single anti-Christian work composed by Jews living within western Christendom.[5] Down through the end of the first millennium, the Jews of the world, concentrated in the realm of Islam, were hardly obsessed with Christianity and Christians.[6]

With the displacement of the center of Jewish population to western Christendom, serious engagement from both sides had to begin. Jews and Judaism penetrated the Christian consciousness in a far more immediate way than heretofore. This meant the augmentation of anti-Jewish argumentation, the adumbration of more extensive policies for the Jewish minority living within western Christendom, the evolution (perhaps deterioration would be more accurate) of Christian imagery of Jews, and the eruption of new forms of anti-Jewish animus and violence. For the Jewish minority, the changes were equally momentous. Jewish life was now constrained by new policies and new dangers; Jews were now regularly exposed to the blandishments of the majority Christian religious faith; Jewish leaders had to learn more about that majority faith and to fashion anti-Christian argumentation that would enable their Jewish followers to resist missionizing pressures and remain loyal to Judaism.

The story of medieval Jewry in western Christendom constitutes a critical element in the saga of the Jewish people; at the same time, this story illuminates significant aspects of majority life in medieval western Christendom. As scholarly attention has shifted away from the leadership groups on the medieval scene – popes, bishops, emperors, kings, and dukes – toward a broader swath of humanity, awareness has developed of the variegated nature of what once seemed a monolithic society. The Jews have come to occupy a significant place in recent study of medieval western Christendom. They provide an intriguing litmus test for treatment of out-groups in an overwhelmingly Christian society; they are especially valuable in that – unlike most other out-groups – they have left a literature of their own, to supplement the data available from the majority perspective.

Indeed, for most of the time period we shall be studying, and most of the geographic areas under consideration, there was a very special quality to the Jews as a minority presence in western Christendom. Generally, the Jews constituted the only legitimate dissenting religious group in all of society.[7] Minority status is never easy; to be the only legitimate religious minority is even more precarious. Often, as we shall see, the negative aspects of this minority status have been highlighted, and there surely was much that was limiting and harmful. At the same time, the successes of the venture should by no means be overlooked. In many ways, the Christian majority – or at least

Map 3 Europe, 1490

Only those political units
referred to in the text
have been labeled.

LITHUANIA

POLAND

LANDS OF
THE BOHEMIAN
CROWN

HUNGARY

GERMAN

PRINCIPALITIES

NAPLES

PAPAL
STATES

SICILY

MEDITERRANEAN SEA

ENGLAND

FLANDERS
BRABANT

BURGUNDY

SAVOY

FRANCE

ARAGON

NAVARRE

CASTILE

PORTUGAL

GRANADA

0   150   300   450 km
0   150   300 miles

elements of it – and the Jewish minority cooperated effectively in fostering Jewish presence and activity that proved of immediate and long-term benefit to majority and minority alike.

The spatial boundaries of this study are easy to delineate and are hardly controversial. The designation "western Christendom" points to the distinction between the eastern and western areas of the Christian world, with the eastern centered in the imperial court at Constantinople and the western centered in the papal court at Rome. On another level, eastern Christendom was constructed around Greek language and culture, while western Christendom was constructed around Latin, its linguistic derivatives, and its culture. With the passage of time, these two segments of the Christian world pulled further away from one another. This process of disengagement and differentiation culminated in the bloody Fourth Crusade of 1204 and the sacking by western Christian troops of the eastern Christian imperial city of Constantinople.[8]

While there was considerable unity within western Christendom – religious, cultural, and political – that unity should by no means be overstated. This vast area harbored considerable differences as well. The fault lines were both horizontal and vertical. Perhaps the most significant fault line lay in the distinction between the Mediterranean lands of southern Europe and the more remote lands of the north. The Mediterranean lands of the south had been fully absorbed into the Roman Empire and had been richly infused with Roman civilization and culture. Remnants of Roman civilization and culture were (and are) everywhere palpable across the southern tier of Europe. In contrast, the lands of northern Europe had been only brushed by the contact with Rome and had preserved much of their Germanic heritage.[9] In a general way, the southern sector of medieval western Christendom was far more advanced in the year 1000 than were the areas of the north. That situation, however, was to change rapidly and dramatically.

The remarkable vitalization of western Christendom subsequent to the year 1000 took place most markedly in the heretofore backward north. By the year 1500, England and France had emerged as large and powerful monarchies on the Western scene, contesting Spain for preeminence. Indeed, part of the French kingdom's success lay in its absorption of previously independent southern territories into the expanded royal domain, centered in the north. Paris and London were the greatest cities of medieval western Christendom by the year

1500; strikingly, they had both been backward provincial towns five hundred years earlier. There is perhaps no more eloquent testimony to the centrality of northern Europe in the great awakening of medieval western Christendom that took place between 1000 and 1500.[10]

There is a second major fault line as well, one that proceeds on a vertical axis, and that is the distinction – particularly noteworthy in the north – between western Europe, on the one hand, and central and eastern Europe on the other. In the year 1000, the most potent political authority in western Christendom seemed to be the German emperor. Rooted in imperial lore and tradition, the German throne seemed likely to remain the strongest political power among the emerging states of western Christendom. Such was not, however, to be the case. The far less imposing kings of France, England, and Spain learned how to manipulate the feudal system to their advantage, slowly converting local rule and royal prerogative into large, stable, and increasingly puissant monarchies. Germany slipped far behind its more westerly neighbors in economic development, political maturity, and cultural creativity. Further east, at the fringe of medieval western Christendom, such kingdoms as Hungary and Poland slowly began to develop by the end of our period.

Finally, there is yet one more important geographic distinction, involving interior areas of western Christendom and those exposed to outside forces. On many levels, differences emerged between those lands generally insulated from outside aggression and with a relatively homogeneous population (in which Jews were prominent as the only legitimate dissenters), on the one hand, and territories that bordered on other realms and in which populations were heterogeneous, on the other.[11] The lands of the east – Italy in the south and Hungary and Poland in the north – were very much exposed to external intrusion, as was the Iberian peninsula in the southwest. There were salient differences between exposed and interior areas in terms of majority self-image and in terms of the populations with which the Christian majority (even in a few instances the Christian ruling minority) had to deal.

We shall have to be constantly aware of these important geographic distinctions. They will play a key role in understanding the roots of Jewish life in the south, the establishment of important Jewish communities in the rapidly developing north, the banishment of these new Jewish centers to the eastern peripheries of northern Europe toward the end of our period, and the eventual disappearance of almost all Jewish life from the western sectors of Europe by the year 1500. It is impossible to make the kind of generalizations necessary in an overview such as this without occasionally slighting one or another geographic sector of large and complex medieval western Christendom. Ideally, there should be available more focused studies of medieval Jewish life for each of the geographic regions included in medieval western Christendom.[12]

While the geographic parameters of this study are fairly easy to specify, the temporal boundaries are somewhat more difficult. The designation "medieval" is fraught with problems. Medievals would never of course have identified themselves as medievals; they very much saw themselves as *moderni*, that is to say moderns, the latest link in the chain of human history. The terms "Middle Ages" and "medieval" came into being as the medieval synthesis began to unravel; they were terms of opprobrium, used to highlight the alleged backwardness and benightedness of the period that stretched from late antiquity to the onset of the Renaissance. Generally, this negative sense of the Middle Ages focused on the purportedly suffocating centrality of religion in every sphere of human endeavor. This centrality of religion – monotheistic religion at that – contrasted with the more open society of ancient Rome and with the more open society that the men and women of the Renaissance hoped to create. Out of this backlash the pejorative term "medieval" was fashioned.

In practical terms, how does this view of the Middle Ages translate into tangible dating for the beginning and end of the medieval period? This is an extremely difficult question to answer. Scholars have differed regularly as to the onset and conclusion of the Middle Ages. Happily, for our purposes, the debate over the beginnings of the Middle Ages is irrelevant. As already noted, significant Jewish presence in medieval western Christendom did not emerge until the end of the first Christian millennium, the point in time when the region began its long ascent toward dominance in the Western world. Thus, whatever "medieval" might mean in the abstract, for this specific study of the Jews of medieval western Christendom it identifies a period that begins around the year 1000.[13]

The end point for this study is more problematic. Once again, there is considerable scholarly dispute as to marking the close of the Middle Ages. Clearly, the Middle Ages ended at different points in time in diverse sectors of western Christendom – generally earlier in the western areas and later in the eastern areas. Since by the fourteenth century the process of removal of the Jewish population to the eastern edges of western Christendom was well under way; for the bulk of European Jewry medieval conditions ended quite late. For the purposes of this study, however, the adjective "medieval" will be attached to western Christendom, not to the Jews. This will be a history of the Jews in medieval western Christendom, rather than a history of medieval Jewish circumstances in western Christendom. As the medieval synthesis began to disintegrate, toward the close of the fifteenth century, our story will conclude, even though Jews continued to live under medieval conditions for centuries to come in the northeastern areas of Europe.

The divergences within the Jewish communities of medieval western Christendom make the terminal date of 1500 sometimes irrelevant, sometimes inappropriate, and in one major case highly appropriate. The year 1500 is obviously irrelevant to English Jewry, whose history came to a close in 1290, and to French Jewry, whose creative history ended in 1306. It means little for the history of German and eastern European Jewish history. The year 1500 is actually problematic for the history of Italian Jewry, for which most historians see the fifteenth and sixteenth centuries as a unified epoch.[14] 1500 is of course highly appropriate for Iberian Jewry, given the expulsion from Aragon and Castile in 1492 and from Portugal in 1497. Again, the date has been chosen out of consideration of the Christian majority, rather than any special sector of the diversified Jewish minority.

Thus, the temporal boundaries of this study will be the years 1000 and 1500. During this five-hundred-year period, the old Jewish communities of the south expanded markedly and a new set of Jewish communities was created in the north; both sets of Jewish communities developed through the thirteenth century with measures of success and failure; they disintegrated subsequently in the more advanced areas of western Europe and were reconstituted on the eastern peripheries of western Christendom, especially in the north. Despite all the shortcomings and failures, the bulk of world Jewry made its transition into the rapidly developing Christian orbit, a change that would not be undone down to the present.

In some ways, the shortest word in my title – "of" – has presented the most difficulties. I vacillated regularly between *The Jews in Medieval Western Christendom* and *The Jews of Medieval Western Christendom*. The first title suggests the relative isolation of the Jews whom we shall be studying; the second integrates them somewhat into their

European ambience. I ultimately opted for the latter title, out of the strong conviction that medieval Europe was far more than simply a terrain on which Jewish life unfolded. Problems aside – and they were manifold – the Jews upon whom we shall focus were very much a part of the medieval European scene. They spoke the language of their land; they were integrated into the economic and political structures of their societies; their cultural and religious lives were deeply affected by their environment; they influenced – for good and ill – the majority ambience within which they found themselves.[15]

Reconstructions of the past are ultimately determined by the source materials bequeathed to posterity. Where the data are rich, the reconstructions can be dense and nuanced; where the data are thin, so too must be the historical account. To what extent are sources available for reconstructing the story of the Jews of western Christendom from 1000 to 1500? How fortunate or unfortunate are we with regard to the evidence? The simple answer is that we are moderately fortunate. The data are far richer than those available for the first half of the Middle Ages; they are, at the same time, far poorer than those available for reconstructing the experience of modern Jewish communities. Not surprisingly, availability of source materials for reconstructing the history of the Jews in medieval western Christendom is much influenced by the temporal and geographical distinctions just now drawn.

During the period between 1000 and 1500, as the various sectors of medieval western Christendom and their Jewries matured, increasing quantities of source material were compiled and maintained. As we approach the close of this period, the sources – at least in certain parts of western Christendom – become truly copious and diversified. As the same time, the geographic distinctions just noted played a significant role. The southern and northwestern sectors of Europe, for example Italy, Spain, southern France, England, and northern France, provide extremely rich documentation; the north-central and north-easterly areas, for example Germany, Hungary, and Poland, provide far less. The removal of Jews from the more advanced areas of western Christendom has deprived us of considerable data; the Jews, as noted, relocated in those areas where documentation remains sparse. Thus, we are differentially provided with data. For some periods and places, the data are rich; for others, they are poor.

Since the focus of this study is the interrelated activities of majority and minority in fostering Jewish presence and creativity in medieval western Christendom, we shall necessarily depend on the evidence provided by both the Christian majority and the Jewish minority. With regard to the former, one of the most important developments of our period was the maturation of authority, both religious and temporal. A critical element in this maturation was the creation of stable institutions and reliable record keeping.

The first truly potent institution to emerge in medieval western Christendom was the papacy. The papal court quickly developed all the appurtenances of power, including scrupulous record keeping. Papal documentation grew exponentially from the twelfth century on. While Jews constituted a fairly minor element within the complex of Church priorities, they were important enough to generate thousands of papal documents and conciliar decrees. This rich documentation was among the first bodies of non-Jewish source material to be exploited for reconstructing the history of medieval Jewry.[16]

The pioneering secular authority in record keeping was Angevin England, beginning in the latter decades of the twelfth century. The records of the Angevin monarchy are extremely rich, and data concerning the Jews are copious. Indeed, no one has been yet able to control this vast documentation. At the same time that the royal records were multiplying at an astonishing rate, so too were the archives of the various ecclesiastical institutions of England. An increasingly large number of literary sources – histories, poetry, early theater pieces – were produced and preserved as well. Thus the relatively small English Jewish community is documented with a richness nowhere else available for medieval western Christendom at this early point in time.[17]

The French monarchy matured slightly more slowly than its English rival, and the same is true for its archives as well. Since the Jews were expelled from France at the beginning of the fourteenth century, the explosion of royal documentation that began during the thirteenth century does not fully illuminate the medieval experience of French Jews. At the same time, the rich local court and notarial records of southern France have preserved valuable evidence of Jewish life and activity. An increasing volume of Christian literary evidence also began to accumulate prior to the expulsion.

The kingdoms of medieval Spain were yet slower to develop the institutional and archival maturity of England, but eventually they did. Since medieval Spanish Jewry far outlasted its English counterpart, by time we reach the latter decades of the thirteenth century and on into the fourteenth and fifteenth centuries, Spanish records become increasingly voluminous.[18] Much interesting research is currently being done on the Jews of Spain, based on the available documentary evidence.[19] Once more, literary evidence grew at a rapid pace as well. Both historical accounts and belle-lettristic compositions serve to round out the evidentiary base for reconstructing the history of the Jews of medieval Spain.

For Italy, the proliferation of principalities and the longevity of the Jewish communities have resulted in extensive archival deposits. A voluminous set of documents has been published over the past few decades, providing a rich evidentiary base for the reconstruction of Jewish life all across the peninsula, at least for the latter centuries of our period.[20] The process of working through these materials and integrating them into a synthetic view of the Jewish experience in medieval Italy has proven most difficult. In the north-central and northeastern areas of Europe – Germany, Hungary, and Poland – the volume of non-Jewish source materials diminishes.

There are, unfortunately, almost no Jewish documentary materials available from our period. Record keeping within the Jewish communities of medieval western Christendom may well have begun during our period; however, the upheavals occasioned by expulsion resulted in the destruction of most of the documentary evidence created by the Jews of medieval western Christendom. Thus, our major Jewish sources are literary compositions of one or another kind.

Most valuable for our purposes are historical narratives. Medieval Jews – in western Christendom and elsewhere – were not deeply drawn to the writing of broad histories, as were their Christian neighbors. Recurrently, however, unusual events moved Jewish observers to record what they had seen or heard, sometimes in order to warn contemporaries against danger, sometimes in order to memorialize fallen heroes, sometimes in order to lodge a plea before the divine audience, and sometimes in order to engage difficult questions associated with Jewish suffering. The resultant narrative records, sparse though they are, provide invaluable evidence of the minority perspective on important developments on the medieval scene. The related literary genre of poetry, especially liturgical poetry, provides similar evidence of important developments, although generally providing less in the way of specific detail.[21]

A genre that became increasingly popular with the passage of time was polemical literature, which constituted a Jewish response to enhanced Christian proselytizing. While there is an element of the timeless – and often an element of the tedious – in polemical literature, in many instances these compositions provide valuable evidence of accelerating religious pressure exerted by the majority on the minority and of creative minority response.[22]

The literary genres most favored by the Jews of medieval western Christendom revolved around what the Jews viewed as their two revelations, which they designated their Written Torah, i.e. the Hebrew Bible, and their Oral Torah, i.e. the classics of rabbinic teachings. Biblical and talmudic commentaries and codes of Jewish law, which are central to an understanding of Jewish cultural and intellectual activity, generally shed minimal light on the quotidian lives of the Jews of medieval western Christendom. The one popular genre of rabbinic law that does provide considerable insight into everyday Jewish life is the rabbinic *responsum*. Beginning with a query, normally generated by a real-life situation, the medieval *responsa* literature reveals much about the interactions between Jews and their non-Jewish neighbors, as well as much about internal interactions within the Jewish community. As was true for the non-Jewish materials, so too the Jewish evidence is spotty, occasionally extremely rich and sometimes quite poor.

Specific data – sometimes rich and sometimes sparse – provide the underpinning for modern historical reconstructions. In approaching this particular historical reconstruction, the first important decision I had to make involved the alternative paths of narrative versus topical organization, each with advantages and disadvantages. Given the remarkable changes in Jewish fate from the year 1000 to 1500, my decision has been – probably not surprisingly – for narrative reconstruction. This option enables fullest focus on the evolution of the Jewish communities of medieval Latin Christendom. The major disadvantage of this choice is the loss of social history. Topics such as religious practice and the role of family and women do not lend themselves well to the basic narrative format I have utilized.

Having opted for a basically narrative approach, I quickly concluded that the complex nature of medieval western Christendom and its Jewish communities precluded a single narrative treatment. The Jewries of medieval Latin Christendom were simply too divergent one from another to allow for one encompassing narrative. Thus, the narrative account of Jewish fate in medieval western Christendom has been divided into four chapters – the first treating the one major pan-European institution, that is the Roman Catholic Church; the second describing the older Jewish communities of southern Europe; the third focused on the new Jewish communities of the northwest, i.e. northern France and England; and the fourth portraying the Jewish communities of north-central and northeastern Europe, i.e. the German lands, Hungary, and Poland.[23] These four narrative chapters will then be followed by a chapter that attempts to draw together the material aspects – positive and negative – of medieval European Jewish experience and a second chapter that attempts to make sense of the Jewish spiritual and intellectual experience.[24]

The efflorescence of studies in medieval Jewish history has been noted, and it has raised a number of important issues, two of which deserve to be addressed. In the first place, as the parameters of interest in medieval western Christendom have expanded, and as the Jews, along with other marginal groups, have become increasingly a focus of interest, the circle of those reconstructing the medieval Jewish experience has – happily – expanded. In addition to the more traditional group of historians whose training and central interest has been in the Jewish past, a growing number of general medievalists have devoted themselves to projects involving the Jews of medieval western Christendom.[25] This development has contributed richly to our expanding knowledge of the Jews of medieval Europe. On occasion, there has seemed to be a tension between treatment of the Jews within the context of overall Jewish history and acknowledgement of the embeddedness of these Jews in their medieval milieu.[26] The stance of this study will be that neither context can be dismissed; in fact, the combination is what shaped the fate of the Jews of medieval western Christendom. For this reason, the book will insist on acknowledgement of both the diachronic and the synchronic aspects of the Jewish experience, that is to say the Jewish experience as shaped to an extent by the overall trajectory of the Jewish past and the Jewish experience as shaped by the specific contours of one or another area of Europe. The book thus begins with discussion of the legacies imposed upon and introduced by the Jews of medieval Latin Christendom prior to indicating how these legacies were preserved and altered in the new European contexts. The dual focus on the diachronic and synchronic will be maintained throughout.

The expanded perspectives brought to the study of medieval history in general and medieval Jewish history in particular raise yet another important issue. As noted, attention has moved from the leadership groups on the medieval scene – both lay and ecclesiastical – to the more nuanced sense of medieval society as composed of numerous elements and classes, each of which must be understood in its own terms to the extent possible. The lively new interest in the Jews of medieval western Christendom in fact flows from this new and more open stance on the part of scholars. However, in writing a composite history of the Jews of medieval western Christendom, I have found myself forced to make some assessments I would have preferred not to make, to highlight certain issues and to submerge others. In effect, I have had to move in the direction of identifying "major" facets of medieval Jewish experience. I have found this necessity distasteful, but unavoidable.

Opting for a basically narrative structure necessitates some central image or set of images, often called a meta-narrative or a master narrative. While regularly lamented, this imagery is in fact indispensable. Data must be organized in some coherent fashion, and the master narrative affords this coherence. To be sure, the data and the imagery must ultimately reinforce one another. Radical disjuncture between the data and the master narrative suggests that the latter is inappropriate.

Quite often, master narratives turn out to be quite judgmental, in effect to reflect one or another ideological predisposition. The history of the Jews in medieval western Christendom has conjured up much negative imagery among the descendants of these Jews. For subsequent Jewish memory, the Jewish experience in medieval Latin Christendom has been synonymous with persecution and violence; it has meant bloody crusading assaults, anti-Jewish slanders and the popular attacks they spawned, the dreaded inquisition and the pain it inflicted. These memories have been deeply embedded in the ritual and liturgy of medieval and modern Jews.[27] While persecution and suffering have been projected as *leitmotifs* of the two-thousand-year experience of Jewry in exile, an overwhelming majority of the catastrophes memorialized in post-exilic Jewish ritual and liturgy derive from experience under medieval Christian rule.

As noted and analyzed by Yosef Hayim Yerushalmi, history writing was undertaken only fitfully by medieval and early modern Jews. That limited body of historical writing very much reinforced the popular perception of medieval Christian persecution and Jewish suffering.[28] When fuller integration into historically conscious nineteenth-century European society stimulated the onset of modern history writing within the Jewish world, the prior memory patterns created the framework through which historical data were interpreted. For the first great historian of the Jews, Heinrich Graetz, the dominant patterns of pre-modern Jewish history were suffering inflicted by the outside – preeminently Christian – world and heroic Jewish commitment to life of the intellect through which the suffering was transcended. When Graetz's romantic and intellectually oriented framework was challenged by a newer nationalist and more specifically Zionist historiography, the emphasis on persecution and suffering was yet more pronounced, with the Jewish experience in medieval Latin Christendom once again highlighted, without the redeeming creativity suggested by Graetz.

Majority Christian perceptions of the Jewish experience in medieval western Christendom have been similarly simplistic and one-sided. While this experience looms very large in Jewish memory, its impact is considerably reduced in Christian memory. The little recollection that remains is, once again, highly negative, although with an opposing valence. For Christians, the folk recollections involved Jewish hostility, which took a number of forms, including political treachery, for example bringing the Muslims onto the Iberian peninsula during the eighth century; vicious anti-Christian rage, which led Jews to murder; and the harm inflicted by Jewish moneylenders and moneylending. For Christian memory, there was no counterpart to Graetz's insistence on Jewish creativity; there was no awareness of the Jews as involved in anything other than relating negatively to the Christian majority.

General medieval historiography has likewise been affected by much ideological prejudgment, both negative and positive. As noted, the very terms "Middle Ages" and "medieval" reflect damning indictments made by Renaissance thinkers, determined to forge a new European civilization. For the men and women of the Enlightenment, the Middle Ages constituted a deplorable interlude in European history. Not surprisingly, rejection of these negative perspectives resulted in the creation of a highly romanticized view of medieval Latin Christendom, a world viewed in this camp as rich in ideals and meaningful achievements, enlivened by a great Church and chivalric commitments, achieving heights of human creativity. Again, the relation of these views of the Middle Ages to important assessments of nineteenth- and twentieth-century realities and issues is patent.

Recent historiography – both Jewish and general – has moved in new and different directions. Historians of the Jews have come to see their Jewish subjects in all periods as living within majority environments that challenged them in multifarious ways – not only through persecution and violence – and that stimulated the Jewish minority to wide-ranging creativity. For the study of Jewish life in medieval western Christendom, this has meant a decided movement away from the folk and earlier historiographic emphasis on suffering and toward a fuller appreciation of the many dimensions – both positive and negative – of the Jewish experience in medieval Europe. At the same time, as the study of medieval western Christendom in general has abandoned its earlier focus on the ecclesiastical and secular authorities, the tendency toward the judgmental has diminished markedly, replaced by a desire to understand the complexities of medieval European society and life.

The present account of the Jews in medieval western Christendom is very much anchored in the new tendencies discernible among historians of the Jews and historians of medieval Europe. It begins by rejecting the sense of the medieval Jewish experience as consisting essentially of suffering. To the contrary, one of the most striking aspects of the Jewish experience in medieval western Christendom involves the growing number of Jews who became part of the Christian ambience. To be sure, some of these Jews came into Christendom involuntarily via conquest; others, however, made a conscious decision to leave the Muslim world and to immigrate into Christendom, which suggests positive imagery of Christian society on the part of such Jews. Even those Jews who passed into Christian territory via conquest still had the option of leaving and generally chose not to exercise that option. Perhaps more strikingly yet, as the situation of the Jews in medieval western Christendom deteriorated, the overwhelming majority of these Jews opted to stay within their Christian ambience, rather than abandon it.

The changing material fortunes of the Jews in medieval western Christendom will be tracked carefully, with no sense that Jewish fate was preordained from the outset. There were positive factors working on Jewish fate and negative factors as well. Both sides of the story will be presented. There was certainly enough of the positive to encourage considerable voluntary Jewish migration into medieval Latin Christendom and to maintain the desire of most Jews to remain with its confines. The decline of Jewish life is palpable as we move into the fourteenth and fifteenth centuries, and that decline will necessitate considerable description and analysis. There is, however, no intention to project a teleological vision of Jewish history in medieval western Christendom, a sense that Jewish life was doomed in this environment from the outset. Put differently, the Jews who made their way into medieval western Christendom and elected to stay there will not be treated in this book as myopic, unaware that there was no hope for a Jewish future in Christian Europe. They will, rather, be projected as vigorous and adventuresome pioneers, willing to tie their fate to the most rapidly developing sector of the Western world. In the process, these pioneering Jews achieved much and lost much, but such is the way of the world.

The interactions of Christian majority and Jewish minority will by no means be limited to the material realms of demography, economics, and politics. Medieval western Christendom was alive with intellectual and spiritual vigor. The Jews of medieval western Christendom were challenged by this dynamic environment, both directly and indirectly. Directly, the Christian majority became increasingly committed to a program of conversion. Occasionally, these efforts were carried out violently, in contravention of ecclesiastical teachings. More often, the modalities of convincing the Jews were peaceful and ecclesiastically legitimate, ranging from informal suasion to formal preaching and disputation. Whatever the modality of persuasion, Jewish leadership was called upon to identify salient differences between the two faiths, emphasizing of course Jewish strengths and Christian shortcomings. Less directly, the sheer vigor and dynamism of the Christian majority stimulated enhanced creativity among the Jewish minority. Living in a dynamic majority, even an often hostile dynamic majority, moved the Jews of medieval western Christendom to a rich creativity of their own. The Jewish creativity celebrated by Heinrich Graetz was not unrelated to the Christian environment that he decried.

Finally, it must be acknowledged that focusing on the Jews and the effort – in part Jewish and in part non-Jewish – to establish viable Jewish life in medieval western Christendom has meant projecting developments, to a significant extent, from an essentially Jewish perspective. History generally involves conflict of one sort or another, and historical accounts are always written from a particular point of view. The War of American Independence reads differently from an American perspective than it does from a British perspective. The

conquest of the American West is perceived differently by the victorious settler population than by the native American victims of that
conquest. Telling the story of the medieval Jews from an essentially
Jewish perspective means, for example, seeing Jewish resistance to
Christian missionizing as a success, although the same development
was perceived by ecclesiastical leadership as a failure on its part and
on the part of the Jews as well. Likewise, the expulsions from the
westerly sectors of Latin Christendom will be portrayed from a Jewish perspective, that is to say as a negative outcome. To be sure, there
were many in western Christendom for whom expulsion of the Jews
was a signal victory. The present account will not be framed from
their perspective.

The story that will unfold herein is a complex amalgam of successes
and failures, on the part of both the Christian majority and the Jewish
minority of medieval western Christendom. It involves the best and
worst of human characteristics; it is filled with contingencies at every
point; it has no plot resolution, either happy or sad; it concludes
open-ended, with benefits and liabilities extending far beyond the
year 1500, indeed down into our own times. Those seeking a clear-
cut and obvious moral to this tale will be disappointed. Hopefully,
the complex saga of the Jews in medieval western Christendom –
not at all reducible into simple conclusions and lessons – will provide
useful insights into the Jewish, Christian, and human conditions.

I

PRIOR LEGACIES

Jews were settled in medieval western Christendom prior to the year 1000, although in relatively small numbers. Those early Jews left almost no evidence of their existence to posterity.[1] They seem to have exerted little impact on the larger number of Jews who came to populate a rapidly changing western Christendom subsequent to the year 1000. We find very few references in that later period to precedents from earlier Jewish life in Europe.

This is not to say that, as Jewish numbers expanded in medieval western Christendom, these later Jews and their Christian neighbors were unaffected by pre-existent legacies and innovated freely with respect to Jewish circumstances. To the contrary, Jewish life, as it expanded all across medieval western Christendom from south to north, was deeply affected by inherited structures and attitudes. By the year 1000, Jews across the globe had evolved a rich social and intellectual framework for living as a creative minority within monotheistic majority societies. At the same time, the Christian majority was heir to a set of complex and ambivalent policies toward and perceptions of Judaism and the Jews. Surprisingly, perhaps, we must begin with the prior legacy of Islam and its stances toward Jews living under its rule. Since so many of the Jews who were absorbed into medieval western Christendom after the year 1000 came – involuntarily (through Christian conquest) or voluntarily (through immigration) – from the Muslim sphere, their circumstances and expectations played a significant role in the Jewish experience in medieval western Christendom.

THE MUSLIM LEGACY

While it may seem somewhat strange to begin with the Muslim legacy as part of the necessary backdrop to this study of Jewish life in medieval western Christendom, there are a number of justifications for so doing. First of all, prior to the year 1000, the bulk of world-wide Jewry – as we have seen – was to be found within the Muslim sphere. This meant that the Muslim world had enjoyed far greater contact with a Jewish minority than had western Christendom and had, as a result, developed far fuller policies for dealing with toler-ated minority communities in general and with the Jews in partic-ular. The Jews absorbed into medieval western Christendom from the year 1000 onwards had their expectations fashioned in no small measure from their prior experience in the Islamic world. Equally important, the Jews absorbed into medieval western Christendom were deeply steeped in the vibrant culture of the medieval Muslim world and brought much of that culture with them into their new Christian environment. Finally, the situation of the Jews in the Mus-lim sphere will recurrently offer enlightening contrasts with Jewish life in medieval western Christendom.[2]

Islam emerged onto the world scene very much in the mold of biblical Israel, as a political and religious unity. In utterly unexpected fashion, the Muslim armies broke out of the Arabian peninsula and conquered in almost every direction, creating one of the Western world's great empires in the process. The populations subjugated by the Muslim armies were vast and heterogeneous. The victori-ous Islamic authorities divided the non-Muslim subject population into two camps, that of the polytheists who had no intrinsic rights and that of the monotheistic precursors of Islam, meaning essentially Jews and Christians. This latter group did have a set of basic rights, to be enjoyed in *quid pro quo* fashion. Jews and Christians were entitled to physical security and the right to observe their own traditions, in return for political loyalty to the Muslim regime, tax revenues, and acknowledgement through a set of stipulated limitations of a status inferior to that of what ultimately became an Islamic majority.

The guarantees of physical and spiritual security were by and large maintained throughout the early centuries of the Middle Ages. There are few recorded instances of Muslim infringement on these rights during this period. In return, the Jews did prove loyal to their Muslims rulers and did produce the obligatory tax revenues. The demand for inferior Jewish status had a checkered history. To an extent, it was maintained; to an extent, it was neglected. Jews recurrently evaded the restrictions supposedly incumbent upon them and rose to heights of wealth, social standing, and political power. One of the areas in which the restrictions were most regularly evaded and in which Jews frequently achieved wealth and power was the Iberian peninsula, where eventual Christian conquest was to bring into the Christian orbit large numbers of Jews accustomed to considerable latitude in lifestyle.

As we shall see, Jews in post-1000 Christendom were subjected to more or less the same set of theoretical policies. The differences, however, are instructive. As Islam developed, Jews were only one of its monotheistic precursors; fundamental Christian stances toward the Jews were formed at a point when Jews were the sole monotheistic precursor community, making the Christian–Jewish relationship much more focused and intense. Whereas Islam saw itself simply as the third and final of the monotheistic revelations, the Christian relationship to Judaism and the Jews was – as we shall shortly see – much more involved, convoluted, and emotionally charged.[3] Moreover, the population of the medieval Muslim world was far more heterogeneous than its Christian counterpart; this heterogeneity again provided an ease and latitude by and large missing in western Christendom.

Westerners today often fail to appreciate the extent to which the Islamic world far outstripped its Christian counterparts through the first half of the Middle Ages. We have earlier utilized the Jewish traveler Benjamin of Tudela to convey some sense of this imbalance, which was military, economic, technological, and cultural. The last is especially important for our purposes. The Jews living in the vibrant Muslim sphere were thoroughly conversant with majority culture. They, like medieval Jews in general, spoke the language of their environment, which in this case was Arabic. Since Arabic was the written language as well, Jews had entrée into the dominant high culture and were creatively challenged by it. The Jews immigrating into medieval western Christendom brought with them the high culture of the Islamic world, which constituted simultaneously a challenge to Jewish identity and a stimulus to Jewish creativity.

The institutional framework for maintaining Jewish life as a minority community in the medieval Muslim world was fully developed. Alongside a rich complex of local institutions, there existed a set of centralized institutions that claimed roots well back in antiquity.

The exilarchate housed in Baghdad claimed direct descent from the Davidic dynasty; the great academies likewise housed in Baghdad could be traced back into the period of the evolution of the Babylonian Talmud. The antiquity and central authority of these institutions contrasts strikingly with the sense of newness and limited authority of the Jewish institutions of medieval western Christendom.

The creativity of the Muslim environment and its Jewish minority resulted in considerable augmentation of an evolving Jewish cultural legacy. The traditional areas of Jewish study, focused around the Bible and the Babylonian Talmud, were much enhanced. In biblical studies, a new emphasis on lexical and grammatical accuracy emerged; in rabbinic studies, the first efforts to examine closely and mine the rich and diffuse talmudic corpus are discernible. In addition, new avenues of cultural creativity developed. The most prominent of these innovative areas were theological and philosophical speculation and secular poetry. In both instances, the broad and stimulating environment encouraged the Jewish minority to experiment with new forms and ideas. Quickly, these Jews made the new cultural outlets their own. To be sure, such innovation inevitably raised hackles in some sectors of the Jewish community. Conflict around the new creativity was inevitable and quickly materialized.

While Jewish identity in the medieval Muslim world was not directly challenged by a majority propensity toward missionizing, Islam was successful nonetheless in attracting polytheists, Jews, and Christians to its ranks. Precisely how deeply these conversions cut into the Jewish community is not clear. In any case, the conversions were not the result of concentrated Muslim efforts to reach out to the other monotheistic communities. There were no identifiable structures for regularly engaging Jews and Christians with Islamic truth, and there is relatively little in the way of Muslim anti-Jewish and anti-Christian polemical literature. As a result, there is likewise relatively little in the way of an anti-Islamic polemical literature created by the Jews, since there was no genuine defensive need for such a literature.

The greatest challenge to Jewish belief and identity emanated from the philosophic inclinations of the period. Medieval Islamic culture engaged profoundly the riches of Greco-Roman civilization, preserved much of that civilization through extensive translation, and expanded the Greco-Roman legacy in its own terms. Many of the foundations of Greco-Roman thought were inimical to monotheistic principles, challenging simultaneously traditional Islam, Judaism, and Christianity. The best minds of the period – Muslim, Jewish, and Christian – were absorbed by the effort to mediate between their received religious traditions and the impressive philosophic legacy of Greece and Rome.

Jews lived all across the medieval Muslim world, from the great centers of the Middle East across North Africa and over onto the Iberian peninsula. People and ideas passed freely from east to west and back. The large Jewish communities of North Africa and especially the Jewish settlements of the Islamic Iberian peninsula constituted a considerable reservoir of new Jewish recruits to medieval western Christendom. In some instances – particularly in the Iberian peninsula – the transition was involuntary, as Christian armies added ever larger portions of Spain to the realm of Christianity. In other instances, movement from the Islamic sphere to western Christendom represented a conscious choice on the part of Jews attracted by the dynamic development of western Christendom. In both cases, the Jewish communities of western Christendom were demographically and culturally strengthened by the flow of immigrants. The enlarged Jewish population heightened Christian sensitivity to the Jewish minority, reinforcing traditional concerns and creating new anxieties. These Jews who had now become, in one way or another, part of western Christendom brought with them expectations of the ruling majority, patterns of minority existence, and a richly developed cultural legacy.

THE CHRISTIAN LEGACY

Awareness of the Islamic legacy provides us, on the one hand, with an understanding of the backdrop for Jewish life in post-1000 western Christendom, since so many of the immigrants came from the Muslim sphere and brought with them political and social expectations and a rich cultural legacy. At the same time, awareness of the Islamic stance toward Judaism and the Jews affords us a number of extremely useful contrasts, which serve to highlight the special tensions that shaped Jewish experience in the Christian orbit; this awareness indicates how unusual Christian–Jewish relations have been over the ages, how complex the stances with which Christianity has encountered its Jewish rival.

Two contrasts are especially helpful. The first involves the early development of the two faiths and their accession to power. As noted,

Islam emerged from its earliest days – like biblical Israel – as a religious polity, with a conviction that the political and religious spheres of life were unified. Islamic tradition projected Muhammed as a prophetic communal leader and ruler, along the lines of the Israelite Moses. Muhammed both brought laws and led the way toward their implementation. He was also a military conqueror, in this sense combining the roles of both Moses and Joshua in Israelite history. By contrast, the founding figure in Christianity, Jesus, exercised no worldly power, sending forth his disciples on a distinctly religious mission of teaching new truth to the world. It was only centuries later, at a point when Christian missionizing had been highly successful and an effective ecclesiastical hierarchy had been fashioned, that power over the political apparatus of the pre-existent Roman Empire was achieved.

For the history of the Jews in medieval western Christendom, this contrast had potent implications. It meant that the Jews in Christendom found themselves in an environment pervaded by the notion of both ecclesiastical and temporal leadership. To an extent, this bifurcated authority held out benefits to the Jewish minority; it allowed for the playing off of one leadership cohort against the other. At the same time, the bifurcated authority was in some respects harmful, in that it accorded considerable power to an ecclesiastical leadership group that could afford to be relatively unconcerned with temporal gain and loss. In any case, bifurcated authority was a reality with which the Jews of medieval western Christendom regularly had to contend.

Far more important for Jewish fate was the importance of proselytizing in the Christian scheme of things. A faith that had come to power through religious suasion could never forget the importance of that suasion. There were of course periods in which the missionizing impulse was relatively dormant; it could never, however, be neglected in the long term. The extent to which Jews might become the objects of missionizing involved complex and contradictory considerations. There were good reasons to make the Jews secondary, given for example their relatively small numbers and long record of resistance. As we shall see, there were equally compelling reasons to make missionizing among the Jews a very high priority.

A second contrast between Islam and Christianity has to do with their relationships to Judaism and is – from the Jewish perspective – yet more significant. Islam developed on the Arabian peninsula among a new human community of believers. It quite simply proclaimed itself an innovative religious vision. Fully aware of the prior monotheistic traditions of Judaism and Christianity, Islam venerated these prior traditions to an extent, but proclaimed its supersession of both. The break was clean – a new place, a new people, a new revelation, and a new corpus of authoritative Scripture. By contrast, Christianity emerged out of a geographic and physical Jewish matrix and developed an extremely complex and tormented relationship to that matrix. The complexities of that relationship form the most critical element for the evolution of Jewish life in medieval western Christendom. For centuries, the complex Christian–Jewish relationship was central to Christian thinking only in theoretical terms and exerted little impact on Jews, who were concentrated in the Muslim realm. The augmented Jewish presence in the western Christian world made this complex relationship far more important than it had previously been to the Christian majority, crucial to the fate of the Jewish minority, and critical to our understanding of the history of the Jews in medieval western Christendom.[4]

Because of the very special circumstances of its early history, Christianity has had a complicated and ambivalent relationship toward the Jewish matrix out of which it was spawned. This complicated and ambivalent relationship includes elements of deepest respect and – at the same time – elements of deepest hostility. For Christians, Jews have been viewed, over the ages, as the very noblest of humanity in some senses, while being perceived in other respects as the very worst of the human species. This ambiguous and ambivalent Christian relationship with Judaism and the Jews set the terms for Jewish life throughout medieval western Christendom and demands explication as the critical element in the pre-1000 legacy that would affect subsequent Jewish life in medieval western Christendom.[5]

In order to gain some sense of this complexity and ambivalence, we must briefly trace broad lines of early Christian history (which created the complexity and ambivalence), identify the apologetic stance developed by Christians to differentiate themselves from Judaism and Jews, examine the ecclesiastical doctrine and policies established at the point in time that Christians ascended to power in the Roman world, and conclude by ascertaining the major elements in Christian imagery of Judaism and the Jews. Superficially, it was the doctrine and policies of Christianity – more specifically the doctrine and policies of the Roman Catholic Church – that overtly affected the Jews of medieval western Christendom. At a less obvious, but even deeper level, Jewish life in medieval western Christendom was shaped by the imagery that everyday Christians bore of their Jewish neighbors. Christian policy toward and imagery of Judaism and the Jews set the stage for Jewish life in medieval western Christendom.

Our initial focus on pre-1000 Christian doctrine, policy, and imagery should by no means be taken to imply that they were destined to remain static during the period between 1000 and 1500. Religious thinking is generally characterized by organic growth and development. One of the critical elements in declining Jewish circumstances – as we shall see – was a hardening of ecclesiastical policy toward the Jews and a corresponding deterioration of the image of Judaism and the Jews. Both these processes will be examined as important components in the history of the Jews in medieval western Christendom. For the moment, we shall turn our attention to the pre-1000 legacy, a legacy already rich and complex. This legacy set important parameters for evolving Jewish circumstances in medieval western Christendom.

The history of Jesus of Nazareth and his immediate followers cannot be reconstructed in modern scholarly terms. Our inability to recapture the reality of Jesus and his disciples results from a total lack of data from his immediate time period and circumstances. What we today know of Jesus is derived from sources composed many decades after his death, when the vision he enunciated had undergone considerable alteration. Now, if we do not have sources from the lifetime of Jesus himself, why are modern scholars so certain that the sources we do have – composed a number of decades after his death – come from altered circumstances and reflect shifts in his original vision? The answer to that question lies in historical realities of which we can be relatively certain.

It seems obvious to the majority of students of early Christianity that Jesus and his immediate followers lived within the fractious Jewish community of first-century Palestine and were part and parcel of that Jewish community, sharing its assumptions, its concerns, and its uncertainties. The Jewish community of first-century Palestine lived under the stress of Roman domination, with its members taking differing stances toward their Roman overlords. Some first-century Palestinian Jews were comfortable enough with Roman rule; others found it utterly intolerable. This Jewish community, plagued by dissension in the realm of politics, was further fragmented by religious contention as well. Alternative visions of the historic covenant between God and the people of Israel were abroad in the land at this time.

Happily, we do have some first-century evidence of Jewish life during this frantic period. The first-century Jewish historian Josephus alerts us nicely to some of the fragmentation in first-century Jewish life. Yet more strikingly, from the writings of the first-century Dead Sea community we gain the sense of one vibrant sub-group of Jews, wiped out during Roman suppression of the Jewish uprising that began in the year 66. In these writings, we encounter a group of Jews deeply critical of the official leadership in Jerusalem, committed to what they believed to be purification of Jewish faith, and very much Bible-centered in their view of history. In fact, as they read closely the words of the prophets of Israel, the members of the Dead Sea community became convinced that these prophets were in fact predicting important events in their own communal experience.

In the tumultuous setting that spawned the Dead Sea community, Jesus of Nazareth preached his own particular vision of the covenant between God and Israel. He brought this vision to his Jewish followers in the language of his community (either Hebrew or Aramaic) and was surely viewed by friend and foe alike as a Jew, one of those – like the Dead Sea group – highly dissatisfied with current religious leadership and norms. Unlike the Dead Sea community, however, Jesus and his immediate followers did not leave us their Hebrew or Aramaic writings.

The very first writings from the Jesus movement that have come down to us derive from the pen of a diaspora, Greek-speaking Jew named Saul of Tarsus, who took the name Paul upon his acceptance of the vision of Jesus. Saul, who never encountered Jesus first-hand, thought and wrote in Greek, not the Hebrew or Aramaic of Jesus and his immediate followers; his preaching was addressed largely to diaspora Jews, not the Palestinian Jews among whom Jesus circulated; in many cases, Paul brought his message to non-Jews as well. Thus, even without certainty as to Jesus' original message, the important linguistic and social shifts reflected in the activities and writings of Paul suggest that his teachings were hardly identical to those of Jesus and his immediate Palestinian Jewish circle. Indeed, Paul's writings and the account of his life in the book of Acts reflect considerable disagreement with the original followers of Jesus.

Paul's stance toward Judaism and the Jews is both complex and ambiguous. Modern scholars are deeply divided on the issue of

Paul's views of Judaism and the Jews.[6] For our purposes, it is sufficient to note that Paul's own letters and the account of his activities in the book of Acts include elements of deep respect toward Judaism and Jews, on the one hand, and elements of sharp disparagement, on the other. This ambiguity, troubling to scholars seeking to clarify the Pauline stance, may in fact be the most important aspect of his teachings on Judaism and the Jews.[7] Paul was surely aware of the growing gulf between the Jewish world, in which he had been raised, and the gentile Christianity he vigorously fostered. He was deeply conscious of the need to differentiate the two. This differentiation had to emphasize the truth of the gentile Christian views and the errors of the Jews. Yet, Paul seems to have been unwilling to dismiss the Jews entirely, recognizing their past greatness and holding out hope for their future redemption.

With the further passage of time, the Palestinian Jewish group declined in importance within the nascent Christian community; the diaspora Jewish groups eventually declined as well; the gentile subgroup came to dominate the young faith community. Here again, there was much room for changes that would reflect a new social grouping, a new linguistic and cultural milieu, and new forms of spirituality. To be sure, much of the original message was undoubtedly retained; at the same time, much was altered. Exactly what remained and what was changed is the key question, to which no precise answer has yet won – or is likely to win – a consensus of scholarly support. What we do know is that the Gospels, on which subsequent knowledge and imagery of Jesus are based, post-date the social, linguistic, and ideational changes just now depicted. Thus, they reveal a Jesus as perceived by later observers far removed from the original Palestinian ambience within which Jesus himself lived and taught.

In this new gentile Christian setting, determined to maintain a sense of continuity with the earlier and somewhat different Jesus movement, the Jews constituted a vexing problem. On the one hand, there was much in the new faith that involved traditional Jewish thinking and that was deeply and inextricably bound up with the Jesus legacy. For example, it was clear that Jesus and his followers were Jews, that the ethical and spiritual norms of the Hebrew Bible were central to their early vision, that miracles of biblical proportions played a key role in their thinking, and that fulfillment of biblical prophecy was a crucial element in the early Jesus movement. At the same time, there was obviously much criticism of the established

Jewish leadership on the part of Jesus and his earliest followers. Such criticism did not of course remove Jesus and his disciples from the Jewish community, just as it did not break the bonds of the Dead Sea community with Palestinian Jewry either. The imputation to Jesus of critical remarks by no means signals rejection of Judaism and the Jews.

Fairly quickly, however, as the Jesus movement evolved into an independent and overwhelmingly gentile Christianity, it became increasingly clear that the bulk of the Jewish world rejected the message of Jesus, his immediate followers, and those who took over leadership subsequently. These developments required for the young Christian group a clear break with Judaism, decisive differentiation between the two faith communities, and requisite proof of the superiority of the new vision over its older rival.[8] What emerged was the notion of profound Jewish error, including the failure to recognize the overwhelming evidence presented for the messianic role fulfilled by Jesus of Nazareth. Jesus' Jewish contemporaries were intended to be the recipients of the blessings of messianic advent. They, however, consistently failed to recognize the obvious signs of his role – his miracles for example and his fulfillment of prophetic prediction for the Messiah and his activities.

The failure to recognize the divinely predicted Messiah was compounded by the purported sin of doing that Messiah to death. Jesus' crucifixion was a Roman punishment, imposed by a Roman official. Whatever might have been the original reality, the Gospel accounts all remove the Romans to the periphery and make the crucifixion of Jesus a Jewish responsibility. Thus, in the Christian reconstruction, much more was involved than simply an internal Jewish dispute between Jesus and his Jewish contemporaries. The bulk of the Jewish world, in this view, committed an unthinkable crime, which had to occasion divine wrath and in fact did. Distressed by the failure of the people whom he had originally singled out, God had – as it were – no alternative but to reject the Jews and to transfer the blessings and responsibilities of the covenant to a new people, the Christians. It is in this sense that the Jews were projected as the best of humanity, the original covenant people, and at the same time as the worst of humanity, a covenant people that had lost its blessings through obtuseness and sinfulness.

Canonization of Christian Scripture enhanced the complicated and ambivalent Christian stance thus far elaborated. Christian

Scripture became an amalgam, composed of an Old Testament, which is more or less the set of sacred books revered by the Jews, and a New Testament, composed of subsequent writings centered around depictions of the life and activities of Jesus and the epistles of Paul. For Christians, these two sets of books fit together perfectly. The Old Testament was intended to prefigure the New Testament and to find its fulfillment therein; the New Testament laid bare the deepest meanings of the Old. This canon of sacred literature accorded relevance and respect to the Jews, at least in the earlier portions of their history; at the same time, it constituted clear repudiation of Jewish understanding of the Hebrew Bible. Jewish understanding was superficial and ultimately erroneous; it was Christian understanding of the Hebrew Bible that revealed its true meaning. Again, the contrast with the sacred literature of Islam is instructive. Incorporating none of the books of Judaism or Christianity, Islam made its break with the prior monotheistic faith communities relatively neat; there was none of the complexity and ambivalence inherent in the Christian absorption and reinterpretation of the sacred literature of its Jewish predecessor.

While differentiation of Christianity from Judaism and explanation of the superiority of the former over the latter obviously played a central role in the self-definition and self-justification of the Christian faith, the resultant negative imagery of Judaism and the Jews was to plague Jewish life over the ages. To the extent that the bulk of the Jewish world was centered in the Muslim sphere, prior to the year 1000, the impact of this imagery on Jewish life was minimal. As a larger number of Jews were absorbed into the Christian realm, this deleterious imagery came to play a central role in setting the parameters within which Jewish life was to develop. To the extent that Jews were viewed as the one-time covenant people who had lost their mission and function, they were saddled immediately with heavy negative overtones. When the emotional imagery of the Crucifixion was added to this mix, the potential for evocation of powerful anti-Jewish feelings was high.

What has been said thus far revolves around religious argumentation and resultant imagery. By the early fourth century, a new ingredient was added. By that time, the Christian community had grown sufficiently to establish patterns of ecclesiastical organization and to be concerned with maintaining hard-won achievements. Thus, at the Council of Elvira, one of the earliest Church councils whose proceedings have come down to us, it was decreed that Jews must not cohabit with Christians and must not bless Christian fields. Reflected in these stipulations is a defensive stance, a concern lest Jews intrude on Christians and their beliefs in one way or another. Relationships in which Jews might exercise power over Christians, such as slave-owning, public office, and marriage, were particularly dangerous and were eventually prohibited.

The special dangers that Jews might pose to a Christian society flowed from the close relationship between the two faiths that has already been delineated. Obviously, divergent views always pose a danger to any religious or ideological community. The dangers posed by Jews, however, were special. Since so much of Christian thinking was rooted in the Jewish world and since Judaism's Scriptures were embedded in Christianity's sacred canon, there always lurked the possibility of Christians questioning the accepted sense of Christian rectitude and Jewish error. With so much Jewish thinking at the disposal of Christians, might not some of them question the authoritative view and suggest that the Jewish version of Scripture and history might possibly be correct? Because of the intimacy of the Christian–Jewish relationship and the ready availability of knowledge of Jewish views, protection of the Christian populace against the threat of Judaism took on heightened significance.

A truly critical turning point came with the change of direction in Roman governance initiated by Emperor Constantine the Great, who ruled the Roman Empire in its totality from 324 to 337. Constantine reversed the prior policy of persecution of Christians, beginning a process that eventuated in Christian power over the entire empire. Here was a new phenomenon – a vast Western state ruled in the name of a monotheistic faith. New issues had to be raised. One of these issues – neither the most nor the least significant – involved the status of another monotheistic people, the Jews. What emerged from Constantine's ground-breaking regime was, on the one hand, reinforcement of the prior Roman status for Judaism as a permitted religious faith. At the same time, the defensive concerns noted already in the Council of Elvira were now to have the backing of the secular authorities. Constantine decreed, for example, that Jews were not to seek or accept converts to their faith. Quite specifically, he singled out the situation of slaves. Slaves both Christian and non-Christian were not to be circumcised by Jewish owners. On the other hand, those who changed faith in the other direction, moving from Judaism to

Christianity, were never to suffer reprisal from disappointed Jews. The recognition of Jewish rights within the newly Christianized Roman Empire was of decisive importance for subsequent Jewish life in the Western world. The sense that Jewish life, while legitimate, was subject to requisite restrictions was equally momentous.

Many of these disparate strands of theory and policy were woven together by one of the great figures in antiquity, Augustine, the bishop of Hippo in North Africa. The Augustinian synthesis was solidly grounded in profound knowledge of the Hebrew Bible and the New Testament and of the histories of Greece, Rome, Israel, and the Church. Augustine's view of Judaism and the Jews is not ambiguous and unclear, as was the case for Paul; it is, however, grounded in much the same ambivalence discerned in Paul. Augustine also understood fully the importance of the Constantinian position on the legitimacy of Judaism within a Christian world and was determined to provide for that political decision requisite theological grounding.[9]

On the positive side, Augustine was deeply aware of the greatness of early Israelite/Jewish history, contrasting this God-centered history with what he saw as the errors of paganism reflected in Greece and Rome. The Jews, recognizing the one true God, had led a blessed existence on the terrestrial level. To be sure, they did not reach the fullest possible understanding of God's ways. Their deficiencies led to their undoing, with the appearance of Jesus as God's appointed Messiah. The failure of the Jews to read properly the prophetic message led them to spurn Jesus and eventually to insist on his death. All these traditional motifs – with their positive and negative implications – find a place in the Augustinian synthesis.

In particular, Augustine laid a solid foundation for the Constantinian recognition of the legitimacy of Jewish existence in a Christian state and society. Whereas Constantine may well have been guided by little more than imperial precedent and the normal inclination to preserve the status quo, Augustine approached the issue of the Jews from a distinctly theological perspective. He insisted, on theological grounds, that Jews must live a protected existence within Christian society. Citing an enigmatic biblical verse, Psalm 59:12 – "Slay them not, lest my people forget" – Augustine argued that God himself had ordained that the Jews were not to be killed. Rather they were to be scattered in order to serve divine purposes.

What were these divine purposes that required preservation of the Jewish people? According to Augustine, God intended that the

Jewish people be preserved in order that they serve as witnesses to Christian truth, in one of two prominent ways. In the first place, Jews acknowledge before all humanity the divine origins and thus the truth of the prophetic corpus. By insisting that the words of Isaiah, Jeremiah, and the other prophets of ancient Israel were God-given, the Jews create an obvious basis for Christian claims about Jesus. Isaiah predicted – in the Christian view – that a virgin would conceive and give birth. By bearing witness to the divine origins of such a statement, the Jews buttressed Christian truth claims. To be sure, Jews did not themselves understand the real import of the Isaiah message. Nonetheless, their disinterested – as it were – insistence that the Isaiah message was divinely inspired served as a powerful weapon in the Christian effort to bring truth to the pagan world. Obviously, this grounding for protection of Jews had again its positive and negative implications. It was positive in that it pointed once more to the Jewish legacy of biblical truth; it was negative in that it again highlighted Jewish failure to understand the truth they themselves had brought to humanity.

Augustine adduced yet another grounding for protection of the Jews. This second rationalization was more decidedly negative. Augustine offered what had become a widely accepted Christian sense of history, more specifically of the working of sin and resultant divine punishment throughout history. For Augustine, as for many Christians, the Jews had sinned grievously in their failure to acknowledge Jesus and in their responsibility for his death. The consequences of this sinfulness were obvious to those who knew how to read the record of history. The Jews sinned and were almost immediately punished by God with loss of their political independence, with destruction of their political and religious capital, and with permanent exile from the land promised to them. It is hard to imagine, for Augustine, a clearer manifestation of sin and divinely imposed punishment. Here the negative implications dominate.

Finally, Augustine – following the Psalmist and Paul – makes one last point. God is a God of mercy. Furious at the Jews for their failures, God stripped them of their role in covenantal history and consigned them to harsh punishment. Nonetheless, the merciful God always holds out love and hope, even for those whom he severely chastises. The Jews must be preserved within and by Christian society, because in the fullness of time they will yet return in repentance and win once more divine love and grace. Here, the Pauline hope for eventual

Jewish recognition of truth – in effect by repudiating Judaism – and for resultant reconciliation with an ever-forgiving God finds full expression. Here too we encounter the recurrent underlying ambivalence. On the one hand, there is warmth and hope – the Jews will turn to God and God will once again embrace them. The key to that outcome, however, lies in casting off the Jewish heritage and accepting the Christian vision. In effect, capitulation is the Christian hope for the Jewish future.

This last point leads us to the issue of missionizing among the Jews. Augustine erected a structure that formulated impressively all the ambivalences of prior Christian tradition toward the Jews. He also projected the importance of sympathetic preaching to the Jews. This loving concern was projected as a human extension of divine mercy toward the Jewish people, God's original chosen folk. To be sure, we may suggest yet other elements in the commitment to proselytizing. As noted, Christianity had developed out of the missionizing impulse. Less benignly, Jews posed a considerable threat to Christian well-being, as has already been indicated. While protective steps had been taken by Christian ecclesiastical leadership from early on, successful missionizing was a far better tool for dealing with the Jewish danger. Effective missionizing would make clear to Christian observers that Jews themselves had come round to acknowledgement of the truth of Christianity. Indeed, wholly successful missionizing would obviate the Jewish danger altogether.

Thus, the legacy bequeathed to post-1000 western Christendom from the Christian past was extremely complex and ambivalent. It involved considerable respect for the Jewish past, along with hope for a de-judaized future; it included acknowledgement of Jewish rights of existence within Christian society, a set of defensive limitations on Jewish life aimed at protecting the Christian majority, and a commitment (at least in theory) to preaching among the Jews in hopes of limiting the dangers they might pose and of bringing about the anticipated de-judaized future. This complex and ambivalent legacy was to affect every facet of Jewish existence in medieval western Christendom.

THE JEWISH LEGACY

By the year 1000, the Jewish people was over two thousand years old and had undergone recurrent historical change. Coalescing as a Near-Eastern religious–political community during the first pre-Christian millennium, the Jews had suffered a series of catastrophes that might well have brought their history to an end; instead, they had surmounted the disasters of military defeat and exile by evolving for themselves new political structures and innovative religious stances. By time the Jews of first-century Palestine faced yet another deep crisis, as tensions escalated between them and their Roman overlords, a variety of organizational patterns and religious options were well in place. When the confrontations with Rome ended badly – with devastating military defeats, destruction of the historic capital of Jerusalem, and loss of the religious anchor provided by the Second Temple – the Jews nonetheless had at their disposal alternative possibilities for ongoing political and religious creativity.[10]

A permanent diaspora community became a feature of Jewish life very early in Jewish history, with defeat at the hands of the Babylonian Empire at the beginning of the sixth pre-Christian century (586 BCE). Much of Judean society was exiled to Mesopotamia. Within a relatively short time, it became possible for Jews to return to the Land of Israel, and many did. Nonetheless, a permanent Jewish presence remained in Mesopotamia, with the passage of time secondary to the reconstituted center in Palestine. With the crushing defeats at the hands of the Romans, a slow shift in the balance of power between the Jewish community of Palestine and that in Mesopotamia began. By the end of the third century, the diaspora community had outstripped the homeland community, in size, creativity, and influence. It was, for example, the Talmud created by Mesopotamian Jewry that came to dominate subsequent Jewish religious life, not that of Palestinian Jewry. By the onset of our period, patterns of diaspora existence were fully established among the Jews.

By the year 1000, Jews had long been inured to living as subjects under the rule of others. This was obviously the case for Mesopotamian Jewry from the sixth pre-Christian century onward. Even in the revitalized center of Jewish life in Palestine, the Jews had become accustomed to conforming to the political will and institutions of overlords. During the entire period of the Second Commonwealth, stretching from the late sixth pre-Christian century down through the first and second Christian centuries, the Jews of Palestine had enjoyed political independence under their own Hasmonean rulers for less than a century. For the rest of that lengthy period, they lived under the hegemony of Persians, Greeks, and Romans.

Accommodation to subject status meant, first of all, establishment of effective structures for handling the affairs of the minority community. The (Palestinian) Mishnah and the (Mesopotamian) Babylonian Talmud both show evidence of effective self-governing agencies. Beyond these structural elements, there were attitudinal issues as well. By the year 1000, the Jews who were already resident in or attracted to western Christendom were fully equipped with perspectives that enabled them to live comfortably as a subject community and to cope with the religious implications of lack of the independence once enjoyed by their ancestors.

The requisite foundations of religious life were likewise well in place by the year 1000, all across the Jewish world. Again, we know almost nothing of Jewish existence and religious life in pre-1000 western Christendom. As the growing Jewish communities of this area become known to us, it is clear that they were deeply rooted in rich literary and institutional frameworks. Jewish religious life was grounded in what the Jews viewed as the record of divine revelation contained in Hebrew Scripture. That corpus was, by the year 1000, very well established both as to its overall contents and its precise textual readings. The biblical corpus served as the basis for the extensive set of behavioral guidelines by which Jewish life was ordered; it served, at the same time, as the source for Jewish perspectives on the widest possible range of communal and personal responsibilities.

While the biblical text was very well established, the modalities for reading and understanding that text admitted of considerable flexibility. By the year 1000, traditional homiletic interpretation lived side by side with a newer scientific philology and with innovative philosophic approaches, both developed creatively in the Muslim environment. Alternative modes of biblical exegesis were to become an important issue internally within the Jewish communities of our period. Correct and mistaken reading of the Hebrew Bible was destined to serve as the focal point of much Christian proselytizing among the Jews and of the Jewish polemical literature intended to shield Jews from that proselytizing.

In the traditional Jewish view, the biblical canon, which Jews called their Written Torah, had been supplemented by God with an Oral Torah, the roots of which could also be traced back to the Sinai experience. This Oral Torah was seen as grounded, like the Written Torah, in divine revelation. At the same time, this Oral Torah was acknowledged to have been enriched through ongoing wrestling by gifted Jewish leaders with the exigencies of temporal experience and to have been expanded by the religious intuitions of the Jewish folk. At critical points in time, this oral legacy had been formulated and eventually committed to writing. The first great classic of Oral Torah was the Mishnah, composed in late-second- and early-third-century Palestine. A relatively terse collection of legal injunctions, the Mishnah quickly became the object of investigation and explication in the Jewish study centers of Palestine and Babylonia. In both settings, elaboration of the Mishnah turned eventually into wide-ranging talmudic texts. Of the two Talmuds, it was the later and lengthier Babylonian version that came to dominate subsequent Jewish academic life and behavioral norms.[11]

Institutionally, Jewish life was anchored in the synagogue and the home. The origins of the synagogue are shrouded in obscurity. By the year 1000, however, it was the recognized venue for wide-ranging communal ritual.[12] The system of community ritual involved the daily prayer and observance cycle, the weekly prayer and observance cycle, and the yearly prayer and observance cycle. Religious leadership in the synagogue rested primarily on mastery of the corpus of Written and Oral Law, the ability to guide the community in its practice, and the capacity to exhort the community to fulfillment of its obligations. The synagogue functioned as a center for educating Jews and for inspiring the translation of knowledge into praxis. The home was the locus of family ritual and played an equally, if not more important role in sustaining Jewish life. Much of Jewish practice and teaching revolved around the family and the home. The home, along with the synagogue, served to imbue major life-cycle events and everyday life with deep religious meaning. By time Jews began appearing in western Christendom in numbers, they were well provided with an extensive set of institutions and attitudes that could serve effectively to cushion the pressures exerted by the ruling Christian majority and to guide and enrich the lives of those Jews living within the relatively enclosed Jewish community.

Jewish life under western Christian rule was fairly limited prior to the year 1000. Nonetheless, those Jews living within western Christendom and those who were subsequently absorbed into it had at their disposal a full set of accommodations to living under the rule of others and a full set of justifications for the subservience to which they had become accustomed. Prior Jewish experience under Christian control, of which we know very little, was much supplemented by the fuller experience Jews had amassed under Islam. In addition, those Jews entering western Christendom from the realm of Islam brought with them the beginnings of the medieval cultural and spiritual awakening that was fated subsequently to enrich European civilization. The growing number of Jews in western Christendom was poised to encounter the many and diverse challenges of the coming centuries.

2

THE PAN-EUROPEAN ROMAN CATHOLIC CHURCH

———— • ————

Medieval western Christendom encompassed a vast area and included diverse peoples, languages, economies, political systems, and cultures. This heterogeneity makes a linear history of the Jews in medieval Latin Christendom impossible, necessitating the treatment of diverse sets of Jewries, which will be undertaken shortly. There was, to be sure, one unifying institution in medieval western Christendom, and that was the Roman Catholic Church, hierarchically organized with its center at the papal court in Rome. The Roman Catholic Church was in fact the common element that enables us to speak of western Christendom as a more or less coherent entity. It was also the institution on the medieval scene with the richest heritage as regards Judaism and the Jews, a legacy of late antiquity that demanded respect. Finally, it was the institution in medieval western Christendom with the most intense commitment to clear formulation of doctrine and behavioral norms.

All this is not meant to suggest that consistency was achieved all through western Christendom with respect to theological doctrine, ecclesiastical policy, or imagery of Judaism and the Jews. The diversity of medieval western Christendom and the varying perspectives of different groupings within majority society and even within the Church itself precluded unanimity with respect to the Jews or any other issue. In this chapter, the focus will be on broad issues of doctrine, policy, and imagery of the Jews, as reflected largely in papal pronouncements. On occasion, a relatively authoritative non-papal voice will be introduced. Again, this is not meant to imply unanimity within the Church. At a number of junctures – here and in subsequent chapters – divergent ecclesiastical positions will be highlighted. At the same time, it is important to be aware of an underlying consensus with respect to many aspects of the Church's stance on Judaism and the Jews.

This chapter will also by no means imply that Church doctrines, policies, and perceptions remained static throughout our period. To the contrary, the dynamism of these centuries precluded maintenance of an unchanging stance on the Jews. There was considerable evolution in theological doctrine, ecclesiastical policy, and the imagery the Church – knowingly or unknowingly – fostered, and that evolution had enormous impact on the fate of medieval Europe's Jews in their varied settings.[1]

THEOLOGICAL DOCTRINE

The so-called Augustinian synthesis constituted a complex theological doctrine that absorbed many of the disparate elements in prior Christian thinking about Judaism and the Jews. It offered theoretical justification for what seems to have been a political *modus vivendi* fashioned by Constantine between victorious Christianity and the Jewish inhabitants of the Roman Empire. As we have seen, Augustine preserved the ambivalence originally articulated by Paul vis-à-vis Judaism and the Jews, with elements of deep respect on the one hand and elements of profound denigration on the other. In part, this synthesis was oriented toward the past – the Jewish failure to recognize Jesus as Messiah, Jewish responsibility for the Crucifixion, divine punishment through defeat of the Jews and their exile; in part, it was oriented toward the future – eventual Jewish acceptance of Christian truth and reconciliation with God. Conspicuously absent was any serious engagement with the Jewish present and the actual contours of Jewish existence in Augustine's own times, the fifth century. These matters were relegated to the realm of ecclesiastical policy, as we have also seen.

Prior to the year 1000, the Augustinian synthesis could be readily maintained in the Latin West, since there was little in the way of Jewish presence to raise innovative and disturbing questions or issues. As Jewish presence in western Christendom began to grow after the year 1000, new issues inevitably developed. Concern with Jews as a potential danger quickly emerged; as a result, the effort to segregate the Jews intensified; unprecedented Christian knowledge of Jewish behaviors and the teachings of rabbinic Judaism was generated; a new Jewish economic posture evolved and posed significant problems that had to be addressed; in a more aggressive Latin Christendom, the commitment to converting Jews deepened; and highly charged imagery of Jewish hostility and harmfulness proliferated. All these developments influenced the adumbration of new policies relative to Judaism and the Jews.[2] Occasionally, these developments led to a rethinking of the fundamental Augustinian doctrine on the place of Judaism and the Jews within Christian society.[3]

A fascinating example of this occasional rethinking can be found in Alexander of Hales's *Summa theologica*. Alexander of Hales was one of the giant intellects of the thirteenth-century Church. A native of England, Alexander made his way to Paris and studied in its young but vibrant university, eventually joining the faculty. Alexander entered the Franciscan Order, thereby securing a faculty place at the university for the order. Alexander's *Summa theologica* is a classic of scholastic theology; it raises fundamental theological issues, presents a range of views on these issues, offers a resolution of the differing views, and then explains the meaning and significance of positions that have been rejected. Alexander's treatment of Judaism and the Jews is set in the context of his discussion of sins against God, specifically those sins through which divine omnipotence is dishonored. Judaism is thus treated, *ab initio*, as a set of beliefs that dishonor the divinity. This placement does not preclude serious consideration of Judaism and the Jews and judicious weighing of a variety of positions, some negative and some positive.

Alexander of Hales clearly grounds his treatment of Judaism and the Jews in the Augustinian synthesis and ultimately ends by reaffirming that synthesis. However, along the way, Alexander introduces many of the troubling issues that had emerged by the thirteenth century from the realities of Jewish life in medieval western Christendom, and uses these issues as a basis for challenging the regnant Augustinian position. For our purposes, Alexander of Hales's *Summa theologica* will provide a sense of continuity, tempered by the introduction of new issues and attitudes that were proving unsettling to concerned ecclesiastical observers.

Alexander opens, reasonably enough, with the question of the tolerability of the Jews and – by extension – Judaism, the question earlier addressed by Constantine and subsequently by Augustine. While the

Augustinian position was clear-cut on this issue, the driving curiosity of the twelfth and thirteenth centuries, new developments within Christendom in general and among its Jews in particular, and fuller knowledge of Judaism combined to move Alexander to raise the question and to begin his answer by taking the position that Jews are in fact not to be tolerated, a reversal of the Augustinian position.

The reasons Alexander advances for non-toleration of the Jews are three: (1) "They blaspheme against Christ and against the Blessed Virgin; they take revenge on the Catholic faith; they do injury to the sacraments and the ecclesiastics, as is indicated in the *Decretales*. According to the Old Testament, blasphemers are to be subjected to death. Therefore, Jews are not to be tolerated, but should be consigned to death, especially those who behave in this fashion." (2) "Moreover, in their book, which is called Talmud, many statements are contained that relate to blasphemy of Christ and the Blessed Virgin. Since they must observe the doctrine of that book as law, they along with these books should be dispersed." (3) "Also, Christians persecute those pagans who hold the Holy Land to the death. However, contempt of the Redeemer is a great injury. Therefore, Christians ought to persecute to the death those who perpetrate such contempt. Therefore, the Jews are not to be tolerated."[4]

All these charges involve developments, information, and perceptions that postdate the year 1000. Thus, Alexander of Hales is suggesting that these new considerations should lead to the conclusion that Judaism and the Jews ought not be tolerated in Christian society; he is in effect subverting the Augustinian emphasis on a distant past and a distant future in favor of an emphasis on the present and its contours. Let us look a bit more closely at these three contentions, which abandon the more abstract Augustinian considerations and address current realities or at least new Christian awareness of prior realities. We shall rearrange somewhat the order of Alexander's presentation to correspond to chronological developments in western Christendom, within the Christian majority and the Jewish minority.

We begin with the third of Alexander's arguments against toleration of Judaism and Jews. This argument is grounded in popular perceptions of the meaning of crusading, which was of course a new phenomenon on the late-eleventh-century medieval scene. In 1095, Pope Urban II called the warriors of western Christendom to free the sacred sites of Christianity from Muslim hands. It is certain that the papal call did not mention Jews, nor did it envision any possibility that the call might have implications with respect to the Jews.

For some – but by no means all – of the crusading armies formed in response to the papal announcement, the call to battle against the Muslims in the Holy Land did in fact have implications with respect to the Jews. An anti-Jewish crusader slogan is attested by both Christian and Jewish sources. In the words of the oldest of these sources, a narrative account of the violent crusader assaults in the Rhineland in 1096: "They [the crusaders] said to one another: 'Behold we travel to a distant land to do battle with the kings of that land. We take our lives in our hands in order to kill and subjugate all those kingdoms that do not believe in the Crucified. How much more so [should we kill and subjugate] the Jews, who murdered and crucified him.'"[5] This popular reasoning, grounded in the new phenomenon of crusading, was soundly repudiated by the leadership of the Church at the outset of the Second Crusade. Bernard of Clairvaux opposed to this popular reasoning the old Augustinian synthesis.[6] Here, however, Alexander of Hales resuscitates the popular sloganeering, to be sure in more genteel fashion. Alexander is not calling for mob violence against the Jews. He is, nonetheless, posing a provocative *a fortiori* case: Christians legitimately persecute the Muslims, who deny Christ; Jews are at least as bad as – if not worse than – the Muslims in their contempt for Christ; therefore treatment of the Jews should be at least as harsh as – if not harsher than – treatment of Muslims. For Alexander, this should mean minimally non-toleration of Judaism and Jews.

In terms of chronological development, Alexander's initial argument for non-toleration of the Jews is the second to emerge during the medieval centuries. In the wake of the heightened sense of the enmity of the Islamic world, there evolved as well an intensified perception of the Jews as internal enemies of the Christian faith. As we shall see, this perception expressed itself in a variety of modalities, including Jewish blasphemy against Jesus and Mary, Jewish maltreatment of Christian *sancta*, Jewish oppression of Christians, and even Jewish murder of Christian neighbors.[7]

The *Decretales* mentioned by Alexander is the collection of papal rulings organized by Raymond Penaforte in the 1230s as a supplement to the earlier authoritative code of Church law, Gratian's *Decretum*. In the collection of twelfth- and thirteenth-century papal epistles fashioned by Raymond, there is a full section on Jews and Muslims. Within this section, there is recurrent reference to Jewish enmity and Jewish blasphemy. Following are a few examples, taken from the letters of Pope Innocent III (1198–1216): (1) "We most especially forbid anyone [this is found in a canon of the Fourth Lateran Council that deals with Jews and Muslims, with a focus on the Jews] to break forth into insults against the Creator. Since we cannot shut our eyes to insults heaped upon him who washed away our sins, we decree that such presumptuous persons shall be duly restrained by fitting punishment meted out by secular rulers, so that none blaspheme against him who was crucified for our sake."[8] (2) "As we have heard, certain ones among them [again Jews] do not blush to go out on such days [Easter week] more than usually ornamented and do not fear to poke fun at Christians who display signs of grief at the memory of the most holy Passion."[9] (3) "We have heard that the Jews make Christian women nurses for their children, and – something that is an abomination not only to utter, but even to think – whenever it happens that on the day of the Lord's Resurrection they take in the body and blood of Jesus Christ, the Jews make these women pour their milk into the latrine for three days before they give suck to the children."[10] These allegations are taken from the authoritative collection of papal expressions; other papal missives detail even more heinous Jewish crimes; and popular imagination was yet more extreme. Basing himself only on authoritative papal depictions of alleged Jewish blasphemy and hatred, Alexander suggests that, since biblical law demands death for blasphemers, Jews should by no means be tolerated in Christian society.

Alexander's middle argument for non-toleration of Judaism and Jews was the last to develop. Prior to the twelfth century, there is almost no evidence of Christian awareness of the central role played by the Talmud in Jewish life. During the twelfth century, a few Christian thinkers, especially the Spanish convert Petrus Alfonsi and the militant abbot of Cluny, Peter the Venerable, brought some sense of the Talmud into western Christendom, mostly in order to denigrate it and to deride the Jews, who allowed themselves to be guided by it. During the 1230s, however, another convert from Judaism to Christianity, Nicholas Donin, originally from southern France, appeared at the papal court, bearing allegations that the Talmud contained matter intolerable in Christian society. Nicholas Donin was sent forth to subject the Talmud to careful scrutiny, with an ultimate objective of clarifying whether the charges were accurate or not. If accurate, then harsh and innovative steps were required.

The papal appeal to the ecclesiastical and secular authorities of western Christendom generated one major response, and that was in the France of the pious King Louis IX. There, large quantities of Talmud manuscripts were confiscated in 1240, and the Talmud was subjected to careful examination. Large segments were translated, with the translations then organized into a set of accusations. At the heart of these accusations lay charges of blasphemy against Jesus and Mary and encouragement to, perhaps even requirement of anti-Christian activities. The Talmud was then brought to trial, with a number of northern-French rabbis serving as witnesses. The trial, the precise nature of which is a matter of some uncertainty, ended with condemnation of the accused text. Condemned Talmuds and related rabbinic materials were subjected to public burning in Paris in 1242.[11]

In his second argument against toleration of the Jews, Alexander does not point to all the elements in the condemnation of the Talmud, but singles out the evidence of blasphemy in the Talmud, reinforcing his prior anti-Jewish point. While in that first argument, he had quoted papal letters, here he can bring to bear evidence from the literature of the Jews themselves. Since the Jews overtly indicate that they must "observe the doctrine of that book as law," there can be no question as to the accuracy of this information or its authoritative standing.

The case made against toleration of the Jews seems to be rather strong. It is created out of a series of developments that are distinctly medieval. Alexander has, in effect, marshaled arguments based on medieval realities in order to undermine the Augustinian position, grounded in the past and the future.

Alexander ranges against these new arguments the weight of the Augustinian position. He advances three claims. The first and third are fairly parallel to one another, citing alternative proof texts. The first biblical citation – Psalm 59:12: "Slay them not, lest my people forget" – is heavily emphasized by Augustine himself and is taken to mean that the Jews are to be "dispersed, so that they might be invited to conversion." The closing biblical verses – Isaiah 22:10 and Romans 11:5 – are similarly read to mean that a remnant of the Jews will repent and return to God. "Now, remnants cannot be saved, unless the seed of the Jews remains." Therefore, the Jews must be preserved and thus tolerated. The middle claim repeats the basic Augustinian contention that the Jews serve an extremely useful function by attesting to the sanctity of the biblical text they themselves do not understand. Again, if the Jews were to disappear, they could no longer serve that valuable function. The conclusion is that the Jews must be tolerated. In the process of reaching that conclusion, however, Alexander has advanced a potent anti-Jewish case, which he must proceed to address.

With respect to the argument from crusading, Alexander distinguishes between the Muslims "as unjust holders of the Holy Land and violators of a sacred space." Clearly, the Jews do no such thing, and thus their benefits outweigh their liabilities. Of course, "if they transgress openly against Christ, they are to be coerced by the appropriate punishment." Likewise, some Jewish blasphemy is simply rooted in the belief that the Messiah has not yet come. If Jews proceed beyond such a simple assertion and blaspheme Jesus or Mary or Christian *sancta*, then they deserve punishment. To the extent that the Talmud is guilty of blasphemy, it should be destroyed. Thus, Alexander does not deny anti-Christian thinking and behavior on the part of Jews. Where it exists, it must be rooted out. For those Jews willing to live appropriately in Christian society, the old Augustinian considerations still hold good.

We have focused on Alexander of Hales, because he provides a most useful instance of new anti-Jewish perceptions – the fruit of real experience with Jews in medieval western Christendom – clashing with the older and more abstract Augustinian view of Judaism and the Jews. While the older view dominated as a theoretical framework, the new concerns were compelling and minimally led to an emphasis on watchfulness with respect to the Jews of medieval western Christendom. To the extent that Jews might prove themselves docile and harmless, the old Augustinian view would ensure their ongoing existence in Latin Christendom; to the extent that they could be proven harmful, they must suffer punishment on the individual level or some sort of corporate punishment for the group.[12]

An important and regularly promulgated papal document, the so-called *Constitutio pro Judeis*, embodies – albeit with far less detail – the Augustinian position. At the same time, this often enacted statement of Jewish rights serves as a useful bridge from theological doctrine to practical policy, since it includes elements of both. The earliest extant *Constitutio pro Judeis* was promulgated by Pope Alexander III; however, there are references to yet earlier versions of the document enacted by Pope Calixtus II and Pope Eugenius III. The heart of the document lies in a formula introduced in the sixth century by the important Pope Gregory the Great: "Just as license ought not be granted to the Jews to presume to do in their synagogues more than the law permits them, just so ought they not suffer curtailment of those things which have been conceded to them." This is an overarching statement of Jewish rights, meant to serve as a preamble to key protections owed to the Jews. It lacks any explanation for the rights; it simply asserts them.

While this is the opening of the earliest versions of the *Constitutio*, the powerful Pope Innocent III, already cited for a number of fulminations against Jewish blasphemy, expanded the older version through the addition of a new opening and new closing to the document. The new opening reads as follows: "Although the Jewish perfidy is in every way worthy of condemnation, nevertheless – because through them the truth of our own faith is proven – they are not to be severely oppressed by the faithful. Thus, the prophet says: 'Do not slay them, lest they forget your law.' Put more sharply, you must not destroy totally the Jews, so that Christians will not be able to forget your law, which they – although they do not understand it – display in their books to those who do understand." This is, again, the Augustinian view, but it is couched in unusually vituperative terms.

The new closing reinforces the negativism of the opening. "We wish to place under the protection of this decree only those who have not dared to plot against the Christian faith."[13] This is a hint of what was later to emerge in Alexander of Hales. Jews have the potential to do great harm to Christianity, Christians, and Christendom. The Augustinian toleration of the Jews is to be extended only to those Jews who live peaceably and harmlessly within Christendom; anti-Christian behaviors, increasingly perceived subsequent to the year 1000, thus modify the theoretical guarantees extended by Augustine.

ECCLESIASTICAL POLICIES

Even the theological doctrine of toleration of Jews in Christian society was shaken by the realities of a growing Jewish presence in medieval western Christendom. In policy terms, the growing Jewish presence in Latin Christendom had far greater impact. As noted, the Augustinian synthesis looked back to the past and forward to the future; it was relatively unconcerned with the present. Church policy, by contrast, was thoroughly oriented to here-and-now Jews, to their needs, and to the dangers they presented. If even the more abstract theory was brought into question by the evolving realities of medieval Jewish life, then we might well anticipate even greater diversity and change in the sphere of ecclesiastical policy, and that expectation is in fact met.

Church policy toward the Jews involved from early on a complex balance between protection of the Jews and limitations imposed on them. While neither side of the balance was abandoned, the period between 1000 and 1500 saw accelerating emphasis on limitation over protection, the intensification of older limitations, the introduction of new limitations, and the onset of serious efforts to convert the Jews of medieval western Christendom.

Let us begin with the protections. The *Constitutio pro Judeis* spells out the most basic of protections, beginning with prohibition of forced conversion, which represents a critical safeguarding of Jewish spiritual rights. This is then followed by protection of Jewish physical rights: "Without the judgment of the authority of the land, no Christian shall presume to wound their persons, to kill them, or rob them of their money." Jewish worship sites and burial grounds are to be immune from assault as well.[14] The sum of protections accorded was wide-ranging and – from the Jewish perspective – invaluable.

Did the leadership of the Church follow through on the promise of protection? Did ecclesiastical leaders in fact intervene in the face of impending abrogation of Jewish rights? The answer is affirmative in many instances. The Church's protective stance was a constant all through our period, and the Jews of western Christendom regularly lodged complaints with leading churchmen, up to and including the pope himself, over dangers they faced. In many instances, these ecclesiastical leaders intervened energetically on behalf of Jews, particularly in the face of dangers from what both the ecclesiastical leaders and the Jews saw as illegitimate distortions of Church initiatives. Two salient examples of such initiatives that ultimately led to ecclesiastical intervention on behalf of Jews involved crusading and moneylending.

As noted, the First Crusade and its successors clearly included no specific anti-Jewish message. However, the popular exhilaration that gripped western Christendom in the wake of the call of Pope Urban II in 1095 resulted in unanticipated assaults by a minority of popular crusading bands against Jewish communities in the Rhineland. The archbishops and bishops of the area rejected these calls to violence and attempted to protect their Jews, with only limited success.

As the leadership of the Church prepared for the Second Crusade in the 1140s and as reports of new incitements to anti-Jewish violence surfaced, the great spiritual figure of the Second Crusade, Bernard of Clairvaux, rejected the arguments for anti-Jewish violence and laid out a powerful case for maintenance of Jewish security, a case grounded – not surprisingly – in the Augustinian position on Judaism and the Jews. Bernard's case for Jewish safety involved four arguments, two rooted in Scripture and two in empirical considerations. Bernard quotes both Psalms and Paul to show that God himself had decreed the punishment of exile for the Jewish sin of rejection of Jesus as Messiah. In the face of this divine decision, calls for human revenge – reflected in the crusader slogans – are utterly inappropriate. Moreover, according to Bernard, the Muslims became objects of Christian assault because they had in fact attacked first. Were the Muslims willing to live docilely under Christian control, they too would be immune from Christian violence. Since Jews in fact live docilely under Christian control, they are not legitimate objects of Christian violence. Finally, Bernard urges the Christian warriors to remember that the Jews are a people "from whom we have a law and a promise and whose flesh was shared by Christ."[15]

Despite the vigor of Bernard's denunciation of anti-Jewish violence, revenge continued to be preached in the Rhineland, especially by a Cistercian monk named Ralph. Not content with warning against anti-Jewish attacks, Bernard eventually went to the area of danger and ordered Ralph back into his monastery. The Rhineland Jews were well aware of Bernard's efforts and appreciated them. Ephraim of Bonn, the Jewish chronicler of the limited anti-Jewish violence of the Second Crusade, acknowledges fully the role Bernard of Clairvaux played in minimizing Jewish casualties during the turbulent early months of the Second Crusade. As we shall see in more detail, the leadership of the Church, of the German Empire, and of German Jewry combined to protect endangered Jewish life during the early months of the Third Crusade.[16]

Jews continued to suffer, however, during the less organized crusading movements that sprang up from time to time. Such was the case, for example, in the western areas of France during the 1230s. The anti-Jewish violence spawned by that anarchic crusading movement moved the Jews to approach Pope Gregory IX, who responded with eloquent pleas on behalf of the Jews. In these pleas, the pope depicted in extremely moving terms the suffering of the

Jews, indicated that the Jewish leadership of France had laid its request for assistance before him, and presented once again the case for Jewish safety and security. The papal letters were addressed to the archbishops and bishops of France and to the king, who were all ordered to intervene on behalf of beleaguered Jews and to ensure restitution for Jewish suffering.[17]

As we shall see shortly, by the late twelfth century, considerable ecclesiastical attention focused on the new Jewish economic specialization in moneylending.[18] In the wake of numerous anti-usury measures promulgated by the Church, some of the secular authorities of western Christendom utilized the ecclesiastical campaign as a vehicle for brutal exploitation of Jewish moneylenders. Aware of the Church's proclaimed policy of safety and security for the Jews, Jewish spokesmen turned to Church leaders with pleas on behalf of badly mistreated brethren. Such pleas fell on responsive ears, with extensive efforts made to insure that the anti-usury campaign was carried out properly and that mistreatment of Jews end.

An especially moving letter of protestation against Christian cruelty was elicited by the anti-usury campaign of the French crown and the French barony during the 1230s. Pope Gregory IX addressed the archbishops and bishops of France in 1233, describing in considerable detail the violence and abuses associated with the anti-usury efforts. Gregory begins with an overarching generalization: Many of the authorities of France are guilty of torturing Jews "horribly by means of hunger and thirst, by the privations of prison, and by intolerable tortures of the body." He then proceeds to specifics, noting the imposition of a four-year period for the repayment of debts, with annulment of anything beyond the principal, "though all this was contrary to the contracts into which they had publicly entered." According to Gregory, "at the end of four years, however, the Jews were seized and were kept for a long time under custody in prison, until, having pooled all the debts due them from Christians, they gave the lord of the place whatever security he thought proper that, within a stated period of time, they would not demand any payment of their debts." Jews thus in effect lost everything. Those unable to raise the security money remained in prison. Gregory's case reaches a crescendo with the following: "Certain of these lords rage against these Jews with such cruelty that, unless they pay them what they ask, they tear their finger-nails, pull out their teeth, and inflict upon them other kinds of inhuman torments." The legitimate anti-usury efforts of the Church had been, in papal eyes, exploited for illegitimate cancellation of honest debts and – more strikingly – for inhumane torture of Jews. The pope concludes by urging the archbishops and bishops of France to intervene on behalf of the suffering Jews, to halt the physical torture, and to insist upon the honoring of legitimate obligations.[19] Once again, the Church exhibited special sensitivity to Jewish suffering that resulted from a campaign it had set in motion.

What then of the other half of Church policy, the limitations on Jewish behaviors? The oldest of ecclesiastical concerns with respect to the Jews was protection of Christians from Jewish influence. Because Judaism and Christianity were, in so many ways, closely allied in thinking and because Christian Scripture included books sacred to the Jews as well, Jews posed a special danger to Christians. While in point of fact the likelihood of minority Jews being swayed to majority Christianity was far higher, the Church was anxious over the possibility of Jews seducing Christians out of their faith. In antiquity, protection of Christians from Jewish harm meant particularly prohibition of circumstances where Jews might exercise power over Christians, for example through political office, slaveholding, or marriage. The fear was that Jewish power over Christians might translate into religious influence. All possibilities of Jewish power were outlawed by Church councils in antiquity, and these prohibitions were maintained throughout the Middle Ages.

During the twelfth and thirteenth centuries, as the number of Jews in western Christendom increased and Church concern over the influence Jews might wield grew as well, the effort to limit potential Jewish impact on Christians took on greater significance. In fact, a measure of social segregation developed early on, as Jews clustered in relatively separate neighborhoods, out of both their own desire and the will of the Christian majority. As we shall see more fully, when the bishop of Speyer wished to entice Jews to settle in his town, one of the boons he offered them was a separate area encircled by a wall.[20]

The growing number of Jews and the Church's accelerating concerns about potential Jewish influence elicited more extreme demands. The Third Lateran Council of 1179, called by Pope Alexander III, prohibited Christians from living and working in Jewish or Muslim homes. The prohibition was double in force, aimed at Jewish or Muslim employers and Christian employees. "Jews and Saracens shall not be permitted to have Christian servants in their homes, for the purpose of nursing their children, or for domestic service, or for any other purpose. Those who dare live in the homes of Jews or Saracens shall be excommunicated."[21] This stipulation moves beyond the earlier concern with relationships in which Jews exercised power to relationships that involved considerable proximity and contact.

The next step in segregation of the Jews was yet more drastic. The Fourth Lateran Council of 1215, called by the powerful Pope Innocent III, made the following stipulation: "Whereas in certain provinces of the Church the difference in their clothes sets Jews and Saracens apart from Christians, in certain other lands there has arisen such confusion that no differences are noticeable. Thus it sometimes happens that, by mistake, Christians have intercourse with Jewish or Saracen women and Jews or Saracens with Christian women. Therefore, lest these people under the cover of error find an excuse for the grave sin of such intercourse, we decree that these people [Jews and Saracens] of either sex and in all Christian lands and at all times shall be distinguishable from other people [i.e. Christians] by the quality of their clothing."[22] In the drive to limit Christian–Jewish contact, this was a major turning point. Jews were to be identifiable at all times, with the intention of avoiding untoward mixing between Christians and Jews.

The legacy from antiquity envisioned the possibility of negative Jewish impact on Christians and also negative Jewish impact on Christianity. Both concerns occasioned important prohibitions. As Jewish presence grew in medieval western Christendom and as hostility deepened between the two communities, the leadership of the Church became increasingly concerned with Jewish blasphemy against the *sancta* of the Christian faith. We have already noted a number of examples of this concern from the letters of Pope Innocent III included in the *Decretales*. Pope Innocent III and his successors railed repeatedly about reported Jewish blasphemy against Jesus, Mary, the saints, and the Church.

A turning point in ecclesiastical awareness of Jewish blasphemy came in 1236, with the appearance of a convert from Judaism to Christianity named Nicholas Donin at the papal court. Donin claimed that the relatively unknown Talmud was reprehensible on many levels and deserved to be banned within Christian society. Precisely what he first argued is not available to us. Our earliest evidence comes from a series of letters sent forth by Pope Gregory IX in 1239, letters addressed to major secular and ecclesiastical authorities throughout western Christendom. The papal letters, like most indictments, are wide-ranging in their charges. They allege: that the Talmud represents Jewish dismissal of the divinely revealed Bible in favor of a human work; that the Talmud contains material "so abusive and so unspeakable that it arouses shame in those who speak of it and horror in those who hear it;" that the Talmud is the chief factor in the obstinacy of the Jews, the major impediment to their acceptance of Christian truth. In view of all this, the pope asks that the books of the Jews be seized on a Sabbath morning and entrusted to the Dominicans and Franciscans of the capital city.[23] The Dominicans and Franciscans were chosen for their special role for a number of reasons, including their central position in the developing University of Paris and their role in assuring the doctrinal purity of Christian society.

Extensive citations – deemed problematic – from the Talmud were translated into Latin in Paris. These translations were organized into a series of allegations against the Talmud.[24] In 1240, a tribunal was organized to hear the case against the Talmud, with Nicholas Donin serving as prosecutor and four northern-French rabbis serving as witnesses for the defense. Two records of the trial have survived, one a Latin account of the purported confessions of two of the rabbis, Rabbi Yehiel of Paris and Rabbi David of Melun, and the second a Hebrew narrative of the court proceedings. Not surprisingly, the two sources provide drastically different portraits of what took place.

Whatever precisely happened in the court hearing, there is no doubt as to the outcome. The Talmud was found guilty and was condemned to burning. Large quantities of rabbinic literature were collected and were burned at a major plaza in central Paris in 1242. The impact of the burning was profound, for both sides. For Jews, loss of the books they deemed sacred constituted a catastrophe of major proportions. For Christians, condemnation and burning of the Talmud seemed to confirm the prior sense that Jewish religious tradition was deeply hostile to Christianity, its central figures, and its core doctrines.

The aftermath of the burning of the Talmud is illuminating as well. It reveals a Jewish community still capable of defending itself in vigorous negotiations, a papacy caught up in the conflict of competing ecclesiastical positions, and a northern-French Church leadership committed to extreme stances. Two years after the burning of the Talmud in Paris, the new pope, Innocent IV, repeated the strictures of his predecessor, commended the king of France for his

energetic anti-Talmud actions, and urged that the anti-Talmud campaign be extended throughout the length and breadth of the French
kingdom.[25]

Three years later, however, Jewish leaders made their case before
Pope Innocent IV, arguing that stripping the Jews of their Talmud
was tantamount to prohibiting them from living as Jews. Since the
right to live as Jews was a basic guarantee for Jewish existence in
Christian society, prohibition of the Talmud in effect created internal
inconsistency: Jews were promised the right to live according to their
own religious vision and then were denied that same right. In a sense,
the criticisms of the Talmud penned by Gregory IX and Innocent IV
recognized something akin to the Jewish claims, since both described
the Talmud as the chief element in the maintenance of Jewish identity.
Nonetheless, Pope Innocent IV heard the Jewish pleas and responded,
requesting that the issue of the Talmud be reopened in Paris and that
sections of the Talmud found tolerable be returned to the Jews.[26]
We shall later see that the reexamination in Paris did not lead to
the return of the Talmud to the Jews of France, as the pope had
projected.[27] Nonetheless, the position enunciated by Pope Innocent
IV in 1247 – toleration of the Talmud, with excision of sections
deemed offensive – became normative subsequently for the Church
and most of western Christendom.

The prohibition of Jews doing harm to Christians and Christianity
had an inherent elasticity that is readily understandable – patterns of
alleged Jewish harmfulness might of course evolve. From the minority
perspective, this elasticity was quite dangerous, since it allowed for
ever-expanding infringements on Jewish life. We have already seen
how the notion of obviating Jewish influence on Christian neighbors
could be extended to the point where Christian–Jewish contact was
profoundly impeded and Jewish status lowered. The notion of Jewish
harm could also be extended into new domains. The most striking
example of such extension developed out of the increasing Jewish
involvement in moneylending, first in the northern areas of Europe
and then on into the areas of older settlement in the south.

Jewish moneylending was a complex phenomenon, with which we
shall deal repeatedly and in a number of contexts. For the moment,
suffice it to note that this moneylending was highly useful in the
expanding European economy of the twelfth century and that the
way for this specialization was paved by the Church itself. Maturation
of the economies of western Christendom – especially the more

rapid process of maturation that took place in the northern a
generated widely recognized needs for the flow of capital.
taking was augmented, and projects of all kind were undertaken at
increasingly extravagant levels. Money had to change hands in order
to support such risk-taking and such projects. At the same time, the
Roman Catholic Church had been strengthened as well and had
embarked on a vigorous campaign to reform itself and Christian
society at large. Among the targets of these reforming efforts was
Christian usury, that is to say the lending of money at interest by
Christian to Christian.

The roots of the prohibition of Christian usury lay in Deuteronomy 23:20: "You may not take interest from loans to your country-
men, whether in money or food or anything else that can be taken
as interest."[28] The twelfth- and thirteenth-century Church effort
to extirpate the sin of Christian taking interest from Christian was
intense and protracted.[29] Critical to our understanding of the development of Jewish moneylending is the very next verse, Deuteronomy
23:21: "But you may deduct interest from loans to foreigners." Over
the ages, both Jews and Christians had understood the latter verse
to permit cross-denominational taking and giving of interest. Thus,
in the particular circumstances of twelfth-century western Christendom, with its enhanced need for the flow of capital, Jews were
understood – at least initially – to have the right to lend money at
interest to Christians, and they did so.

Just as the leadership of the Roman Catholic Church was especially
sensitive to Jewish suffering that was grounded in its own initiatives,
so too was it especially concerned with Jewish abuses emanating from
its own initiatives. Since the stance of the Church on Christian moneylending played such a significant role in steering Jews toward this
sector of the burgeoning European economy, ecclesiastical leadership
quickly turned its attention to a variety of problems associated with
the new Jewish economic specialization.

Jewish moneylending – like banking in general – generated problems of all kinds. Before long, complaints surfaced, and significant
issues were raised. Initially, the Church was deeply concerned for
itself. Christians sometimes deposited sacred objects with Jews as
collateral for loans, a procedure that was inherently offensive from an
ecclesiastical perspective and that in addition raised the possibility of
Jewish mistreatment of such objects. Jewish loans against land sometimes resulted in foreclosure, with the mortgaged property coming

into Jewish possession and thus no longer subject to Church tithes. Complaints about loss of ecclesiastical revenues quickly emerged.

A special issue involved Jewish lending and protection of crusaders. The Church was deeply concerned with protecting those who committed themselves to the sacred mission. One of the elements in this protection involved obligations owed by crusaders. The Jewish chronicler of the Second Crusade, Ephraim of Bonn, suggests that the king of France annulled debts owed to Jews, which seems rather unlikely. We do know that Pope Eugenius III, on the eve of the Second Crusade, provided a series of financial protections for departing crusaders. With respect to financial obligations, the papal bull stipulated: "All those who are burdened by debt and have, with pure heart, undertaken so holy a journey, need not pay the interest past due and, if they themselves or others for them have been bound by oath or pledge, by apostolic authority we absolve them." While this is not a call for annulment of obligations, absolving crusaders of the need to pay interest constituted a major boon for crusaders and a major loss for lenders. To be sure, the papal demand did not mention Jewish lending specifically; however, given the ubiquity of Jewish lending, the provision would seem to have affected Jews considerably.[30]

As in so many other spheres, the pontificate of Innocent III brought clearer and more far-reaching policy with respect to protection of crusaders. Pope Innocent III was deeply committed to crusading and attempted to clarify and improve the lot of the crusader. With respect to crusader debts, he stipulated the following: "If any of those about to depart be held bound by an oath to pay usury, you, brother archbishops and bishops, shall force their creditors in your dioceses, by means of the same measure [ecclesiastical censure] and with no obstacle of appeal, completely to absolve the crusaders from their oath and to desist from any further exaction of usury. But if any of the creditors should compel them to pay usury, you shall by similar punishment without appeal force him to return it." Unlike his predecessor Eugenius, Innocent adds specific reference to Jewish lending: "We order that the secular powers shall compel the Jews to remit their usury, and – until the Jews have done so – they shall be forced to do so under pain of excommunication. Moreover, for those who are unable at the present time to pay their debts to the Jews, the princes shall procure the needed moratorium, so that, until their death or return be definitively established, they shall not suffer the inconvenience of accruing interest."[31] Loans owed to Jews were to cease bearing interest from the moment the crusader took the cross; interest collected by the Jews in contravention of this stipulation was to be returned; crusaders unable to pay their debts were to enjoy a moratorium, that is to say an interest-free loan.

With the passage of time, ecclesiastical concern over Jewish lending broadened considerably. From an initial focus on Church objects, Church revenues, and crusaders, ecclesiastical leadership began to exhibit concern with the broad population of Christian borrowers and the harm Jews might inflict upon them. This constituted a considerable expansion of the earlier notion of limitation of Jewish behaviors deemed harmful to Christians and Christianity. Whereas the early sense of harm to Christians involved the religious sphere, now the Church saw itself a protector of Christians in the realm of the material as well. Again, the fact that Church policy had opened the way for Jewish specialization in moneylending may well have played a role in this expansion of concerns.

Rules were established, for example, as to precisely who might and who might not borrow from Jews or what might be left and what might not be left as pledges for loans. Perhaps the best known of these limitations was the stipulation enacted at the Fourth Lateran Council, prohibiting Jews from charging excessive interest on their loans: "The more the Christian religion refrains from the exaction of usury, the more does the Jewish perfidy become used to this practice, so that in a short time the Jews exhaust the financial strength of Christians. Therefore, in our desire to protect Christians in this matter, that they should not be excessively oppressed by the Jews, we order by a decree of this Synod that, when in the future a Jew – under any pretext – extort heavy and immoderate usury from a Christian, all relationship with Christians shall therefore be denied him [the Jew] until he shall have made sufficient amends for his exorbitant exactions."[32]

There are a number of noteworthy aspects to this decree of the Fourth Lateran Council. In the first place, the objective of protecting endangered Christians is patent. To be sure, the remedy is a curious one. Normally, when making stipulations about the Jews, Church leaders asked the secular authorities to enforce its edicts. Here, social isolation is decreed for Jews charging excessive interest. The reason for this rather strange punishment seems fairly clear. Because Jewish moneylending was so lucrative to the secular authorities, they could not be depended upon to follow the Church's lead in rigorously limiting Jewish usury. After insisting on social isolation of Jews exacting exorbitant usury, the decree proceeds to ask the secular authorities "not to be aroused against the Christians [who observe the decree] because of this."

With regard to Jewish moneylending, as was true for so many issues, churchmen expressed a wide range of views. Limitation of Jewish moneylending – the official position of the papacy – was ultimately the milder Church reaction to the perceived threat posed by Jewish lending. Beginning in the late twelfth century, some preachers began to call for total prohibition of Jewish banking business, with suggestions that failure on the part of the Jews to comply with this demand should result in their removal from Christian society. A number of expulsions of Jews from the baronies of northern France in the closing decades of the twelfth century were set in motion by a reformist preacher and his vigorous condemnation of Jewish usury. During the middle decades of the thirteenth century, the pious King Louis IX of France ordered his Jews to desist from moneylending or to leave his realm. Quite clearly, many of the king's Jews chose the latter option. Toward the end of the thirteenth century, the Jewish crime of usury – as defined by the Church – served as justification for wide-ranging expulsions of Jews.[33]

The Church's policy toward the Jews included both protection and limitation. As the Jewish population of western Christendom expanded, the commitment to protection was by no means abandoned; however, the concern with limitation of the Jews came to dominate. Old limitations were intensified, and new areas of Jewish life were opened to regulation. Beyond protection and limitation lay one more stance, the complicated matter of proselytizing among the Jews.

Missionizing among the Jews involved complex issues. On the one hand, there was much to encourage it. As we have seen, Christianity came to power in the Roman world through missionizing, thus creating an ongoing commitment to winning new recruits to the faith. Among the potential objects of missionizing ardor, the Jews seemed, from some perspectives, to constitute a most likely target. Since they were already committed to part of the revealed literature that Christians held sacred, using that literature would seem to have represented a fairly simple tactic. On the other hand, medieval churchmen were aware that Christian missionizing efforts among the Jews had been conspicuously unsuccessful. The efforts of Jesus himself and subsequently the apostles had achieved little. Given the relatively small size of the Jewish target audience, other communities of potential converts might have seemed more promising. Yet, precisely the failures of prior preaching efforts aimed at the Jews spurred some churchmen to try yet once again, out of a sense that success would represent a historic achievement. By the thirteenth century, there already existed within Latin Christendom a group of converts from Judaism to Christianity who were especially zealous in carrying Christian truth to the Jews.

The period prior to the year 1000 shows no signs of significant missionizing among the limited Jewish population of western Christendom. With the growth of the Jewish population and the enhanced militancy of western Christendom, missionizing among the Jews inevitably increased. By the middle decades of the twelfth century, the first Jewish anti-Christian polemical works began to appear in western Christendom, suggesting that Christian pressures were accumulating and that Jewish responses were required. One of the resultant Jewish polemical tracts, the *Milḥamot ha-Shem* of an unknown Jew named Jacob ben Reuben, sets itself in the context of the friendship between the author and a Christian cleric. When the latter began to urge his Jewish friend to recognize the truth and convert, the Jew concluded that a guide to Christian argumentation and Jewish rebuttal was required, and he set about composing such a manual.[34]

By the middle decades of the thirteenth century, a more formal Church commitment to missionizing among both Muslims and Jews had evolved. Schools for language training were established, intended to equip Christian preachers with the linguistic skills needed to plumb the religious literature of both Muslims and Jews. Techniques were also developed for bringing together audiences of Muslims and Jews to hear the Christian message. The simplest of these techniques involved governmental force imposed on Muslims and Jews to present themselves before Christian preachers and to hear conversionist sermons. Set in a number of venues, these forced sermons became a feature of Jewish life first in the southern sectors of Europe and then elsewhere. They certainly were viewed as a serious danger by the Jewish leadership.[35]

A milestone of sorts in the new missionizing campaign was reached in 1263, in the great city of Barcelona. There, the leaders of the Dominican Order convinced the king of Aragon, James I the Conqueror, to sponsor a forced disputation between one of the new-style converts from Judaism, a Dominican friar named Paul Christian, and the Jews. Either at Christian initiative or Jewish request, the Jewish side was represented by the distinguished rabbi of Gerona, Moses ben Nahman. While often portrayed as a religious debate, implying an open exchange of views, the Barcelona encounter was in fact a carefully contrived proselytizing engagement, with structured ground rules.

According to these ground rules, the discussion was to be based entirely on rabbinic texts. In contrast to more traditional Christian–Jewish argumentation, Friar Paul did not intend to cite either biblical proof-texts or arguments from reason. Rather, the friar set out to show the rabbi and the assembled Christians and Jews that rabbinic sources themselves acknowledge major Christian truths. The four Christian truths singled out to be proven through citation of rabbinic texts were: (1) that the Messiah has already come; (2) that the Messiah was intended to be both divine and human; (3) that the Messiah was intended to suffer and die; (4) that, with the advent of the Messiah, Jewish law and ritual had lost their force. While these four claims were age-old, buttressing them through citation of rabbinic sources was highly innovative. Besides being new, this tactic meant that Christian belief could by no means be challenged in this engagement. From the Christian point of view, a total victory by the rabbi would mean only that rabbinic sources could not be utilized for proving Christian truth, hardly a serious matter for the Christian side. By contrast, the friar's success would mean a devastating blow to Spanish – indeed all of European – Jewry.[36]

We do not know precisely what happened during the four days of the Barcelona engagement. Two accounts have reached us. The first is a rather dry Latin resume, proclaiming utter Christian victory, with the defeated Jewish spokesman fleeing ignominiously. The second is a far fuller and more dramatic Hebrew narrative, written by Rabbi Moses ben Nahman himself. The rabbi portrays himself as demolishing every argument advanced by his adversary on the basis of rabbinic sources. He further portrays himself as circumventing the ground rules, regularly discussing biblical proof-texts, and arguing for the rationality of Jewish views and the irrationality of Christian beliefs. He portrays the friar as bumbling, himself as learned and resourceful, and the king as a decent and relatively objective observer. In the end, he suggests that this relatively objective observer, who could not of course declare the rabbi victorious, sent him away with a monetary reward and honor.

Attention to the subsequent activities of the two sides suggests that the claims of victory advanced by both the Christian and Jewish reporters were exaggerated. Christian claims of success, culminating in humiliation of the Jewish spokesman, are clearly unfounded. There is in fact no sign of conversions generated by the Barcelona exchange. To the contrary, there is considerable evidence of Christian recognition of shortcomings in the argumentation of Friar Paul, necessitating the more extensive collection and interpretation of rabbinic material by Friar Raymond Martin, to be discussed shortly. In parallel fashion, the sense conveyed by Rabbi Moses that he had totally demolished the case made by Friar Paul and exposed the latter as a bumbling fool is belied by the fact that Friar Paul continued to preach his message, in fact winning the support of King Louis IX of France for yet another major confrontation with rabbis in Paris at the end of the decade. The effort expended by Friar Raymond Martin to improve the line of missionizing argumentation initiated by Friar Paul implies recognition of shortcomings, but also the conviction that the new missionizing tack was potentially useful and should be pursued. Indeed, the post-1263 writings of Rabbi Moses ben Nahman himself suggest that he considered it important to drive home the lessons of the Jewish position, indicating that his performance in Barcelona had not brought about thorough repudiation of Friar Paul or the new Church argumentation.

Reference has been made to the post-1263 missionizing manual composed by Friar Raymond Martin, the *Pugio fidei*. Friar Raymond was not Jewish by birth; he was, rather, the product of the new language schools, mastering both Arabic and Hebrew. Leading what seems to have been a team of researchers, he combed through rabbinic literature, amassed thousands of rabbinic citations, translated them scrupulously into Latin, and organized them into a set of arguments for the truth of a wide range of Christian doctrines. Friar Raymond's *Pugio fidei* was far richer in rabbinic citations than were Friar Paul's rudimentary efforts at Barcelona and Paris; his understanding of the rabbinic materials was far more sophisticated than Friar Paul's; the range of issues he addressed was far broader; it was indeed comprehensive.

Efforts to convert the Jews of western Christendom continued all through the thirteenth through fifteenth centuries. New converts from Judaism to Christianity continued to play a prominent role in these efforts, but the commitment was far broader. As noted, the disputation at Barcelona seems to have resulted in no actual conversion

on the part of Jews. A century and a half later, yet another such missionizing disputation was held in Tortosa. Once again, the engagement was engineered and led from the Christian side by a recent convert, and once again the tactic involved citation of rabbinic sources to
establish Christian truth. In many other ways, however, the Tortosa
disputation was quite different from that of Barcelona. In the first
place, it took place at a time of crisis in the history of medieval
Spanish Jewry, that is to say in the wake of the fearful violence of
1391, when tens of thousands of Jews had perished and additional
tens of thousands had converted in order to save their lives. The
Jewish community of Spain was thus in a mood of extreme despair.
Moreover, the engagement was far more protracted, lasting not four
days but two years. Finally, the results were far different. In their weakened state, many Jews were moved by the give-and-take at Tortosa
to abandon Judaism and accept baptism.[37]

Intensified missionizing was the last of the major policy initiatives
of the medieval Roman Catholic Church vis-à-vis the Jews. It was
generated by a combination of the broad militancy of the medieval
Church and by the growing Jewish community living within western
Christendom. To an extent, missionizing among the Jews constituted
an effort to fulfill a major Christian obligation, sharing the truth with
others. To an extent, this proselytizing represented a peaceful, yet radical solution to the "Jewish problem" of medieval Latin Christendom.
Thoroughly successful proselytizing among the Jews would eliminate
all Jewish threats and would in addition serve as ringing evidence of
Christian truth.

IMAGERY OF JUDAISM AND THE JEWS

One more modality of Church influence on Jewish life in medieval
western Christendom involved the imagery that leadership of the
Church projected of Judaism and the Jews. Of the three modalities
of Church impact on the Jews, doctrine was – as we have seen –
the most resistant to change; policy was somewhat more flexible,
adjusting itself to the evolving realities of Jewish life; imagery was
surely the most fluid of all and the least amenable to the influence
of the central agencies of the Church. Imagery of the Jews varied
more widely from area to area and from century to century than
did doctrine or policy. Nonetheless, while the central organs of the
Church had far less influence on perceptions of Judaism and the Jews

than they did on doctrine or policy, the imagery projected by the papacy and by widely acknowledged leaders of the Church deserves at least brief treatment, in part as a reflection of changing societal views of Judaism and the Jews, in part for their authoritative impact, limited though that impact might be.

The pre-1000 legacy of Christian imagery of Jews and Judaism was quite diverse. Beginning with the Gospels and the Pauline letters, there was much highly charged negative imagery, along with occasional positive statements and images. Once again, Paul's essentially ambivalent stance toward Judaism and the Jews should be recalled. That ambivalence was reprised, as we have seen, in Augustine as well. The leadership of the Church, as well as the common believer, thus had much upon which to draw when contemplating Jewish neighbors or associates.

Since Judaism and the Jews often appeared in the preaching of medieval clergy, the tendency toward the exaggerated rhetoric often characteristic of sermons should be borne in mind. The objective of the preacher was to move his audience, and medieval audiences – like modern audiences – were generally moved by extremes, rather than by moderation. Representations of Jews that elicited excitement, often by highlighting dangers associated with the Jews, were especially likely to draw listener attention. The source material available to us from the central agencies of the Church tends, by contrast, toward the rational and the temperate. When even papal sources are rich in intemperate statements on the Jews, we may well conclude that these intemperate statements reflect widespread perceptions and that these intemperate statements were likely to reinforce the more damning of popular perceptions.

The overwhelming image of the Jews bequeathed to medieval Christendom involved opposition to and denial of Jesus in his messianic role. This opposition and denial eventuated, according to the Gospel accounts, in Jewish responsibility for the Crucifixion. The Roman authority in Palestine was purportedly prepared to release Jesus, according to the Gospel accounts. It was the Jews who insisted on his death. This imagery of Jewish hostility and opposition lay at the core of Christian perceptions of the Jews over the ages. As we have seen, the explosion of anti-outsider sentiment unleashed by the call to the First Crusade elicited in certain Christian circles the sense that revenge ought to be taken, first of all, against the Jewish enemy, who was after all the most heinous of opponents.

We recall the opposition mounted by Bernard of Clairvaux to these views at the onset of the Second Crusade. In denouncing the popular crusader thinking, Bernard did not challenge the imagery of the Jews as historic enemies. He fully accepted this imagery, but insisted that God himself had already meted out punishment to the Jews, the punishment of perpetual exile. Given this divine punishment, crusaders had no right to seek further revenge on the Jews. A bit later in his important statement, Bernard notes explicitly that medieval Jews, while the heirs of their ancestors' opposition to Christ and Christianity, had in fact resigned themselves to living peaceably in Christian society. Were the Muslims to resign themselves similarly to docility, there would be no need for crusading at all. Bernard's great contemporary, Peter the Venerable of Cluny, did not share the former's sense of Jewish docility. On the eve of the Second Crusade, Peter sent a letter to the king of France suggesting that the Jews of the twelfth century were as hostile as their ancestors had been, finding endless ways of blaspheming the sacred figures and objects of the Christian faith. While Peter eschewed anti-Jewish violence as the proper response to purported Jewish enmity, he did urge that the Jews be forced to defray some of the cost of the crusade as punishment for their ongoing hostility to Christianity and Christians.[38]

While notions of historic Jewish enmity must be fully anticipated in papal writings, the accelerating sense of current Jewish hostility is striking. We return once more to the powerful and innovative Pope Innocent III. We have noted Innocent's innovations in the area of policy; now we must attend to his innovations in imagery of the Jews. We have already noted his addition of a new opening and a new closing to the traditional *Constitutio pro Judeis.* Innocent's new version of the *Constitutio* opens with: "Although the Jewish perfidy is in every way worthy of condemnation," an unusually harsh formulation in its identification of Judaism as a perfidy and its specification of the condemnation of which this perfidy is deserving. We have also noted that the closing indicates the existence of Jews who plot against the Christian faith, with the stipulation that such Jewish plotters may not enjoy the protections that the *Constitutio* provides.

Innocent's further letters are rich in anti-Jewish rhetoric. In a 1205 letter to the king of France, Innocent begins by acknowledging the acceptability of Jewish life under Christian princes in Christian society. He castigates, however, "[princes] who prefer the sons of the crucifiers, against whom the blood cries to the Father's ears, to the heirs seed is Sown for religion — economic *

of the Crucified Christ."[39] In this complaint about royal and baronial favoritism to the Jews, depiction of the Jews as "the sons of the
crucifiers, against whom the blood cries to the Father's ears" reflects
imagery of the Jews that is intense and likely to evoke profound
anti-Jewish sentiment in broad segments of the Christian populace.

Innocent's profound sense of the Jews as here-and-now enemies
of Christianity and Christians is reflected in a slightly later letter to
the archbishop of Sens and the bishop of Paris. In this letter, the
pope again complains of Jewish behaviors in northern France and of
royal and baronial favoritism to the Jews. Innocent begins his letter
by pointing to Christian piety that accepts the Jews, "who by their
own guilt are consigned to perpetual servitude, because they crucified
the Lord, although their own prophets had predicted that he would
come in the flesh to redeem Israel." He suggests that the Muslims
rebuke the Christian world for tolerating the Jews under such circumstances. Nonetheless, such is the nature of Christian piety. In the
face of such piety, "the Jews ought not be ungrateful to us and ought
not requite Christian favor with contumely and intimacy with contempt." Yet the Jews do in fact show themselves ungrateful. "While
they are mercifully admitted into our intimacy, they threaten us with
that retribution that they are accustomed to give to their hosts, in
accordance with the common proverb, 'like a mouse in a pocket, like
the snake around one's loins, like the fire in one's bosom.'"[40] This
imagery of the Jews transforms them from historic enemies to here-
and-now dangers. Such a transformation took place all across western Christendom, beginning in a prominent way during the twelfth
century. It seems that, in this transformation, Pope Innocent III was
by no means an initiator; he seems to have been, rather, a follower.
Nonetheless, papal pronouncement of these views assured them wide
dissemination throughout Latin Christendom and enduring impact
on medieval Christian thinking.

In his letters, the actions that Innocent singles out as proof of
this Jewish ingratitude and hatred encompass a variety of purported
Jewish crimes, including blasphemy against Jesus, blasphemy against
the host, and oppression of Christians through usury.[41] As we shall
see, the sense of Jewish enmity eventuated — even prior to Pope
Innocent III — in the conviction that Jews take every opportunity to
kill Christians, out of simple hatred of the Christian faith. Innocent
lent the prestige of his office to that allegation as well. In his letter to
the king of France, he includes toward the end the following: "They

take advantage of every wicked opportunity to kill in secret their Christian hosts. Thus, it has recently been reported that a certain poor scholar has been found murdered in their latrine."[42]

To be sure, the papacy and high-ranking churchmen often protected the Jews against the most radical of the anti-Jewish calumnies that began to proliferate during the twelfth and thirteenth centuries. The blood libel accusation – the claim that Jews kill Christians and use their blood for Jewish ritual purposes – was recurrently investigated by the papacy, discredited, and rejected. At the same time, other such claims were often buttressed by the papacy. In particular, the claim of host desecration was often reinforced by ecclesiastical support for the erection of sanctuaries on the sites of the purported desecrations, which also became sites of impressive miracles. As we shall see, the early and important host desecration allegation in Paris in 1290 received the powerful backing of the papacy through recognition of the shrine erected there.[43] The record of the central agencies of the Church with respect to the potent anti-Jewish allegations was mixed.

As noted already, the papally-supported investigation and condemnation of the Talmud contributed not a little to the declining Jewish image in western Christendom. Pope Innocent IV did call for reconsideration of the total destruction and prohibition of the Talmud enacted in Paris in 1242. Generally, the papal position favored censorship of the Talmud, that is to say elimination of those sections deemed offensive. The harsh language with which the Talmud was depicted, however, suggested that popular perceptions of the Jews as alien and enemy elements in Christian society were in fact justified. In this sense, the Church, out of its concern with Jewish blasphemy, intensified considerably the anti-Jewish perceptions that developed broadly across western Christendom from the twelfth century on.

CULTURAL AND SPIRITUAL CREATIVITY: DANGER, CHALLENGE, STIMULUS

We have focused thus far on Church doctrine, policies, and imagery related directly to Judaism and the Jews, all of which had profound influence on the Jews of medieval western Christendom. There was, however, yet one last mode of Church impact – less direct and more difficult to track, but powerful nonetheless. The five centuries under consideration, especially the twelfth and thirteenth centuries, constituted a period of remarkable cultural and spiritual creativity in western Christendom. These centuries saw, *inter alia*, the development of a brilliant new architectural style, stunning achievements in the visual arts, the emergence of rich and innovative literatures, the founding of European universities, major advances in science and philosophy, intensified interest in and knowledge of a wider cross-section of humanity, the emergence of new forms of pietism and spirituality. The twelfth century in particular has so impressed recent scholarship as to be designated a "renaissance."[44] The bulk of this creativity emerged out of the Christian religious vision, and the Church absorbed much of it. On occasion, the new creativity crossed what ecclesiastical leadership perceived to be the line of acceptability and was rejected. Identification of "heresy" and the effort to destroy it were major ecclesiastical concerns from the twelfth century on. In any case, both "normative" and "heretical" creativity had to be acknowledged by the Jewish minority as a reflection of Christianity and its vigor. Living in such an environment impacted powerfully the Jews of western Christendom.

In part, the cultural and spiritual efflorescence produced new threats to the Jewish minority of western Christendom. The vigor and depth of the new culture provided a sense within the Christian majority that the religious vision underlying the intellectual and spiritual creativity was surely true and that competing religious visions were obviously deficient. This is an interesting variation on the "might makes right" thinking common in many societies. Emboldened by its creativity, the Church and churchmen made an intensified commitment to missionizing, which – as we have seen – was a core Christian value. While the central focus of proselytizing energy was the world of Islam, the great competitor faith for medieval Christendom, the historically significant Jews were also caught up in the intensified commitment to carrying the message of Christian truth into the sphere of the non-believers.

The multi-faceted Christian creativity resulted in the exploration of multiple avenues for winning over the Jews. Primary among these was the traditional Christian argumentation from the Hebrew Bible. To be sure, such argumentation can be traced back into the earliest strands of extant Christian literature, the letters of Paul and the Gospels. With the passage of time, however, Christian thinkers became increasingly aware of a rich Jewish tradition of scriptural exegesis that read key biblical verses in alternative fashion. With the twelfth- and thirteenth-century expansion of biblical studies, those committed to proselytizing among the Jews became convinced once more that the "plain truth" of the biblical text could be achieved and that such "plain truth" must necessarily be convincing to Jews.

The same set of developments can be traced among those committed to philosophic inquiry and to the use of philosophy for buttressing Christian truth. Again, this tendency goes back into the early days of Christianity. It is hardly accidental that Justin Martyr was simultaneously among the first of the Church's philosophers and the first of its powerful polemicizers. Thomas Aquinas's remarkable effort to construct an argument for Christian truth on philosophic grounds alone had little real impact on medieval Muslims and Jews; the Aquinas synthesis was simply too complex to serve as an effective proselytizing tool. This mammoth effort represents, however, a useful index of the confidence of medieval western Christendom, of its sense that intellectual achievement – in this case philosophic inquiry – validates the truth of the Christian religious vision.

The vigorous new effort to expand the world-view of medieval western Christendom, to learn more of the complex physical world outside of Christendom and of the spiritual realms outside of Christianity also impacted the missionizing enterprise. This new interest stimulated an effort at identifying and then translating the foundational texts of other religious traditions. These translated texts quickly became vehicles for effective proselytizing. In the case of the Jews, utilization of revered rabbinic sources became a staple of Christian proselytizing argumentation from the mid-thirteenth century on. Jews were confronted with the claim that their own rabbinic texts supported Christian readings of the Hebrew Bible.

For example, traditional Christian claims for the messianic role of Jesus were drawn from Isaiah 52–53, the lengthy and moving description of a Suffering Servant of the Lord. Jesus, it was claimed, obviously fulfilled this messianic prediction in every possible way. Medieval Jews regularly rejected this claim, arguing that the Isaiah passage did not describe the Messiah; rather, it was an accurate depiction of the persecution and suffering to be inflicted on God's chosen people, the Jews themselves.[45] The new missionizing efforts adduced rabbinic passages that made Isaiah 52–53 a portrait of the Messiah, seemingly deflating the standard medieval Jewish view of the passage and validating Christian claims.

In addition to rabbinic exegesis of key biblical verses, free-floating rabbinic dicta were regularly cited in the new missionizing argumentation as proofs of the rabbi's recognition and acknowledgement of Christian truths, such as the prior advent of the Messiah or the multifaceted nature of the godhead. Jews' intellectual and spiritual leaders created responses to these new thrusts, but the thrusts – engendered by the cultural creativity of western Christendom – were potent.

Perhaps the most piercing Christian thrust involved the vitality and power of western Christendom and the contrastive circumstances of Jewish life. Steeped in a sense of Christian dynamism and achievement, churchmen argued that the triumphs of Christendom and the obvious failures of Jewry could only be interpreted as divine favor for the former and divine abandonment of the latter. Interestingly, this is the Christian argumentation that the Jewish polemical sources reflect most tellingly and that they go to the greatest lengths to combat. While Jewish leaders did provide responses for their followers, this thrust was deeply troubling.[46]

Beyond the specific attacks generated by this rich cultural creativity, a more general challenge was posed. As noted, one of the most potent Christian arguments for conversion of the Jews was drawn from empirical realities. Jews were confronted with the sharp contrast between Christian ascendancy and Jewish decline. The contrasting circumstances of the two faith communities were made to suggest divine embrace of the former and divine rejection of the latter. Generally, the proofs of Christian ascendancy and Jewish decline were drawn from the material realm – demography, economy, political power. Jews were equipped with replies to these claims, grounded essentially in the sense that physical achievement by no means reflects spiritual truth. To acknowledge, however, cultural and spiritual inferiority would have been another matter. Thus, in the face of Christian cultural and spiritual achievement, Jews were deeply challenged to a cultural creativity of their own, a cultural creativity that would match or – at least in Jewish eyes – exceed Christian achievement.

We encounter this sense of Jewish cultural and/or spiritual superiority early in our period, in the violent assaults on Rhineland Jewry that accompanied the early stages of the First Crusade. Interestingly, the Jewish narrators of these events made no effort to assign base motives to the undertaking; rather, they – like their Christian contemporaries – saw it as a reflection of spiritual values, albeit spiritual values that were sullied in Jewish eyes by the errors of the Christian

faith. The Jews of 1096 knew that the crusading warriors saw themselves in heroic terms, but the Jewish victims themselves or at least
those who chronicled their behaviors were convinced that the Jews
were the genuine heroes, while the grandeur of the Christian attackers was vitiated by the vacuity of their religious vision. The Jewish
victims and their chroniclers knew of the exalted crusading goal
of Jerusalem, but claimed that the Christian concern was with the
physical Jerusalem. In contrast, the Jewish martyrs of 1096 – it was
asserted – were erecting a spiritual Jerusalem and a spiritual Temple
on the banks of the Rhine River. This is a stunning reversal of the
traditional Christian sense of itself as Israel of the spirit and of the Jews
as Israel of the flesh; it reflects a deep Jewish sense of competition
with a vibrant Christian society.

This same competitive sense is reflected in the new Jewish biblical
exegesis of the twelfth century. Here, we have considerable evidence
of Christian–Jewish interaction. As Christian exegetes committed
themselves more firmly to the plain sense of the biblical text, they
inevitably were drawn in the direction of Hebrew study and utilized the language skills of their Jewish neighbors.[47] Jews, aware of
these new directions in Christian exegesis, pursued their own study
of the plain sense of the biblical text, convinced that their analysis far
exceeded that of their Christian contemporaries in depth and accuracy. The Christian creativity reflected in a new-style biblical exegesis
stimulated a Jewish effort in the same general direction, with Jewish
assertions of greater achievement.[48]

The Jewish sense of meeting and exceeding Christian achievement is palpable in other domains as well, although the evidence for
Christian–Jewish interaction is less direct. Scholars have long noted
striking methodological parallels between the new dialectical modes
of canon law study and the innovative tendencies in talmudic study
that emerged during the early decades of the twelfth century in northern France. Here – unlike the arena of biblical study – there is no
evidence for avenues of contact. Nonetheless, it does not seem at all
unreasonable to suggest Jewish familiarity with the new-style thinking abroad in society, absorption of that new style, and a conviction
of fuller usage of it.[49]

Philosophic interests first emerged in the Muslim world in the
tenth and eleventh century. This early immersion in the philosophic
legacy affected directly the Jews living in the Muslim sphere, producing an outpouring of philosophic inquiry that culminated in the

thinking and writing of Rabbi Moses ben Maimon. Muslim preservation and cultivation of the philosophic legacy eventually was absorbed by medieval western Christendom and its Jews, especially those of the south. Again, Jews became convinced that Christian philosophizing was superficial, that the essential irrationality of Christianity – as Jews saw it – precluded serious and genuine philosophizing. Jewish philosophy, on the other hand, was a natural outgrowth – so it was claimed – of the inherent rationality of the Jewish religious vision.

Perhaps the most interesting cultural sphere in which Jews were challenged by their Christian environment was Jewish mysticism. While mystical tendencies have been part of the Jewish heritage from biblical times onward, the commitment to mystical speculation took on special force in western Christendom from the twelfth century onward, reaching a height of sorts in the late thirteenth century, with the composition of the *Zohar* as the classic Jewish mystical text. This mystical speculation was deeply embedded in the broad religious tendencies of medieval western Christendom. The effort to bridge the gap between the divine and the human and to see the godhead as a dynamic and multi-faceted unity characterize both Christian and Jewish mystical thinking of this period. At the same time, the Jewish mystics were unceasing in their denigration of Christianity, in their attribution to it of much of the evil in their world.[50] Again, it seems that Jews were influenced by the central lines of majority creativity and were simultaneously emboldened to assert the basic error of Christian ways and the basic superiority of the Jewish vision.

To this point, I have treated the Christian–Jewish relationship as adversarial, with the Jewish minority challenged by the creativity of the Christian majority and asserting its superiority. This is of course not the only way in which the relationship worked. To a significant extent, Jews simply lived in an exciting environment and absorbed the dynamism of that environment. Much of the Jewish creativity in medieval western Christendom was spawned in this simpler and less adversarial manner.[51]

LOOKING AHEAD

The Roman Catholic Church's doctrines and policies regarding Judaism and the Jews played a major role in the fate of the Jews in medieval western Christendom, as did the imagery it purveyed. At the same time, the Church's impact must not be exaggerated; it was but one element – to be sure, a major element – on the medieval scene. It was hardly as unified as it wished to be, with considerable latitude for regional variation and for chronological change. We must now proceed to a discussion of the diverse Jewries that inhabited medieval western Christendom. In this discussion, we shall encounter recurrently the Roman Catholic Church's theological doctrines, ecclesiastical policies, and broad imagery of Judaism and the Jews. We shall see how these doctrines, policies, and images interacted with local realities, needs, and traditions to result in the diversity of Jewish life encountered in the various Jewries of Latin Christendom.

We shall also trace the burgeoning creativity of the various Jewish communities of medieval western Christendom, stimulated in no small measure by their dynamic environment. To an extent, the Jews were simply influenced by the creative directions of this vigorous environment. Jews had to acknowledge the cultural dynamism of their surroundings and were impressed by it. At the same time, Jews felt deeply threatened by this dynamism, which they – like their Christian contemporaries – associated with the Christian religious vision. As a result, the Jews of medieval western Christendom felt compelled to denounce the majority faith and its cultural and spiritual achievements and to trumpet the superiority of the Jewish religious vision and its attendant cultural and spiritual creativity. Just as the Christian majority was deeply ambivalent toward the Jewish minority in its midst, so too the Jewish minority was ambivalent and uncertain about the majority Christian ambience in which it found itself.

3

THE OLDER JEWRIES OF THE SOUTH

Study of the Jews of medieval western Christendom must properly begin with the older Jewish communities of the south.[1] By the year 1000, the Jewish settlements scattered throughout the Christian principalities along the northern littoral of the Mediterranean Sea were well established, although not particularly large.[2] They could trace their origins far back into antiquity. With the extension of Roman rule into the eastern Mediterranean basin and the conquest of Judea toward the end of the first pre-Christian millennium, the way was clear for increasing numbers of Jews to move westward across the southern and northern shores of the "Roman lake," and they did so, establishing Jewish enclaves that would last through antiquity, on into the Middle Ages, and – in some cases – down into modernity as well.

We shall treat first the Jewry of southern France, which by virtue of its more interior position was less exposed to the incursion of external forces.[3] Part of a broad Mediterranean culture that stretched from Spain in the west through Italy in the east, southern France was from the beginning of our period through its end fully within the Christian orbit. The history of southern France thus has a somewhat linear quality to it. We shall next proceed to the Iberian peninsula, which at the beginning of our period lay largely under Muslim control. The history of Spain during our period is very much a story of ongoing Christian conquest and ongoing absorption of the conquered areas into the fabric of western Christendom. Lastly, we shall treat the Italian peninsula, where the creation of a unified polity, toward which both southern France and Spain were moving, did not take place. The story of the Italian peninsula is the most disjointed and fragmented we shall encounter in all the areas of western Christendom.

Modern observers perceive southern France as part of a large political and cultural unit that stretches vertically from the Mediterranean Sea in the south into the reaches of northern Europe, a unit bound together by language, history, and political destiny. Such perceptions would have been unimaginable to pre-thirteenth-century medieval observers. They would have seen southern France as part of a linguistic and cultural composite that stretched horizontally from the northern areas of the Iberian peninsula through the south of France and onto the Italian peninsula. A medieval traveler moving across that swath of territory – as in fact Benjamin of Tudela did – would have been linguistically relatively comfortable, sensing only dialectical differences in the various areas visited. In contrast, someone journeying from Narbonne in the south to Paris in the north would have found the language of the latter city and region more or less incomprehensible.

Southern France was, at the beginning of our period, fragmented into a welter of small independent principalities. Since there was no extended period of Muslim control, reconquest of territory from the forces of Islam was not a preoccupation and did not offer the opportunity for either the coalescing of increasingly large and powerful political units – as happened in Spain – or invasion from the north, the pattern in Italy. Like Italy – albeit with a different dynamic – southern France became the object of attraction for many of the emergent monarchies of western Christendom. Threatened by a number of these outside forces, southern France eventually fell during the thirteenth century into the hands of the Capetian kings of the north, setting it on the course that has been maintained ever since.[4]

The Jews of southern France, like their confreres on the two peninsulas, began to settle in late antiquity, under Roman rule. Again like their peninsular brethren, they tended to cluster along the shores of the Mediterranean, moving further inland only slowly and fitfully. The number of Jewish inscriptions from late antiquity found in southern France is much the smallest for any of the Mediterranean areas, suggesting a somewhat limited Jewish population.[5] The same inference might be reached from the lack of early cultural creativity in the area. Whereas both Spain and Italy show signs of significant intellectual and spiritual activity prior to the year 1000, such indications are missing from southern France. The first identifiable figure from the area is the eleventh-century Moses ha-Darshan of Narbonne, whose writings are known only from citations by later authors. There is in the *oeuvre* of Moses, focused on the midrashic tradition, no sign of the rich impact of the non-Jewish environment that we shall note on both the peninsulas.

It is worth journeying with Benjamin of Tudela again, as he made his way from Spain across to Italy. Benjamin made the following stops in southern France: Narbonne, Béziers, Montpellier, Lunel, Posquières, St. Gilles, Arles, and Marseilles. In Marseilles, Benjamin boarded a ship and journeyed by sea to Genoa. A few observations on the geography of the Jewish communities visited by Benjamin are in order. First, it is striking that all eight towns are extremely close to the Mediterranean coastline. This was surely the easiest route eastward for Benjamin. At the same time, it probably reflects the demography of the Jewry of southern France as well, with the major settlements located in proximity to the sea. Secondly, five of the eight towns are in Languedoc, that is to say west of the Rhone River. Only Arles and Marseilles are in Provence, east of the Rhone. During the twelfth and thirteenth centuries, the Jewish communities of Languedoc were the most creative Jewries of southern France. That creativity was brought to a close by the absorption of Languedoc into the Capetian royal domain during the middle decades of the thirteenth century, which resulted in the removal of the Jews from Languedoc as part of the overall expulsion of 1306. As we shall see, some of the banished Jews managed to find refuge elsewhere in southern France, although by the end of our period only tiny Jewish enclaves remained across the area.

Benjamin was struck during the course of his journey by differing aspects of the Jewish communities he visited – sometimes numbers, sometimes economies, sometimes intellectual and moral qualities. In the towns of southern France, the eight Jewish communities he visited were of varying size, with the largest consisting of three hundred Jews, that is to say on the order of the Jewish communities he knew in northern Spain. Curiously, Benjamin, who often tells his readers about the economic activities of the Jews whom he encountered, does not do so for the Jews of southern France. He does convey a sense of the southern-French towns as centers of trade and of their Jews as quite comfortable economically. Jewish economic activities across southern France seem to have been rather diverse, although with the passage of time the new specialty of moneylending made its appearance. As noted, the Church's assault on Christian usury paved the way for Jewish involvement in this sector of the economy.

What most impressed Benjamin in the Jewish communities of southern France was the high level of talmudic studies, with great teachers and academies attracting students from far and wide. He was also impressed with the philanthropic largesse of the well-to-do southern-French Jews. Let us note Benjamin's depiction of the Jewish community of Lunel.

From Montpellier it is four parasangs to Lunel, in which there is a congregation of Jews who study the Torah day and night. Here lived Rabbenu Meshullam, the great rabbi since deceased, and his five sons, who are wise, great, and wealthy. [They are:] R. Joseph, R. Isaac, R. Jacob, R. Aaron, and R. Asher the recluse. He [R. Asher] dwells apart from the world and pores over his books day and night, fasting periodically and abstaining entirely from meat. He is a great student of the Talmud. At Lunel, there lives also their brother-in-law R. Moses the head rabbi; R. Samuel the elder; R. Ulsarnu; R. Solomon ha-Cohen; and R. Judah the physician ibn Tibbon the Sephardi. The students who come from distant lands to learn Torah are taught, boarded, lodged, and clothed by the congregation, so long as they attend the house of study. The community includes wise, understanding, and saintly men of great benevolence, who lend a helping hand to all their brethren both far and near.[6]

Benjamin was obviously taken with this and other Jewish communities of southern France.

Benjamin's impression of well-attended talmudic academies in southern France is accurate. Twelfth-century southern-French Jewry produced many outstanding rabbinic scholars, who devoted themselves to intensive study of and commentary upon the Talmud, to furthering the development of Jewish law through engagement with immediate issues raised in their vibrant environment, and to organizing the vast and often chaotic materials of rabbinic law into manageable compendia. The luminaries of twelfth-century southern France, such as Rabbi Abraham ben Isaac of Lunel, Rabbi Zerahiah ben Isaac ha-Levi also of Lunel, Rabbi Abraham ben David of Posquières, and Rabbi Jonathan of Lunel, occupy a place of distinction in the history of medieval rabbinic learning. Benjamin was surely justified in his appreciation of this aspect of Jewish creativity in the south of France.

While Benjamin was perceptive in his acknowledgement of the rabbinic culture of twelfth-century southern France, he was at the same time somewhat limited in his vision of the creative horizons of the southern-French Jews. For twelfth-century southern France was in general a hotbed of intellectual and spiritual ferment, and its Jews likewise were engaged in the wide range of intellectual activities and spiritual explorations found among their Christian neighbors. The general creativity of southern France was fed, in part, by its proximity to the Mediterranean and the Muslim world, from which a host of new ideas and inclinations flowed; it was also abetted by the lack of any centralized control, by the freedom offered by the small and independent principalities of southern France. Innovative ideas flowed vigorously throughout the area, and new spiritual outlets were cultivated. This innovative creativity regularly crossed the bounds of acceptability, and southern France – especially the western areas, that is to say Languedoc – became synonymous, in the eyes of many then and now, with heresy. This heresy is often depicted in theological and doctrinal terms, with dualistic concepts allegedly imported from the East seen as decisive. At the same time, other modern researchers see the wellsprings of the purported heresy in simple yearnings for a new and purer Christianity. Whatever the case may be, the innovative spirit of southern France inevitably impacted the Jewish minority of the region.

We do not know how Benjamin made his way into the various Jewish communities he visited, who hosted him, and how he met the specific leaders he cites. Interestingly, for Narbonne he notes four Jewish luminaries and for Lunel ten. While these figures are known, it is striking that Benajmin does not mention the Kimhi family of Narbonne and cites Judah ibn Tibbon of Lunel as the very last of the ten Jewish leaders he mentions. Both the Kimhi family and the ibn Tibbon family were wide-ranging in their intellectual interests and distinguished over a number of generations. It seems fair to suggest that they eclipsed the rest of the worthies designated by Benjamin.

Benjamin identifies Judah ibn Tibbon as a physician and a refugee from Iberia. He was, however, much more. His move from Spain to southern France provided him with impressive linguistic tools and with a sense of the importance of the translation enterprise. Determined to make the riches of the Jewish culture of Muslim

Spain available to the vibrant Jewish communities of southern France, Judah ibn Tibbon led the way in translating Judeo-Arabic classics into Hebrew. After him, his son Samuel continued the effort, as did Samuel's son-in-law Jacob Anatoli. The ibn Tibbons constituted the most important family of contributors to the important effort of cultural transmission.[7]

Samuel ibn Tibbon translated widely, but his crowning achievement was his rendering into Hebrew of Maimonides' *Guide of the Perplexed*. For Samuel, this particular translation was crucial, for it involved transplanting into southern France the great philosophic classic created in the Muslim world. Deeply devoted to philosophizing, Samuel saw the *Guide* as crucial to the development of indigenous philosophic speculation in his new homeland. He himself contributed to the enterprise a number of original works. Many sensed in the broadly directed philosophizing by Samuel ibn Tibbon and others like him the serious dangers posed by philosophic speculation.

Yet another family transplanted from Muslim Spain to southern France was the Kimhi family, which found its refuge in the town of Narbonne. Joseph Kimhi, the immigrant who resettled his family in Narbonne, was also a translator; he was, in addition, a linguist, a biblical exegete, and one of the very earliest of the Jewish polemicists of western Christendom. In the 1160s, Joseph Kimhi harnessed his linguistic, exegetical, and philosophic skills to Jewish rebuttal of the intensifying Christian thrusts, penning what is the very first of the Jewish polemical tracts composed in western Christendom that have survived. Written in the form of a dialogue between a Christian and Jew, Joseph Kimhi's *Sefer ha-Berit* moves gracefully from issue to issue. In effect, Joseph Kimhi portrays his Jewish protagonist emerging victorious from philosophic argumentation, from close scrutiny of key biblical proof-texts, and from a comparison of the moral achievements of the two rival religious communities.[8]

As was the case for the ibn Tibbons, so too the Kimhi family excelled intellectually over more than one generation. Joseph Kimhi had two talented sons, who followed in his footsteps. The older son Moses is known only minimally through fragments of his biblical commentaries. The younger son David was destined to emerge as one of the premier biblical exegetes produced by medieval Jewry. His commentaries show unmistakable signs of the father's convictions; they are distinguished by close attention to textual and grammatical accuracy, by a concern with the Hebrew Bible as the source of much Christian–Jewish contention, and by a thoroughgoing rationalism. Not surprisingly, when the furor broke out in southern France over the writing of Maimonides, David Kimhi involved himself as an important voice in the rationalist, pro-Maimonidean camp.[9]

The dynamic and volatile spiritual atmosphere of southern France produced innovation in yet another area of Jewish religious life, loosely designated mysticism. As noted, many of the Christians of southern France were in search of a purer Christianity. Confronted with the worldly splendor and power of the Roman Catholic Church, many in the Christian majority of southern France committed themselves to finding the deeper religious truths behind what they perceived to be the shallowness of the organized Church with which they lived. In some instances these new spiritual impulses were acknowledged by the ecclesiastical authorities and integrated successfully. In other instances, the spokesmen for these impulses were denounced by the Church leadership, were projected as heretical, were engaged in intellectual and spiritual battle, and were brought to account through inquisitorial proceedings. Southern France was perceived to be uniquely endangered, a hotbed of heresy. Thus, the support of the secular authorities was enlisted, and the new inclinations were subjected to physical persecution and suppression. In this seething environment, new Jewish mystical inclinations not surprisingly manifested themselves.

Throughout prior Jewish spiritual history, there is recurrent evidence of efforts to probe beneath surface realities and the surface explication of traditional Jewish literature and praxis in order to discover the deeper truths embedded in creation and the Torah. By time we reach the late twelfth century, there was an accumulated body of such speculation, not readily available, however, in concentrated and coherent form. Southern France became the initial locus for the clarification and expansion of this tradition. The first important composition in this direction – if indeed it can be called a composition – was the *Sefer ha-Bahir* (*The Book of Brilliance*). Like many of the mystical works from this period, it claims to project the teachings of earlier Jewish authorities, from the time of the Mishnah. It has little organizational structure, and modern scholars are uncertain as to its precise provenance. The uncertain consensus suggests that its writing took place not too long prior to its emergence in late-twelfth- or early-thirteenth-century southern France. It sounded many of the themes that would be worked out in medieval Jewish mystical thinking and writing over the ensuing century. These included a basic emanationism, which posited an unknown and unknowable divinity made manifest in ten dynamically interrelated *sefirot*. The interactions between these spheres of the emanated divine and humanity are complex, but likewise interactive. Humans affect the divine spheres through their behaviors, which can influence the flow of forces either for good or ill.[10]

These mystical speculations are often viewed as providing an alternative to philosophic speculation, which was under considerable attack in southern France at this time. A stark contrast between philosophical and mystical speculation is, however, too simplistic. The early kabbalists of southern France, including the author or collector of the *Sefer ha-Bahir*, were clearly much influenced by the Neoplatonic thinking popular in both the Muslim and Christian worlds. Both sets of speculators – the philosophic and the mystical – were committed to discovering the truth that lies beyond normal sensory experience and the surface reading of the record of revelation. Nonetheless, a contrast can be noted in the difference between the role of religious praxis in the philosophical circles and the mystical circles. In the philosophical circles, ritual could be explained in a way that might ultimately make it superfluous; in the mystical circles, the nature of the deity and the universe made ritual the key to divine–human interaction.

A vibrant setting like southern France, with both the Christian majority and the Jewish minority exploring new avenues of intellectual and spiritual activity, was not conducive to consensus building and harmony; indeed, it was likely to produce passionate disagreement as to what was licit and illicit, what fit the mold of traditional thinking and practice and what was unacceptably innovative. This is in fact what happened within the Christian majority, as we shall soon see, and similar tensions developed within the Jewish minority as well. Among the Jews, the inflammatory issue was philosophizing, and that issue was to divide Jews for centuries. It is by no means surprising that the initial explosion of hostility toward philosophic speculation and the initial reaction to that hostility should have erupted in southern France. While there had earlier been negative reactions to some of the teachings of the great Maimonides, during the 1230s a traditional leader in the town of Montpellier attacked the philosophizers. This led to a ban on philosophy, to a counter-attack by the philosophically inclined, to emissaries from both camps reaching out beyond southern France to other Jewish centers, and to eventual efforts at compromise. Above all, the controversy over philosophic speculation reveals a Jewish community in southern France alive with innovative thinking and the dangers that such thinking always poses.

Jews were limited in the measures they could initiate against perceived intellectual and spiritual threats. The Roman Catholic Church was far less limited. As noted, the dynamic intellectual and spiritual explorations that characterized southern-French Christian society – especially its westerly sectors – were related to the impact of Mediterranean and Muslim culture on this centrally located area; they were also fostered by the permissiveness of the ruling class of the small principalities that dotted the southern-French landscape. In part, the Church marshaled its own intellectual and spiritual resources to meet the challenge of what it perceived as heterodoxy. The Dominican Order was established specifically to do battle against the southern-French heretics, by formulating the requisite intellectual argumentation and by offering a counter-image of orthodox piety and poverty. The spiritual engagement had some success, but was proceeding too slowly for the taste of many in the leadership of the Church. More immediate and more tangible measures were demanded.

During this period, the inquisition emerged as a powerful force within the Church, attempting to identify those in error, to convince them of their error if possible, and to prosecute those unwilling to acknowledge what the Church defined as their crime. The foundation upon which the success of the inquisition rested was the cooperation of the secular authorities, and the barons of southern France proved remarkably resistant to taking steps the Church deemed necessary.

During the early decades of the thirteenth century, the energetic and powerful Pope Innocent III committed his Church to the battle against the external enemies of Christendom, that is to say the Muslims, and to the extirpation of internal enemies, that is to say the heretics. To the latter end, Innocent III extended the notion of crusading, originally viewed as the war against the Muslim foe, into bearing arms against all the enemies of the Church, whether external or internal. He called in effect for a crusading campaign to unseat the barony of Languedoc, allegedly indifferent to the spread of heresy in the area, in favor of new rulers who would aid the Church in purging the area of heterodoxy.

A number of the most powerful rulers of medieval western Christendom answered the papal appeal, partly out of their sense of religious obligation and partly out of the desire to add the rich and attractive areas of Languedoc to their territories. For a time, it seemed that the ultimate victor in this struggle would be the Crown of Aragon, the confederation of principalities that extended across the northeast sectors of the Iberian peninsula. In many ways, this would have been a reasonable outcome, since the Aragonese and the southern French shared so much culturally. It is interesting to speculate for a moment as to the fate of southern-French Jewry had the rulers of Aragon been successful. But in fact they were not. Rather, it was the Capetians of the north who emerged victorious, extending their rule southward to the Mediterranean Sea. It was the misfortune of the Jews of Languedoc – the most creative of the Jewish communities of southern France – to have their home area subjected to Capetian domination at precisely the point in time when the policies of the kings of the north were turning decisively negative toward their Jews and when Jewish fortunes in the north were in the process of reversal.[11]

We are fortunate in having at our disposal a set of writings from Narbonne that reveal much of the dislocation occasioned by the imposition of Capetian rule. Rabbi Meir bar Simon of Narbonne was a talmudic scholar of note, inclined toward a moderate version of Maimonidean rationalism and rather critical of the new mystical thinking. He was deeply involved in the polemical effort to protect his fellow-Jews from the blandishments of Christian missionizing, speaking and writing at the time that the informal proselytizing of the twelfth century was beginning to morph into the organized and aggressive proselytizing of the thirteenth. Rabbi Meir has left us a paraphrase of a counter-sermon he delivered in the synagogue of Narbonne, after a missionizing address by a Dominican preacher. In a sprawling collection known as the *Milḥemet Mizvah* (*The Obligatory War*), Rabbi Meir has bequeathed a number of polemical compositions of enormous value for understanding the mid-thirteenth-century Christian missionizing assault and Jewish response.[12]

Rabbi Meir's composition is also a valuable source for the transition from the Languedoc of small principalities to Capetian Languedoc. In his writing, we see, first of all, evidence of warm relations between the Jews and their southern-French overlords. Rabbi Meir details a discussion with the archbishop of Narbonne, whom we can identify as Guillaume de Broue. Arguing against Jewish taking of interest from Christians on the basis of Deuteronomy 23:20–21, which distinguished between lending to brethren and strangers, with the former prohibited and the latter permitted, the archbishop claimed that the Jews have no better brother in the world than he has been, protecting them regularly against the depredations of royal (i.e. Capetian) officials. Given this brotherly behavior on the part of the archbishop, the Jews can surely not treat him – and by extension other Christians like him – as a stranger. Interestingly, Rabbi Meir mounts no opposition to the archbishop's case. He acknowledges the prelate's support and seeks to ground Jewish taking of interest on completely different foundations. At the same time, this fascinating passage does indicate the evolution of ecclesiastical anti-usury sentiment. The friendly archbishop has concluded that his Jews must desist from their new business.[13]

Rabbi Meir has much negative to say about the new Capetian rulers. Included in his collection is a Hebrew version of a curious letter purportedly addressed to none other than King Louis IX of France. Rabbi Meir addresses the monarch respectfully and notes his reputation for religious conviction and righteousness. The rabbi proceeds to identify the religious shortcomings inherent in the new royal anti-usury legislation, which we shall track in some detail.[14] He attempts to argue in effect that true religiosity would have prevented the king from instituting such unfair and immoral innovations.[15] While Rabbi Meir's protestations obviously were ineffectual, they illuminate for us a painful transition period for southern-French Jews.

King Louis IX of France, with a profound sense of personal responsibility for the Jewish presence in his kingdom, attempted to submit the Jews of the southern areas that had now become part of his realm to the policies that had been developing for a number of decades in the north. This effort was by and large successful, although, occasionally, local rulers – for example in Narbonne – were able to maintain prior control and policies. Thus, Narbonne became briefly an oasis of moderation for southern-French Jews seeking to escape the new policies of the Capetian rulers. These Jewish efforts at evading the new restrictions were, however, doomed to failure. Fairly rapidly, the Jews of the south found the prior way of life altered in the same directions already suffered by their brethren in the north.[16]

Acceleration of the anti-Jewish policies of the Capetian authorities moved inexorably in the direction of expulsion, especially once the precedent of thirteenth-century royally sponsored expulsion had been established by King Edward I of England. In 1306, King Philip IV ordered the Jews out of royal France, which now included much of the south.[17] The most vital and creative Jewish communities of southern France were affected by the expulsion of 1306. Jewish life in the towns of Languedoc – established more than a thousand years earlier and so warmly depicted by Benjamin during the middle of the twelfth century – came to a stunning close.

Since royal territory did not include all of southern France, refuges were available both to the east and to the west. The more important refuge seems to have been eastward, in areas of the south that had not been taken over by the Capetians. Jewish life in these areas, especially the County of Provence, was to last to the end of our period, with occasional flashes of cultural brilliance. Toward the end of the fifteenth century, however, the circumstances of Jewish life in Provence began to deteriorate markedly. Popular outbursts against the Jews are notable from the 1470s onward. When the County of Provence was added to royal domain in 1481, first some local expulsions were decreed, followed in 1500 and 1501 by expulsion of the Jews from the county in its entirety. Interestingly, a majority of the Jews of the county seem to have opted for conversion, rather than exile.[18]

The second alternative for the Jews expelled from Languedoc in 1306 was to head westward into the territories of Navarre, Aragon, and Majorca. In some instances this even meant remaining on the eastern side of the Pyrenees, in French territories belonging to one or another of the Spanish kingdoms. Thus, for example, the County of Rousillon – already home to a Jewish community – offered itself as a refuge to the Jews expelled by Philip IV. Thus, Jewish life remained a feature of Rousillon until the end of the fifteenth century, when the Jews were expelled as part of the banishment from the Crown of Aragon.

Despite the shattering impact of the expulsion of 1306, Jewish creativity across southern France did not end in the early fourteenth century. In those areas still open to Jewish presence both east and west of Languedoc, the Jewish communities, reinforced by some of the refugees, continued to create along the lines already developed during the preceding centuries. Indeed, major figures dot the history of these fourteenth- and fifteenth-century Jewish communities. One of the most prominent names is that of Rabbi Menahem ben Solomon Meiri of Perpignan, who was born in the middle of the thirteenth century and outlived the expulsion of 1306 by a decade. The Meiri was yet another of the multi-faceted creative figures that grace the history of southern-French Jewry. He wrote in many different genres, and his work reflects the prior diversity of southern-French Jewish culture. The most important of his works was his massive Talmud commentary, entitled the *Bet ha-Behirah*. This commentary, devoted to the direct meaning of the talmudic passages and to their implications for Jewish practice, was a major contribution to medieval rabbinic literature.

A younger contemporary of the Meiri was Levi ben Gerson of Orange, one of the areas still open to Jewish settlement east of Languedoc. Deeply steeped in talmudic and biblical studies, Gersonides penned important commentaries on most of the books of the Hebrew Bible. His commentaries follow the tradition of literal and philosophical exegesis already noted for such predecessors as David Kimhi. Gersonides is equally well known for his scientific and philosophical writings. He wrote on arithmetic, geometry, trigonometry, and astronomy, with his work in the last of these fields winning him high repute. His major philosophical work is *Sefer Mihamot Adonai (The Book of the Wars of the Lord)*, viewed as one of the major works of medieval Jewish philosophic thinking.[19]

By the end of our period, Jewish life had disappeared from almost all of southern-French territory. Only tiny enclaves were left. This disappearance – especially the absorption of the most creative areas into the Capetian kingdom – extinguished much of the sense of a separate Jewish community and culture. As was true for southern France in general, southern-French Jewry by and large lost its communal and cultural identity. Subsequently, because of the relatively small size of southern-French Jewry and the diffusion of its Jews, there remained little continuity for what had once been a flourishing and dynamic Jewry.

Medieval Spanish Jewry was sufficiently large and powerful to transcend its expulsion from the Iberian peninsula and to transplant its heritage to a variety of places of refuge. The mistaken contemporary sense of world Jewry as divided into Ashkenazic or Sephardic components is testimony to the achievement of the Jews of medieval Iberia. Italian Jewry was much smaller than Iberian Jewry. It had, however, the virtue of persistence or at least the good fortune of maintaining its presence on the Italian peninsula down to the present. Of the three southern-European Jewries, that of southern France has been the most unfortunate. Relatively small, absorbed to a significant extent into Capetian France during the thirteenth century and then expelled, with remnants spread eastward and westward and slowly removed, it enjoyed neither the power and strength of Iberian Jewry nor the continuity of Italian Jewry. It has thus been accorded minimal attention. This is lamentable, since the Jews of medieval southern France constituted a community with a fascinating history all its own, a history of resilience and cultural creativity. Many of the innovative tendencies of twelfth- and thirteenth-century western Christendom first manifested themselves in the south of France, affecting the Christian majority and the Jewish minority alike, making the latter a spiritually vital and adventuresome element on the medieval Jewish scene.

CHRISTIAN SPAIN

The history of the Iberian peninsula and its Jews shows some significant similarities to that of the Italian peninsula and its Jews. Like Italy, Spain also was situated at the contact point of western Christendom and its neighbors; as was the case on the Italian peninsula, segments of the Spanish peninsula were conquered by these neighbors; like the Jews of Sicily and southern Italy, the Jews of Spain were deeply affected by the period of Muslim domination; in both cases, the conquering Christians maintained major features of prior Jewish life under Islam; in both areas, the Jews played a role in transmission of classical and Islamic thought into western Christendom; on both peninsulas, Jewish intellectual and spiritual creativity was stimulated by the encounter with multiple civilizations and cultures.

Overall, however, the differences between the two peninsulas were more striking than the similarities. The Iberian peninsula passed almost completely into Muslim hands for nearly five hundred years; medieval Christian Spain was for centuries profoundly engaged in an ongoing struggle against the Muslim foe, with that struggle defining important aspects of Christian Spanish governance and culture; medieval Christian Spain encompassed a large Muslim subject population, along with a sizeable Jewish minority as well. Although the small northern Christian kingdoms of the Iberian peninsula enjoyed considerable assistance from outside warriors in their effort to recapture what they saw as their Spanish patrimony, the rulers of medieval Christian Spain proved capable of creating and sustaining large and effective political units, enabling them to maintain their independence, without falling victim to conquest by others, as was the case in Italy.

The Jews of medieval Christian Spain were deeply influenced by all these special features of Iberian history. They enjoyed a number of centuries of living in the more variegated society of medieval Islam, creating Jewish communities that were demographically well rooted and economically diversified; they imbibed major aspects of medieval Islamic culture; they were positively impacted by the compelling needs of an aggressive and expansionist Christian Spanish society; they were, at the same time, negatively impacted by the aggressiveness and expansionism of Christian majority society. As a result of these special circumstances, the Iberian peninsula was the last sector of the more advanced western monarchies of medieval Latin Christendom to expel its Jews, following a number of centuries later the examples of England and France. Put differently, the rich Jewish experience in these more advanced western states of Europe was longer and fuller in Spain than anywhere else. The unusual Iberian Jewish experience resulted in the creation of a branch of the Jewish people – the Sephardic branch – that maintained its sense of uniqueness long past the end point of our study and down into the contemporary world.[20]

Jewish life on the Iberian peninsula – like Jewish life in southern France and on the Italian peninsula – had deep roots in antiquity. Jews reached Spain under Roman rule and settled there in seeming comfort. The record of Jewish life prior to the year 1000 shows signs of both equilibrium and disequilibrium. From the meager repository of source materials available for reconstructing Jewish experience under Visigothic Christian rule during the sixth and seventh centuries, it would seem that the Jewish community was relatively large, economically important, and politically influential.[21] During the seventh century, with conversion of the Visigothic rulers from Arian Christianity to Catholic Christianity and the growing threat posed by Muslim advances across North Africa, the authorities of Church and state in Spain seem to have sponsored some sort of forced conversion that led in turn to serious problems of backsliding and judaizing. The combination of forced conversion and subsequent backsliding, to be repeated in more fully documented forms in the late fourteenth and fifteenth centuries, led to some sort of expulsion, which was clearly not comprehensive.

The Jews remaining in Visigothic Spain were, in all likelihood, hardly distressed by the Muslim conquest of Spain at the beginning of the eighth century. All through the Middle Ages, Christian lore insisted that the Jews of Visigothic Spain had colluded with the Muslims and had in fact brought the Muslims onto the peninsula. Modern research suggests a different picture, with disaffected Christian elements inviting Muslim intervention. The Jews seem to have distanced themselves from the Christian–Muslim struggle. Prudence normally dictates that minority communities avoid taking sides in the face of threats to the ruling majority, at least until the outcome of the struggle might be clarified. This seems to have been the stance of the Jews of Visigothic Spain. While they were by no means responsible for bringing the Muslims onto the peninsula, once Muslim success was reasonably assured, the Jews of Spain were quite comfortable in cooperating with their new rulers.

The interlude of Muslim rule created a Jewish community in Spain that differed markedly from the Jewish communities elsewhere in Europe. To begin with, the Jewish communities of Muslim Spain seem to have grown considerably larger than their counterparts elsewhere in Europe. As was true for Jews throughout the Muslim world, there were few impediments to a diversified Jewish economy in Muslim Spain. Jews involved themselves in almost all economic activities, with the exception of agriculture, in which they only dabbled. They occupied the lowest rungs of the economic ladder and the highest as well. Particularly noteworthy are the successful and influential Jewish physicians of Muslim Spain. The Muslim authorities were aware of the useful political role Jews might play and freely engaged Jewish courtiers, in contravention of established Islamic norms. These Jewish courtiers had unusual access to non-Jewish court life and played dominant roles as negotiators between the Jews and the Muslim authorities and as patrons of Jewish culture both traditional and innovative.[22]

Since Arabic was the language of the street and the literary language as well, Jews were comfortably integrated into the intellectual life of the majority milieu. New cultural outlets developed, in particular a Jewish concern with science, philosophy, and secular poetry. At the same time, the new cultural interests influenced the more traditional Jewish intellectual domains of talmudic and biblical study. Imagery of a golden age of Jewish prosperity and cultural creativity in Muslim Spain developed already during the Middle Ages and has become a staple of modern Jewish historical thinking.

Significant signs of Jewish intellectual creativity emerged on the Iberian peninsula even prior to the year 1000. The Spanish-Jewish physician Hasdai ibn Shaprut is the first major figure known to us from Muslim Spain. He was an eminent practitioner of medicine and utilized his language skills to pursue the scientific study of medicine through immersion in the classics of medical knowledge. Hasdai, in addition, distinguished himself in service to the court of the Muslim rulers of his day and as a major patron of Jewish culture, again in both its traditional and innovative forms.

During the eleventh century, as the once unified Spanish Muslim state disintegrated into a welter of competing principalities, the cultural creativity of the Muslim majority and the Jewish minority flourished. Through the eleventh century and on into the twelfth, Spanish Jewry produced a galaxy of cultural heroes – talmudists, linguists, biblical exegetes, poets, scientists, and philosophers. Let us cite but one illustrative example. During the eleventh century, a young Jew from a rather pedestrian background, Samuel ibn Nagrela, was able to lift himself out of poverty, to find a place in the court of Granada, to emerge as vizier of that small city-state and commander of its army, to master the intricacies of the Talmud, to pen polemical works, and – above all else – to compose some of the most striking poetry in the history of the Hebrew language.

The vitalization of western Christendom, discernible toward the end of the tenth century, quickly expressed itself in a new Christian aggressiveness toward the external world, especially toward the Muslim foe. On both the Iberian and Italian peninsulas, indigenous Christians, reinforced by Christian warriors from the heartland areas, particularly France, began pushing back the Muslims. The battle on the Iberian peninsula was difficult and protracted. Crusading in the broad sense of a Christian battle against Islam began in Spain, lasted longest there, and there had its fullest and most pervasive impact on Christian society and its minority communities.

During the very first stages of Christian reconquest of the Iberian peninsula, which began during the middle decades of the eleventh century, there is evidence of the deflection of anti-Muslim sentiment against Jews as well. In a revealing letter, Pope Alexander II praised the bishops of Spain, who had protected endangered Jews against the threat of violence at the hands of Christian warriors.

We are pleased with the report we have heard concerning you, that you have protected the Jews living among you, lest they be slain by those who set out to war against the Saracens in Spain. These warriors, moved surely by blind cupidity, wished to bring about the slaughter of those whom divine charity had predestined for salvation. In the same manner, Saint Gregory also admonished those who agitated for annihilating them [the Jews], indicating that it is impious to wish to annihilate those who are protected by the mercy of God, so that – with homeland and liberty lost, in everlasting penitence, damned by the guilt of their ancestors for spilling the blood of the Savior – they live dispersed throughout the various areas of the world. The situation of the Jews is surely different from that of the Saracens. Against the latter, who persecute Christians and drive them out of their cities and homes, one may properly fight; the former, however, are prepared to live in servitude.[23]

Obviously, the Jews of Spain were subjected to the threat of violence, stimulated by the anti-Muslim sentiment animating the Christian warriors, and the bishops of Spain intervened on their behalf. Pope Alexander's theoretical foundation for Jewish safety is of course reminiscent of Augustinian thinking. Jews must be preserved, because God predestined them for salvation and because they serve as an object lesson for the working of human sin and divine punishment. In addition, the pope adds a contemporary consideration. The Muslims persecute Christians and must therefore be fought; the Jews live in servitude and must therefore be spared.[24]

While the warriors from northern Europe may have failed to distinguish the traditional Jewish foe from the contemporary Muslim enemy, the Spanish kings leading the reconquest effort were fully sensitive to the distinction. The conquering Christian rulers had genuine need of assistance from the conquered population. As had already happened in the eighth century, during the Muslim conquest of the Iberian peninsula, the victors required considerable cooperation on the part of the subject population in order to maintain the prior level of civilization in the conquered territories. The subject population during the eleventh through the thirteenth centuries was composed of a Muslim majority and a considerable Jewish minority, and the new Christian rulers could obviously trust the Jews more readily than their Muslim neighbors. Thus, not surprisingly, the Jews of Spain fairly quickly threw in their lot with the new Christian authorities and received valuable safeguards and privileges in return.

In 1115, King Alfonso I of Aragon conquered the town of Tudela, which was to be the hometown of the traveler Benjamin. The king made the following provisions for the Jews of Tudela:

(1) He commanded them by his grace that all those who had left return to Tudela to live, with all their possessions and goods.

(2) He commanded them by his grace that they might remain securely in their homes and that no one might quarter either a Christian or a Moor in their homes.
(3) He commanded them by his grace that the levy they have to pay they must give in one term annually.
(4) He commanded for them by his order the *fuero* of the Jews of Najera in all their cases . . .
(5) The king commanded them by his order that no seigneur nor anyone, living in Tudela or in any other place, who sees this charter shall contravene it nor do other than stipulated in this charter.[25]

In 1149, when the count of Barcelona, Raymond Berenguer IV, conquered Tortosa, he accorded the Jews of that town a yet more generous charter. The count allocated to these Jews an entire neighborhood of Tortosa, in which they "shall remain and live securely and peacefully with all your goods for all times." Indeed, the count further stipulated that, "if more Jews come to settle, I shall give them homes to occupy and inhabit."[26] This last note alerts us to a new and significant mid-twelfth-century development on the Iberian peninsula – the slow voluntary movement of Jews from Muslim territories into Christian lands.

Thus far, we have noted the absorption of Jews into Christian territory via conquest, and have seen that a symbiotic relationship developed early on between the conquering Christian authorities and the Jews of the conquered areas. The process of Christian conquest was, however, hardly linear. After an initial set of late-eleventh- and early-twelfth-century Christian victories at the expense of the militarily weak Muslim city-states, Islamic Spain attracted reinforcements from North Africa, first the Almoravides and subsequently the Almohades. The latter were especially militant and zealous. They halted the Christian advance down the peninsula through the second half of the twelfth century. At the same time, these new Muslim rulers introduced harsh internal measures that destabilized the prior Muslim–Jewish equilibrium in the Islamic portions of the peninsula. While the sources are sketchy, some sort of forced conversion to Islam was decreed, a move that severely shook the Jews of Islamic Spain.

Major Jewish thinkers of mid-twelfth-century Muslim Spain, where the center of intellectual and spiritual gravity for the Jews of the peninsula still remained, were convinced that Jewish life on the Iberian peninsula was coming to an end. The twelfth-century Jewish historian and philosopher Abraham ibn Daud wrote a complex, but moving historical record, the *Sefer ha-Kabbalah* (*The Book of Tradition*). On the one hand devoted to a defense of rabbinic tradition, ibn Daud's historical account was at the same time a dirge for a Jewish experience in Spain that he believed had reached its final stages. Hundreds of years of productive Jewish life were – in his view – coming to a close. Ibn Daud looked back fondly on centuries of Jewish creativity in a number of spheres and on a way of life he deeply esteemed. His religious convictions led him to reassure his fellow-Jews that God had provided new centers of Jewish creativity for the future, but he nonetheless mourned what he saw as the demise of the great center in Spain.[27]

Many other Jewish intellectuals shared ibn Daud's sense of the demise of Jewish life in Spain. They went further, however, in proposing programs of reaction to the catastrophe. The famed poet and philosopher Judah ha-Levi saw his people in Spain trapped between the hammer of militant Christianity and the anvil of a counter-militant Islam. For Judah ha-Levi, the radical, but ineluctable, solution to the Iberian dilemma was a return to the Holy Land. His Zionide poetry, written out of that conviction and during his own journey eastward, became a landmark in medieval Jewish poetry and thought.

Others agreed with Judah ha-Levi's negative assessment of the circumstances of Jewish life in Spain, but were less ideological in the solutions they offered. Numerous Jewish families decided to relocate off the peninsula. The most famous of these families included the young prodigy, Moses ben Maimon. His distinguished family left Iberia for the eastern Mediterranean, that is to say for a safe refuge in the world of Islam. Sojourning briefly in the Holy Land, the family of Maimonides eventually settled in Egypt, where the young genius grew into his eventual role as physician, communal leader, and supreme intellectual force. Others chose to travel shorter distances and to leave the orbit of Islam completely, relocating in adjacent Christian areas. The Jewish communities of southern France – as already noted – were much enriched by the arrival of families like the ibn Tibbons and Kimhis during the second half of the twelfth century.[28]

Not everyone agreed with Judah ha-Levi's imagery of a Christian hammer and an Islamic anvil, and many Jews rejected Abraham ibn Daud's conviction that Jewish life on the Iberian peninsula had come to an end. For some, the storm in Islamic Spain would pass, and life there would return to its prior contours. No relocation at all was required; all that was needed was patience. For others – and these are the Jews of interest to us at the moment – Christian Spain offered rich and exciting possibilities. These Jewish observers concluded that the future of the Iberian peninsula lay ultimately with the Christian side. They were fully aware of the aggressiveness of the Christian kingdoms of the north, but saw beyond the aggressiveness. They were convinced that, beyond the militant ideology of reconquest, lay normal societal needs. As the peninsula changed hands once more, the Christian conquerors would require assistance from within the conquered population and would naturally turn to the Jewish minority as a talented and trustworthy group that might provide considerable support. Precisely this attitude on the part of the Christian rulers is reflected in the charters for Tudela and Tortosa already noted.

As the Christian reconquest of the Iberian peninsula resumed during the opening decades of the thirteenth century, those Jews whose homes had already been overrun by the Christian armies found themselves increasingly more comfortable under Christian rule. In addition, many Jews opted to move voluntarily into the Christian areas and to link their fates with those of the expanding Christian principalities. Finally, even those Jews who remained in place in Muslim territories were more fully prepared to cooperate with the Christian forces that, during the great thirteenth-century Christian push southward on the peninsula, absorbed their home territories.

The bond of cooperation between the Jews of Spain and the increasingly potent Christian authorities enabled Jewish life to thrive across most of Spain, as the Christian share of the peninsula continued to grow. Jewish economic and cultural well-being was so pronounced as to lead many modern students of medieval Spanish Jewry to speak of a second "golden age" in Iberia. For these recent observers, the prior golden age under Muslim rule – the eleventh and early twelfth centuries – was succeeded by a thirteenth-century repetition under Christian auspices. The splendor of this second golden age is seen in terms of Jewish economic and political power, the ongoing role of well-placed Jewish courtiers in the royal courts of Christian Spain, and the explosion of spiritual and cultural creativity all across the peninsula.[29]

Economically, Jews maintained the prior lines of Jewish activity under Muslim rule. Especially prominent were the wealthy Jewish

families that continued to serve the ruling class, now no longer the
Muslim ruling class but that of the Christians. The one innovation
obvious during the thirteenth century was the introduction into Spain
of the new Jewish specialization in moneylending, already noted
in our discussion of the Church and southern-French Jewry. Once
again, the needs of a rapidly developing society and the intense opposition of the Church to Christians exacting usury from Christians
combined to open an important new area of the economy to Jewish
entrepreneurs. As already noted, moneylending has never been a
popular profession, and in the various areas of medieval western
Christendom the new Jewish specialty was fostered by the ruling
class and despised by many others.[30]

Acceptance by the new Christian authorities of the Jews of the
conquered areas and cooperation with them was the cornerstone of
the efflorescence of Jewish life in increasingly Christianized Spain.
This same acceptance and cooperation were deeply resented in sectors
of Christian society. The barons of Spain, acceding much of their
prior power to the monarchies, resented the strong alliance between
the kings and the Jews. The baronial convocations of the Spanish
kingdoms became centers of recurrent anti-Jewish agitation. The
urban populations of the Spanish kingdoms had their own grievances
against the Jews, who were largely seen as economic competitors. In
both cases, barons and city folk who fell victim to economic need
and then to Jewish moneylenders felt especially aggrieved.[31]

Perhaps the most important of the negative elements in Spain was
the Roman Catholic Church. Many of the expedients adopted by
the Christian rulers ran counter to traditional ecclesiastical policies.
Particularly noteworthy in this regard was the utilization of Jewish
courtiers for assistance in governance. A holdover from the role Jews
had played in Muslim Spain (where it also ran counter to traditional religious dictates), such political power vested in the hands
of Jews contravened one of the oldest concerns of the Church –
the specter of Jews in positions of power vis-à-vis Christians. Complaints about Jewish courtiers dot the correspondence of the popes
of the thirteenth century and of the prelates of the Spanish Church
as well. The more general thirteenth-century Church insistence on
enhanced segregation of the Jews surfaced in Spain as well. As knowledge of rabbinic literature accelerated during the middle decades of
the thirteenth century, traditional ecclesiastical concern with Jewish
blasphemy took on new urgency. Calls for censorship of the Talmud

and related rabbinic literature multiplied. The result of all this was considerable church–state tension and a complex balancing act on the part of the rulers of Christian Spain, aimed at appeasing the ecclesiastical pressures while enabling ongoing utilization of the human and fiscal resources provided by the Jews.

The most striking of the innovative ecclesiastical initiatives pursued in thirteenth-century Spain involved missionizing among the Jews. As noted, proselytizing was built into the core fabric of Christianity. This essential Christian value took on heightened significance in thirteenth-century western Christendom in general and on the Iberian peninsula in particular. The aggressiveness spawned by the rapid development of western Christendom first manifested itself during the eleventh century in military terms. Before long, however, voices in the Christian world suggested that the proper mode for engagement with the enemies of Christianity was through a war of words, rather than a war of arms. The new Christian propensity for missionary engagement with the world of Islam was buttressed by the growth in the early thirteenth century of the European universities, in which intellectual leaders sought to make peace between the dictates of Christian faith and the teachings of philosophy. As that daring enterprise gained force, Christian thinkers became yet more confident of their ability to vanquish the Muslim foe – and other foes as well – by the force of argumentation. In addition, fuller awareness of the non-Christian world and readiness to learn the ways and the thoughts of that world moved Christian circles to undertake extensive translation efforts aimed at making the underpinnings of Muslim thinking accessible. All these elements combined to strengthen Christian resolve to engage the world of Islam in religious dispute.[32]

In the process and almost inevitably, the Jews became yet another target of missionizing ardor. The Jews certainly constituted a less significant foe, at least in terms of strength, resources, and the threat they posed. On the other hand, Jews were age-old dissenters, indeed the very first to reject the teachings of Jesus and his disciples. The Jews, as the group seemingly best situated to acknowledge the truths of Christianity, had a long history of recalcitrance, which often seemed quite threatening. If the new militancy, buttressed by philosophic sophistication and enhanced knowledge of the other, might eventuate in winning over the oldest of the dissidents, that would constitute a signal achievement indeed.[33]

While these sentiments were shared all across western Christendom, it was on the Iberian peninsula that the commitment to both military and intellectual engagement with the Muslim world was most intense. In fact, the protracted military engagement with the forces of Islam lent special force to the intellectual engagement as well. It hardly seems accidental that the earliest Jewish polemical works to be composed in medieval western Christendom were penned in Christian Spain and adjacent southern France.

One early Spanish work – the *Milḥamot ha-Shem* (*The Wars of the Lord*) of the otherwise unknown Jacob ben Reuben – is rich and fascinating.[34] The author portrays himself as exiled from his home community. He claims that, in his place of refuge, he was befriended by a distinguished local cleric, from whom he learned much about philosophic and theological issues. At some point, the friendly exchanges purportedly moved the Christian to urge the Jew to abandon his ancestral faith and his beleaguered ancestral community. This conversionist turn in the relationship seemingly moved Jacob to compose his polemical manual, in which a variety of Christian arguments are depicted and then rebutted. The portrayal of Christian argumentation is detailed, and the Christian figure in the dialogue is hardly a straw man, easily dispatched. Rather, the exchanges are protracted, with the Christian defending his position repeatedly and vigorously. To be sure, in the end the Jewish position always emerges victorious. Toward the close of the twelve-chapter work, Jacob goes on the offensive, citing key passages from the Gospel of Matthew in Hebrew and attacking from a number of perspectives the views embedded in these passages. *Milḥamot ha-Shem* suggests, on the one hand, close relations between Christians and Jews, with accelerating Christian knowledge of Jews and Judaism and – likewise – accelerating Jewish knowledge of Christians and Christianity. The book also suggests augmented twelfth-century religious pressures on the Jews of Christian Spain to abandon their faith and join the Christian majority.

A measure of success in these Christian efforts is reflected in the evidence for a number of thirteenth-century converts from Judaism to Christianity who came out of the center of the Jewish communities of southern Europe, rather than from their margins. Some of these converts joined the ranks of the missionizers, bringing with them both zeal and intimate knowledge of Jewish religious tradition, sensibilities, and vulnerabilities. By the middle decades of the thirteenth century, Christian pressures for conversion of both Muslims and Jews in Iberia had proceeded from the informality encountered in *Milḥamot ha-Shem* to an organized and well-financed campaign. The assistance of the authorities was enlisted to enforce Muslim and Jewish attendance at conversionist sermons delivered by Dominican preachers. Spain, with its large population of subject Muslims and Jews, became the center of this organized campaign. At the same time, the effort to discover new lines of argumentation that might discomfit Muslim and Jewish audiences was relentlessly pursued. Key to this effort was richer Christian knowledge of Muslim and Jewish tradition and thirteenth-century Muslim and Jewish thinking. Chairs in Arabic and Hebrew were established, so that Christian scholars might plumb the sacred literature of both the Muslim and Jewish communities. As noted, learned converts from Judaism provided instant access to knowledge of Jewish tradition and literature.

We have noted already the important missionizing confrontation organized in Barcelona in 1263 by the Dominicans, under the sponsorship of King James the Conqueror of Aragon.[35] While both sides trumpeted victory, in fact the subsequent activities of both the Dominicans and the Jews suggest a measure of success and a measure of shortcoming. From the Jewish side, Rabbi Moses ben Nahman committed himself to combating both the old and the new Christian missionizing thrusts; from the Christian side, Friar Raymond Martin elaborated the new proselytizing argumentation in his massive *Pugio fidei*.

A few decades after the Barcelona encounter, a yet more impressive former Jew made his mark as a Christian proselytizer. Abner of Burgos was a respected leader in his Jewish community, fully immersed in the traditional Jewish curriculum and in the new areas of cultural creativity such as philosophy and mysticism. He was a Jewish leader to whom his co-religionists regularly addressed their concerns and doubts. Unbeknownst to his fellow-Jews, he himself was wracked with doubts about the truth of his faith. He seems to have been affected in particular by the growing Christian emphasis on historical fate, on the good fortune of the Christian world as contrasted with the suffering of the Jews. Shortly after the beginning of the fourteenth century, Abner came to the decision to leave his ancestral community and join the Christian camp. Like Friar Paul before him, Abner – now Alfonso of Vallodolid – embarked on an effort to bring his former co-religionists along with him. Whereas Friar

Paul's medium was oral presentation, via sermons and disputations, Abner/Alfonso was a man of the written word. He composed treatises and letters addressed to the Jews. These works were written in Hebrew, were replete with profound Jewish learning, and were couched in the style of rabbinic argumentation. A reader focusing on the style of Abner/Alfonso's writings only, without attention to their content, would come away with a sense of encountering carefully honed rabbinic compositions. The great historian of medieval Iberian Jewry, Yitzhak Baer, considered Abner/Alfonso the most serious proselytizer the Jews of medieval Spain encountered.[36]

The Church assault was intense, and some of the best minds in Spanish Jewry committed themselves to the defense effort. We have noted the role of Rabbi Moses ben Nahman, one of the giants of thirteenth-century Jewish creativity, at the Barcelona disputation. Subsequent to the encounter with Friar Paul in Barcelona, Rabbi Moses harnessed his remarkable literary and exegetical abilities to a series of compositions intended to buttress Jewish faith in the face of the intense Christian assault. The intellectual leaders of medieval Spanish Jewry, from the late twelfth century on, regularly produced significant anti-Christian polemics, aimed at reinforcing the faith of beleaguered Jews. The Hebrew writings of Abner/Alfonso in particular generated a spate of Jewish responses.

While much Jewish intellectual activity was oriented in this direction, Jewish cultural and spiritual energies were hardly exhausted in this important defensive effort. As noted, there is a perception of the thirteenth century as a second material and spiritual golden age for the Jews of Iberia. One of the first tasks on the spiritual plane involved adjustment to the new language circumstances of Iberian Jewry. As noted, under Muslim rule, the Jews of Spain used Arabic as both their vernacular and literary language. This meant ready familiarity with the majority literature of their environment and rich Jewish creativity in Judeo-Arabic. The transition to Christian rule introduced major cultural changes. The Jews of Christian Spain no longer used Arabic in their everyday discourse and thus lost access to both the multi-faceted Arabic literature that had enriched Jewish creativity during the first golden age and the remarkable Jewish literature composed in Judeo-Arabic. In Christian Spain, the everyday language of the Jews became the local Romance dialect. The literary language of the Christian milieu – Latin – was largely closed to the Jews of Christian Spain, making Hebrew the Jews' literary language. These changes necessitated, on the one hand, recapturing the legacy of Jewish creativity in the Islamic world through a major translation effort and, at the same time, honing medieval Hebrew to accommodate its new role as the dominant literary language of the Jews. Happily for the explosion of Jewish creativity, both tasks were successfully accomplished.

To an extent, these Jews of thirteenth-century Spain continued to be nourished by the legacy of the halcyon days of Islamic Spain; at the same time, they were stimulated by the increasingly vibrant culture of western Christendom as well. The result of these twin stimuli was accelerating Jewish creativity in a variety of cultural domains. Talmudic and biblical studies remained the central focus of the Jewish curriculum, and major works of exegesis of both classical literatures were fashioned. We have noted the public role of Rabbi Moses ben Nahman as Jewish spokesman in the missionizing encounter engineered by the Church in Barcelona in 1263. As indicated, Nahmanides followed up his oral presentation with a series of post-disputation compositions intended to drive home the polemical lessons that Jewish reading of Scripture was utterly accurate, that Jewish moral standards were the highest and Christian moral standards debased, and that Jewish suffering by no means reflected divine rejection. The same Nahmanides was a major figure in both talmudic and biblical exegesis. His comments on the Talmud are seen as the beginning of a new era in Spanish Jewish study of the Talmud; his commentary on the first five books of the Hebrew Bible has become a classic, studied regularly in Jewish schools from the thirteenth century down through the twenty-first. Both commentaries are distinguished by the remarkable range of the author's command of prior Jewish sources and his profound sensitivity to literary style. In particular, the literary skill reflected in Nahmanides' brilliant narrative account of the Barcelona proceedings is reflected in his biblical commentary as well, as he probes the storytelling style of the biblical account.[37]

A concern with philosophy was one of the major legacies inherited from the Jews of Islamic Spain. The pursuit of philosophy was controversial during the Middle Ages in all three monotheistic faith communities. As noted, it was felt by many that philosophic inquiry, bequeathed to the West by the Greeks, was ultimately incompatible with revealed religious truth and could only lead monotheistic believers astray. Alternatively, if such inquiry did not lead believers astray, it would introduce into religious thinking and belief views that would dilute essential Islamic, Christian, and Jewish doctrine. The defenders of philosophy of course saw things differently. For them, philosophy could not be incompatible with religious truth, because both had as their ultimate source the one and only God in the universe. Thus, philosophy could by no means lead believers astray, nor could it dilute essential religious doctrine. To the contrary, a religious tradition that does not wrestle with the questions posed by philosophy stands in jeopardy of fossilization and of losing many of its adherents.

For many – if not most – medieval Jews, philosophic inquiry was synonymous with one dominating figure – Rabbi Moses ben Maimon, born in Spain, nourished by the culture fashioned by the Jews of Islamic Spain, and eventually transplanted to the east-ern end of the Mediterranean basin. Within a few decades of his death, the writings of Maimonides had already begun to spark seri-ous controversy, which broke out initially in the towns of southern France.[38] Fairly quickly, the two sides to the dispute turned to the larger and neighboring Jewish communities of Spain, where pro- and anti-Maimonidean factions developed. Interestingly, the same Rabbi Moses ben Nahman, whom we have already encountered in a num-ber of connections, played a decisive role here as well. He projected a moderate position, which acknowledged both the legitimacy and the dangers of philosophic inquiry. In the face of this complexity, he urged limitations on philosophic study, intended to maximize the gains deriving from it while minimizing the dangers.[39]

The commitment to philosophic inquiry suggests that at least some Jews were no longer satisfied with received religious tradition and were seeking new and greater depth for their religious commitments. Yet another index of such seeking was the efflorescence of mystical speculation during the late twelfth and on into the thirteenth century. This mystical speculation involved an effort to discern the deeper truths hidden behind the surface phenomena of everyday life and the surface meaning of Scripture. While mystical inclinations are patent in the literature of the Jews from biblical times down through the Middle Ages and beyond, in our period these inclinations intensified and assumed the dimensions of movements.[40]

The first major glimmerings of the new mystical propensities emerged in southern France toward the end of the twelfth century. As we have seen, the general societal backdrop of religious search-ing made southern France an appropriate venue for the new Jewish mysticism.[41] Fairly quickly, the interest manifested itself in Catalonia as well, then spread further westward into Castile. The rapid maturation of this new impulse is striking. By the end of the thirteenth century, the new inclination had produced the great classic of Jewish mystical literature, the *Zohar* (*The Book of Illumination*). Written in a purposely archaic Aramaic and presenting itself as the work of a great second-century rabbi of Roman Palestine, the book presented the teachings of circles of Spanish kabbalists who sought to penetrate the secrets hidden behind surface realities.[42]

The Christian setting for the new Jewish mysticism is by no means irrelevant. One of the major concerns of mystical speculation in general is to narrow the distance between the human believer and the divine (which the philosophic tradition tends to magnify). For Jews living in thirteenth-century Spain, this issue was especially vexing. The traditional Christian emphasis on a variety of divine forces and – increasingly – on the intercessory role of Mary, the mother of Jesus, raised issues for Jews. On the one hand, Jewish polemicists delighted in attacking these notions of multiple forces on the divine scene; at the same time, some Jews clearly found the notions of a caring and responsive deity and a central feminine figure appealing. The new Jewish mystical circles projected a complex divine arena, an arena of ten *sefirot*, replete with a multiplicity of interacting forces. The divine–human interaction was thus made intense and intimate, constituting in effect a response to the challenge of Christianity. At the same time, and understandably, the Jewish mystical circles painted an extremely negative picture of Christianity as a distorted view of the dynamics of the divinity and of the divine–human relationship.

The first "golden age" of Spanish Jewry, under Muslim rule, ended with the onset of the Christian reconquest and the introduction of the Almoravides and Almohades onto the Iberian peninsula; the second "golden age," under Christian rule, ended with the broadly disastrous fourteenth century – the set of pan-European demographic and economic setbacks, deepened by the plague that affected all areas of western Christendom at the midpoint of the century. The Iberian peninsula suffered along with all other sectors of Europe, and the Jews of Spain endured both the direct and indirect consequences of the crisis. Directly, they were affected by the economic and political retrogression and by the ravages of the plague; indirectly, they bore the traditional lot of minorities in periods of economic decline; also indirectly, the new perceptions of Jews as hostile to their Christian surroundings resulted in widespread allegations that the plague was the working of Jewish malevolence.

The incredible devastation of the plague years meant a breakdown of normal societal authority and constraints. While the rulers of Christian Spain and the authorities of the Church attempted to maintain law and order, they were regularly foiled by the force of popular hysteria. With regard to the Jews specifically, a general pattern is manifest. There were numerous assaults on the Jewish communities of Iberia; the authorities of Church and state attempted to protect the endangered Jews; in some instances, the protection was effective; in other cases, it was not. Thus, the Jews suffered doubly, succumbing on the one hand to the plague itself and at the same time enduring the collateral damage occasioned by majority panic and the accumulated imagery that pointed to the Jews as responsible for the disaster.

The crisis of 1348–1349 for the Jews of the Iberian peninsula was a prelude to a far greater tragedy, which struck at the end of the fourteenth century. Starting in the late 1370s, an especially zealous preacher in the southern areas of Castile named Ferrand Martinez aroused the populace against the Jews. He painted alleged Jewish malevolence in unusually inflammatory colors and urged a set of anti-Jewish actions that went far beyond what was canonically permitted. With the death of the king of Castile in 1390 and a weak regency serving on behalf of the very young successor, the stage was set once again for a breakdown of normal law and order. The storm broke out in early June of 1391 in Seville, the town in which Martinez was most active. The Jewish quarter was obliterated; the synagogue became a church; many Jews were killed; many more Jews accepted baptism and thus saved their lives. From Seville, the violence spread throughout the southern areas of Castile, relatively new to Christian control, and on into the northern areas of Castile as well. By early July, the anti-Jewish agitation had spread across the border into Aragon. The royal authorities made intensive efforts to quell the agitation and resultant violence, but to little avail.

When the summer of 1391 was over, the Jewish communities of both Castile and Aragon lay in shambles. Jewish quarters had disappeared; synagogues were gone; thousands of Jews had lost their lives; many more had accepted Christianity and thus maintained themselves. This last aspect of the tragedy imposed a new dimension to it. The conversions of 1391 were the most numerous ever suffered by the Jewish communities of medieval western Christendom, shocked the remaining Jews, and begged explanation. Not surprisingly, the prior cultural battles of Spanish Jewry set the parameters for these explanations. For many, the chief factor in the loss of Jewish faith was the commitment to philosophy. Philosophic teaching had sapped the inner strength of the Jews of Spain, making them vulnerable – in the face of popular violence – to the blandishments of Christianity. Modern historians, sensitive to the contrast with the Jewish martyrdoms of 1096, have extended the allegation. The Jews of the Rhineland, unsullied by philosophy, responded to their attackers in 1096 with an unprecedented outburst of martyrdom; the Jews of Spain, attenuated by their flirtation with philosophy, wilted in the face of the violence of 1391.[43]

This medieval/modern explanation for the conversions of 1391 is surely overly simplistic. The differences between 1096 and 1391 are numerous and extend well beyond the issue of philosophy. In the first place, the two Jewish communities involved were radically different one from the other. As we shall see, the Rhineland Jewish communities were young, small, and socially rather isolated from their majority environment. In contrast, the Spanish Jews of 1391 constituted an old and large community fairly well integrated into its surroundings. Moreover, the two sets of attacks were hardly the same. In 1096, the Rhineland Jews were assaulted as an outgrowth of remarkable religious exhilaration, flavored by millenarian fervor. They were attacked in the name of the Christian faith, and this attack generated a Jewish counter-crusade commitment, the commitment to battle Christianity in the name of Judaism. Death in such a battle constituted a victory of sorts.[44] In contrast, the attacks of 1391 were the result of socio-economic and ethnic grievances. Meeting such assaults with Jewish martyrdom hardly seemed an appropriate or meaningful response. Finally, the study of philosophy may have blunted to an extent the commitment to Jewish identity; however, the century and a half of intense Christian missionizing probably did far more harm to that commitment. Indeed, one of the major emphases in the new missionizing was the proof of Christian truth from Christian ascendance and Jewish suffering. Thus, precisely such a disaster served to underscore this important Christian thrust. Jews reeling from the physical tragedy had to contend with the damaging Christian interpretation of it.

Whatever the wellsprings of the massive conversion of 1391, it left a residue of problems for the Jewish minority and for the Christian majority. On the simplest level, the deaths and conversions – espe-cially the latter – created a mood of despondency among the surviv-ing Spanish Jews. The reality of such devastating losses, some through physical violence and others through abandonment of the commu-nity, struck deep at the psyche of the Jews of the Iberian penin-sula. In addition, the massive conversion meant rich new fodder for Christian argumentation. Missionizing preachers could now point to the numerous converts, living in close proximity to those who had remained Jewish. These preachers could pose painful questions: Are there compelling reasons to suggest that these converts, many for-merly respected and upstanding members of the Jewish community, erred? Indeed, is it not likely that those who held fast to their Jewish identity were the ones in error? The propriety of conversion was much reinforced by the reality of so many converts.

In fact, well aware of the crisis created by the conversions of 1391, the Church pressed on with its proselytizing efforts. In 1413, the Church initiated at Tortosa yet another missionizing disputa-tion. Once again, the Christian case was advanced by a convert. The Christian spokesman, the former Jew Joshua ha-Lorki, subsequently known as Hieronymus of Sancta Fide, seemed to have been more Jewishly learned than Friar Paul of the thirteenth century, although the technique of argumentation was precisely that initiated by the lat-ter. Hieronymus set out to prove, over a lengthy period of time and with considerable patience, that rabbinic sources acknowledged that the Messiah had already come. Given the realities of world history, this could only mean that Jesus was in fact the promised Messiah. The Tortosa disputation was lengthier, more closely monitored, and far more successful from the Christian perspective than that at Barcelona. As it unfolded, significant numbers of additional Jews left their faith community.

Strikingly, the Jewish communities of Spain were able to rebuild themselves in considerable measure. While some Jewish enclaves dis-appeared forever, many were slowly rebuilt over the course of the fifteenth century. The leaders of the Jewish communities banded together to analyze elements in the disaster that might be amenable to amelioration and undertook what they saw as the required cor-rectives. Extravagant Jewish behaviors, which might arouse Christian envy and animosity, were carefully limited; the internal Jewish tax structure, which might have fed Jewish dissatisfactions, was modified; the Jewish schooling system, key to maintenance of Jewish identity, was analyzed and reformed. The achievements of the Jewish communal leadership were impressive, and these leaders received considerable support and assistance from their traditional allies, the monarchs of Aragon and Castile. Difficulties notwithstanding, functioning Jewish communities once again dotted the Spanish landscape during the fifteenth century.[45]

While the Jews of Spain encountered formidable obstacles in the wake of 1391, the problems created by the massive conversions were no less challenging to the Christian majority. Despite the time-honored commitment to the goal of converting the Jews, the reality of large-scale conversion entailed difficulties. At one level, the problems were social. The Christians of Spain suddenly found themselves confronted with a new Christian population, a population of folks who had heretofore been Jewish and had suddenly joined Christian ranks. Social acceptance of these newcomers was far from easy. In many cases, they lived in the same neighborhoods they had previously inhabited as Jews and plied the same trades. To a significant extent, they maintained prior social and marital linkages within the convert population. Thus, changing attitudes to them was sometimes difficult for many of their old-line Christian neighbors. Moreover, in some instances those newly christianized quickly moved into economic and political positions once closed to them, attracting all the antipathy that is normally the lot of parvenus. Many long-time Spanish Christians recoiled from contact with the newly christianized.

A curious terminology emerged, which distinguished between Old Christians and New Christians. In theory, there was no place for such terminology, since the newly christianized were theoretically fully Christian. Yet the terminology did develop, with a racist focus on biology following not long after. Spaniards became attracted to notions of blood purity, which meant simply a long lineage within the Christian fold. By the middle years of the fifteenth century, an identifiable New Christian class had emerged, had attracted much of the animosity normally focused on the Jews, and had even become the object of popular violence.

Beyond the problematic of social integration, there were religious issues as well. The first involved the status of those converted under duress. Since — as we have seen — Christianity from early on prohibited forced conversion and promised Jews freedom from such coercion, many of the converts assumed that their conversion would have no meaning and that, when life returned to normal, they would of course be permitted to return to their prior Jewish identity and community.[46] In fact, however, ecclesiastical doctrine on this issue had become highly complex, distinguishing between absolute force – where the person in question had no physical alternative whatsoever – and conditional force, in which human volition could still be exercised. Conversion through absolute force was meaningless, since it involved no willing consent whatsoever; conversion through conditional force – for example offering the alternatives of baptism or death – was prohibited, but was at the same time irreversible, because the victim did in fact exercise his or her will and consented to the baptism. Thus, the conversions undergone by the Jews in 1391, while prohibited and lamentable, could not be undone.

Thus, the converts of 1391 consisted of a number of sub-groups. There were those for whom the violence was the very last straw, pushing them over a precipice and into the Christian camp. These converts genuinely wished to join the Christian majority. At the other extreme were those Jews who had always intended to remain Jewish, who had assumed that their conversion would have no validity, and who were thus ensnared in a Christian identity for which they had no desire. Finally, there was also a group of skeptics, Jews who no longer believed in the Jewish religious vision and thus could not bring themselves to die for it. At the same time, such skeptics were highly unlikely to accept the doctrines of Christianity. They were, from the outset, utter disbelievers. Integrating the first sub-group might be difficult because of the numbers involved. The second and third groups posed enormous difficulties to those committed to making the newly christianized truly christianized.

Within the Spanish Church, a number of views emerged as to how best to deal with the large and problematic group of newcomers to Christianity. One wing of the Church called for loving acceptance, careful instruction, and much patience. Acknowledging that change of religious identity is a complex phenomenon, this sector of the Spanish Church argued for a long-term vision and a long-term solution to the problem of the converts. A second wing of the Church saw the issue in starker terms. Christians who failed in their Christian obligations, either of practice or belief, could not be tolerated, no matter what the specifics of their circumstances. Such Christians were simply miscreants; in the language of the Church they were heretics. The crime of heresy had long been perceived as a threat to the Church and to all of Christian society. In dealing with this crime, effective modalities had long been available and must now be utilized. The key element in this response to widespread heresy was the inquisition.

The term "inquisition" has a fearsome quality associated with it. In fact, in the medieval world the term simply designated a special ecclesiastical court, assigned a unique set of problems with which to deal and armed with a number of unique judiciary tools with which to engage those problems. These special courts had emerged into prominence in southern France during the outbreak of what the Church defined as heresy in the twelfth century. Because of what was perceived as the seriousness of the danger associated with heresy and the difficulties of rooting it out, the inquisitorial courts were permitted to hide the identity of those providing evidence against the heretics and to use torture in order to obtain evidence. By the fifteenth century, these unusual and dangerous judicial procedures had become an established part of the inquisitorial system. Also, the special province of the inquisitorial courts – that is to say the identification and destruction of heresy – gave them a special place within the ecclesiastical hierarchy, a position of remarkable power.

When an inquisitorial court was established in a given area, its first step was normally the announcement of an edict of grace, a proclamation inviting those guilty of heresy to come forth and confess. Those confessing were punished with a variety of penances. More important, those confessing heresy had to furnish full information on confederates in heretical activity. Thus, the grace period was simultaneously the beginning of the creation of dossiers of information on the alleged heresy of people other than those coming forward to confess.

Upon the completion of this initial phase, the process of gathering information accelerated. The broad populace was informed of the signs of heresy and urged to come forward with evidence of heretical behavior. The evidence thus provided was carefully recorded, with – as noted – the identity of the witnesses protected. Obviously such protection of identity might have encouraged false testimony, but the penalties for lying were heavy. The extent to which false testimony was elicited is a subject of considerable dispute among historians of the inquisition. Those arrested were intensely interrogated, with torture one of the tools of interrogation. While the application of torture was carefully controlled, the extent to which false confession was obtained is yet another point of contention among students of the institution. The objective of all this was confession on the part of the heretic and return to the orthodox fold. Those proven guilty of the crime of heresy, but unwilling to confess and retract, were judged to be the most dangerous of criminals and were turned over to the secular authorities for execution. Heretics were burned in public ceremonies intended to reinforce societal condemnation of the crime, to instill fear of committing the crime of heresy, and to elicit broad willingness to assist in its suppression.

In fifteenth-century Spain, the overwhelming majority of the heretics thus pursued were accused of the specific crime of judaizing, that is to say returning to their earlier Jewish roots, practices, and beliefs. As noted, some of the New Christians of the Iberian peninsula had by no means intended to embrace the Christian faith when they had been forcibly baptized; others had been non-believing Jews turned into non-believing Christians; even some of those who had fully embraced their new faith and had hoped to find a place in the Christian world were disillusioned by the negative reception they perceived on the part of their Christian neighbors. Thus, backsliding into Jewish practice and belief was surely a reality, although precisely how widespread a reality is again a matter of dispute.[47]

All the common inquisitorial procedures described just now made their appearance in fifteenth-century Spain. Especially intriguing are the signs of heresy announced by the inquisitorial courts as they embarked on the information-gathering phase of their activity. Spanish Christians were encouraged to report neighbors who seemed to tidy up their homes on Friday afternoons, whose chimneys seemed to cease producing smoke on Saturdays, who seemed to avoid certain foods, who seemed to refrain from eating altogether on a given day in the early fall. All these unusual behaviors might be interpreted as signs of backsliding into prior patterns of Jewish behavior and would be worthy of reporting to the inquisitorial court. The range of those haled before the tribunal was wide and included common men and women, the well-to-do of both sexes, and some who had risen to high place in both secular and ecclesiastical circles. The special status of the inquisitorial courts made them immune to intervention on the part of the secular and ecclesiastical establishment.

As the inquisitorial investigations proceeded into the 1480s, evidence seemed to mount of massive backsliding on the part of the New Christian population of the peninsula. A sense emerged that inquisitorial prosecution could by no means contain the crimes and the danger they presented to Christian society at large. It was increasingly urged that a major factor in the backsliding was the presence of the large Jewish population of the peninsula and the ongoing connections between the New Christians and their Jewish former friends and neighbors. The solution proposed for the seemingly monumental problem of heresy among the New Christians was to eliminate the contact with Jews through expulsion and then to proceed relentlessly against the New Christians, who would be deprived of their living and immediate connections to Judaism.

Lurking behind this suggestion of expulsion were some prior elements of reality and theory. There were the realities of a seventh-century banishment from the Iberian peninsula, of which little was (and still is) known. More immediately and more importantly, the Jews of England and France had been expelled, the former in 1290 and the latter first in 1306 and then again (a much reduced community of returnees) at the end of the fourteenth century. These well-known thirteenth- and fourteenth-century precedents – and many more localized and lesser-known precedents – were not capricious acts. They were grounded in the fundamental ecclesiastical theory we have already examined. Jews had a legitimate place in Christian society, so long as they in no way brought harm to their Christian hosts. In the thirteenth- and fourteenth-century expulsions from England and France, Jewish usury – claimed to be harmful and a problem that had proven intractable – served as the legitimating grounds for the decision to expel the Jews. In fifteenth-century Spain, voices began to argue that Jews were bringing harm on Christian society through their very presence and their encouragement of backsliding among the New Christians. This harmfulness was advanced as the grounds for expulsion.

Obviously, the Church voices had to win the backing of the secular authorities in order to become effective. As noted, the kings of Aragon and Castile had long engaged in a complex balancing act, playing off the utility of the Jews against the combined pressures of ecclesiastical demands, the resentments of the barony, and the anti-Jewish inclinations of the urban population. As the end of the fifteenth century approached, major developments on the royal scene took place. The first was the marriage in 1469 of Isabella, heiress to the crown of Castile, and Ferdinand, heir to the throne of Aragon. In 1474, the couple became rulers of Castile; in 1479, they acceded to power in Aragon. Isabella and Ferdinand were energetic and capable; they immediately set about reforming major aspects of governance in both Castile and Aragon. A core tendency of their rule involved amassing as much power as possible in the throne; they were highly committed to the centralization of authority. They were, at the same time, also deeply committed to achieving homogeneity on the peninsula and within Christian society. They were determined to uproot the last vestiges of Muslim power on the peninsula, and in 1492 they were successful in so doing. They were likewise committed to destroying heresy within Christian society and became zealous supporters of the inquisition. Eventually, they became convinced that the removal of the Jews was essential to the extirpation of heresy and thus to the creation of a homogeneously orthodox Christian society in their realms. This conviction was played out in 1492, ending the long and illustrious history of the Jews on most of the Iberian peninsula.

The Jews expelled from Castile and Aragon faced a limited number of refuge options. England and France – both northern and southern – were by now closed to Jewish settlement. Large numbers of Jews made their way to nearby Portugal, where their presence was briefly encouraged. The desire to effect a marriage alliance with the rulers of Castile and Aragon, however, led to the demand from the latter for expulsion from Portugal. The result, in 1497, was a bizarre combination: an order of expulsion, withholding of all opportunities for flight, and consequent proclamation of de facto conversion. In effect, the Portuguese option was quickly closed off.[48]

The only remaining realistic option within western Christendom was Italy, but the possibilities there were slim, as we shall shortly see. For most of those expelled from the Iberian peninsula and fortunate enough to make their way elsewhere, the realistic refuge lay in the rapidly developing areas of the Turkish Empire, which by and large welcomed the forced Jewish émigrés. Old centers in the Middle East became home to Iberian Jews, who settled into their new homes with a very strong sense of business and spiritual superiority and who insisted on maintaining their own language and culture. The extent to which the Sephardic element in the diversified Jewish populations of the Near East rose to leadership is reflected in the fact that these old Jewries came to be identified as Sephardic with the passage of time, obliterating by and large the reality of the older Jewish elements long housed in this area.

One of the descendants of the exiled Jews mused subsequently on the origins of his community. The sixteenth-century Solomon ibn

Verga suggested that the roots of the Jewry to which he belonged lay all the way back in the sixth pre-Christian century, the time of the destruction of the First Temple in Jerusalem by the Babylonians. According to ibn Verga, the Babylonian king needed assistance and called upon the king of Spain. When the conquest of Jerusalem had been successfully completed, the Babylonian king offered his Spanish ally first choice of the spoils. The clever Spanish monarch chose the Jews of the finest neighborhood of the conquered city and took them back with him to the Iberian peninsula. As history, this tale is risible; as a reflection of the Sephardic sense of belonging on the Iberian peninsula, it is precious, revealing – alongside the belief in antiquity – the Spanish Jewish sense of aristocracy, of descent from the Jews of the choicest neighborhood of biblical Jerusalem and evolution into the cultural aristocracy of subsequent Jewish life.

ITALY AND SICILY

The history of the Jewish communities of Italy and adjacent Sicily is *sui generis* and most difficult to reconstruct, far more difficult than that of the Jews of either southern France or the Iberian peninsula. While both of the latter areas showed considerable diversity, there were in both cases sufficient commonalities to allow for a reasonably linear presentation. No such commonalities are available for the Italian peninsula, which constituted a complex of diverse geographic and socio-economic areas that failed to achieve anything approaching political unity during the Middle Ages.[49] Parts of Italy constituted the oldest areas of Jewish habitation during our period, while other parts of Italy were devoid of Jews in the year 1000 and only gained a Jewish population during the later medieval centuries. Put differently, sectors of Italy were very much southern European in terms of their Jews, housing old and economically diversified Jewish communities, while other sectors were distinctly northern European, with new Jews immigrating and settling into limited niches of the economy.[50] In addition to these internal differences, the political and military weakness of medieval Italy invited outside interference, invasion, and conquest. Thus, the history of Italy and its Jews is often a reflection of attitudes and policies spawned elsewhere in medieval Europe. The story of medieval Italian Jewry is, as a result, utterly fragmented and disjointed.[51] In view of this fragmentation, we shall have to adopt a somewhat different strategy from the prior depictions of the Jewries of southern France and Spain and from the subsequent depictions of the Jewish communities of northern France, England, Germany and eastern Europe. We shall in effect tell – somewhat briefly – three separate tales: the first of the Jewish communities of Sicily and southern Italy; the second of the special Jewish communities of the papal states and Rome; and the third of the later developing Jewish communities of the north.[52]

Benjamin of Tudela once again provides valuable insight, this time into the demography of twelfth-century Italian Jewry. On his way eastward, he visited the following towns on the Italian peninsula and indicates the Jewish population of each: Genoa – two Jews; Pisa – twenty Jews; Lucca – forty Jews; Rome – two hundred Jews; Capua – three hundred Jews; Naples – five hundred Jews; Salerno – six hundred Jews; Amalfi – twenty Jews; Benevento – two hundred Jews; Melfi – two hundred Jews; Trani – two hundred Jews; Taranto – three hundred Jews; Brindisi – ten Jews; Otranto – five hundred Jews. On his way back westward, he also visited Sicily, for which he cites Messina with its two hundred Jews and Palermo with its fifteen hundred Jews.[53]

A number of interesting conclusions emerge from this somewhat strange list. First, the center of Jewish population on the Italian peninsula in the twelfth century was very much in the south. The Jewish populations in the northern cities of Genoa, Pisa, and Lucca were minuscule compared to some of the larger Jewish communities of the south, such as Naples, Salerno, Otranto, and especially Palermo. Second, the larger Jewish populations of the towns of southern Italy – five hundred to fifteen hundred – exceeded by a considerable margin the Jewish populations of any of the towns that Benjamin had visited in the northern portions of the Iberian peninsula, in southern France, and in northern Italy. Finally, the fragmentation of the Italian peninsula was manifest as well. Benjamin notes recurrently the localized rule he encountered, and the fact that Jewish population in southern Italy could vary so widely between many hundreds on the one hand and ten and twenty on the other hand suggests a high level of local idiosyncrasy.

During the first half of our period, the center of Jewish population lay in the south, with Sicily probably accounting for more than half the Jews of Italy. Down into the eleventh century, Sicily was ruled by the Muslims, and parts of southern Italy by the Byzantines. Under Muslim rule in particular (as was the case on the Iberian peninsula),

Jews enjoyed the advantages of a multi-religious, multi-ethnic environment and flourished. Valuable insight into the Byzantine areas of the peninsula during this early period is provided by the *Megillat Ahima'az*, composed by Ahimaaz ben Paltiel. An expansive account of family and Jewish life in Italy over two centuries, the narrative provides – despite much imaginative material – remarkable insight into the vagaries of Jewish life in a southern Italy divided into Muslim, Byzantine, and Latin Christian spheres.[54]

Jewish economic life in the south was rooted in the long history of the Jews in the area and shows a high degree of diversification. Jews were involved in agriculture to a limited degree, crafts, business, and medicine. This diversification contributed significantly to the strength of the Jewish communities of Sicily and southern Italy. Jewish involvement in medicine is particularly noteworthy; as was the case in Muslim Spain, it involved traditional practice and expertise, on the one hand, and knowledge of the literature of science on the other. Jewish connections across the Mediterranean world and resultant Jewish knowledge of a variety of languages played a major role in Jewish mastery of the inherited scientific literature.

The Jews of Sicily and southern Italy have left us early indications of intellectual and spiritual creativity that preceded the year 1000. Some of these indicators are embedded in Jewish memories that are difficult to substantiate. Nonetheless, the recollection that the four Jewish captives who allegedly set in motion the later European centers of talmudic study – a story cited and made popular by the twelfth-century Abraham ibn Daud – set sail from Bari in southern Italy is striking.

While these memories and perceptions cannot be substantiated, there is considerable evidence that suggests they were by no means unfounded. Gravestone inscriptions indicate the increasing use of Hebrew across southern Italy during the early Middle Ages.[55] More important is the preservation of Hebrew poetry from the tenth century in the later *Megillat Ahima'az*, which shows mastery of the Hebrew language and a high level of poetic sophistication. Yet more striking is *Sefer Yosippon*, widely believed to be a product of tenth-century southern Italy. Purported to be a Hebrew version of the writings of Josephus, the flowing Hebrew narrative became a major medieval source of Jewish knowledge of late antiquity.

Even before the year 1000, a major creative figure emerged in southern Italy. His name was Shabbetai Donnolo, and he was a physician, scientific writer, linguist, talmudist, and mystical speculator. Donnolo, born in Oria, was a practicing physician-pharmacist, with extensive knowledge of Greek and Latin manuscripts. His *Book of Remedies* was innovative for Italy, where it was written, and for the Hebrew language, in which it was composed. Donnolo's commentary on the mystical *Sefer Yezirah* constitutes a very early index of Jewish attraction to mystical thought in western Christendom.[56]

Muslim and Byzantine hegemony over Sicily and southern Italy fell victim to the resurgence of western Christendom in general and its northern areas in particular. The first of the conquerors, the Normans, took control of these areas during the eleventh century – at roughly the same time that the Christian reconquest of the Iberian peninsula began – and made them a permanent part of Christian Europe. The Normans were displaced by the Hohenstaufens, who ruled from the late twelfth through the mid-thirteenth century. The Hohenstaufens were replaced briefly by the Angevins, who were succeeded more lastingly by the Aragonese.

So far as we can tell, the Norman conquerors did nothing to disturb the prior patterns of Jewish existence in the territories they conquered. Like their Iberian Christian counterparts, they seem to have concluded that the Jews could be useful allies in the effort to maintain the high level of civilization in the areas now under their control. Indeed, the Jewish population of Sicily and southern Italy was enhanced during the twelfth century by immigration from Iberia and North Africa spawned by Almoravide and Almohade persecutions, especially the latter.[57] Jews seeking refuge from this unusual persecution made their way northward on the Iberian peninsula, over into southern France, across into Sicily and southern Italy, and on occasion even further eastward in the Mediterranean basin. Those Jews who settled in Sicily and southern Italy under Norman rule seem to have found a hospitable reception.

The Hohenstaufens as well seem to have changed little in the circumstances of the Jewish communities of Sicily and southern Italy. Under Emperor Frederick II in particular, the Jews of Sicily and southern Italy played an important role in the transmission of knowledge from the Muslim and Byzantine worlds into the rapidly developing intellectual circles of western Christendom. As noted already, the Muslim world had preserved much of the intellectual legacy of antiquity through translation of scientific, philosophic, and literary masterpieces into Arabic. During the twelfth and thirteenth centuries, as western Christendom began its rapid ascent to power in the West, yet another stage of transmission was required, with the eventual creation of a corpus of influential texts available in Latin. The Jews of Sicily and southern Italy played no small role in this important process. As a result of contacts all through the Mediterranean world, many Jews were equipped with considerable language facility, which included Hebrew, Arabic, Greek, Latin, and early Italian. To an extent, these Jews worked on their own, with a concern for making Arabic classics available in Hebrew. At the same time, some of them worked in tandem with Christians, often under governmental patronage, with the goal of creating a Latin corpus. Frederick II's court was especially renowned for its commitment to the translation enterprise, with Jews prominent in this process.

During the thirteenth century, the southern-Italian Jewish propensity for wide-ranging cultural creativity continued to manifest itself. Jewish schools were active, and Jews composed works in a wide variety of literary genres. As was true generally for the various Jewries of medieval western Christendom, rabbinic studies stood at the center of the curriculum, and creativity in this domain was highly prized. Likewise, the Jews of Italy – like their confreres elsewhere – devoted themselves to study of the Hebrew Bible in a number of modalities, ranging from close scrutiny of the literal meaning of the biblical text to concern with the philosophic and mystical import of key biblical passages.

We have noted the early attraction of southern-Italian Jews to medicine and science, and that interest was maintained. Jewish physicians abounded during the thirteenth century, many of them achieving eminence in non-Jewish circles as well. The interest in medicine and science led easily to concern with philosophic issues and texts. Southern-Italian Jewish thinkers were very much part of the thirteenth-century Jewish tendency all across western Christendom to explore the issues of philosophy, often through the prism of the great twelfth-century legalist and philosopher, Moses ben Maimon. Reflections on the *oeuvre* and thinking of the famed Maimonides were undertaken by a number of Jewish savants. Inevitably, the reaction against philosophy in general and against Maimonidean doctrine in particular, which began already in the early years of the thirteenth century in southern France, made its way to southern Italy as well during the course of the century.

An interesting figure, who illustrates much of the foregoing, is the thirteenth-century Hillel ben Samuel. Hillel, like so many Jews of this period, seems to have moved from place to place, with stops noted at Rome, Capua, and Naples at least. Scion of a distinguished rabbinic family of Verona, he was a physician and scientific writer and, at the same time, a talmudist. He is best known as a philosopher, whose major work was *Tagmulei ha-Nefesh* (*The Rewards of the Soul*), a rambling composition in which reflections on key elements and works of prior philosophic speculation are undertaken. Hillel's philosophic writings indicate familiarity with some of the scholastic thinking developing in contemporary Christian circles. Hillel became intimately involved in the controversy that resurfaced at the end of the thirteenth century over the writings of Maimonides. He was a zealous defender of Maimonides and philosophic inquiry, attempting – with considerable success – to rally the supporters of philosophy against its opponents.

The mystical speculation that had begun to enliven Jewish life in western Christendom during the twelfth century and had achieved maturity during the thirteenth made its way into Italy as well. In part, this was a movement of people, in part, a movement of books and ideas. One of the major creative figures of thirteenth-century Jewish mysticism, Abraham Abulafia, made his way to Italy and there interacted with a number of Italian Jewish thinkers. Even without this immediate personal contact, Italian Jews began to read the works composed further westward and to add their own particular contribution to the burgeoning mystical corpus.

Under Aragonese rule from the late thirteenth century on, Jewish life in Sicily and southern Italy was, for a considerable time, maintained in its prior contours. By the end of the fifteenth century, signs of change were in the offing. Increasingly rabid anti-Jewish preaching emerged, sparking popular anti-Jewish rioting. The end was not far off. The edict of expulsion of 1492 included the Jews of the areas under Aragonese rule in the eastern Mediterranean as well, despite objections lodged by the local authorities.[58] A long and distinguished history came to a precipitous close.

The second of the sectors of Italy with which we shall deal is found in the middle of the peninsula; it is the area controlled by the papacy, most particularly the city of Rome itself. The Jewish community of Rome had of course distinguished roots in antiquity. Of the early Jewish communities on the peninsula, it was that of Rome itself that was the largest and most important. Valuable evidence for the Jewish communities of southern Europe in late antiquity comes from inscriptions, and the distribution of the extant inscriptions is revealing. In the most recent collection of European Jewish inscriptions from late antiquity, there are a mere three inscriptions from southern France; eleven from Spain; nineteen from Sicily; one hundred twenty-one from sites in southern Italy other than Rome; and five hundred fifty from Rome itself.[59] The overwhelming centrality for Jewish life of the southern sectors of the Italian peninsula and especially the city of Rome during this early period is patent.

The centrality of ancient Rome and its Jewish community is easy to understand. The great city was the commercial, political, and cultural hub of the Mediterranean world of late antiquity, the dominant urban enclave in a sprawling empire. As such, Rome became a magnet for adventurous Jewish migrants. Economic, social, and cultural opportunities abounded in the capital city, and Jews responded to the lure. Ensconced at the center of the empire, the Jews of Rome came to play an especially critical role in Jewish political life in late antiquity. The Jews of Rome negotiated with the Roman authorities on behalf of their brethren throughout the empire. The often beleaguered Jewry of Palestine was in constant contact with the Jewish community of Rome, sending delegations to plead its causes before the imperial authorities and exploiting the political, economic, and social strength of the Jews of the capital city.

Medieval Rome bore many vestiges of the greatness of antiquity, and the Jews of medieval Rome were cognizant of that earlier greatness. Benjamin of Tudela has left a striking account of his visit to the former imperial city. Overall, he notes that "there are many wonderful structures in the city, different from any others in the world." More specifically, "in the midst thereof [the twenty-four mile circumference of Rome], there are eighty palaces belonging to eighty kings who lived there, each one called *imperator*, commencing from King Tarquinius down to Nero and Tiberius, who lived at the time of Jesus the Nazarene, and ending with Pepin, who freed the land of Sepharad from Islam and was the father of Charlemagne." Benjamin describes extravagantly a number of such structures: the purported palaces of Julius Caesar, Titus, and Vespasian.[60] It is reasonable to assume that Benjamin's guides to these sites must have been the Jews of twelfth-century Rome, whom he depicts admiringly and who must have been justly proud of their home city's prior stature.

However, medieval Rome and Italy were much changed from the Rome and Italy of late antiquity. Centralized control of the western portions of the Roman Empire dissipated from the fifth century on, as did control of the peninsula itself. Italy, weakened by its own internal divisions, became an attractive prize for powerful and aggressive forces – from outside western Christendom the Byzantines and the Muslims, from inside western Christendom the Normans, Germans, French, and Aragonese. In the medieval world, Italy was no longer at the center, as it had been in antiquity. Rather, the vagaries of change transformed the Italian peninsula into an exposed area, poised on the borders between western and eastern Christendom and – even more important – between the Christian world and that of Islam; even within western Christendom, it was regularly prey to the ambitions of others.

In one respect, however, Rome retained its former glory and centrality in the West. No longer the capital of a powerful empire, Rome remained nonetheless the center of the far-flung world of Roman Catholicism. Seat of the papacy, Rome sent forth its emissaries throughout the length and breadth of western Christendom and received delegations from far and wide in return. To be sure, the papal throne was often endangered by the incessant battles for supremacy over the peninsula. On numerous occasions, the pope had to flee Rome and find refuge elsewhere in Italy or even outside of Italy. Nonetheless, the sense of papal Rome, its greatness, and its authority survived all these challenges. Once again, albeit in new ways, the Jewish community of Rome came to play an important role because of its location at the heart of authority, this time religious authority.

The sense of the importance of Rome as the seat of the papacy is well captured in an early Hebrew source from far-off northern Europe. While the details of the story may be suspect, the perception of the importance of the papacy, of Rome, and of Rome's Jewish community is manifest. According to this Hebrew account, the Jews of northern Europe were threatened early in the eleventh century by some of the leading barons of northwestern France, who ordered conversion or death. Supposedly, a major Jewish leader, one Jacob ben Yekutiel, challenged these barons with the argument that only the pope in Rome possessed the authority to issue such an edict. Purportedly, the Jewish leader was sent off to Rome, where he was hospitably received by the Jews of Rome and made his case successfully with the pope. Whatever the reality of this incident, the distant northern-European Jewish perception of the power of the papacy, Rome, and its Jews is clear.[61]

Once again, our helpful traveler, Benjamin of Tudela, provides useful evidence. Benjamin begins his depiction of Rome by noting: "Rome is the head of the kingdoms of Christendom and contains about two hundred Jews, who occupy an honorable position and pay no tribute. Among them are officials of the Pope Alexander, the spiritual head of all Christendom."[62] Noteworthy here is Benjamin's sense of the standing of the pope throughout Christendom and his perception of the positive relationship between Rome's Jews and the papal court. It is generally felt that the important *Constitutio pro Judeis*, which from the twelfth century onward served as a basic statement of Jewish rights, was in fact regularly transmitted to the Jewish community of Rome.[63] The Jews of Rome during our period served much the same intercessory role with the papacy that their ancestors in antiquity had served with the Roman emperors.

The medieval Jewish community of Rome was the stablest of the Jewish settlements in medieval Italy. While it regularly endured difficulties, it also enjoyed long periods of material ease and spiritual creativity. Indeed, it was the only Jewry of Italy to survive as a significant Jewish community from beginning to end of our period without interruption. While flux in Jewish life is prominent throughout Italy, Rome was a continuous home to a considerable Jewish community from 1000 to 1500.[64] In some measure, this stability was grounded in the long and rich past of the Jews in Rome. Probably more important was the papacy and its long-standing policy of moderation vis-à-vis the Jews.

Besides playing a major intercessory role, the Jewish community of Rome exhibited its own rich cultural creativity. Especially noteworthy in this regard is Nathan ben Yehiel of Rome. A contemporary of the creative eleventh-century figures in Iberia and the first intellectual giants of northern Europe, Nathan grew up in Rome, studied there at the talmudic academy headed by his father, and eventually acceded to leadership of that academy. Nathan composed a lexicon of terms that appear in the Talmud and midrashim, explaining these terms in detail. The book took its place as a classic of rabbinic literature; it was widely copied, regularly cited, and eventually recurrently printed.

The Jews of Rome continued to involve themselves in the traditional domains of Jewish scholarship, that is to say rabbinic and

biblical studies. At the same time, they also made their mark in the
newer domains as well, perhaps most strikingly in the field of poetry.
One of the most intriguing creative Jewish figures of this period
was the poet Immanuel of Rome. Seemingly born and brought up
in Rome, Immanuel – like so many of his co-religionists – moved
about regularly. Immanuel has left a series of *mahbarot*, modeled
on the Arabic *maqama*. Stylistically, Immanuel was immersed in the
Hebrew poetry of Iberia, which betrays the profound influence of
Arabic poetry. At the same time, he was also conversant with the
Italian poetry of his epoch – the age of Dante – and influenced by it.

The content of Immanuel's *mahbarot* varies widely, from the light
and frivolous to the deeply serious. The most interesting *mahberet*
of all is the closing one in Immanuel's collection, entitled *Mahberet
ha-Tofet ve-ha-'Eden* (*The Maqama of Hell and Heaven*). Immanuel's
journey through hell and heaven reflects full awareness of the great
Dante poetic epic – critics have suggested direct borrowing for some
of the episodes. Immanuel's verse constitutes one of the highlights of
medieval Jewish poetic creativity.

The Jewish community of Rome was hardly distinguished by its
size; it was, however, distinguished by its longevity, stability, mediating
role with the head of the Roman Catholic Church, and ongoing
creativity. It stands out as a bastion of stability in the rapidly changing
world of the Jewries of medieval western Christendom.

During the thirteenth century, the demography of Italian Jewry
began to change markedly. On the one hand, the old Jewish centers
of the south were subjected to new pressures, in considerable measure
imported from outside the Italian peninsula. More important, new
centers of Jewish life were created in the central and northern parts
of the peninsula, areas in which Jewish presence had previously been
quite sparse. It is suggested that, prior to the thirteenth century, Jews
were known to inhabit less than twenty towns throughout central
and northern Italy; by the end of our period, the number of Jewish
communities reached into the hundreds, mostly quite small to be
sure.[65]

The growth of the Jewish communities of the north resulted from
a combination of factors, some external and some internal. These
factors begin with the demographic. By the second half of the thirteenth century, Jews were on the move, both on the Italian peninsula
and elsewhere, seeking new areas in which to settle. Some southern-
Italian Jews were periodically prepared to move northward into areas

heretofore devoid of Jews. Jews were also on the move from the newer Jewish settlements in the northern areas of Europe. By the middle decades of the thirteenth century, many of these new Jewries were in full-scale decline. The Jews of England were eventually expelled in 1290, but decline was evident by the middle decades of the thirteenth century. The Jews of France were similarly banished in 1306, but the lengthy reign of King Louis IX (1230–1270) constituted a turning point in French Jewish history. In Germany, accelerating violence took a fearful toll on the Jews, and many were prepared to seek their fortunes elsewhere.[66]

Of course, more was required than simply a Jewish desire for refuge and change. There had to be some kind of economic opportunity to attract and maintain a new Jewish population. Such economic opportunity was associated with the new Jewish specialty that had emerged in the middle of the twelfth century in northern Europe. There, broad societal need for capital and the Church's campaign against Christians taking interest from fellow-Christians had combined to open for the recently settled Jews of northern Europe a new economic specialization in moneylending. This Jewish activity took many forms, from high-level and lucrative banking to everyday loan activities on a petty scale. By the latter decades of the twelfth century and the early decades of the thirteenth century, this same process began to repeat itself across the northern areas of Italy.[67] New Jewish settlements, grounded economically in the lending of money, began to spring up. These new settlements were generally buttressed by some kind of formal agreement with the disparate authorities of the various principalities of the north.

The young Jewish communities of the north were hardly immune to the dislocations of the difficult fourteenth century, including economic setback and the mid-century plague. However, Jewish suffering in the northern regions of the peninsula was not as devastating as it was elsewhere, for example in Germany. Italian Jewry's relative freedom from extreme violence is not meant to suggest that Jewish life was free of tension and pressure. It surely was not. Traditional Church policies and imagery almost guaranteed the generation of problems. Indeed, there was a more immediate factor, namely the emergence of Jewish moneylending and Jewish moneylenders across northern Italy. In general, moneylending has never been a popular profession. The need to repay and the penalties imposed for non-payment regularly elicit considerable emotional resistance to the lender and the

lending process. In addition, there is in moneylending a stigma associated with the sense of profit unearned, and this stigma was embedded in both the philosophic and ecclesiastical traditions. Finally, by
time moneylending made its appearance in Italy, a body of ecclesiastical objection to Jewish lending had emerged. While elements
in the Church continued to sanction Jewish taking of interest, other
reputable Church leaders had come to reject it, to resent bitterly
Jewish involvement in the lending business, and to agitate vigorously
against it.

In northern Italy, there emerged a particular element in the Church
that was militantly opposed to Jewish lending, and that was the so-
called "Observantine" wing of the Franciscan Order. The Franciscan
Order had been founded by St. Francis of Assisi, with a profound
commitment to poverty. With the passage of time, the new order
took on special responsibility for preaching to the poor urban population of the towns of western Christendom, for amassing the intellectual tools to battle heretics and infidels, and for carrying the struggle into the field against heretics and infidels, including the Jews.
Often, original spiritual messages are obscured, and segments of
the Franciscan community in Italy came to believe that the original emphasis on poverty had diminished in their order. These more
rigorous Franciscans were – not surprisingly – much concerned with
the plight of poor Christians indebted to Jews and to the wealth that
Jews were seemingly amassing at the expense of these Christian poor.
The denunciation of Jews by rigorous Franciscan preachers during
the latter decades of the fourteenth century reached a fevered pitch.

Church concern – especially on the part of the Franciscans – with
the poor and their indebtedness led to a movement to create charitable
loan institutions that would displace the Jewish lenders – the *monti di
pieta*. The conception was fairly simple: lending institutions built on
a concern for the poor would be much preferable to the depredations
of Jewish lenders. While the conception was simple, establishing and
maintaining such institutions were not. The movement encountered a
variety of problems in its effort to succor the poor and to minimize the
business activities of the Jewish moneylenders. The latter continued
to ply their trade, despite the efforts to displace them.

The onset of Renaissance sensibilities, especially in the north,
served as a counterpoint to the intense ecclesiastical agitation against
the Jews. In many ways, the fifteenth century was a time of successful
expansion for the young Jewish communities of northern Italy. One

of the most important developments of this period was the establishment of Jewish printing houses in a number of the towns of northern Italy. This influential new technology was to alter the culture and cultural climate of western Christendom in general. The emergence of printing establishments devoted to the language and literature of the Jews had great significance for modern Jewish cultural life.[68]

Studies of the Jewish communities of northern Italy during our period have come to emphasize a special feature of these Jews of northern and central Italy. As noted by Michele Luzzati, "the most astonishing behaviour of the Jews of northern and central Italy is not, however, just simply their geographic mobility, but their outright nomadism, an 'itinerism,' to use this neologism . . . These Jews, themselves descended from 'immigrant' families (from Rome, southern Italy, Germany, etc.), were not satisfied with moving only once from one town to another, but changed their residence several times during their lifetimes, so that they eventually became known as 'habitores' of four, five, or more cities or towns." This mobility was to become a significant characteristic of modern Jewish existence.[69]

The story of Italian Jewry is special in many respects, perhaps most notably its longevity. Of all the Jewries we shall study, it was only Italian Jewry that maintained itself in unbroken fashion from the beginning of our period to the end. Indeed, the history of Italian Jewry extended from more than a millennium prior to our period and has continued down into the twenty-first century. With the demise of many old Jewish communities in the contemporary Muslim world, Italian Jewry has emerged as one of the very oldest Jewries in existence. The fragmented Jewish communities of medieval Italy show a considerable measure of resilience in meeting the diverse challenges with which they were recurrently presented. They show a readiness for change – for example change of venue and change of economy – that is impressive. The Jews of medieval Italy also contributed significantly to the cultural legacy left by medieval Jewry in western Christendom. The importance of medieval Italian Jewry has tended to be somewhat overshadowed by the larger Iberian (Sephardic) Jewish community and the yet larger amalgam of northern European (Ashkenazic) Jewries. As a smaller and separate entity, medieval Italian Jewry has often been neglected. Given the richness of the Italian Jewish experience, this is most unfortunate.

4

THE NEWER JEWRIES OF THE NORTH: NORTHERN FRANCE AND ENGLAND

•

All the Jewries of northern Europe were new, much newer than the Jewish communities of the south. The Jewries of northern Europe did not have roots in the Roman world; they were not located in areas conquered and held by the Byzantines or the Muslims; they did not build a reservoir of experience under the rule of these conquerors; there was no experience of Christian reconquest to affect them for good and ill. Northern-European Jewish life was a *tabula rasa*, a blank slate to be shaped by the interaction of Christian majority and Jewish immigrant minority during our period, influenced to be sure by prior Church doctrine, policy, and imagery with respect to Judaism and Jews.

What is so striking about the evolution of northern-European Jewry is that, alongside the broader shift of the center of gravity in the Jewish world from the realm of Islam to western Christendom, there was an internal shift as well, as the Jewries of northern Europe began the slow process of exceeding the Jewries of the south in size and power. While the Jewish experience in northern Europe was decidedly mixed, with much that was negative from the Jewish perspective, the Jewish immigrants to the northern lands and their Christian neighbors were successful in laying the groundwork for the emergence of what is often designated Ashkenazic Jewry, which became the dominant Jewish sub-group on the modern scene.[1]

Division of the broad portrayal of medieval European Jewry into the preceding chapter on the one hand and this one and the next on the other reflects the important divide between southern Europe and Europe of the north. The decision to begin with Mediterranean Europe flows from the greater antiquity and the rich pre-1000 history of the Jewries of the south. For the ordering of this chapter and the next, a further line of demarcation within medieval western Christendom comes into play – that between northwestern Europe on the one hand and north-central and northeastern Europe on the other, involving divergent medieval fortunes and differing patterns of Jewish experience.[2]

Early Jewish settlements in northern Europe were established toward the close of the first millennium, first in the heartland areas of France and Germany; these early settlements then spread westward from France into England and eastward from Germany into Hungary and Poland. The Jewish community of northern France will be discussed first, for a number of reasons. France constituted the very core of medieval Latin Christendom, the most normative and typical of its central areas. The French experiment at powerful monarchy was, from a number of perspectives, the most successful in all of Europe; the French alliance with the Church in general and the papacy in particular was the most durable of such alliances; many of the characteristic institutions and movements of the Middle Ages originated in France. In his meticulous study of the Capetian kings and their Jews, William Chester Jordan goes even further, arguing that the thirteenth-century Capetian monarchy established many of the foundations for subsequent Western governance altogether. "Certain distinctive features of Western state formation, without which we cannot understand later developments, emerged earliest and most characteristically in France: binding legislation in the absence of direct consent; governance through salaried non-noble officials who were not native to their locality of administration; the principle of non-extinguishability of regalian right; the necessity of religious conformity within the polity . . . It is by no means an exaggeration to say that the blend of these elements was new in thirteenth-century France and became an example to most other princes."[3] Jordan's careful analysis of Capetian theory and praxis with respect to the Jews indicates that French treatment of the Jews, in its ebbs and flows, was similarly innovative and precedent-setting. We shall thus see in northern France developments illuminating for Jewish life in medieval Latin Christendom in its entirety. We shall begin with France and then proceed westward to the small, but important derivative community in England.

Subsequent to this treatment of French Jewry and its English off-shoot, we shall in the next chapter turn our attention to the other major set of Jewish settlements in northern Europe, the fragmented Jewish communities of Germany. The German area differed significantly in its economic, political, and cultural history, and thus – not surprisingly – the history of the Jewish minority diverged markedly from that of French and English Jewry.

German Jewry too sent forth colonies, in this case the Jewish communities of eastern Europe, more specifically Hungary and Poland. Like the mother communities – France and Germany – which differed radically, so too did the offshoot communities – England on the one hand and Hungary and Poland on the other. The English Jewish community was the very first to disappear in medieval western Christendom. In contrast, the Jewish settlements of eastern Europe were by the end of our period well on their way to becoming the demographic centers of Jewish life in Latin Christendom, indeed throughout the world.

NORTHERN FRANCE

While we have already noted the paucity of data for the history of the Jews in eleventh- and twelfth-century western Christendom, this point deserves special emphasis as we approach the history of the Jews in northern France. In effect, we have very few sources for the formative and flourishing period in the history of this set of Jewish communities. In contrast, we have considerable documentation for the period of decline, i.e. the thirteenth century. The lack of documentation for the period of development and the contrasting richness of documentation for the period of decline may lead to greater emphasis on the latter, which must be resisted. The story of northern-French Jewry, like the story of the Jews in medieval western Christendom altogether, involves a complex combination of success and failure. Neither should be neglected.[4]

There are random traces of Jewish settlement in northern Europe prior to our starting point, the year 1000. This early and ephemeral Jewish life in northern France has left neither physical remains nor any traces in the subsequent writings and thinking of the Jewish communities that began to evolve during the eleventh and twelfth centuries. Medieval northern-French Jewry never seriously claimed for itself roots in antiquity. The origins of this important Jewry lay in the vitalization of northern Europe that commenced at the turn of the millennium. The desire of Jewish traders to settle in northern Europe – more specifically in northern France – is understandable. Happily for these Jews, their desire was matched by the interest of a number of northern-French rulers in supporting Jewish immigration.

A curious source noted in the previous chapter provides valuable insight into the symbiotic relationship between the immigrating Jews and their baronial protectors. We have noted the Hebrew account that depicts a persecution in early northern France and the pur-ported mission of a Jewish leader to Rome and the pope in order to save his fellow-Jews. Supposedly, the mission was successful, and a papal enactment was secured, thus ending the threat. This interest-ing narrative ends by focusing on the Jewish hero. We are told that, subsequent to his successes in Rome, the Jewish leader – Jacob ben Yekutiel – returned to his home in the north "and lived there for twelve years. Eventually, Baldwin, count of Flanders, contacted him, writing [to say] that the [Jewish] leader should come to him and that he might bring with him thirty Jews – his friends and associates – to settle in his [Baldwin's] land. He [Jacob] arose and went to him [Baldwin]. They received him with great honor, along with his two sons, Isaac and Judah. He [Jacob] tarried with him [Baldwin] for three months, and there he passed away."[5]

This story is illustrative on many levels. It reflects the mobility of the Jews, the interest of key rulers in encouraging Jewish settlement, and the role of the barony in northern France at this point in time. All through the eleventh and twelfth centuries, northern France was a conglomeration of independent principalities, some of them much larger in extent than the holdings of the king, centered around the Ile-de-France. Jewish life prospered under the rule of many of these barons, in such counties as Normandy in the west and Champagne in the east, although we are poorly informed as to these successes.

Sources to illuminate the economic underpinnings of Jewish life in eleventh- and twelfth-century northern France are sparse. It seems that the mainstay of Jewish life was, at the outset, trade. Jewish businessmen seem to have done local and more wide-ranging busi-ness. While we cannot follow the process of change, twelfth- and thirteenth-century sources indicate that, during the course of the twelfth century, as western Christendom rapidly matured, the Jews of northern France shifted into the lucrative and at the same time dangerous enterprise of moneylending.

Already during the middle decades of the twelfth century, Bernard of Clairvaux, in protecting Jews from the threat of crusading violence, used the verb *judaizare* (to behave like Jews) as a synonym for moneylending.[6] By the end of the twelfth century, a popular preacher, Fulk of Neuilly, agitated – successfully in many cases – for the expulsion of Jews from the principalities of northern France, in order to expunge what he saw as the sin of Jewish moneylending. The early-thirteenth-century biographer of King Philip Augustus, Rigord of St. Denis, rooted the anti-Jewish actions of the young monarch in a set of Jewish activities, many of which were related to moneylending.[7] The earliest royal enactments relative to the Jews all featured, in one way or another, Jewish moneylending. Indeed, the proliferation of such enactments over the course of the thirteenth century is stunning. Thus, despite the absence of evidence for the specifics of this evolution, it seems clear that a significant shift in Jewish economic activity in northern France took place during the twelfth century.

While the combination of accelerating need for capital and the Church effort to suppress Christian usury opened up a new field of endeavor for Jews throughout western Christendom,[8] the element of need was especially potent in the rapidly maturing areas of France and England. These northwestern sectors of Europe were in the position of attempting to overtake older European economies with richer and deeper roots. Risk-taking and investment were critical to success, and capital was critical to risk-taking and investment.

The Jews on their own could not have succeeded at this endeavor in the banking business. Success required some measure of governmental assistance. Ultimately, all business activity, whether in trade or banking, requires minimally governmental adjudication of inevitable conflict. Thus, rules of adjudication had to be established and enforced. Such rules for adjudication of conflict with respect to Jewish lending emerged all across Europe, most especially in the German lands.

There was yet a more forceful form of governmental involvement in the new Jewish lending business. The most important collateral available in medieval western Christendom was land. Thus, large-scale lending had to take place against landed property. Since Jewish lenders – or any other lenders, for that matter – could not, in case of default, take over property by force, Jewish lending against landed property could only take place with the promise of governmental support. This more advanced and lucrative form of lending necessarily involved the Jews deeply with their baronial or royal lords. Clearly, many of the rulers of northern France (and England) were willing to provide such support. This willingness on the part of the ruling class was grounded in the altruistic sense of the need for flow of capital within society at large and in the more self-serving potential for considerable taxation of Jewish gains from the banking business, which often translated into expropriation of a considerable portion of Jewish profit. Both the need for flow of capital and for reliable sources of tax revenue were especially acute in northern France (and England), and this led to an unusual level of support for the new Jewish economic specialty.

While the new Jewish specialization in moneylending was useful to the Christian economy, profitable to the baronial protectors of the Jews, and lucrative to the Jewish lenders, it entailed as well significant liabilities for the Jewish bankers and their co-religionists. The first was intensification of Jewish reliance upon baronial and royal protectors. Successful Jewish immigration into northern Europe could only have taken place with the support and protection of the ruling class. Such support involved, first and foremost, protection in the face of majority hostility against newcomers who were, more specifically, Jews. Now, a further layer of dependence was added. Jews became dependent on these same rulers for extensive business support as well. This enhanced dependency involved at least two problems. In the first place, it could and did open the Jews to intensified economic exploitation. In addition, it posed the threat that anti-authority sentiment might readily be deflected against obvious and weak allies of the ruling class, the Jews.

There was an additional set of negatives as well, negatives intrinsically associated with moneylending itself. Ecclesiastical policy had opened the way for this new Jewish economic specialization. To the extent that the Church was successful in eliminating the taking of usury by Christians, it created the circumstances for Jewish involvement in moneylending. Yet the matter was hardly that simple. By virtue of its anti-usury campaign, the Church in effect stigmatized the Jews who picked up the economic slack. While there were reasons why Christians were forbidden and Jews permitted to lend at interest, such differentiation was often lost in the rush of ecclesiastical anti-usury rhetoric. Fairly quickly, reforming churchmen such as Fulk of Neuilly, cited above, began to reject the distinction between Christian and Jewish lending and to insist that Jews as well were included in the prohibition of Deuteronomy 23:20. Less dramatically, Church leadership became seriously engaged with the social problems associated with Jewish moneylending, attempting to safeguard the more vulnerable classes of European society from the suffering regularly associated with the banking business. Finally and most directly, moneylending – while a necessity – has rarely been a popular pursuit. Bankers and moneylenders have historically been portrayed in negative terms, and our period was no exception. The moneylender, generally perceived to be self-interested, calculating, and ruthless, was all the more loathed if he were a Jew to boot.

A number of additional developments on the eleventh- and twelfth-century scene in western Christendom in general and in northern France in particular served to further diminish the image of the Jews. The same aggressive vitalization that brought the Jews to northern Europe expressed itself in a new militancy against the outside world, meaning in effect the Muslim world that bordered on medieval Latin Christendom from almost every direction. Anti-Muslim aggression began, as we have seen, within Europe itself, on the Italian and Iberian peninsulas. Far more dramatic was the call to free the sacred city of Jerusalem, first announced in 1095 by Pope Urban II. Papal hopes and plans for an organized Christian army under Church control were quickly frustrated. A series of baronial and popular armies sprang up in the mid-1090s, intending to make their way eastward to the Holy Land. Northern France was a center of crusading fervor, although neither the king nor leading northern-French barons took part in the First Crusade.

There is evidence for only one instance of First-Crusade-related violence against the Jews of northern France, an incident at Rouen that claimed the lives of but a small number of Jews. At the same time, our earliest and best Jewish source for the First-Crusade anti-Jewish violence was well aware of the roots of the crusade in northern France and of anti-Jewish animus associated with French crusading fervor. This early source notes fear and consternation among the Jews of northern France, pleas sent off to the great Rhineland Jewish communities, and misguided reassurance offered by the leaders of Rhineland Jewry. Composed in the Rhineland after the crusaders had made their way eastward out of both France and Germany, the extant Hebrew narratives in fact knew of no significant persecution of French Jews.

The Hebrew First Crusade narratives note the passage of popular French crusading forces under the leadership of the charismatic Peter the Hermit. Our earliest Hebrew source makes general reference to these French crusaders: "When the crusaders [meaning the French] began to reach this land [the Rhineland], they sought funds with which to purchase bread. We gave it to them."[9] A subsequent Hebrew account, in detailing events at Trier, is somewhat fuller. It specifies the leadership of Peter the Hermit and notes that "he brought with him a letter from France, from the Jews, [indicating] that, in all places where his foot would tread and he would encounter Jews, they should give him provisions for the way. He would then speak well on behalf of Israel, for he was a priest and his words were heeded."[10] This seems to suggest that French Jews did more than turn to their Rhineland brethren for spiritual support. They developed a practical strategy for dealing with Peter, and this strategy – economic assistance – seems to have by and large worked.

While the anti-Jewish rhetoric associated with the First Crusade was grounded in recollections of the historic Jewish sin of deicide and calls for Christian vengeance, by the middle of the twelfth century perceptions of Jews as here-and-now enemies of Christendom, poised at every moment to bring harm to Christian society, proliferated. The powerful abbot and militant thinker Peter the Venerable of Cluny urged the king of France, on the eve of the Second Crusade, to make the Jews bear a portion of crusading expenses because of their incessant hatred of Christianity and their ongoing blasphemy against the *sancta* of the Christian faith.[11]

The most dangerous of these perceptions of here-and-now Jewish hatred and malevolence involved the conviction that Jews regularly murder Christian neighbors, to be sure underhandedly and surreptitiously. In most instances, the victim of purported Jewish aggression was a child, implying both defenselessness and innocence. The murder allegation surfaced all across northern Europe during the middle decades of the twelfth century, rapidly embellished with the sense that the murders were committed out of religious antipathy and that the Christian victims of alleged Jewish hatred were thus martyrs to their faith. These convictions further evolved into allegations of the ritualization of such murders, for example claims that the killings were carried out by crucifixion, as a blasphemous reenactment of earlier Jewish animosity and violence, or that they were committed as part of a renewed Jewish sacrificial cult.

An especially striking instance of the claim of Jewish murder took place in the northern-French town of Blois in 1171. This episode and its aftermath, both richly depicted in a series of Hebrew letters, were unusual in a number of respects. First, the allegation was made in the absence of a Christian corpse – no victim was ever discovered or even reported. Second, the allegation was accepted – at least provisionally – by a major northern-French baron, Count Theobald of Blois, who ordered a trial by ordeal of the accused Jews. The trial resulted in conviction of the Jews of Blois and execution of more than thirty of them. Finally, the trial and execution deeply frightened the Jews of northern France, who feared that Count Theobald's actions would reinforce the growing perception of Jews as murderers.[12]

In the face of this threat, the Jews of northern France organized an extensive campaign to rebut the allegation through meticulous reconstruction of the events that took place in Blois and to secure repudiation of the slander by major northern-French authorities. Count Henry of Champagne, a brother of Count Theobald, rejected the murder allegation, as did King Louis VII, a brother-in-law of Count Theobald. A meeting held between the king and leading Jews of his realm was particularly important. According to the Jewish report, the king disavowed the actions of Count Theobald, noting that similar claims of Jewish murder had been leveled in his domain, in the towns of Pontoise and Janville, and that he had rejected them. The monarch purportedly concluded with broad reassurance for his frightened Jewish subjects: "Now then, be aware, all you Jews of my land, that I harbor no such suspicions. Even if a body be discovered in the city or in the countryside, I shall say nothing to the Jews in that regard. Therefore, be not frightened over this matter."[13] The king's pronouncement was reinforced by a written charter, circulated to royal officials throughout his domain.

The royal stance in the wake of the Blois incident is reflective of the generally protective posture of the ruling class of northern France. The Jews of northern France seem to have been well protected by their lords during the First Crusade – with only the Rouen incident reported, in stark contrast with the loss of Jewish life further eastward in the Rhineland. With the onset of the Second Crusade, the authorities of Church and state and the Jews as well were all aware of the potential that crusading bore for the arousal of anti-Jewish sentiment. The great spiritual figure behind the Second Crusade, Bernard of Clairvaux, in rallying Christian warriors to the undertaking, warned explicitly against the infliction of violence upon Jews. The Jewish chronicler of the events of the Second Crusade, Ephraim of Bonn, has little wide-ranging violence to report, even for the Rhineland areas that had seen the massacres of the First Crusade.

For northern France, Ephraim notes one frightening incident, in which the life of Rabbi Jacob ben Meir, spiritual and temporal leader of northern-French Jewry, was threatened and then saved. After detailing this incident, Ephraim adds: "In the rest of the [Jewish] communities of France, we have not heard of anyone killed or forcibly converted. However, the Jews lost much of their wealth. For the king of France commanded: 'All who volunteer to go to Jerusalem shall have their debts forgiven, if they are indebted to the Jews.' Since most of the Jews' loans in France are by charter, they lost their monies."[14] While there were a number of allegations of Jewish murder during the second half of the twelfth century, the rulers of northern France again seem to have protected their Jews effectively, since the reports do not indicate loss of Jewish life at the hands of agitated mobs.

To be sure, the protectors of the Jews could on occasion turn against them. We have already noted the incident at Blois in 1171. Count Theobald of Blois was responsible for the death of more than thirty Jews, ostensibly as the result of a judicial procedure. One of the Hebrew letters noted above suggests a complex set of romantic and political circumstances behind the count's unusual actions. A yet more powerful ruler – the young king of France, Philip Augustus – initiated an assault on a Jewish community in a principality adjacent to the royal domain that cost the lives of more than eighty Jews. The royal attack was grounded in claims of Jewish murder and the need to set matters aright. There may have been, in addition, political calculations as well.[15] In any case, the actions of Count Theobald of Blois and King Philip Augustus constitute the exception. By and large, the rulers of northern France protected their Jews effectively through the tumultuous twelfth century.

The Jews of northern France organized themselves with increasing effectiveness during the eleventh and twelfth centuries and – against the backdrop of a vibrant majority culture – created brilliantly in a number of fields of spiritual endeavor. The heart of Jewish organizational life lay in the local community apparatus. We lack detail, but it is clear that the local Jewish communities of northern France created an effective taxation and disciplinary structure for themselves already during the eleventh century.[16]

As the twelfth century proceeded, it became increasingly important for the Jews of northern France to proceed beyond the local level
and organize themselves more broadly for effective self-protection
and self-regulation. The Blois incident illuminates the capacity of
the Jews of northern France to move beyond the local level in order
to confront a wide-ranging challenge to Jewish well-being, through
negotiation with a variety of ecclesiastical and secular authorities.
These Christian authorities were spread all across northern France,
and Jewish leaders from a number of principalities had to cooperate effectively in reaching all of them. At the center of this multi-
faceted defensive activity was the great spiritual leader of northern-
French Jewry at this point, Rabbi Jacob ben Meir, a resident of the
town of Ramerupt in the county of Champagne. His Jewish part-
ners in the effort included the leadership of the Jewish community of
Troyes in Champagne and the leadership of the Jewish communities
of Paris and Orleans in the royal domain. The authorities approached
included the king, the counts of Champagne and Blois, and the archbishop of Sens. The capacity for such wide-ranging Jewish action was
clearly crucial to Jewish survival in twelfth-century northern France,
which lay on the threshold of considerable centralization.

Jewish inter-communal cooperation involved more than defensive activity. Rabbi Jacob ben Meir and his brother, Rabbi Samuel
ben Meir, were instrumental in bringing together representatives of
a broad swath of Jewish communities to draft and ratify a number of
ordinances meant to aid Jewish leadership in coping with the many
challenges of twelfth-century Jewish affairs. A number of communal
ordinances widely accepted across northern France and even beyond
have survived. While the circumstances that gave rise to these decrees
and the issues they addressed were less dramatic and pressing than
the response to the frightening events in Blois, the ordinances again
indicate the capacity for wide-ranging cooperation among the leaders of twelfth-century northern-French Jewry and the special role
played by the distinguished brothers Jacob ben Meir and Samuel ben
Meir. The Jews of northern France recognized the growing centralization across the rapidly maturing principalities within which they
found themselves and forged the tools for adapting to that accelerating
centralization.[17]

The same creative energy manifest in Jewish business and communal success is reflected in the sphere of Jewish culture as well. The
impressive Jewish cultural creativity in eleventh- and twelfth-century

northern France seems to have been stimulated by the vibrant general
environment of the area. There is, to be sure, a problem in clarifying
this synergy. It is fairly easy to indicate the impact on Jewish cultural
creativity of the medieval Muslim ambience, since both the Muslim
majority and the Jewish minority shared a written language and could
access readily one another's writings. By contrast, the language circumstances in western Christendom, with its Romance vernaculars
and its Latin literature, makes understanding connections and discerning influences more difficult. Nonetheless, in some areas of southern
Europe, for example Italy, it was possible for us to discern broad
cultural influences on – for example – the poetry of Immanuel of
Rome, whose poetic style was so obviously innovative. For the Jewish
cultural creativity of northern Europe, expressed in fairly traditional
Jewish terms, identifying precisely the impact of majority society
and the lines of transmission of such impact is impossible. Thus, the
best we can do is to simply assert that the richness of Jewish creativity must bear some relationship to the vibrancy of majority society and to point to some parallels in minority and majority cultural
productivity.

Toward the end of the first third of the eleventh century, a Jew
appeared in the town of Troyes in the important county of Champagne, destined to serve as a remarkable cultural pioneer in this set
of young Jewish communities. Rabbi Solomon ben Isaac, a native
of Troyes, made an important decision to immerse himself in the
then-richest Jewish culture of northern-European Jewry, centered in
the Rhineland. He traveled eastward to study and, at a certain point
in time, returned westward to Champagne to share the learning of
the Rhineland Jewish academies and to innovate. Rabbi Solomon
ben Isaac, known throughout the subsequent Jewish world as Rashi,
was remarkably productive. He composed two extensive bodies of
commentary, one on the Bible and the other on the Babylonian
Talmud. These works have become normative for subsequent Jewish
intellectual life. The works would have been utterly remarkable under
any circumstances; they are all the more noteworthy for being the
products of such an early stage in the material and cultural history
of northern-French Jewry. No other Jewish cultural classics have
emerged at such an early stage in the history of a community.

Beyond the grandeur of his own works, Rashi is further notable
for setting in motion new tendencies in talmudic and biblical commentary, tendencies that were to play themselves out for more than

a century subsequent to his death. In the case of the new tendencies in talmudic commentary, they in fact came to dominate the field of Talmud study from the twelfth through the twenty-first centuries. The specifics of Jewish cultural creativity in the spheres of both biblical and talmudic commentary will be detailed as a later point in the book.[18] For the moment, suffice it to indicate that the young Jewry of northern France matched its innovativeness in economic and communal affairs with equal or greater creativity in key areas of Jewish cultural and religious life.

Twelfth-century Jewish life and creativity in northern France took place against the backdrop of a vigorous majority ambience, in which political diversity was the order of the day. All that was to change in the thirteenth century. During the thirteenth century, northern France was consolidated under the Capetian kings, ruling from their capital city Paris over larger and larger sectors of the north and subsequently over much of southern France as well. The move toward centralized authority proved in some ways a boon for the Jews, who had – as we have seen – organized themselves increasingly across the borders of individual principalities. At the same time, centralization had its liabilities. Jewish fate now lay to an alarming extent in a single set of hands. When a number of the rulers of twelfth-century northern France expelled their Jews toward the end of the twelfth century, the Jewish refugees could readily find new homes in alternative principalities without traversing long distances or incurring major economic and cultural dislocation. When King Philip the Fair expelled his Jews early in the fourteenth century, a vast territory was subjected to the royal edict, and Jewish refugees had to traverse long distances to find refuge in new and strange societal settings.[19]

The architect of much of the centralization was King Philip Augustus (ruled 1179–1223). Philip's reign was a turning point in the history of northern France and of northern-French Jewry. He acceded to the throne as a young man, limited in land and resources, possessed of few regalian rights, and challenged by a powerful coalition of barons. At his death, he left a much enlarged royal domain, rich resources, and royal prestige unknown to his predecessors. Precisely where the Jews stood on Philip's list of priorities and precisely what his view of his Jewish subjects was are unclear. The record shows considerable shift, so much so that William Chester Jordan has labeled Philip's policies vis-à-vis the Jews erratic.[20] There is unfortunately no clear royal statement to aid us in comprehending the alternating royal stances. The importance of his reign to the Jews of northern France, however, is indisputable. His centralization of authority in general and his evolving Jewish policy in particular paved the way for the thirteenth-century history of northern-French Jewry and for the eventual demise of this Jewry in its entirety.

The difficult circumstances of Philip's early years formed the backdrop to a series of anti-Jewish moves on the part of the young monarch. The first was a wide-ranging confiscation of Jewish goods, followed by a ransoming of the sequestered goods. This *captio* seems to reflect the economic well-being of northern-French Jewry and its potential to provide considerable financial resources for a strapped monarchy; it was a precedent to be repeated a number of times throughout the thirteenth century. The next royal step reflects the growing Jewish specialization in moneylending and the accelerating antipathy toward this Jewish activity. King Philip Augustus ordered the remission of debts owed to the Jews, with one-fifth of the total to be paid to the royal treasury.[21] The third and final royal move was expulsion of the Jews from the royal domain in 1182, with Jewish property – excepting synagogues, which were granted to the Church – ceded to the royal treasury.

While Philip's biographer Rigord attempts to root each of these actions in Jewish misdeed and royal determination to fulfill the religious responsibilities of a "most Christian king," in fact the common denominators in these moves are financial windfall, satisfaction of ecclesiastical interests, and adroit courting of public opinion. Each of the moves – confiscation, remission of debts with one-fifth to be paid to the royal treasury, and expulsion with confiscation of Jewish landed property – added significant financial resources to an impoverished crown. Remission of debts was surely viewed positively in reforming Church circles, in which agitation over Jewish moneylending had been increasing, and allocation of synagogues to the Church was yet another step intended to win ecclesiastical acclaim. The royal biographer Rigord serves as an excellent index of the success of the king's effort to garner ecclesiastical approbation. For Rigord, the anti-Jewish moves constituted the major achievements of Philip's early years. Finally, remission of debt surely won popular appreciation, at least on the part of those in debt. Payment of twenty percent to the royal treasury had to seem like an excellent bargain. Expulsion of the Jews was, in all likelihood, viewed favorably by large segments of the Christian population. The royal attack on the Jewish community of a neighboring principality, portrayed once again by Rigord as fulfillment of the religious responsibilities of the monarch, may also have involved public relations considerations.

Rigord, enthused over the young king's early anti-Jewish moves, was distressed by the royal decision to readmit Jews to the royal domain in 1198. This new direction in royal policy was stimulated in part by the availability of Jews on the move, owing to the demographic upheaval occasioned by the successful preaching of Fulk of Neuilly. With Jews once more in motion, the king seems to have been determined to attract some of them to his domain, thus reviving the business stimulation of Jewish moneylending and reinstating the taxation opportunities associated with Jewish banking.

The mature years of the reign of Philip Augustus, which stretched down to 1223, were dominated by three major developments with respect to the Jews. The first involves the rapid expansion of royal territory, with the resultant augmentation of the number of Jews living directly under royal control. Philip's successful dislodging of the Angevin monarchy from the large and important duchy of Normandy, for example, brought a number of important Jewish communities under royal protection, royal control, and royal taxation. Even in those areas that remained under baronial rule, the impact of the king and his influence was increasingly felt. King Philip Augustus took the lead, for example, in establishing new policies for Jewish moneylending, which – with the assent of key barons – became normative across much of northern France. In 1206, he and two major baronial holders of Jews agreed on a set of stipulations regarding Jewish moneylending. The fact that these three figures simultaneously introduced these regulations meant that Jews in all three domains were affected and that there could be no movement from one to another in order to avoid the imposition of the new limitations. Philip Augustus utilized the Jews as vehicles for the expansion of royal power and prerogative.

The second thrust of post-1198 Jewish fate involved enhanced royal control over the Jews, a process that was intended to foster more effective exploitation of Jewish wealth and that eventuated in considerable restriction of Jewish movement and diminution of Jewish status. As noted, prior to this point Jewish movement was fairly simple and widely attested. Even the royal expulsion of 1182 and the baronial expulsions of the 1190s seem to have been absorbed with minimal problems by the affected Jews, who were able to find refuge in nearby unaffected principalities. Upon readmitting Jews to the royal domain, Philip Augustus proceeded quickly to establish control over his new Jewish subjects. For example, he struck a treaty with the count of Champagne, a major holder of northern-French Jews, in which the king promised the following: "Let all whom the present letter reaches know that we have conceded that we shall retain in our land none of the Jews of our most beloved and faithful nephew, Theobald, count of Troyes, unless with the consent of that count." For his part, the count made a parallel promise with respect to the Jews of the king. In the process, each of the signatories to the treaty assured himself full control of his Jews. Jewish ease of movement was, in the process, seriously impaired. With the conquest of Normandy, King Philip Augustus moved quickly to stabilize Jewish presence and, again, to assure himself of control of the Jews of that large and rich principality. Jews were enrolled and forced to give sureties for their continuing presence in the duchy and thereby for their continuing acceptance of royal control. Thus, the king established greater control in part by working with fellow holders of Jews and in part by obligating the Jews directly. The result of these alternative techniques was limitation of Jewish movement and more effective exploitation of Jewish wealth.

The post-1198 history of the Jews under the rule of Philip Augustus shows one new and major *captio*, reminiscent of the confiscation he had ordered early in his reign. In 1210, Jews all across northern France were arrested and their goods confiscated. Once more, this led to imposition of an extremely large payment on the Jews, a payment that continued to afflict the Jews and their debtors for years to come. Again, firmer control of the Jews precluded any significant escape from this onerous exploitation.

While royal cupidity seemingly lay at the core of the new policy of controlling Jewish movement and occasionally expropriating portions of Jewish wealth, there was a countervailing tendency and third thrust in the policies of Philip Augustus, which can only be understood against the backdrop of royal commitment to the Church and royal acceptance of the need to placate ecclesiastical leadership.[22] As noted, ecclesiastical concern with Jewish moneylending had accelerated during the second half of the twelfth century. This concern expressed itself in a number of ways. For some churchmen, Jewish moneylending resulted in abuses that had to be addressed and eliminated; for others, Jewish moneylending was inherently wrong – Deuteronomy 23:21

could not be read as license for Jews to take interest from Christians. In the papal court, it was the former view that dominated, leading *inter alia* to the canon of the Fourth Lateran Council of 1215 that prohibited excessive Jewish usury, which seems to have been defined as an interest rate of more than twenty percent per annum. As was often the case, the ecclesiastical leadership of northern France seemed to gravitate to the more extreme position. We recall, for example, the campaign of Fulk of Neuilly at the end of the twelfth century, to extirpate Jewish moneylending in its entirety from northern France, out of a sense that Jewish taking of interest was inherently illegitimate.

Already in 1205, the powerful Pope Innocent III addressed a vigorous letter of rebuke to King Philip Augustus. The first and most telling of the papal complaints involved Jewish usury: "Know then that news has reached us to the effect that, in the French kingdom, the Jews have become so insolent that by means of their vicious usury, through which they extort not only usury, but even usury on usury, they appropriate ecclesiastical goods and Christian possessions. There seems to be fulfilled among the Christians that which the prophet bewailed in the case of the Jews, saying: 'Our heritage has been turned over to strangers, our houses to foreigners.'"[23] The papal complaint does not project Jewish usury as sinful in and of itself; the focus is upon the unwelcome repercussions of Jewish usury – Jewish appropriation of church vessels and dispossession of Christian property.[24] Some accommodation to ecclesiastical demands had to be forthcoming, and in fact it was.

Philip Augustus set in motion a sequence of limitations on Jewish usury that surely impacted severely Jewish profits from the banking business. The first of these limitations was enacted – as noted – in an edict of 1206, issued in conjunction with the countess of Champagne and the lord of Dampierre; the edict's most important provision specified a maximum interest rate of twenty percent per year, anticipating the demand of the Fourth Lateran Council of 1215. The second major provision ordered that Jewish loans could not be called within the first year, seemingly addressing the issue of compound interest highlighted in the papal letter of 1205. Toward the end of his reign, in 1219, Philip Augustus once more addressed ecclesiastical concerns with the abuses associated with Jewish moneylending. In this later legislation, he addressed, above all else, the indebtedness of the poorer elements in French society and of religious houses and their officials, attempting to protect these relatively defenseless sectors of French society against the ills flowing from indebtedness to the Jews.

The lengthy reign of Philip Augustus was, as noted, a landmark in the development of royal France and a turning point for the Jews as well. While his policies show elements of capriciousness, the core concerns with enhanced control of the Jews, occasionally severe exploitation of their goods, and imposition of a series of limitations that cut deeply into the Jewish moneylending business were augurs of what was to come. It can reasonably be suggested that the downturn in Jewish fate in northern France began during the lengthy and effective reign of Philip Augustus, although arguably the Jews living under his rule had no reason to see things in this way.

In his penetrating analysis of the Capetian kings and their Jews, William Chester Jordan suggests three distinct phases to the process of decline inaugurated by Philip Augustus: (1) the brief reign of Louis VIII and the early years of Louis IX (1223–1242); (2) the mature years of Louis IX and the reign of Philip III (1242–1285); (3) the reign of Philip IV and the expulsion (1285–1306). The Jews were readmitted to royal France in 1315, under circumstances that will be briefly discussed, but the real history of medieval northern-French Jewry came to a close with the expulsion of 1306.

In the first of these stages, the often disparate tendencies of the reign of Philip Augustus were better integrated. Royal expropriation and opposition to Jewish usury on grounds of principle went hand in hand. At the very beginning of the reign of Louis VIII, in 1223, the king, in an assembly of barons, ordered that all debts owed to the Jews were to cease bearing interest and were to be paid off in installments over a three-year period to the royal treasury. This was yet another confiscation of Jewish wealth, with appropriate concern for not having the funds contaminated by usury. More significant for the long haul was the stipulation that "the Jews shall henceforth not have seals for sealing their debts."[25] In Jordan's words, "an entire structure was collapsing."[26] Jewish lending in northern France had been carried out with the support – perhaps collusion might be more accurate – of the baronial and royal authorities. That support was now being removed. The increasingly pious rulers of royal France were going to distance themselves from all hints of involvement with Jewish lending. Not surprisingly, these stipulations, undertaken by twenty-six northern-French barons, were accompanied by insistence on the maintenance of control of the Jews. "We and our barons have decreed and ordained, concerning the status of the Jews, that none of us may receive or retain the Jews of another." This was intended for those agreeing to the ordinance as well as those who did not. Jews' flight from domain to domain was no longer possible.

Seven years later, early in the reign of the young king Louis IX, the regents of the kingdom adumbrated the principles of 1223 more sharply. "We and our barons shall henceforth cause no contracted debts to be repaid to the Jews."[27] The king and the barons of northern France utterly removed themselves from Jewish banking business. This did not mean that Jews themselves were prohibited from taking interest, although that further step was in the offing; it meant that the governing authorities would henceforth be free of any contamination associated with Jewish usury. The non-retention issue, which had been developing for decades, received its fullest formulation. "Wherever anyone shall find his Jew, he may legally seize him as his serf, whatever the custom the Jew may enjoy under the rule of another or in another kingdom."

Over the first decades of the thirteenth century, moneylending, which had become the mainstay of Jewish economic existence in northern France, was progressively eroded, through limitations and then through removal of the governmental backing that had buttressed the most lucrative kinds of Jewish banking activity. In 1235, the royal authorities went yet one step further, ordering that Jews "live by their own labor or by trade, but without usury."[28] To be sure, there were no teeth provided for this demand. Nonetheless, it went beyond the withdrawal of governmental support and ordered Jews themselves to desist from moneylending at interest.

At the same time, that is to say in the late 1230s and early 1240s, the royal authorities launched yet another devastating campaign against the Jews, this time aimed at the foundations of their religious life. As noted recurrently, the Talmud was little known in western Christendom prior to the thirteenth century. During the 1230s, far fuller knowledge of the Talmud became available, and that knowledge was utilized for more practical purposes. The Talmud was projected as, on the one hand, criminal and, on the other hand, a potential source for innovative proselytizing argumentation. While King Louis involved himself and his government in both of these directions, it was the former direction that was pursued earlier, more fully, and more tellingly.

As has been noted, the attack on the Talmud was initiated by a convert from Judaism named Nicholas Donin. Donin appeared at the papal court in 1236, claiming that the relatively unknown Talmud was in fact reprehensible on many levels and deserved to be banned within Christian society. Precisely what he first argued is not available to us. Our earliest evidence comes from a series of letters sent forth by Pope Gregory IX, letters addressed to major secular and ecclesiastical authorities throughout western Christendom. The routing of these letters through the bishop of Paris and a special letter sent to the same bishop, the Dominicans of Paris, and the Franciscans of Paris, ordering them to examine the Jewish books and have those found guilty burned, suggest that the pope may well have anticipated that action would be taken only in the kingdom of the pious Louis, and that in fact is what happened.[29]

Jewish books were confiscated, were subjected to trial in Paris, and were burned there. The Jewish leadership of royal France was successful some years later in gaining an audience with Pope Innocent IV and making the case that deprivation of the Talmud was tantamount to outlawing Judaism. The pope accepted their claim and ordered that the Talmud be reexamined, that offensive passages be excised, and that the rest be returned to the Jews. As noted, this became the normative Church position on the Talmud. However, the call to return the Talmud to the Jew was rejected in Paris, where the prior conclusion that the Talmud was literally intolerable was repeated and became the normative French stance toward the Talmud.[30] Once more, the ecclesiastical and lay leadership of France was attracted toward the most extreme views current in the Church. While talmudic study was not in fact totally eliminated across northern France, the great days of rabbinic creativity in northern France had come to an end.[31] The royal assault had targeted, along with the economic base of northern-French Jewry, its spiritual foundations as well.

According to Jordan, the next stage in Capetian policy, which took place between 1242 and 1285, was set in motion by the religious agitation for Louis IX's first crusading venture and the radical religiosity sparked by the commitment to crusading. From this period, we have two testimonials to Louis's anti-Jewish sentiment. The first gives us a formal perspective on royal anti-Jewish sentiment. When approached by advisors who suggested that the 1253–1254 royal prohibition of Jewish usury, accompanied by an order of expulsion for those unwilling to abide by the edict, would simply encourage Christians to enter the vacuum created by removal of the Jews from moneylending, the king is purported to have indicated that Christian usury was the responsibility of the Church and churchmen. The Jews, however, were present in France with his protection, and they constituted his responsibility. For the purity of his soul, he had no choice but to eliminate any sinfulness that might accrue from Jewish behavior. Three points are noteworthy here: the royal sense of overarching responsibility for Jewish presence in France; the profound concern of King Louis IX, eventually to become St. Louis, for the purity of his soul; his conviction that Jewish usury was illegitimate and sinful. Once again, the northern-French reading of Church policy tended in radical directions.

The second testimonial to Louis IX's anti-Jewish proclivities comes from the great crusade historian Jean de Joinville, who recounts in his *Life of St. Louis* a chilling account of visceral royal sentiments. According to Joinville, the king told the story of a debate held at Cluny, at which a knight opened and quickly closed the debate by physically attacking the Jewish spokesman. The moral the king drew from the story was grounded in his conviction that the knight's behavior had been correct, that inter-faith discussion might threaten Christian beliefs. "I agree myself that no one who is not a very learned cleric should argue with them [the Jews]. A layman, as soon as he hears the Christian faith maligned, should defend it only by the sword, with a good thrust in the belly, as far as the sword will go." Given Louis's reputation as a man of peace – at least between Christian and Christian, this is a stunning report, suggesting animosity of the deepest sort.

The mature Louis IX and his son Philip III pursued the lines of policy on Jewish moneylending established from 1223 through 1242. The great inquiries into the state of the realm launched in 1247 revealed evasions of the anti-usury edicts and precipitated another *captio* of Jewish goods. More strikingly, the king sent a letter from the East to his officials in 1253, ordering that the prior stipulation that Jews refrain from usury be enforced by expelling those Jews unwilling to abide by the prohibition. This order was reinforced by the king upon his return in 1254. Precisely how many Jews left the kingdom at this point is unclear. King Philip III maintained the anti-usury policies of his father assiduously.

One new element in Jewish policy during this period (1242–1285) involved Louis IX's support for the innovative missionizing efforts of Friar Paul, whom we have encountered already in Spain. As noted, Friar Paul's proselytizing involved the utilization of rabbinic teachings to argue the case for Christian truth. One of the advantages of this tack was to remove Christian truth from contention. The argument involved whether talmudic teachings do or do not support Christian truth claims; it did not address the substance of Christian truth claims. Friar Paul, who had earlier won the backing of King James I of Aragon for the engagement in Barcelona, now garnered the support of the king of France for a parallel endeavor in Paris. We possess an extended Hebrew record of the encounter, indicating royal support, the frightening circumstances of public debate, and deep Jewish anxieties. To be sure, the Jewish author claims that no Jews were swayed to conversion.

The last act in the drama of Jewish life in medieval northern France was written by King Philip IV. Early in his reign, he simply followed the Jewish policies established by his forebears. A number of late-thirteenth-century developments moved him to opt for a massive expulsion of his Jews. The most important of these developments were: accelerating public animosity toward the Jews; the diminishing resources and economic utility of these Jews; the spate of expulsions from a number of northern-French principalities, capped by the banishment of English Jewry in 1290. The expulsions, especially the expulsion from England, highlighted for many observers the combination of public antipathy and limited Jewish resources.

Both medieval and modern commentators note the special impact of the host desecration charge leveled in Paris itself in 1290. The story involved a poor Christian woman indebted to a Jewish pawnbroker, the Jewish pawnbroker, his family, and the ecclesiastical and secular authorities of Paris. The Jew allegedly offered relief from debt to the Christian woman if she would provide him with a host wafer, which she did. The Jew then purportedly tried to torture the wafer, was eventually discovered, was sentenced to death by an ecclesiastical court, and was burned by royal officials.[32]

The host allegation was yet one more spin-off from the original twelfth-century perception of Jews as here-and-now enemies of Christ, Christianity, and Christians. As noted earlier, this broad sense of Jewish hatred gave rise to notions of Jewish murder, generally of weak and innocent children. These Christian victims were identified with the innocent Jesus, who suffered at the hands of hostile Jews, and were regularly memorialized as martyrs. At the hands of Thomas of Monmouth, the English chronicler of the life and miracles of one such alleged martyr, the Jewish murder was carried out

in ritualized form, that is to say through crucifixion.[33] Late-twelfth-
and thirteenth-century evolution of these themes introduced into the
murders elements of Jewish ritual practice, either through renewal of
the sacrificial cult of antiquity or through contemporary Jewish religious rituals, such as those of the Passover festival. The host desecration charge is clearly an offshoot of all this, an offshoot reflecting the
accelerating Church emphasis on the doctrine of transubstantiation.

Important for our purposes is the evolution of the attitudes of
French ecclesiastical and lay leadership to the anti-Jewish allegations.
We recall that, during the 1170s, the archbishop of Sens had intervened energetically on behalf of the Jews of Blois, who had been
executed by his brother, Count Theobald, on the charge of murder.
Likewise, King Louis VII had indicated to a delegation of Jewish
leaders that the charge of malicious murder had been leveled in two
of his towns and that he had rejected the allegations. He assured these
Jewish leaders that such would be his policy in the future. In contrast, by 1290 the bishop of Paris and the king of France accepted
the new allegation, condemned the alleged Jewish malefactor, and
worked toward the creation of a suitable monument to the miracles
associated with the allegedly purloined host wafer, thereby enhancing
public acceptance of the charge through ritualized memorialization
of the event.

Precisely what role the 1290 incident played in the royal decision
for expulsion is by no means clear. In all likelihood, the king was
persuaded by the combination of broad factors already noted and
the anti-Jewish sentiments reflected in his behavior in 1290. In all
events, the Jews were ordered to leave royal France in its entirety
in 1306. This was by far the most devastating expulsion yet suffered by the Jews of medieval western Christendom. It was hardly
unprecedented – we have noted a number of prior banishments
already, including the expulsion from the French royal domain in 1182
under Philip Augustus. However, none of the precedents involved
anything like the number of Jews affected by the edict of 1306, nor
had any prior expulsion involved such drastic problems of relocation
as that of 1306.[34]

From the royal perspective, whatever the stimuli might have been,
Philip IV was determined to make this the most lucrative of the anti-
Jewish moves in the history of the French kingdom. While the Jews
were permitted to take their moveable goods with them, their landed
property escheated to the crown. A bureaucracy was established to

sell off Jewish property and realize maximal revenue. Yet more important, Jewish business records were impounded, and royal bureaucrats
became the collectors of sums owed the Jews, with reduction of those
sums so as to preclude any possibility or even appearance of royal
profit from usury. These efforts did not go well. There is abundant
evidence of malfeasance on the part of royal officials. Nonetheless,
royal profit was considerable, surely dwarfing the profits from earlier
arrests, confiscations, and ransoms.

The difficulties in realizing maximal profit from the expulsion
seems to have been the major factor that moved Philip IV's heir,
Louis X, to allow the return of some Jews to the royal domain in
1315. The edict of return is interesting from many perspectives.[35]
It begins with elaborate justification for the reversal of Philip IV's
expulsion. Factors include: biblical teaching, which holds out the
promise of Jewish conversion; the doctrines of the Roman Catholic
Church, which preserve the Jews as a constant memory of the Passion
and also in hopes of converting them; the legacy of St. Louis, who
had purportedly expelled the Jews and then recalled them; and the
alleged clamor of the people, which is a bit difficult to believe.

The invitation to return included a multiplicity of clauses intended
to limit Jewish behaviors, of which we shall note only a few. The
Talmud remained a condemned book, and Jews were prohibited from
disputing matters of faith with Christians. Jews were to be readily
identifiable through the special badge that had been introduced over
the course of the thirteenth century. Control of the Jews was firmly
established: "No other lord in our kingdom . . . may hold in his land
Jews of another lord by origin and by legal right." While there is
some possibility of freedom of movement, only the king might take
over Jews belonging to another.

Not surprisingly, the focus remained on Jewish economic activity, and many of the evolving prohibitions of the thirteenth century
were restated. These prohibitions are lumped together in ways that
are ultimately internally inconsistent, but the combination is fascinating. The most radical of the stipulations is Louis IX's pronouncement
that Jews "must live by the labor of their hands, or they must trade
in good and reliable merchandise." To be sure, this was stated without Louis IX's insistence on expulsion for Jews refusing to abide by
this pronouncement. The milder notion of governmental withdrawal
from the sinfulness of Jewish usury was also reiterated: "No one may
be forced by us to pay interest of any sort to a Jew." A further retreat

involves moving backward to the 1206 order of Philip Augustus. The wording is striking: "Since the Jews must work and labor with their hands or must trade, as has already been said, it is not our wish that they be permitted to lend at interest, and we forbid it expressly. If it should happen that they perchance do lend, they may take no more than two pence per pound per week." To this was added the earlier order that Jewish lending – forbidden in theory, but permitted in practice – only take place against pledges, with no governmental documents playing a role. The 1315 document, with all its inconsistencies, provides us with an illuminating look backward at evolving Capetian anti-usury policy that stretched out over decades.

Equally interesting are the stipulations governing prior property of the returning Jews. The most significant of these items provides that "they may recover and hold a third – while we hold two-thirds – of the debts that were owed them prior to their expulsion." This stipulation seems to provide the major explanation for the change of policy. Jews were allowed to return to royal France in hopes that they might assist in tracking down yet more of the money owed them prior to 1306. A two-thirds/one-third split would benefit both parties – the royal protector of the Jews and the Jews themselves.

Jewish property sold off after 1306 was to remain in the hands of Christian buyers. Special notice is taken of Jewish public space, i.e. synagogues and cemeteries. "Their synagogues and cemeteries shall be returned to them, upon payment of the price for which they were sold to those who bought them, unless there are very large buildings there or other reasons why they may not be taken away. If there are any still held by us, which were not sold, they shall be returned to them." Jews might recoup their sacred places, but at a price, unless they had not been sold off. "If perchance they are unable to recover their synagogues and cemeteries for good reason, we shall see that they receive sufficient buildings and grounds for a suitable price." Payment is everywhere in these stipulations.

The Jews did return in some numbers, but the creative period in the history of the Jews of medieval northern France had passed. Individuals and families resettled, and some communities reemerged, but without the vibrancy and creativity that had distinguished Jewish life in northern France from the eleventh through the mid-thirteenth century. When a final expulsion was decreed in 1394, it had little impact on the overall fate of northern-European Jewry. The Jewish community dismantled in 1394 was a mere shadow of its earlier self.

ENGLAND

Medieval English Jewry emerged out of northwestern France. Jewish settlement in England does not seem to have existed prior to the Norman Conquest. In a move reminiscent of the invitation extended by Baldwin of Flanders to the Jew Jacob ben Yekutiel, King William the Conqueror seems to have invited Jews from his Norman possessions to settle in England. The settlement of Jews in England began much later – and eventually ended earlier – than the mother settlements of Jews in northern France.[36]

The newer English Jewry shows many of the salient characteristics of its northern-French progenitor, but always in more extreme fashion. Northern-French Jews were immigrants and were widely perceived that way. The immigrant status of English Jewry was far more pronounced. English Jews were associated with the new Norman monarchy and thus a part of the conquering class that had imposed itself on the English people. Northern-French Jewry was limited in its economic outlets, slowly gravitating over the course of the twelfth century to the useful, lucrative, and dangerous specialty of moneylending; English Jewry was yet more limited, specializing almost from the outset and much more narrowly in the banking business. Northern-French Jews eventually became deeply dependent on the French monarchy, with the barons of northern France losing their grip on the Jews. English Jews from the outset "belonged" to the kings of England, with the barony only rarely gaining control of them. The combination of banking business and growing royal control resulted, in northern France, in the potential for considerable royal exploitation of Jewish wealth; in England, this potential and its actualization were more extreme. Finally, in northern France, the combination of newcomer status, traditional Christian anti-Jewish motifs, Jewish moneylending, and the alliance with the monarchy resulted in popular hostility toward the Jews. In England, since the newcomer status, the moneylending, and the alliance with the monarchy were all far more pronounced, anti-Jewish hostility was considerably more intense.

One striking difference between northern-French and English Jewry involves the cultural legacy of the two Jewries. As we have seen, northern-French Jewry was remarkably creative through the eleventh, twelfth, and early thirteenth centuries. Especially impressive was the fact that such creativity could emerge so early in the development of a set of Jewish communities. English Jewry shows nothing like this cultural creativity; it was – in cultural terms – a mere appendage to the vibrant Jewry of northern France.

There was yet a second contrast between the northern-French and English Jewish experience, a contrast that affects the reconstruction of the history of the two communities. While we have noted the development of a royal bureaucracy and royal records in thirteenth-century France, the English monarchy pioneered in both regards. The bureaucracy and the archives of England developed far earlier and far more fully than those of France, and, as a result, much more copious data are available for reconstructing the history of English Jewry. The non-Jewish documentary sources for twelfth- and thirteenth-century English Jewry are literally many hundreds of times richer than those for France.

In England, a full-blown bureaucratic office for Jewish affairs – the Exchequer of the Jews – was established already in the twelfth century. Five volumes of calendars of thirteenth-century plea rolls of the Exchequer of the Jews have been published.[37] Nothing remotely like this treasure trove of material exists for any other thirteenth-century Jewry. If we today possessed nothing more than the plea rolls of the Exchequer of the Jews, English Jewry would be far and away the best-documented Jewish community in thirteenth-century Latin Christendom. In fact, there is much more. All the major sets of governmental records are replete with references to Jews and Jewish-related issues, to say nothing of the extensive references in the documentation of ecclesiastical institutions. It is worth adding that – not surprisingly, given the lack of cultural creativity – the Jewish evidence for medieval English Jewry is woefully sparse, creating a striking imbalance between the rich governmental and ecclesiastical data and the sparse Jewish evidence.

As a result of the copious governmental and ecclesiastical documentation, fuller historical reconstruction of medieval English Jewry has been achieved than for any other Jewish community in twelfth- or thirteenth-century medieval western Christendom. English medievalists exhibited an early and abiding interest in the Jews of medieval England. Already in the early eighteenth century, Blossier de Tovey, an English vicar and subsequently Principal of New Inn Hall, Oxford, composed an elaborate history of medieval English Jewry, exploiting the rich records we have noted. Publication of much of the Exchequer of the Jews documentation has been carried out by distinguished English medievalists, and many of these scholars have also reconstructed aspects of medieval English Jewish history. To note but a few recent examples, H. G. Richardson has written an important study of the English Jews at the end of the twelfth and on into the early thirteenth century; R. B. Dobson has contributed a number of valuable studies of specific Jewish communities; Robert Stacey has expanded our knowledge of Jewish fortunes during the important reign of Henry III; and Robin Mundill has provided extensive depiction of the expulsion of 1290.[38] The lack of Jewish documentation has made it yet easier for such general medievalists to focus on the Jews of England from the eleventh through the thirteenth centuries. We are more fully informed at least as to the material circumstances of English Jewry for these centuries than we are for any of the older and larger Jewries of southern or northern Europe.

The rich governmental records begin to proliferate toward the end of the twelfth century. For the first century of Jewish history in England (the 1060s to 1150s), we are in much the same situation encountered already for northern France – a minimum of data. Nonetheless, the fragmentary evidence suggests an immigrant Jewish community originally limited to a number of major towns but slowly expanding outward, a set of Jewish settlements developing under royal protection, economic specialization in the money trade, and considerable popular hostility.

The earliest record of the royal exchequer, the pipe roll of the thirty-first year of King Henry I (1131), already shows evidence of a number of wealthy Jewish financiers. These wealthy Jewish businessmen are often portrayed as benefiting from royal assistance in realizing obligations owed to them. At the same time, they are also portrayed as occasionally losing moneys owed to them, as a result of sums paid to the crown by their debtors for release from obligations. The common denominator in both cases is royal profit. In a number of instances, the Jewish businessmen are seen making small advances to the crown. This is a procedure hard to grasp. It may reflect a kind of Jewish business or, alternatively, a veiled payment for royal protection and assistance.

We are probably justified in suggesting that hostility toward the Jewish immigrants developed fairly early on, for the reasons already noted – immigrant status, traditional Church teachings, limited and problematic business, and alliance with the foreign monarchy. The strong early Norman monarchs seem to have been successful in damping down this hostility. Problems would necessarily arise for the Jews during periods of governmental instability, for example the civil war waged by King Stephen and the Empress Mathilda in the 1140s. Jews were very much caught up in the crossfire, with an opportunity for the combatants, their partisans, and the population at large to exploit Jewish vulnerability and to express pent-up anger.

The Norwich incident of the 1140s shows us some of the depth of this anger; it at the same time suggests that anti-Jewish sentiment was by no means universal and that the government was generally able to protect its Jews effectively. The story begins at Easter-time in 1144. The mutilated body of a young tanner named William was found outside of town. Suspicion – at least among part of the Christian populace of Norwich – fastened upon the Jews. It is important to note, however, that our major source for the incident, composed a number of years later, indicates clearly that many of the townsmen of Norwich were equally convinced that the Jews had nothing to do with the crime. In any case, the local sheriff effectively protected the Jews of Norwich from any reprisals that might have been occasioned by Christian suspicions.

The sense among some inhabitants of Norwich that the Jews had killed the young lad involved also the conviction that the sole motive for the crime was Jewish hatred for Christ and Christianity. The victim seems to have been a fine boy, thus suggesting the lack of any reasonable basis for the killing. The conviction that William had died because of Jewish enmity transformed the victim of the alleged crime into a martyr for his Christian faith. As a martyr, William's gravesite was venerated, and miracles were quickly reported to have taken place there. Once again, the townsmen of Norwich were divided in their assessment of the saintliness of William – some convinced of his martyrdom, others uncertain, yet others sure that he was not a martyr and saint. Some years later, a newcomer cleric undertook the task of proving William's saintliness. For Thomas of Monmouth, there were three indices of William's saintliness – his blessed and irreproachable childhood; death as a martyr at Jewish hands; and the miracles associated with his gravesite. Clearly, the middle element – a martyr's death – was key to Thomas's case, and he spun out the tale of William's demise in great detail.[39]

According to Thomas's unsubstantiated reconstruction, the Jews of Norwich lured the unsuspecting young tanner into their clutches and then fell upon him without warning. The chronicler describes alleged

Jewish savagery in great detail. He claims that the Jews "were so cruel and so eager to inflict pain that it was difficult to say whether they were more cruel or more ingenious in their tortures. For their skill in torturing kept up the strength of their cruelty and ministered arms thereto." The tortures purportedly inflicted on the youngster already suggest overtones of Jesus' suffering. Thomas proceeds to make the identification overt. "Thus, while the enemies of the Christian name were rioting in a spirit of malignity around the boy, some of those present adjudged him to be fixed to a cross in mockery of the Lord's Passion, as though they would say: 'Even as we condemned Christ to a shameful death, so let us also condemn this Christian.'" The emotional impact of this description is of course shattering, making powerfully Thomas's case for William's martyrdom and hence saintliness.

The notion of Jewish murder of a Christian youngster via crucifixion initiated a new stage in the history of Christian anti-Jewish sentiment.[40] Again, it must be emphasized that Thomas's account was necessitated by the objection of some of the Norwich townsmen to the notion of murderous Jewish hatred of Christianity and Christians and concomitant rejection of the sainthood of William. In any case, England provides us with the very first instance of the allegation of religiously grounded Jewish murder of innocent Christians and the claim of murder via crucifixion or ritualized murder.[41] It should be further recalled that Christian anger over the purported crime did not eventuate in overt anti-Jewish violence. The local sheriff was quite successful in protecting the Jews living under his jurisdiction.

The long and by-and-large peaceful reign of Henry II (1154 to 1189) provided the backdrop for further maturation of English Jewry, its business, and its alliance with the monarchy. At the beginning of Henry II's reign, Jewish settlements have been identified in fourteen English towns. By the end of his reign, the number of English towns housing Jews had more than doubled. At the same time, these demographic, business, and political successes also enhanced popular dislike of the Jews.

The expansion of Jewish settlement was intimately linked to the flourishing of Jewish business. From the reign of Henry II, evidence mounts of Jewish banking activity. Especially striking is the emergence of extremely successful Jewish financiers. Some of these included: Brun of London, Isaac of London, the brothers Jurnet and Benedict of Norwich, Vives of Cambridge, Moses of Bristol. Often these financiers worked together in powerful business consortia. Of all the successful late-twelfth-century Jewish moguls, the most prominent was Aaron of Lincoln. According to Cecil Roth, "when he died, about 1186, Aaron of Lincoln was probably the wealthiest person in England, in liquid assets."[42] The list of those to whom he lent is striking; it includes counts, earls, archbishops, bishops, abbots, and towns. Like some of his fellow financiers, he often advanced money to the king himself, in return for a lien on tax revenues. The sums involved in Aaron's business were staggering. Upon his death, his entire estate escheated to the crown. A special office, the *Scaccarium Aaronis*, was established in the royal exchequer, with responsibility for tracking down and collecting the sums due the deceased Jew. The labors of this special office continued for almost a decade, with only limited success. Even that limited success, however, much enriched the royal coffers.

More generally, the business successes of twelfth-century English Jewry translated into considerable revenue for the monarchy. The special arrangements for the estate of Aaron of Lincoln were unusual; exploitation of Jewish wealth was not. Modalities of exploiting Jewish funds included normal taxation, fines for real or alleged trespasses, and special levies. The first of these special tallages came in 1159, on the occasion of a royal expedition to southern France; the last of Henry II's reign came in the late 1180s as Henry prepared for taking the cross. In this instance, the Jews of England were tallaged at one-fourth of their assets, with the intention of raising the enormous sum of 60,000 pounds.

The combination of extended Jewish settlement and thus enhanced contact between Jews and the broad English population, Jewish business success, and the potent Jewish alliance with Henry II and his court exacerbated antipathy toward the Jews. In effect, when the monarchy tightened the screws on its Jews, through one or another of the available fund-raising devices, the pressure was ultimately felt by those in debt to the Jewish lenders. In order to meet the demands of the king, Jews had no choice but to call in debts owed to them. The Jews thus became a vehicle for royal access to Christian funds. Serving as the medium for royal fiscal pressure hardly endeared the Jews to an already hostile population.

The allegation of Jewish hatred of Christianity so intense as to lead to murder of innocent Christians – the allegation that had first surfaced in 1144 in Norwich – appeared with some frequency during the reign of Henry II. It was raised at Gloucester in 1168, at Bury St. Edmunds in 1181, and at Bristol in 1183. In all cases, memorials were established to the purported young martyrs, thus maintaining and spreading the allegation. Once again, however, the authorities seem to have protected the endangered Jews assiduously, with no known reports of reprisals.

Effective royal protection of the Jews gave way rapidly under Henry II's successor, the famed Richard the Lionheart. Two factors seem to have accounted for the outbreak of the violence of the early years of Richard's reign. The first was intense crusade propaganda, which we have already seen to be dangerous to Jewish safety. From the earliest preaching of the crusading campaign to free Jerusalem and the Holy Sepulcher, it became clear that this message, with its focus on the shrine to Christ's suffering, bore the potential for arousing Christian hatred of the Jews, who were purportedly responsible for Christ's death.[43] In addition, royal absence from the realm weakened those agencies that had established an impressive record of effective protection of English Jews.

The first outbreak of violence took place while Richard was still in England; in fact, it coincided with the coronation festivities of late 1189. A deputation of English Jewish leaders presented itself at Westminster Hall and was brutally rebuffed by a guard, which seems to have set in motion popular anti-Jewish rioting at the hall. This rioting in turn was reported back in London as agreeable to the new king, touching off fierce attacks on the Jewish quarter and, eventually, burning of much of the quarter. The precedent was distressing, as was the mildness of the post-violence royal reaction.

When Richard set forth on his crusading venture in early 1190, much more wide-ranging anti-Jewish violence broke out. Attacks took place in Lynn, Norwich, Stamford, Lincoln, Bury St. Edmunds, and possibly elsewhere as well. The most famous – or infamous – of the assaults took place in York. There, the crisis began with assaults on the houses of especially prominent Jews. Those found in these houses were murdered, the contents plundered, and the buildings set ablaze. Quickly, most of the Jews of York made their way to the royal stronghold. A tragic misunderstanding between these Jews and the local sheriff resulted in the effort on the latter's part to recover the castle and oust the endangered Jews. Under the inspiration of a northern-French Jewish spiritual leader, most of the Jews in the castle opted for martyrdom, rather than falling into the hands of their attackers. Those few who chose to survive exited with the intention of converting. In such instances, as we shall see more fully, Jewish life was regularly spared.[44] This, however, was not to be the case in York, where the potential converts were put to the sword. The final step in this violence was an assault on the cathedral, where Jewish bonds were deposited. The bonds were found and burned, freeing many in the area from their indebtedness to the Jews.

While the earlier breach of the peace in 1189 did not elicit profound royal reaction, the violence of 1190 did. Royal troops were dispatched, arrests were made, fines were levied, and property was confiscated. A few years later, after Richard's return from the crusade and captivity, more protracted investigation was undertaken, in an effort to recoup losses suffered during the spate of anti-Jewish attacks. More important, at this point, in 1194, far-reaching changes were instituted to safeguard Jewish business and – perhaps more important – to ensure governmental knowledge and exploitation of that business. Record centers for Jewish business were established, with careful provision for the registration of Jewish loans. All Jewish contracts were to be made out in duplicate, with one copy retained in royal chests. An officialdom of two Christians, two Jews, and two clerks was to monitor Jewish business activity. While one objective was to protect the Jews, the larger goal was to secure governmental profit from the Jews. In the process, Jewish business became increasingly transparent to the royal authorities, with the obvious potential for more effective exploitation of Jewish wealth. Subsequent to the erection of this structure, any effort to lay special levies on the Jews would be preceded by a closing of these centers and an examination of the records, in order to ascertain Jewish resources that might be tapped. Over the succeeding decade, the new structure evolved into the powerful and important Exchequer of the Jews, the valuable records of which have already been noted.

The tumultuous reign of King John – 1199 to 1216 – was disastrous for England in general. We have already had occasion to cite the loss of the crown's Norman possessions, which was as great a success for the French monarchy as it was a blow to England. Strife with the papacy and a series of military setbacks augmented the sense of catastrophe. Under such circumstances, many elements in English society suffered, the Jews among these elements. For a monarchy under enormous fiscal stress, the Jews recommended themselves as a ready target. In general, they were heavily dependent on the crown;

more specifically the new bureaucracy created in the wake of the 1189–1190 turbulence made exploitation of the Jews far easier than it had been heretofore.

During the reign of King John, the earlier practice of exempting debtors from their obligations to Jews for a fee was much intensified. Jewish creditors lost significant sums in this way, with the crown gaining much needed revenue. Fines of extraordinary sums were levied on individual Jews, for example on the wealthy Jewish financier Isaac of Norwich. A series of tallages was enacted, with huge sums thus exacted from the Jews. The tallage of 1210 was especially notable and onerous. The Jews of the kingdom were arrested and their records – now so fully available – carefully studied. Concluding that the Jews had been withholding information and revenue, the king ordered a massive tallage and specified draconian measures for its collection. Once again, we must remember that such pressure on the king's Jews necessarily translated into Jewish pressures on Christian debtors. When money had to be produced, it could only be realized by squeezing those in debt to the Jews. Thus, such tallages were doubly disastrous. They impoverished the Jews, while at the same time intensifying popular animosity toward them.

Not surprisingly, the issue of indebtedness to the Jews made its way into the Magna Carta, King John's concession to baronial demands, often seen as one of the major steps toward the democratic system of modern England. Jews are mentioned in this important document, in an effort to protect debtors from certain kinds of exploitation. These clauses reflect accurately concern with Jewish lending and its repayment, concern very much exacerbated by the depredations of the reign of King John.

For all elements in English society, the accession of King Henry III – as a minor to be sure – seemed to offer the promise of stability. In fact, the reign of Henry III was one of the longest in English history – 1216 to 1272. While this lengthy reign did bring stability in general and for the Jews in particular, the tendency toward support of the Jews largely in order to exploit them became the controlling pattern for the new regime. Jews were supported fairly carefully; their business was monitored closely for their protection and out of concern for potential royal revenue; the exploitation of Jewish business was pursued to the point where the English Jewish community was eventually impoverished, an important step on the road to its demise.

At the outset of the new reign, some of the suffering of the last years of King John was alleviated. Imprisoned Jews were released, and sequestered bonds were returned to them. As preparations for a new crusade developed, requisite steps were taken to insure that the rioting that had accompanied Richard's crusading not be repeated. All these were hopeful signs.

There was one development early in Henry's reign portending new difficulties for the Jews, and that involved augmented ecclesiastical pressure to introduce some of the innovations that had been evolving in Church policy. It will be recalled that the Third and Fourth Lateran Councils had stipulated measures to segregate the Jews more fully. Particularly striking was the introduction by the second of these councils of distinguishing garb for Jews, making them identifiable at all times as Jews. The Fourth Lateran Council had also introduced measures to shield Christian lenders from some of the excesses associated with Jewish banking business. The royal court was amenable to the segregative efforts. In 1218, a royal decree ordained the wearing of distinguishing garb by Jews, a very early instance of secular support for the ecclesiastical innovation. It was not amenable, however, to ecclesiastical efforts to limit Jewish business or to bring Jewish business issues into the jurisdiction of ecclesiastical courts. The Provincial Council of Canterbury, held in 1222, enacted many of the stipulations of the Third and Fourth Lateran Councils, going so far as to prohibit all relations with the Jews of the province, a step that would have made Jewish existence impossible. The royal authorities reacted energetically, forbidding Christians of the province from adhering to the stipulated limitations on contact with Jews.

Emergent ecclesiastical efforts at missionizing among the Jews also struck deep roots in England. During the early years of Henry's reign, Dominicans and Franciscans began to establish themselves in or near Jewish neighborhoods, with the intention of bringing the Christian message to Jewish audiences. In 1232, a *Domus conversorum*, a home for converts from Judaism to Christianity, was established under royal auspices outside of London. The effort to proselytize among Jews was pursued assiduously, and the *Domus conversorum* remained a fixture on the English scene for the rest of the thirteenth century.

Hand in hand with the ecclesiastical pressures went augmented popular animosity. As we have seen, a variety of factors combined to make the general populace of England quite negative in its views of the Jews. Throughout the prior period, the royal authorities had by and large been successful in protecting the Jews against any violence that popular charges might have unleashed. During the reign of Henry III, the number of incidents multiplied, with the royal authorities now supportive of some of the charges. In 1234, a number of Norwich Jews were accused of circumcising a Christian youngster. A hearing before the royal court resulted in passing the case on to an ecclesiastical tribunal. The latter court found some of the accused guilty and sentenced them to death. At the same time, popular rioting took place in Norwich against the Jews.

Such instances began to multiply. The most well known of these incidents took place in Lincoln in 1255, with the discovery of the body of a Christian youngster named Hugh. Once again, the Jews were the center of suspicion. A Jew named Copin was tortured into confession. With the arrival of the king, Copin was immediately hanged and a large number of Lincoln Jews brought to London for trial. Eighteen Jews who demanded a mixed jury of Christians and Jews were immediately executed. The rest were tried and convicted, although eventually released. The story of Little St. Hugh of Lincoln became a staple of medieval English folk literature. The combination of royal support for the ritual murder allegation and popular dissemination of the story further eroded the already negative imagery of Jews in England.

While the accelerating ecclesiastical and popular pressures and the royal responses to these pressures are significant, the most important development of the reign of Henry III was the taxation policy that was innovated toward the end of the 1230s, with the growing control of the monarch and the elevation of a new group of advisors more thoroughly the king's own men. The taxation of Henry III has been studied meticulously by Robert Stacey. Stacey suggests that, "before 1239, Jewish taxation had made a modest but fairly steady contribution to the king's finances of between 2000 and 3000 marks per year under Henry III . . . In 1239, however, this pattern of steady, moderate, effectively annual contributions to the king changed dramatically, when Henry demanded from the Jews the third part of all their chattels, including the value of all unredeemed bonds."[45] This seems to have been the kind of seizure of Jewish property followed by redemption through payment of heavy sums that has been encountered recurrently throughout this chapter. As was predictable, the Jewish chests were closed, with Jewish holdings carefully examined. It seems that the returns from this imposition were disappointing.

This disappointment translated into a more thoroughgoing effort to enjoy the fruits of Jewish wealth. In 1240, the Jewish chests were again closed, with a full-scale investigation of Jewish holdings, capped by the compilation of a census of all Jews in England aged twelve or more. The result of all this preliminary effort was the convocation of an assembly of Jewish representatives in Worcester in February of 1241 and the announcement of an especially heavy tallage of 20,000 marks. The tallage was to be paid in two installments, with the Jews themselves responsible for its collection. A second enormous tallage, this time of 60,000 marks, was levied in 1244 and collected through 1250. Robert Stacey's conclusion is as follows: "The double blows of the 20,000 mark tallage of 1241–2 and the 60,000 mark tallage of 1244–50 ruined the Jewish magnates of England, and effectively decapitated the class structure of medieval Anglo-Jewry. By so doing, Henry broke the financial backbone of the English Jewish community, and permanently reduced its value to the Crown."[46] Inherent in the situation of English Jewry – and, as we have seen, northern-French Jewry in somewhat lesser measure as well – was the potential for such despoliation. The extent to which the Jews were increasingly dependent upon their rulers for both physical security and business dealings and the extent to which Jewish business became increasingly transparent to these rulers made the Jews an enticing source for revenue. Prudence might have dictated measured utilization of this resource, as seems to have been the case during the early years of King Henry III. The combination of accelerating anti-Jewish animosity and pressing fiscal needs regularly served to persuade rulers to abandon moderation. In Stacey's view, the departure from moderation by King Henry III was a blow from which the Jews of medieval England never recovered.

With the accession of Edward I to the throne of England in 1272, the last stage of Jewish life in medieval England was initiated. The most significant difference notable in the reign of Edward I was his allegiance to the objectives and policies of the Church, including prohibition of Jewish usury, enhanced segregation of the Jews, and accelerating efforts at converting the Jews. Edward I's Statute for [English] Jewry, enacted in 1275, was a milestone, echoing the innovations introduced in northern France by King Louis IX. At the heart of this edict lay the demand that Jews no longer occupy themselves with moneylending. The business that had been the mainstay of Jewish economic life in England and that had enjoyed considerable royal support was now disavowed by the monarchy.[47]

The impact on English Jewry was enormous, with some Jews attempting to evade the new legislation and maintain their prior business activities, with others opting to continue their moneylending elsewhere, with some seeking to find legitimate economic outlets, and others turning to crime. Particularly noteworthy in the wake of the 1275 legislation are the repeated accusations of Jewish coin-clipping, the recurrent prosecution of suspected Jewish coin-clippers, and the harsh penalties imposed. Jewish business affairs – in decline in any case – were disastrously affected by the legislation of 1275. This meant, of course, that the potential Jewish contribution to the royal coffers, already minimal, was now nearly non-existent.

On July 18, 1290, King Edward I announced that all Jews must leave England by the following November 1. The history of a ruined community was to come to a formal close. Edward's move was immediately inspired by a need for tax revenues from his barons, who desired the removal of the Jews and were willing to grant the king revenue in return for the edict of expulsion. It reflects, at the same time, much broader developments on the English scene. As noted, because of the richness of the English records, the small Jewish community of medieval England has been widely studied, and numerous views of the factors that led to the expulsion have been articulated.[48] While scholars have occasionally emphasized one element or another, there is broad agreement that there was no one factor that led to the expulsion. Rather, a concatenation of considerations led Edward I to his move. These included: the declining Jewish contribution to the royal treasury, accelerating ecclesiastical pressures for segregation and conversion of the Jews, enhanced royal support of these Church objectives, and – last but surely not least – heightened popular animosity. Edward I had learned that in fact the populace of the continental counties of Anjou and Maine had been willing to pay a price for expulsion of their Jews, and he decided to make much the same move, wringing concessions from his barons for an anti-Jewish action that was highly popular.

The Jews of England faced a stark choice in 1290 between forced migration and conversion. Some chose the latter, most the former. With the demise of medieval English Jewry, a curious experiment in Jewish settlement came to a close. A new Jewish community had been created, had matured and flourished, and had expired, all within the span of little more than two centuries. The Jews expelled from England made their way eastward into royal France, where they added further strains on an already endangered community and where the example of their expulsion would influence the larger and more far-reaching banishment from royal France a mere sixteen years later. Ultimately, the Jews expelled from England amalgamated into the larger entity that came to coalesce as Ashkenazic Jewry, the Jewry pressed ever more insistently eastward into the less developed areas of northern Europe.

5

THE NEWER JEWRIES OF THE NORTH: GERMANY AND EASTERN EUROPE

·

Northern Europe from England in the west to Poland in the east constituted, early in the Middle Ages, the backward area of western Christendom. Subsequently, the remarkable vitalization of Latin Christendom was centered in this northern area, propelling the heretofore lagging area into the forefront of European civilization. This transformation of northern Europe was, however, by no means uniform. While signs of political maturation first appeared in the German areas, ultimately the more westerly sectors – northern France and England – forged ahead. The first powerful government to appear in northern Europe was the German emperor. The imperial title itself bespeaks greater majesty than kingship. Yet with the passage of time, the "mere" kings of France and England outstripped their imperial counterparts and led their monarchies to supremacy in the medieval West. It is difficult to assess the factors in this differential development. Does it reflect greater perspicacity on the part of the French and English leadership; is it a tribute to the resourcefulness of the French and English people, especially the urban elements in the population; is it simply the result of geography and climate; or was some combination of factors decisive?

Whatever the explanation, the reality is that, while Germany became the site for the earliest development of northern-European Jewry, German Jewry – as was true for so many other spheres of German life – was eventually overtaken and outstripped in both material and cultural terms by its western Jewish neighbors. To be sure, German Jews did not suffer the rapid decline and the wholesale expulsion endured by their more westerly co-religionists. The blessings of strong centralized governmental leadership in France and England turned into a curse, as we have seen. The Jews of Germany never enjoyed the blessing and likewise never suffered the curse associated with strong centralized government. German Jewry encountered a different kind of decline, stemming from weak governance, widespread popular animosity, and the recurrent violence spawned by the combination.[1]

As was true further westward, Germany too had its hinterland, the areas of eastern Europe, especially Hungary and Poland. The same dynamic that moved the Jews of northern France to pursue new opportunities further westward in England propelled the Jews of Germany to seek new outlets in the lesser developed areas of eastern Europe. There, however, the parallels cease. Whereas the Jews who made their way to England found an increasingly sophisticated economy and governance structure, the Jews who settled in the most easterly areas of northern Europe encountered the economic opportunities resulting from underdevelopment and political authorities that therefore remained supportive of their presence and activities. Jewish life in England was snuffed out at the end of the thirteenth century. By the year 1500, eastern Europe was well on its way to become the great human reservoir of European – indeed world-wide – Jewry.

GERMANY

Like their counterparts in northern France, the Jews of medieval Germany show no genuine sense of roots in German soil stretching back into the deep past. They fail to note forebears in Germany who predate the year 1000, and they cite no legal or spiritual precedents from that earlier period. Once again, while Jewish traders may well have made their way northward prior to the year 1000, medieval German Jewry took shape during our period. More consciously than the Jews of northern France, however, the German Jews indicate awareness of migrations that brought their ancestors from the Mediterranean world into the reaches of northern Europe. Prominent among these recollections are the purported imperial transfer of the important Kalonymide family from Italy to the Rhineland and the transmission of mystical teachings from the south into the north.[2]

We have noted in the previous chapter two brief reports of invitations to Jews to settle in areas new to them. The first of these reports, composed by a Jewish author, portrays an invitation extended by the count of Flanders; the second, mentioned by a Christian chronicler, depicts the support of William the Conqueror for Jewish immigration into England. For Germany, we have far more detailed information on the settlement of Jews in a town not previously inhabited by them. The town was Speyer, along the Rhine River; the year was 1084; the sources reflect both a Jewish and a Christian perspective. Indeed, the Christian source is the document of invitation itself.[3]

Let us begin with the Hebrew narrative source. It is part of what seems to have been a lengthy communal history of Speyer Jewry, composed during the second half of the twelfth century. Unfortunately, the opening sections of this communal record have been lost. What has been preserved begins with the lengthiest of the Hebrew First-Crusade narratives, edited in the 1140s. The collection, as we now have it, closes with a retrospective look at the history of Speyer Jewry, which depicts its foundation in 1084, its fate during the First Crusade, and the rededication of its synagogue in 1104. The rededication notice concludes with mention of the transfer of the Torah scrolls to the rebuilt sanctuary, "where they remain to this very day." On the morrow, the Jews of Speyer resumed praying in their sanctuary, "where they pray to this very day." Both references suggest the passage of considerable time between 1104 and the penning of this memorial.

According to this retrospective survey of the early history of Speyer Jewry, the Jews of Speyer originated in the nearby and older Jewish community of Mainz. "At the outset, when we came to establish our residence in Speyer – may its foundations never falter! – it was as a result of the fire that broke out in the town of Mainz. The town of Mainz was the town of our origin and the residence of our ancestors, the ancient and revered community, praised above all communities in the empire. All the Jews' quarter and their street were burned, and we were in great fear of the burghers." In this precarious situation, the Jews of Mainz were approached by the bishop of Speyer and invited to settle in his town. "The bishop of Speyer greeted us warmly, sending his ministers and soldiers after us. He gave us a place in the town and expressed his intention to build about us a strong wall to protect us from our enemies, to afford us fortification." Clearly, not all the Jews of Mainz responded to this invitation. Some Mainz Jews did make the move, and the community they created was destined for a long and distinguished history.

The second source for the establishment of Speyer Jewry is the charter of invitation extended to the Mainz Jews by Bishop Rudiger, which corroborates much in the Hebrew report and adds valuable further information. The bishop of Speyer, who was both an ecclesiastical authority and the temporal lord of Speyer, begins by specifying the reason for his invitation. "When I wished to make a town out of the village of Speyer, I Rudiger, surnamed Huozmann, bishop of Speyer, thought the glory of our town would be augmented a thousand-fold if I were to bring Jews." Clearly, Bishop Rudiger was not thinking in terms of a Jewish cultural or intellectual contribution to the development of his town; the Jews were deemed useful for their contribution to the economic well-being of Speyer. Rudiger also specifies the mechanism for attracting Jews to Speyer: "In order to achieve the heights of kindness, I have granted them a legal status more generous than any the Jewish people have in any city in the German kingdom." This claim accords nicely with the Jewish reference to the bishop's kindness.

Rudiger's generosity began with the granting of an area of Speyer that belonged to him – in fact two areas, one in the lower town and one in the upper town – for Jewish settlement. In addition, he provided the Jews with land for a burial ground as well. Recognizing the backdrop of anti-Jewish violence in Mainz, Rudiger added the following: "In order that they not be easily disrupted by the insolence of the mob, I have encircled them with a wall." Reflected here are Christian–Jewish tensions and the generosity of the bishop's invitation. Clearly, the Jews themselves welcomed the extra protection. In later centuries, Church authorities demanded that Jews live segregated from their Christian neighbors. In this much earlier instance, the Jews of Mainz relocating to Speyer were attracted, in part, by this separation.

The Jews migrating to Speyer were merchants, and the economic provisions of their charter reflect mercantile activities. Jews were accorded the right of buying and selling all through the town. Also, Jews quartering with them were to pay no tolls, reflecting more wide-ranging Jewish trade. The later Jewish specialization in moneylending, amply reflected in the prior depiction of the history of the Jews in northern France and England and to be highlighted in some of the thirteenth-century materials from Germany, makes no appearance in this early document.

Two further themes in this document are freedom from Church demands and the right of self-government. The former is reflected in the stipulations that Jews "may legally have nurses and servants from among our people" and that Jews "may sell to Christians slaughtered meats they consider unfit for themselves." The right of self-government is reflected in the following interesting provision: "Just as the mayor of the town serves among the burghers, so too shall the Jewish leader (*archisynagogus*) adjudicate any quarrel that might arise among them or against them. If he be unable to determine the issue, then the case shall come before the bishop of the town or his chamberlain." Once again, the charter does in fact seem unusually generous. The Mainz Jews may well have been attracted by this generosity, as the Hebrew account reports and as Bishop Rudiger intended.

To be sure, what was advantageous to the Jews was, in all likelihood, resented by their new Christian neighbors. The notion that Jews were necessary to the growth and glory of the town surely had an offensive ring to the burghers of Speyer. The granting of land and especially the erection of a wall between the Jews and the Christian burghers was probably resented as well. Finally, the removal of the Jews from municipal jurisdiction, the establishment of a separate Jewish court system, and the reserving of ultimate jurisdiction to the bishop himself must have annoyed Christian burghers intent on expanding their own self-government. In a sense, all this reflects a vicious cycle. The Jews came to Speyer suspicious of their urban neighbors; these suspicions moved them to seek the kind of guarantees that Bishop Rudiger accorded them; the privileges themselves served to further irritate Christian–Jewish relations in the town.

Six years after a Jewish community was established in Speyer, the leadership of the Jewish community, in coordination with Bishop Rudiger, approached Emperor Henry IV for confirmation of Jewish rights in Speyer. The confirmation is likewise a generous grant, somewhat fuller than the original 1084 charter.[4] Again, it begins with guarantees of physical safety for the Jews of Speyer, specified in a number of provisions. Jews are, first of all, protected from physical assault. Should an assault in fact take place, the penalty stipulated in the charter is quite high. Should the perpetrator of violence be unable to pay the assessed fine, the bodily punishment inflicted is extremely harsh. Infringement on Jewish property rights is also prohibited. Once more, violation of this prohibition is penalized harshly. The homes of Jews are inviolable and cannot be used for imperial quartering. Likewise, their horses are not to be requisitioned for imperial or episcopal service. In the spiritual sphere, Jews are protected from forcible baptism. Again, the penalties for contravention are heavy. Even when a Jew expresses a desire for baptism, a three-day moratorium is decreed, in order to be certain that the baptism is totally voluntary.

As in the 1084 charter, the Jews reflected in the imperial dispensation are essentially businessmen, involved in trade. Their trading rights are extensive. An interesting provision addresses the issues of stolen goods, always a bone of contention. "If a stolen item be found in their possession and if the Jew claims that he bought it, he shall substantiate by an oath how much he paid and how much he would accept, and in that way he shall return the item to him to whom it belonged." For Jewish businessmen involved in extensive buying and selling, this was an invaluable safeguard. Jews were protected against certain kinds of judicial ordeals; they were allowed to insist on the use of their own law in cases involving Christians; the Jewish courts were again given the right of jurisdiction in cases that would arise within the Jewish community. Only the court of the bishop could be appealed to beyond the Jewish courts.

Finally, there are a number of useful safeguards against the intrusion of ecclesiastical law into Jewish life. Jews are permitted "to have Christians do their work, except on festivals and Sundays." Although they are forbidden from purchasing Christian slaves, which was of course an established feature of Church law, they are permitted to own pagan slaves. These pagan slaves cannot be seduced away from their Jewish owners through baptism. "They have the right to sell their wine and their dyes and their medicines to Christians." All in all, the imperial charter of 1090 to the Jews of Speyer is – like its 1084 predecessor – very generous in the protections and rights accorded to the Jews. A mid-twelfth-century imperial document extended to the Jews of Worms by Emperor Frederick I depicts itself as a confirmation of an earlier charter given to the Jews of that town by Emperor Henry IV.[5] The parallels in content and language suggest that there was a more-or-less established version of such grants for the Jews of Germany toward the end of the eleventh century.

The Jews of eleventh-century Germany, or more specifically of the eleventh-century Rhineland, are the first important figures in the cultural creativity of northern-European Jewry. As we have already noted, the great northern-French Jewish figure, Solomon ben Isaac of Troyes (Rashi), made his way eastward to the Rhineland, during the middle decades of the eleventh century, in order to further his studies. He clearly perceived the Rhineland academies as constituting the vanguard of Jewish learning at that time.[6]

The dominant figure in this earliest phase of northern-European creativity is Rabbi Gershom of Mainz, accorded the honorific appellation "Light of the Exile." Rabbi Gershom's leadership is reflected in both the communal and literary spheres, although there is much uncertainty with respect to both sets of activities. He was obviously acknowledged as an important authority by his contemporaries and by subsequent Jews. His *responsa* – replies to questions raised about points of Jewish law – carried heavy weight in subsequent halakhic circles. He is reputed to have been the authority behind a number of important communal ordinances, widely accepted across German Jewry, indeed across all of Western Jewry with the passage of time. The best known of these ordinances prohibits polygamy. Associated with Rabbi Gershom, this ordinance has been a mainstay of Jewish family life throughout the ensuing millennium.

We possess little of the literary legacy of Rabbi Gershom and thus cannot identify with certainty the full range of his intellectual activity. His focus clearly lay with Jewish law and its underpinnings in the Babylonian Talmud. He is purported to have copied the Talmud, which is an interesting reflection of a Jewry laying the foundations for its intellectual enterprise. The Talmud is, as we have already seen, a sprawling work, that by virtue of its great length was subject to the vagaries of copyist error. Different readings of the dense talmudic text could play havoc with the meaning of important passages. Creating an authoritative talmudic text, which is what Rabbi Gershom seems to have done, constituted the important step of establishing a sound foundation for the academies of the Rhineland and northern Europe more generally.[7] Whatever the precise range of his intellectual endeavors, Rabbi Gershom was associated in subsequent Jewish thinking with the rise of German Jewry to prominence in rabbinic studies during the eleventh century.

The call to the First Crusade unleashed serious and wide-ranging anti-Jewish sentiment. This anti-Jewish sentiment erupted into uncontrolled violence that is often portrayed as a watershed in the history of the Jews in medieval western Christendom. The assaults of 1096 were, however, highly localized. While there were isolated incidents west and east of the Rhineland, none of those incidents would have been noteworthy in the sweep of history we are studying.[8] It was the Rhineland violence of 1096 that was epochal. The attacks on the Jewish communities of Speyer, Worms, Mainz, and Cologne were intense, unprecedented, and deadly. They surely sapped the creative energies of these important early centers of northern-European Jewish life. Nonetheless, these assaults by no means initiated a permanent downturn in the history of northern-European Jewry in its entirety; in fact, even the affected Rhineland Jewish communities recovered fairly quickly and reemerged as centers of Jewish life and creativity.

The intense anti-Jewish sentiment, the unprecedented anti-Jewish violence, and the extreme Jewish behaviors of 1095–1096 resulted in the creation of remarkable Jewish narrative accounts of the events of this brief but turbulent period. These narrative accounts preserve for us a number of distinctive voices and perspectives. They reveal aspects of pre-1096 Jewish life, along with illuminating important facets of the 1096 experience itself.[9] Of the diverse voices, the earliest and most valuable is that of the so-called *Mainz Anonymous*. This gifted author and thinker, writing shortly after the events of 1096, composed a beautifully crafted narrative that depicts the early development of the crusade in France; the arrival of French crusaders in the Rhineland; the evocation of anti-Jewish sentiment and behavior in Speyer, Worms, and Mainz; the reactions of the authorities and burghers to the new developments; and the Jewish responses as well. The *Mainz Anonymous* was determined to inform his fellow-Jews of the wellsprings of the violence, the behaviors of diverse elements in Christian society, and the multiplicity of Jewish reactions. Beyond these descriptions, crucial to preparing Jewish readers for potential repetitions of the 1096 violence, the *Mainz Anonymous* was also distressed by a Christian interpretation of the events of 1096 that stressed the hopelessness of Jewish circumstances; he presented his readers with an alternative reading that turned tragedy into victory and despair into hope.[10]

Let us begin with the circumstances of pre-1096 Jewish life reflected in the *Mainz Anonymous* (and by the other Jewish voices as well). The Jews of the Rhineland towns were technically – as we have already seen – wards of the German emperor, who was far from the scene and thus essentially irrelevant; at the same time and more consequentially, they lived under the protection of the local Rhineland bishops, who constituted political authority in immediate terms. The Rhineland bishops were unanimous in their determination to protect their Jewish clients. They were, however, uncertain as to how best to achieve that goal, and in many instances they failed dismally in their efforts.

Of the four bishops involved, in Speyer, Worms, Mainz, and Cologne, only the bishop of Speyer – guardian of a very young and still small community – can be truly called successful in his efforts. When a desultory attack was launched against the Jews of Speyer on a Sabbath morning, Bishop John sent his militia to disperse the attackers and punished some of those involved. He then chose to disperse his Jews into outlying fortifications, where they were successfully protected from further violence. The bishops of Worms and Mainz chose to gather their Jews – or most of them – in their own urban fortifications, which failed to preserve the Jews of either town. The bishop of Cologne emulated the Speyer tactic of dispersal of the Jews, but in this case the tactic was a conspicuous failure. The Jews of Cologne were sent off to seven neighboring fortifications. Almost all these enclaves of Cologne Jews were attacked and destroyed.

The burghers of the Rhineland were hardly unanimous in their reactions to the anti-Jewish sentiment whipped up by the French crusaders and expanded by their German imitators. In many instances, the burghers of the Rhineland towns allied themselves with the crusaders. After describing successful negotiations with the French crusaders, which involved funding in exchange for security, the *Mainz Anonymous* continues: "All this, however, was unavailing, for our sins brought it about that the burghers in every town to which the crusaders came were hostile to us, for their [the burghers'] hands were also with them [the subsequent German crusaders] to destroy stock and vine all along the way to Jerusalem." The *Mainz Anonymous*, for example, depicts the locked gate of the town of Mainz opened to the crusading band of Emicho of Flonheim by sympathetic burghers. In contrast, the *Mainz Anonymous* portrays an earlier incident in Mainz, where a ragtag crusading band, led by a woman and her wonder-working goose, taunted the Jews and their hopelessness (a theme to which we shall return) and in the process evoked dangerous anti-Jewish antipathy. In the face of incipient anti-Jewish violence, some of the burghers of Mainz stood courageously alongside their Jewish neighbors and protected them.

The bishops and the burghers were old elements in Rhineland Jewish life, reacting to the new – the crusade and the crusaders. The papal call for freeing the sacred sites of Christianity and for taking revenge on the Muslims who held and allegedly abused these sacred sites included no reference to the Jews and no incitement to anti-Jewish actions. The crusading armies that successfully made their way eastward and conquered Jerusalem were – so far as the available sources tell us – uninvolved in the anti-Jewish violence of 1096. It was in the more popular groups, highly unsuccessful from a military perspective, that anti-Jewish sentiment erupted. The papal call for freeing the Holy Sepulcher and for vengeance against the Muslims seems to have been conflated in extremist circles into the notion that revenge must be taken first upon those who had been responsible for making the Holy Sepulcher a burial shrine, and only then upon those who had more recently abused it. The revenge motif, in conjunction with millenarian exhilaration, seems to have moved these extremist circles to anti-Jewish violence.[11]

While the successful crusading armies seemed to have inferred no anti-Jewish message from the call to crusade, the popular French forces under the charismatic leadership of Peter the Hermit did extract such a message, although they were satisfied with the provisions they managed to extort from the frightened Jews of the Rhineland. The German popular bands that coalesced in the wake of Peter's passage eastward were the most radical in their thinking. According to the *Mainz Anonymous*, the Jewish effort to provision Count Emicho and his followers, in the same way that Peter and followers had been provisioned, was an abysmal failure. The German bands were seemingly determined on the most radical form of revenge, total destruction of Rhineland Jewry – through baptism of those willing to convert and through murder of those unwilling to convert.

The Jews of the Rhineland were not totally unprepared for the eruption of danger. As noted previously, they had been forewarned by their co-religionists in France of the agitation to the crusade and of the anti-Jewish sentiment aroused therefrom. There were, however, no real precedents to guide Jewish behavior in the face of this explosion of popular animosity. As we have seen from the charters of Bishop Rudiger of Speyer and Emperor Henry IV, the established authorities had guaranteed Jewish safety and security. The emperor seems to have been contacted and to have responded with warnings against violence. Given the general turbulence, however, such warnings counted for little. The bishops were on the scene, were similarly committed to Jewish safety, but turned out to be powerless in the face of the unexpectedly strong and unexpectedly militant popular crusading bands. This left the Jews with little leeway. Some did opt for conversion, on the assumption that it would ultimately be meaningless.[12] A larger number – at least so it would seem from the Hebrew narratives – chose to give up their lives, rather than their religious faith.

Jewish loss of life – viewed unequivocally by subsequent Jewish observers as martyrdom – took place in a variety of ways. Some Jews died fighting their crusader attackers, and some Jews allowed themselves to be slaughtered by rampaging crusaders and burghers. More radically, some Jews took their own lives; most radically of all, some Jews slew their wives and children, prior to taking their own lives or letting themselves be slaughtered by their attackers.

One report from the *Mainz Anonymous* on the most radical of Jewish behaviors should be quoted, in order to provide a flavor of its extreme nature and some of the symbolism underlying it. This incident took place in Worms. "There was a certain young man, named Meshullam ben R. Isaac. He called out loudly to all those standing there and to Zipporah his helpmate: 'Listen to me both great and small. This son God gave to me. My wife Zipporah bore him in her old age, and his name is Isaac. Now I shall offer him up, as did our ancestor Abraham with his son Isaac.' Zipporah replied: 'My lord, my lord. Wait a bit. Do not stretch forth your hand against the lad, whom I have raised and brought up and whom I bore in my old age. Slaughter me first, so that I not witness the death of the child.' He then replied: 'I shall not delay even a moment. He who gave him to us will take him as his portion. He will place him in the bosom of Abraham.' He then bound Isaac his son and took in his hand the knife with which to slaughter his son and made the benediction for slaughtering. He then slaughtered the lad. He took his screaming wife from the chamber, and the crusaders killed them."[13]

This is a horrifying portrait, and so it was meant to be. The *Mainz Anonymous* intended to shock and did just that. Radical behaviors, this author clearly believed, had to be graphically recounted. This radical behavior, the Jewish author tells us, was sustained by a belief that it was in emulation of the greatest of biblical figures, the patriarch Abraham. In fact, the reader can easily realize that Meshullam of Worms went far beyond Abraham in his devotion. Abraham was willing to sacrifice his son; Meshullam did so. There were no further familial or personal implications to Abraham's behaviors; the death of young Isaac of Worms was prelude to the further deaths of his father and mother as well.

The rectitude of this extreme act is further rooted in its sanctification through recitation of the blessing normally intoned over the ritual act of animal slaughter. To take matters one step further, in Jewish tradition the near-sacrifice of Isaac by Abraham was associated with the site upon which the later Jerusalem temples eventually stood. Indeed, the biblical story ends with the sacrifice of a ram in Isaac's stead. The Jews who gave their lives in 1096 made this association as well, seeing themselves as sheep and bullocks offered up on the altar of the spiritual temple erected along the banks of the Rhine River. Finally, there can be no missing the conviction of bountiful blessings associated with this radical behavior. The young victim Isaac will be laid in the bosom of Abraham. All through the Hebrew narratives, the conviction of rich and immediate otherworldly reward for the martyrs is patent.

The author of the *Mainz Anonymous* penned his account partly in order to forewarn Jewish readers about crusaders, Christian authorities, and Christian neighbors. In part, the narrative was also an act of filiopietism. Such great self-sacrifice had to be recorded. There was, however, yet a third purpose to the work as well. The *Mainz Anonymous* and the other Hebrew narratives recount numerous incidents in which Christians — sometimes hostile and sometimes friendly — urge Jews to understand what was happening. In the Christian view, the gathering of the Christian armies and the slaughter of Jews can only be understood in one way: God has clearly favored the former and abandoned the latter. Thus, to the despair normally attendant upon catastrophe was added the polemical Christian reading of the tragedy. Jews had to be provided with an alternative understanding of the events of 1096, an understanding that would enable them to maintain their Jewish identity in the face of Christian triumphalism.

The interpretation of the events of 1096 advanced by the *Mainz Anonymous* was audacious, to say the least. The uplifting meaning of the tragedy lay in the tragedy itself. While Christians were arguing that Jewish sinfulness had occasioned divine abandonment and thus the loss of Jewish life in 1096, the *Mainz Anonymous* presented a much different picture. God had by no means abandoned the Jewish people; rather, he had decided to test them, precisely as he had once tested the patriarch Abraham. The difficult test – like that of Abraham – involved the most precious of human possessions, life itself. Like Abraham, in fact well beyond Abraham, the Jews of the Rhineland had passed the test. God completed his testing of Abraham with resounding blessing. The biblical story ends with God announcing: "Because you have done this and have not withheld your son, your favored one, I will bestow my blessing upon you and make your descendants as numerous as the stars of heaven and the sands on the seashore, and your descendants shall seize the gates of their foes. All the nations of the earth shall bless themselves by your descendants, because you have obeyed my command."[14] If all that was promised to Abraham for his mere willingness to sacrifice one son, how much richer would be divine blessing on a generation that in fact carried out the sacrifice of so many sons and daughters.

The preeminence of Rhineland Jewry in northern Europe, especially in spiritual terms, was compromised by the events of 1096. The promise of Rhineland Jewry, or more broadly of German Jewry altogether, was by no means snuffed out, however. Jewish life in Germany, like Jewish life in the great center developing to the west in northern France, continued its upward trajectory during the twelfth century, a period of dynamic growth and development all across western Christendom, but especially in the north. Jewish numbers in Germany continued to expand; the decimated communities of Worms, Mainz, and Cologne were quickly rebuilt; the foundations of Jewish economic life were strengthened. In the spiritual realm, German Jewry may well have slipped behind French Jewry. That, however, was more a function of positive developments in France than of negative developments in Germany. German Jewry continued to create in a variety of spiritual directions.

In material terms, major differences are discernible between the French and the German centers of Jewish life. The slow development of impressive French political leadership in twelfth-century France was not matched in Germany. The twelfth century – and in fact the thirteenth as well – continued to show a number of powerful imperial figures. With their power spread thin over a vast area, however, the German emperors never managed to protect their Jews in the same way as the French barons and monarchs, never managed to support

Jewish economic activities in the same way, and never were able to exploit their Jews in parallel fashion either. From the Jewish perspective, the lack of governmental exploitation was a positive; the lack of governmental support for more sophisticated business operations and the repeated failure to protect Jewish life and property were, however, decidedly negative.

German Jewry was not able to flourish economically during the twelfth century in the way that its French and English counterparts did. Because of the lag in political authority, Germany could never sustain the kind of sophisticated banking arrangements that became the basis for significant Jewish economic achievement in France and England. During the thirteenth century, pawnbroking – decidedly less impressive and profitable than the Jewish banking business in northern France and England – was to emerge as a central Jewish economic activity in Germany. During the twelfth century, however, German Jews seem to have continued the older pattern of trading, carried out on both the local and more wide-ranging level.

Of paramount importance to the German Jews was maintenance of security during a period of continued crusading enthusiasm and in the face of the ongoing threat posed by the anti-Jewish sentiment that crusading evoked. As we have seen, the ecclesiastical authorities were fully prepared throughout the twelfth century for repetition of the anti-Jewish sentiment that exploded in 1096. We have noted the extensive efforts of Bernard of Clairvaux, the spiritual leader of the Second Crusade, to forestall anti-Jewish violence through his letters.[15] Once again, however, anti-Jewish sentiment erupted in the Rhineland, to which Bernard traveled in order to quash the potential for assaults. The Jewish chronicler of anti-Jewish violence during the Second Crusade, Ephraim of Bonn, actually had little to report. Ephraim's detailed knowledge involved incidental attacks by individual crusaders on individuals Jews. He portrays nothing like the massive assaults on entire Jewish communities depicted in the 1096 Hebrew narratives. Ephraim reports three instances in which substantial numbers of Jews lost their lives. These reports are so fragmentary, however, that modern scholars have never been able to identify these three locales with any certitude. Ephraim does not seem to know directly and reliably of any large-scale Jewish casualties inflicted during the Second Crusade.[16]

The reasons for the limited number of casualties associated with the Second Crusade lie in the preparedness of the ecclesiastical leadership, the secular authorities, and the Jews themselves. According to Ephraim of Bonn, the technique of moving Jews outside urban areas into rural fortifications, which had worked well for Speyer Jewry and badly for Cologne Jewry in 1096, was the key to successful protection of the German Jews during the Second Crusade. Ephraim indicates that he himself – a youngster of thirteen during the Second Crusade – was part of a large number of Jews successfully sequestered in the great fortress of Wolkenburg. Jews from other major urban areas found similar refuge all across Germany. The lack of millenarian enthusiasm during the Second Crusade was surely a critical factor in Jewish safety as well.

The same combination of elements – preparedness on the part of the authorities of Church and state, Jewish readiness, the tactic of removal of urban Jews to rural fortifications, and the lack of millenarian exhilaration – served German Jewry well during the Third Crusade also. Rabbi Eleazar of Worms, one of the major figures in the circle of German pietism, has left us a brief memoir of events in Germany during the Third Crusade, as he saw them.[17] Rabbi Eleazar begins his interesting account with an accusation of Jewish murder that was raised in Mainz in mid-1187, to which we shall return shortly. He then tells us that, on the second day of Rosh ha-Shanah, a solar eclipse took place, which was perceived as a divine sign. A few months later, word surfaced that, on that very day, the Muslims had won a major victory in the Holy Land, which served as a prelude to subsequent reconquest of Jerusalem. All this is told by Rabbi Eleazar with obvious relish and with considerable hatred for the *sancta* of Christianity that fell into Muslim hands.

Jewish enthusiasm for Muslim successes was mitigated, however, by the immediate mobilization of Christian forces in Europe for a new crusade. According to Rabbi Eleazar, this mobilization evoked the by-now standard anti-Jewish crusading sentiment. Deeply frightened, the Jews of Mainz and other German towns responded with prayers and fasting, on the one hand, while at the same time preparing to leave their homes for outlying fortresses, where they might find refuge. In March of 1188, the Jews of Mainz, Rabbi Eleazar among them, left their hometown for the safety of the castle of Munzberg, as did the Jews of other German towns as well. "In every town, they [the Jews] divided themselves up into four or five fortified redoubts." Sequestered in Munzberg for slightly less than two months, the Jews of Mainz were able to survive the turbulent early period of crusading preparations, returning by late April to their homes in safety.

Rabbi Eleazar notes that Mainz was the scene of the imperial convocation at which Emperor Frederick Barbarossa and his major followers took the cross, in the presence of the ecclesiastical leadership of Germany. Rabbi Eleazar embedded in his brief memoir a precious letter composed in Mainz by one of the Jews who elected to remain in town in order to carry on negotiations with the secular and ecclesiastical leadership of German society. The depiction of events in this unusual letter is tense and crisp. The Jewish leaders who chose to stay in Mainz were in extreme danger. Crusaders erupted into the Jewish neighborhood of Mainz, with the Jewish delegation exposed to death. Happily – the letter reports – imperial officials intervened decisively and saved the endangered Jews. This imperial intervention was followed by full negotiating success. The Jewish notables secured from the emperor an unequivocal decree: "Anyone who wounds a Jews, his hand will be cut off. Anyone who kills a Jew will be killed." Backing this decree, the assembled bishops announced that crusading privilege could not be invoked to justify escape from these harsh penalties. According to Rabbi Eleazar, the forceful imperial stand constituted a key element in the achievement of Jewish safety in the face of enormous danger.

We have noted that, further westward in northern Europe, the anti-Jewish animosity spawned by the call to the crusade evolved from a perception of Jews as historic enemies of Jesus to a sense that the Jews of northern Europe continued to harbor intense hatred toward Jesus' adherents, hatred so intense as to move them to murder unsuspecting Christians. This new sense of the Jews was first manifest, west of Germany, in the English town of Norwich in 1144.[18] Ephraim of Bonn tells us of a parallel incident in the German town of Würzburg during the Second Crusade. There, in February of 1147, the body of a Christian (interestingly, an adult, rather than a child) was found in the river. The Jews of Würzburg were accused of murdering the Christian out of their hatred for Christianity, and the victim was turned into a martyr, with attendant performance of miracles. This allegation led to attacks on the Jews of Würzburg, with more than twenty killed by the mob. While the accusations were parallel in Norwich and Würzburg, the Jews of Norwich suffered no mob violence; the Jews of Würzburg did. The rest of the Jews of Würzburg made their way to the local fortress and there survived. According to Ephraim, the bishop of the town personally intervened to accord the murdered Jews burial.

Ephraim of Bonn appended to his narrative account of Jewish fate during the Second Crusade a listing of anti-Jewish incidents from all across northern Europe from 1171 through 1196. A number of these incidents were touched off by allegations of Jewish murder. Of these, three involved German Jews. In one of the three, an incident in Neuss in 1186, Ephraim tells us that a Jew did in fact commit murder. According to Ephraim, this Jew, who was deranged, slew a Christian girl. He was immediately killed by enraged onlookers. Subsequently, six more Jews were killed, the Jewish neighborhood was plundered, and the Jewish corpses were publicly displayed in humiliating fashion. A few days later, the mother and sister of the deranged Jew were murdered, and a number of other Jews forcibly converted. Eventually, the Jews paid the bishop of Neuss large sums as a fine, with additional money paid in order to achieve burial for the corpses on display.

Ephraim describes an instance of imputed murder in Cologne in 1180 and another in Speyer in 1196. In the latter case, the imperial authorities, who had warned against harming the Jews, were enraged by the violence inflicted by the Speyer burghers and punished the town severely. Rabbi Eleazar of Worms, in his Third Crusade memoir, begins with a charge of attempted murder, leveled by a Mainz Christian against a Mainz Jew. No violence erupted, but the Jews were fined by the archbishop of Mainz. They also were brought before the archbishop on the second day of Rosh ha-Shanah, where they took an oath, indicating that they had not done the Christian claimant any harm. They also swore that "they [Jews] do not kill Christians on the eve of Passover." The new accusation of groundless murder is, by the end of the twelfth century, widely attested all across northern Europe. In the more western countries, little violence was occasioned by these allegations; in Germany, a considerable number of Jews lost their lives.

The centrality of the Rhineland academies in talmudic study during the eleventh century gave way during the twelfth. This may have been, in considerable measure, the result of the devastation in Worms, Mainz, and Cologne in 1096. To be sure, Jewish life did resume in these towns, and their institutions were rebuilt. Nonetheless, recapturing centrality in a major intellectual sphere may not have been possible. However, too much stress should not be laid on the devastation. It seems likely that part of the shift in centrality was the result of positive developments on the French scene, related in some measure to the ascendance of northern France in Christian intellectual life. New directions were pursued by the French Jews in both talmudic and biblical studies. While we noted that it is impossible to identify channels of influence, the efflorescence of innovative intellectual activity among both the Christian majority and the Jewish minority in northern France and the striking parallels in some of the lines of creativity suggest that the broad environment of northern France played a role for the new tendencies in talmudic and biblical study.[19] Much more than destruction seems to have been involved in the eclipse of the German academies in favor of the northern French.

All this is not meant to suggest that German Jewry lost its creative élan in the wake of 1096. That is surely not the case. New areas of creativity were created, perhaps most notably in the realm of pietistic and mystical thinking. A school of German-Jewish pietism arose, again centered in the Rhineland, with Rabbi Judah he-Ḥasid and Rabbi Eleazar of Worms the dominant figures. The best known work of this new school is a later compendium of pietistic *exempla* and teachings known as the *Sefer Ḥasidim*. This important work reflected the thinking of the Rhineland pietistic circles and in turn influenced subsequent Jewish thinking all across western Christendom.[20]

The pietism of the German-Jewish Pietists was fairly extreme. It was grounded in a sense of normal Jewish religious obligation, which must regularly be exceeded. The commitment to moving well beyond required norms expressed itself in radical asceticism. The *ḥasid* must abstain from a variety of normally permitted experiences; he must also undertake spiritual exercises that test the body beyond its normal limits. A number of modern observers have seen in this tendency toward extremes interesting parallels to some of the twelfth-century Christian pietistic movements. Just as the extreme Jewish martyrological behaviors of 1096 may well have been influenced by the broad exhilaration of crusading and self-sacrifice among the Christian majority, so too with the extreme commitments of the German Pietists and the asceticism in certain reforming Christian circles.

The possibility of majority Christian influence should not be understood to mean any warmth toward Christianity on the part of the German-Jewish Pietists. To the contrary, they exhibit a harsh polemical sense of the absolute rectitude of Judaism and the unfailing error of Christianity. While not mounting intellectual arguments against Christianity of the kind encountered already in southern Europe, their disparagement of Christianity is fierce. Jews who make any sort of accommodation with Christianity do so in error and suffer grievous punishment for so doing. Christianity is errant, and its symbols idolatrous. Jews should maintain every possible distance from these sources of potential contamination.

The German-Jewish Pietists went well beyond their asceticism and pietism. They developed complex mystical doctrines as well. These mystical doctrines are still in the process of being uncovered and understood. Like their counterparts in southern Europe, the German-Jewish Pietists were committed to the effort to move beyond surface realities of all kinds – in the physical world, in society, and in received religious tradition – and to grasp the deeper truths hidden beyond the surface realities. The doctrines of the German-Jewish Pietists were somewhat more traditional and somewhat less dynamic than those adumbrated in southern France and across the Iberian peninsula. They were fated to exert less influence over subsequent Jewish mystical theory and praxis.

By the end of the twelfth century, German Jewry had obviously rebuilt from the localized disasters of 1096, had reestablished its economic and political base, and had struck out in creative new spiritual directions as well. The thirteenth century saw ongoing efforts to expand imperial power and prerogatives, the slow failure of these efforts, the continued encroachment by a variety of forces on imperial authority, and the overall decline of effective government. For the Jews, these developments had considerable implications. On the one hand, Jews found themselves caught up in the conflict between Church leadership and the emperors and between the emperors and their baronial competitors. At the same time, the Jews increasingly found themselves inadequately protected by all these authorities, whose pretensions to power generally exceeded their capacity to control and protect. During the thirteenth century, the Jews of Germany also made the transition into moneylending. The lack of sophisticated governing authorities meant that German Jews could not secure their loans as did their co-religionists in northern France and England; rather, German Jewish lending was secured by the deposition of physical pledges, making the loans of considerably less value and the borrowers a broader spectrum of German society. Finally, during the thirteenth century, the set of anti-Jewish allegations that had begun to proliferate during the second half of the twelfth century expanded, with the incidents in Germany often cost-ing Jewish lives. The thirteenth century ended with massive attacks on German Jewry, an inauspicious augury for the disastrous fourteenth century.

Let us begin with the emergence of moneylending as the mainstay of the Jewish economy. We have seen a number of late-eleventh- and twelfth-century charters to German Jews, none of which addressed aspects of Jewish moneylending. In 1244, however, Duke Frederick of Austria enacted a charter for the Jews of his domain that is heavily focused on protection of Jewish lending. This charter is important from a number of perspectives and will be mentioned recurrently. It reflects the jousting between the imperial authorities and the barony, and it was widely copied by the authorities of eastern Europe as they sought to entice Jews into their lands. For the moment, however, let us examine it primarily for what it tells us of evolving Jewish economic activity in Germany.[21]

Like the charters of Rudiger of Speyer and Emperor Henry IV, Duke Frederick's charter is concerned, above all else, with spelling out important protections for the Jews. These protections involve, first of all, physical safety for the Jews. Reminiscent of earlier edicts, there are stipulations against killing a Jew, wounding a Jew, striking a Jew without drawing blood, raising a hand in violence against a Jewess, and kidnapping a Jewish child. All these actions are forbidden, and the penalties for committing them are extremely harsh. The killer of a Jew must die; one who wounds a Jew must pay a heavy fine to the ducal treasury and indemnify the wounded Jew; likewise for one who strikes a Jew without drawing blood; one who raises a hand in violence against a Jewess is to have his hand cut off; the kidnapper of a Jewish child is to be treated as a thief. In addition to its concern with physical safety for Jews, the document safeguards Jewish synagogues and cemeteries as well.

Another major focus of the charter is Jewish judicial rights. The jurisdictions before which Jews must present themselves are spelled out. There is an effort to safeguard the Jewish court system and to buttress its authority within the Jewish community. If Jews are brought to justice beyond the Jewish court system, then it is only the ducal court to which they must answer. With regard to testimony, the following protection is proffered: "In cases involving money or immovable property or a criminal complaint touching the person or property of a Jew, no Christian shall be admitted as a witness against a

Jews, unless there is a Jewish witness along with the Christian." This is obviously a rather generous stipulation.

While all these protections are important, it is striking that, of the thirty specific clauses in the charter, fully eleven address issues associated with Jewish lending. Moreover, of these eleven, only one discusses the kind of lending against land that propelled northern-French and English Jews to their wealth and importance. This specific stipulation reads: "If a Jew has lent money to a magnate of the country on his possessions or on a note and proves these through a document, we will assign the pledged possessions to the Jew and will defend them for him against violence." Given what we know of Jewish lending against land in northern France and England, this is relatively primitive. Indeed, by this time the sophisticated systems that had long been in place in northern France and England were in the process of being dismantled.

All the remaining protections of Jewish lending address the complex issues associated with pawnbroking, especially with the items deposited as pledges for Jewish loans. There is acknowledgement of the ecclesiastical concerns with regard to Jewish lending noted earlier. The closing item in the charter stipulates a maximum interest rate of thirty-three percent, reflecting the Fourth Lateran Council's prohibition of immoderate Jewish usury. Almost every other stipulation favors the Jewish lender. A Jewish lender "is allowed to receive as pledges all items that may be pawned with him – no matter what they are called – without making any investigation about them, except bloody or wet clothing and sacred vessels, which he shall under no circumstances accept." What then of the claim that the pawned object had been stolen and that it must therefore be returned? "The Jew must swear on that pledge that, when he received it, he did not know it had been removed by theft or robbery. In this oath, the amount for which the pledge was pawned shall also be included. Then, inasmuch as the Jew has brought his proof, the Christian shall pay him the capital and the interest that has accrued in the meantime."

This important protection for the Jewish lenders sets the tone for a series of parallel protections. If a Christian claims that he had pawned a pledge and the Jew deny this claim, if a Christian claims that a smaller amount was lent against the pledge than claimed by the Jew, if the Jew claims that the pledge had already been returned – in all such instances, the Jew takes an oath, and the matter is concluded in his favor. If pledges are lost "through the accident of fire or theft or violence," so long as the goods of the Jew himself were similarly lost, then the Jew need not repay. The protective pattern is clear. More important yet for our purposes, the Jewish transition into moneylending, more specifically pawnbroking, is patent from the inordinate attention paid to this economic activity in the ducal charter of 1244.

We have noted the extent to which the Jews became caught up in the political rivalries of northern France. As the French monarchy began to assert itself, it attempted increasingly to clarify the circumstances of Jews and to assert its own rights over an ever larger number of Jewish clients. Out of this effort emerged an emphasis on Jewish serfdom, which meant the attaching of Jews to a particular domain and penalties for Jews attempting to leave that domain. In Germany as well, the Jews were caught up in rivalries, but the circumstances were quite different. The major rivalry involved the leadership of the Roman Catholic Church ranged against the leadership of the Holy Roman Empire. By the thirteenth century, this contest of wills already had a lengthy history, stretching back for more than a century. The conflict reached a crescendo of sorts during the first half of the thirteenth century, with a series of powerful popes engaged with the potent German emperor, Frederick II. Papal insistence on the servitude of the Jews to the Church, which we have earlier encountered, was more than matched by sweeping imperial pronouncements of the emperor's lordship over the Jews.[22]

One of the most grandiloquent of the imperial pronouncements came in 1236. "Although the preeminence of this august dignity is obligated to extend the arm of its protection to all subjects of the Roman Empire and although it is fitting, for the protection of the faith that stems from celestial dispensation, to treat the faithful of Christ with special favor, nonetheless for the proper management of justice it is required that we rule the non-believers properly and protect them justly, as a special group committed to our care. Thus, living with the faithful under the protection of our majesty, they shall not be violently oppressed by those stronger than they are. Therefore, it is by the contents of the present letter that present and future generations shall know that all the serfs of our court in Germany [i.e. all the Jews] have beseeched our majesty that we deign by our grace to confirm for all the Jews of Germany the privilege of our divine grandfather, Frederick, granted to the Jews of Worms."[23] The language is eloquent, and the sentiments are high-blown. The practical implications of these high-blown statements were, however, minimal.

In fact, despite the grandeur of the imperial announcements, the reality was constant erosion of imperial rights to the barony of the German lands. During the 1230s and 1240s, Emperor Frederick II recognized the authority of a number of barons all across Germany, while at the same time alienating much imperial property to barons and municipalities. We have focused briefly on the charter extended by the Duke of Austria to his Jews in 1244. The circumstances of this charter are illuminating. In 1238, Emperor Frederick II attempted to take over Vienna as an imperial city, in the process granting a generous privilege to the Jews of that town. The charter of 1244, upon which we have focused for its reflection of Jewish economic activity, was the ducal response, announcing ducal rights over the Jews of Vienna and all of Austria. In this battle of charters, it was the duke of Austria who emerged victorious. The slow erosion of imperial rights once again highlights the differing directions taken by political authority in France and England, on the one hand, and in Germany on the other. In the former, the tendency was toward strengthening centralized authority; in the latter, the tendency was toward fragmentation. Each of these tendencies harbored negative implications for the Jews. In the former case, as we have seen, firmer control meant fuller exploitation; in the latter case, political weakness meant greater insecurity for Jews deeply dependent on governmental support.

The need in Germany for governmental support was related to the ever more intense popular antipathy toward the Jews. The spate of anti-Jewish allegations that had begun to develop during the twelfth century deepened during the thirteenth. Indeed, the majestic imperial pronouncement noted just now was occasioned by the first instance of a new manifestation of the sense that Jews in the here-and-now murder their Christian neighbors out of elemental hatred of the Christian faith. We have noted the demand of the archbishop of Mainz in 1187 that the Jews of his town take an oath that "they [Jews] do not kill Christians on the eve of Passover." Precisely what called forth this oath is not clear. To be sure, the Passover holiday is full of blood imagery. The waters of the Nile River are reported in the biblical account to have turned to blood, and the Israelite first-born were saved by the smearing of sacrificial blood on the doorposts and lintels of Israelite homes. With regard to the latter, the biblical story continues: "And the blood on the houses where you are staying shall be a sign for you; when I see the blood I will pass over you, so that no plague will destroy you when I strike the land of Egypt."[24] The oath exacted in 1187 in Mainz would seem to suggest that the notion of Jewish murderousness, widespread by the end of the twelfth century, had morphed into a fear that Jewish celebration of the Passover ritual might have included some kind of use of Christian blood.

While we are not fully informed about the fears that led to the 1187 oath in Mainz, we know more fully of the claim that surfaced in the German town of Fulda in 1235. There it was alleged that Jews utilized the blood of Christian children in their Passover ritual. This new allegation clearly built on the earlier sense we have followed of Jews murderously hostile to their Christian neighbors, the notion that this hostility inhered in Jewish tradition and teaching, and the conviction that Jewish murders involved some kind of ritual. In the earlier stages of this mythology, the sense of ritual was linked to Easter week, with the belief that Jews recapitulate their historic sin of deicide by crucifying Christian youngsters. In the thirteenth-century permutation reflected in Fulda, the ritual became attached to the Jewish celebration of Passover, which takes place at roughly the same time of the year. Given the ubiquity of blood in the Passover story, as already noted, it was but a small step to impute ritualized use of Christian blood to Jews.

The Jews of Germany perceived considerable danger in the new allegation and, in a traditional manner, turned to the highest authorities of Church and state. Pope Innocent IV's letter of repudiation of the new calumny was issued in 1247.[25] More than a decade prior to this, in 1236, Emperor Frederick II had heard Jewish pleas, had investigated the issue quite thoroughly, and had issued a decree denouncing and rejecting the new charge.[26] The imperial investigation involved two stages. In the first stage, the emperor brought together a convocation of leading ecclesiastics and barons. This convocation produced "diverse views on the matter . . . not adequate to produce clear counsel." It was then concluded that "one could not proceed more properly against the Jews accused of the aforesaid crime than through those who had been Jews and have converted to the cult of the Christian faith. They, since opposed to Judaism, would not withhold whatever they might know against the Jews, through the Mosaic books and through the contents of the Old Testament." To be sure, the emperor indicates that he himself and his advisors had been fully convinced of Jewish innocence. The turn to formerly Jewish experts was undertaken in order to remove all doubt and to convince all elements in Christian society, through the findings of a group of experts who would be knowledgeable and at the same time could by no means be suspected of favoritism to Judaism and the Jews. Experts who were formerly Jewish were gathered from all areas of western Christendom, met under the auspices of the emperor, examined the new allegation, and rejected it decisively. Based on their knowledge of Jewish law, these experts concluded that "they [Jews] guard against the intake of all blood, as we find expressly in the biblical book that is called in Hebrew *Bereshit* [Genesis], in the laws given by Moses, and in the Jewish decrees that are called in Hebrew Talmud. We can surely assume that, for those to whom even the blood of permitted animals is forbidden, the desire for human blood cannot exist, as a result of the horror of the matter, the prohibition of nature, and the common bond of the human species in which they also join Christians. More-over, they would not expose to danger their substance and person for that which they might have freely when taken from animals." The finding is fascinating, grounded in knowledge of Jewish sources and in considerations of reason. In the light of these findings, Emperor Frederick II absolved the Jews of Fulda and any other Jews of guilt in such crimes and prohibited attacks grounded in this allegation.

The imperial investigation and edict suggest fear of the new alle-gation and the determination to stamp it out. These are elaborate imperial steps and a ringing imperial conclusion. The fear was cer-tainly well placed. The hope that the special procedures adopted – the convocation of former Jews, their rejection of the allegation, and imperial prohibition of anti-Jewish violence grounded in the allegation – would serve to quash the canard proved to be illusory. Of all the specific charges that emerged during the twelfth and thir-teenth centuries – the broad claim of groundless murder and the more specific charges that Jews crucify Christian youngsters, that Jews ritu-ally sacrifice Christian youngsters, that Jews desecrate the host wafer, and that Jews utilize Christian blood for their religious rituals – it was the last that proved most durable over the ages. The blood libel remained a widely held conviction in popular European mythology from the thirteenth century down into the twentieth and twenty-first centuries.

The combination of proliferating anti-Jewish sentiment and dete-riorating political authority in Germany produced a massive outburst of anti-Jewish violence at the close of the thirteenth century, in the so-called Rindfleisch massacres. These massacres serve as a culmination of the tendencies noted for the thirteenth century and an unhappy introduction to a series of massacres in Germany during the first half of the fourteenth century. During the 1280s, the blood libel accusation – ostensibly disproved by the imperial investigation – resurfaced in a number of German towns. It was supplemented by the new host desecration charge that was first raised in Paris in 1290. In April 1298, in the town of Roettlingen, twenty-one Jews were massacred by a mob led by a German knight named Rindfleisch. The basis for the assault was the allegation of host desecration. After the killings at Roettlingen, Rindfleisch led mobs over the ensuing five months throughout Franconia, Swabia, Hesse, and Thuringia, in a manner reminiscent of the forces that followed Emicho of Flonheim in 1096. In this case, the loss of life seems to have been even greater. Despite imperial prohibition of further violence, the attacks continued into the first years of the new century. The Rindfleisch massacres spanned the thirteenth and fourteenth centuries, highlight the unfortunate combination in Germany of accelerating anti-Jewish sentiment and deteriorating political authority, and serve as an unhappy end to German-Jewish experience during the thirteenth century and an inauspicious beginning for the fourteenth.

We have noted already the broad downturn in European life during the fourteenth century. After three full centuries of remarkable advance, Europe suffered during the fourteenth century devastating setbacks of all kinds. While the best known of these misfortunes came during the middle years of the century, the years of the Black Death, in fact all through the century western Christendom suffered economic hardship, demographic loss, political setbacks, and cultural decline. In England and France, there was little or no Jewish population to suffer the downturn and the attendant majority antipathy; elsewhere in Latin Christendom, the Jews suffered this double liability.[27] Nowhere in Europe, however, was Jewish suffering as intense as it was in Germany.

Early in the fourteenth century, the Jewish communities of western Germany had to absorb numerous refugees from the French expulsion of the Jews. Precise details on this population movement are lacking, but William Chester Jordan has traced some of the movement into the counties northeast of royal France and into the Rhineland. While the numbers of Jews entering these areas were in all likelihood not all that large, their absorption would certainly have imposed some strains on Jewish life and especially on the relations between the Christian majority and the Jewish minority. It would seem that the immigrating Jews were heavily involved in moneylending, which meant the additional economic strain of absorbing not only Jews, but Jewish moneylenders.

The *leitmotif* of Jewish life in Germany during the fourteenth century was – once again – the combination of weak governance and proliferating anti-Jewish sentiment. The Rindfleisch massacres, which ended during the early years of the fourteenth century, were succeeded by the Armleder assaults of the 1330s. These assaults involved lawless lower-class bands, identified by the leather armpieces they wore in lieu of the metal armor of knights. The attacks began in 1336 in Franconia. The following year, a central figure emerged, the tavern-keeper John Zimberlin. Under Zimberlin's leadership, more than one hundred Jewish communities in Alsace were attacked, with massive Jewish casualties. Before too long, the targets of the Armleder assaults expanded to include elements in the Christian population as well. As a result, the bishop of Strasbourg made an extended effort in May of 1338 to end the violence against both Christians and Jews. In August of 1338, an armistice was arranged with Zimberlin, although sporadic anti-Jewish violence persisted. The Armleder violence served as a frightening prelude to the anti-Jewish violence that accompanied the Black Death in the 1340s.

Mention has already been made of the Black Death and its impact on a number of the Jewries of western Christendom. No area of Latin Christendom was spared the effects of the plague. As noted, the toll of the plague was extraordinary, with estimates ranging as high as one-third of the population of Europe perishing over a short span of time. One of the most frightful aspects of the catastrophe was the sense of helplessness it produced. Some saw the plague as divine retribution for societal sinfulness, which then generated unusual levels of penitence to regain God's favor. Another view projected the forces of evil as the source of the disaster, necessitating an effort to identify the human elements in collusion with these forces of evil. While a number of human collaborators were identified, no group recommended itself more readily as the devil's associates in spreading the plague than the Jews, for reasons which by now are quite clear. From the twelfth century onward, the Jews of western Christendom had been increasingly perceived as ranged in enmity toward Christianity and their Christian neighbors. Potent imageries had been created and had been widely accepted in the Christian population at large. Jews were assumed to kill Christian youngsters by crucifixion, to utilize the blood of Christians for their Passover ritual, and to abuse the host wafer. All these images imputed to the Jews hatred so deep as to move them to inhuman acts. Projecting onto the Jews the desire to kill off the entire Christian populace through well poisoning was, for many, a reasonable next step.

There was yet one more element in the widespread conviction of Jewish culpability for inflicting the plague on European society, and that was the extraction of "confessions" from Jews under torture and the subsequent communication of these "confessions" across broad areas. The seeming admission of Jewish guilt added considerably to the predisposition to believe the charge that Jews had brought about the plague by poisoning Europe's water supplies.

The papal court, with its history of protecting the Jews of western Christendom from certain dangers, knew of the growing anti-Jewish allegations of well poisoning and attempted to combat it. Pope Clement VI inveighed against the allegations, invoking powerful arguments from reason. In particular, he noted that the plague was universal and affected locales where there was no Jewish population. Thus, the claim of Jewish causation was obviously incorrect. The German emperor weighed in as well. However, the statements issued by these pillars of the ecclesiastical and secular establishments bore little weight at this time of total societal crisis.

While Jews suffered the double devastation – death directly from the plague and, in addition, popular violence on the grounds that they had brought about the disaster – all throughout Europe, in German lands the toll was especially heavy. In part, the anti-Jewish actions were yet one more in the lengthy string of popular anti-Jewish outbursts in Germany, with which the authorities were unable to cope. The toll from the violence of the 1340s, however, exceeded all prior instances of wide-ranging popular assault. In many of the German cities, the anti-Jewish sentiment expressed itself in milder and less violent fashion, through decisions to forestall further damage by expelling the Jews from the given town. Expulsions – influenced by the various expulsions that had been decreed further westward in the more advanced areas of northern Europe – constituted yet another facet of the fate of the Jews of Germany in 1348–1349.

During the fifteenth century, the process of rebuilding is palpable all across the German lands. To an extent, the Jews of Germany were positively influenced by this rebuilding effort. They continued to suffer, however, from the narrowness of their economic endeavors, from ecclesiastical calls for limitations of Jewish activities, from widespread antipathy on the part of the populace at large, and from weak governance all across Germany. While the circumstances of Jewish life may have been somewhat better in 1500 than in 1400, neither set of circumstances was especially favorable or healthy.

The Jews of Germany remained mired in the limited economic outlets available to them, especially in the business of petty pawnbroking that had emerged as a Jewish specialty in Germany during the thirteenth century. Once again, we must note that this is a useful enterprise, but one that regularly aroused animosity toward the pawnbroker. This economic hostility was readily joined to the broader set of anti-Jewish stereotypes that had, by the fifteenth century, been deeply embedded in the thinking of western Christendom's Christian majority. The fifteenth century is dotted by recurrent allegations throughout Germany of Jewish killing of Christian youngsters for use of their blood and of host desecration. As noted already, such accusations in Germany regularly eventuated in violence, despoiling of Jewish property, and loss of Jewish life.

The Jews of Germany continued to be affected, during the fifteenth century, by the decentralization of political authority. Imperial policy toward the Jews of Germany remained fairly stable. However, the reach of imperial power, which we have seen to be limited from the eleventh century onward, diminished even further. Increasingly, the nobles and the free cities of the German lands came to exercise enhanced authority over their Jews, with instability and inconsistency ever more prominent. We have noted thirteenth-century imperial-ducal contestation over the Jews of Austria, with the dukes winning out. Ducal control of Austrian Jewry solidified during the fourteenth and fifteenth century, but the Austrian dukes were not successful in adequately protecting their Jews or in maintaining a consistently supportive policy. Thus, in 1420–1421, the important Jewish community of Vienna suffered a major outbreak of violence, with more than four hundred Jews losing their lives. In the wake of this persecution, the entire Jewish community was expelled from the city, an expulsion subsequently confirmed in 1453 and 1455. As the cities of Germany garnered increasing control over their own affairs, burgher resentment of the Jews came to play a more important role in the limitations imposed on Jewish life.

While the Jews of late medieval Germany enjoyed none of the advantages associated with the kind of centralized governance that developed further westward in northern Europe, they did suffer one of the major liabilities associated with that more effective governance – the new vehicle of expulsion. With banishment increasingly seen as a reasonable option for dealing with the Jews and the issues they presented, the Jewish communities of Germany suffered recurrent expulsions in the fifteenth century, from principalities large and small. A partial list of towns from which Jews were expelled, at least temporarily, includes: Prague, Mainz, Vienna, Cologne, Augsburg, Mecklenburg, Magdeburg, and Nuremberg; areas from which Jews were expelled include: Austria, Bavaria, Franconia, and Swabia.

In the cultural and religious domains, the Jews of Germany maintained, during the fifteenth century, their prior legacy of talmudic study. The parameters of intellectual life were fairly limited, with rabbinic law and literature dominating. Schools for advanced talmudic study were at the heart of the Jewish religious enterprise, with some of the older schools continuing to function and new schools established as the incessant relocation of the Jewish population took place.

Overall then, it is hardly surprising that the Jews of Germany should have regularly sought new venues for Jewish life, either as a result of being forced to do so or as a result of the less dramatic desire to achieve greater stability and opportunity for self and family. In both cases, the major option available was a move eastward to areas that were in the process of developing, where economic opportunities seemed to be more promising and where the authorities seemed to be more interested in fostering Jewish presence. In many ways, the move into the eastern sectors of northern Europe smacks of a recapitulation of the earlier settlement of Jews during the tenth through twelfth centuries in the western and central areas of the north.

EASTERN EUROPE

The areas of eastern Europe must be understood in terms of two of the three sets of geographic contrasts noted at the outset of this study – the distinction in northern Europe between western sectors on the one hand and central and eastern sectors on the other, and

the broader distinction between interior and exposed areas.[28] The
first of these distinctions involves the greater economic, political, and
cultural progress of the westerly areas of northern Europe and the relative backwardness of the eastern areas. This backwardness worked
to the advantage of the Jews, making their contributions in eastern
Europe useful during the latter centuries of our period, in much the
same way that Jewish contributions had been useful in the western sectors during the eleventh and twelfth centuries. The distinction between interior and exposed areas is equally significant. Both
Hungary and Poland constituted the easternmost reaches of Latin
Christendom; beyond Hungary and Poland lay realms dominated by
alternative religious visions. Hungary and Poland were viewed by
others and viewed themselves as the first line of defense of Latin
Christendom, and both suffered the violence that went with this
exposure. While the economic backwardness associated with location at the eastern extreme of northern Europe worked to the Jews'
advantage, the anxiety and fear of existing on the periphery often
worked to the Jews' disadvantage.

Once again, generalization, even across these eastern areas of
northern Europe, is not possible. General circumstances diverged
considerably in Hungary and Poland, and thus Jewish circumstances
differed markedly as well. We shall begin with discussion of the Jewish
community of Hungary and then proceed to the somewhat larger and
eventually more important Jewish community of Poland.

The history of medieval Hungary began at roughly the year 1000,
which is — perhaps not coincidentally — the starting point of this
study. Medieval Hungary was poised between Latin Christendom to
the west, Byzantium to the southeast, and nomadic territory to the
east and northeast. This exposed position had important implications for medieval Hungary, which suffered pressures from all three
directions. The fundamental decision of the Hungarian authorities
was to align with Latin Christendom, without however falling prey
to German imperial aspirations. In order to limit the impact of the
empire, the rulers of Hungary chose to ally themselves regularly with
the papacy. The Byzantine threat came to an end with the decline
of Byzantium from the early thirteenth century onward. The threat
from the nomadic territories was actualized during the 1240s, with
the incursion of the Mongols. While the devastation was extensive, in
fact Hungary recovered fairly quickly, in the process further strengthening its links to the rest of Latin Christendom.[29]

Hungary's geographic placement involved more than international ramifications; it also affected the internal demography of the
kingdom, which enjoyed or suffered from an unusual diversity of
population – Jews, Muslims, and Cumans. This internal diversity,
as was generally the case, benefited the Jews. Jewish skills and economic abilities were, under normal circumstances, best utilized in
such heterogeneous settings.[30]

While there is some evidence of Jews in the areas that became
the medieval kingdom of Hungary prior to our period, the Jewish
population of medieval Hungary is clearly an offshoot of the Jewries
of northern Europe, especially of Germany.[31] This is seen, first of all,
in the geography of Jewish settlement, which is concentrated in the
northwest corner of the kingdom, that is to say in the areas closest
to the German matrix from which the bulk of medieval Hungarian Jewry originated.[32] Moreover, the basic legal status of Hungarian
Jewry was rooted in King Bela IV's enactment of a grant in 1251 to
the Jews that was essentially a copy of the 1244 charter issued for
the Jews of Austria. This foundational charter was reconfirmed regularly throughout the fourteenth and fifteenth centuries.[33] The Jewish
community of medieval Hungary does not seem to have grown significantly in size; it remained a somewhat small community throughout
our period.

The economic foundations of Jewish life in Hungary began with
trade and craftwork, in the case of the latter especially the minting of
coins. With the passage of time, the Jews of Hungary involved themselves increasingly in moneylending. While by now the Jewish move
into moneylending should hardly evoke surprise, this Jewish activity
in Hungary shows some differences from what we have encountered
elsewhere. On the one hand, there is nothing like the sophisticated
Jewish lending against land we have encountered in England and
northern France; on the other hand, a number of wealthy Hungarian Jews did emerge, some of them with important connections to
the crown and the higher nobility.

Ecclesiastical pressures for the imposition of limitations on Jewish
activity, especially Jewish service to the crown with the attendant
danger of Jewish authority over Christians, were regularly exerted by
the papacy during the later centuries of our period. These demands
indicate the unusual position achieved by a small number of Jews. The
rulers of Hungary, while generally cooperative in their relations with
the papacy, were reluctant to dispense with the services of their Jewish

advisors and officials. As we shall see shortly, the major effort undertaken in 1360 to dispense with the Jews altogether by expelling them
was quickly understood to be counter-productive and was rapidly
reversed.

During the middle years of the thirteenth century, Hungary was
radically disrupted by the invasion of the Mongols from the east.
Death and destruction were widespread, although the kingdom
recovered relatively quickly, suggesting that the basic infrastructure
remained intact. While Jews did suffer along with their Christian
and non-Christian neighbors during the period of invasion, there
is no sign of the Jews being singled out for special persecution by
either the Mongol invaders or – in reaction – by the indigenous
Christian population. The enactment of King Bela IV of the basic
charter for Hungarian Jewry seems to have been part of his program
of reconstruction, with the intention of luring additional Jews into
the kingdom in order to provide economic vitalization. The Jews of
Hungary were less fortunate a century later, at the time of the Black
Death. While they did not suffer the wide-ranging assaults we have
noted elsewhere in western Christendom, the importation of some
of the anti-Jewish motifs previously cited did arouse suspicions and
animosity among the Christian populace. These suspicions seem to
have led to the royal decision to expel the Jews from Hungary in
1360, although this decision was revoked a scant four years later, out
of a sense that it had been misguided.

We know little of the cultural and spiritual life of medieval Hungarian Jewry. Late-medieval synagogue and cemetery sites from western Hungary have been discovered, and they suggest the place of
the Hungarian Jews within the broad culture of medieval Ashkenazic
Jewry. There are recurrent references to intellectual contacts between
rabbinic thinkers in Hungary and their counterparts further westward, but there is no sense of a thriving intellectual center. The Jews
of Hungary seem to have formed an interesting annex to the more
westerly Jewish communities of northern Europe and to the more
rapidly developing Jewish community of neighboring Poland.

The early development of Poland coincides with that of Hungary
and with the emergence of Jewish life in the central areas of northern Europe. The coronation of the first major ruler of the Piast
dynasty, Boleslav the Brave, in 1025 is generally taken as the beginning
of organized active political life in medieval Poland. Polish governance developed in its own idiosyncratic style, exhibiting neither the

overweening claims of the German emperors nor the slow and steady accretion of power of the French and English monarchs. Rather, the monarchy founded by Boleslav the Brave disintegrated fairly rapidly into a congeries of principalities, followed by the slow accretion of power by the Piast rulers, culminating in the major achievements of Boleslav the Great (1333–1370) in revitalizing royal authority. As a result of this unusual evolution, the kings of late medieval and early modern Poland were dependent upon the Polish nobility in a unique way. This special relationship of the royalty and the nobility had major implications for the Jews. On the one hand, the Jews had to establish relationships with both the monarchs of Poland and its noblemen, straining Jewish political acumen somewhat; on the other hand, Jews never became a source of irritation for the nobility, viewed as allies of a centralizing monarchy and thus as detrimental to the aspirations of the barony. As we shall see, these special political circumstances impacted Jewish economic affairs as well.[34]

As was the case in Hungary, in Poland too there is occasional evidence of individual Jewish presence in Poland early on. Real Jewish settlement, however, seems to have begun during the twelfth century, reflective of the generally expansive nature of that creative epoch. Because of the subsequent development of Polish Jewry into a major demographic force on the world Jewish scene, much attention has focused on the origins of Polish Jewry, the places and human elements from which it emerged. In particular, attention has been accorded to the possibility that the roots of Polish Jewry lie in the Khazar kingdom, an eastern-European principality whose leadership accepted Judaism sometime during the first half of the Middle Ages.[35] The possibility of Khazar origins for Polish Jewry has, first of all, something of the exotic and romantic about it; moreover, for many it suggests that the supposed biological and ethnic unity of the Jewish people is in fact chimerical, that the largest Jewish group on the modern scene was not biologically related to earlier Jewish stock. However, the thesis that the origin of Polish Jewry lies with the Khazars has not stood the test of careful examination. In the first place, while there is now a consensus on the historical reality of the Khazar kingdom and the conversion of its leadership to Judaism, little real evidence has survived about the Khazars, their Jewishness, or their subsequent fate. Equally or more important, every aspect of Polish Jewry – geographic placement, political status, economic outlets, and cultural norms – point to the origins of the community further westward in the German lands, parallel to the origins of Hungarian Jewry in the German lands. In fact, the Jewish migration from German territory into developing Poland was part and parcel of a larger phenomenon. The Polish authorities were interested in fostering immigration of urban dwellers in general from the German areas, urban dwellers both Christian and Jewish.

As we have amply seen in this and the previous chapter, there was a steady eastward pressure that brought Jews in the direction of Poland. English Jewry was expelled in 1290 and moved eastward; French Jewry was banished in 1306 and moved eastward; subsequently, the Jews of Germany, in the face of economic limitation and recurrent persecution, began an eastward movement as well. Hungary was one destination for some of these Jews on the move; Poland served even more effectively as a haven for such Jews. The pattern of Jewish settlement in Poland clearly reflects Germanic origins. The major areas of earliest Jewish settlement were in the western parts of Poland, that is to say those areas contiguous with German lands, with movement eastward taking place slowly and fitfully.[36]

Jewish legal status in Poland likewise reflects German origins. In 1264, a major Polish prince, Boleslav of Kalisch, enacted for his Jews a charter clearly grounded in the prior enactment of Duke Frederick of Austria for his Jews in 1244.[37] The dating – like that of the charter of Bela IV of Hungary – suggests the rebuilding efforts in the wake of the Mongol invasion. The first thirty clauses of the Polish charter repeat almost verbatim the Austrian precedent. Only two changes are notable. First, the limitation of interest rate to be charged by Jews as stipulated in the 1244 charter is omitted in 1264; in its place is the indication that "we wish that no one dare to force a Jew to payment of his pledge on his holiday." Both changes clearly are intended for the benefit of the Jews already present in or to be attracted to Poland.

In addition to these thirty stipulations, Duke Boleslav added six additional items that reflect some of the realities of mid-thirteenth-century Jewish life on the eastern periphery of Latin Christendom. One of these additional stipulations indicates the broader economic activities engaged in by Jews in this developing area: "We also order that the Jews may sell and buy all things freely and may touch bread as do Christians. Anyone who impedes them shall be obliged to pay a fine for our palatine." Looking back over this chapter in its entirety, we might suggest that this closing stipulation to the Polish charter of

1264 sounds much like the earliest charters issued to German Jewry in the eleventh and twelfth centuries. In many ways, as already noted, the Jews migrating to Poland were recapitulating the pioneering efforts of their German predecessors of a few centuries earlier. While German Jewry had, by the thirteenth century, moved more completely into the moneylending business, the backwardness of the Polish economy enabled Jews to once again fill a wider variety of useful roles.

The other central theme in the new items in the 1264 charter involves concern over Jewish security. For example, "we order that, if any Jew, compelled by dire necessity, cries out at night and if the neighboring Christians do not bother to provide the proper aid or heed the cry, every neighboring Christian shall be responsible to pay thirty shillings." This is an impressive protection for the Jewish newcomers. More striking yet is the following: "According to the ordinances of the pope, in the name of our Holy Father, we firmly order that henceforth no Jews in our domain be accused of using human blood, since according to the precept of their law all Jews refrain from any blood." The blood libel, first sounded only a few decades earlier, had evoked deep fears among the Jews of northern Europe and had moved them to seek repudiation from both the papal and imperial courts. Duke Boleslav cited the papal repudiation as the grounds for his resolute rejection of the accusation.

Duke Boleslav went yet further. Acknowledging the broader allegation out of which the blood libel had emerged, he addressed the issue of accusations of Jewish killing of Christian children. Such accusations were not inherently unthinkable and might be brought to court. However, the duke's Jews were to be protected from this broader allegation as well. "If any Jew be accused of killing any Christian child, he should be convicted by three Christian witnesses and as many Jewish witnesses. After he has been convicted, he should be punished by the proper penalty for the crime committed. If, however, the aforesaid witnesses and his innocence exonerate him, then the Christian accuser should undergo the punishment that the Jew would have had to suffer for slander." Boleslav's additional stipulations reflect the existence of old and new dangers to Jewish life and ducal intentions to afford maximum protection in the face of these dangers.

The German origins of Polish Jewry are reflected in both its geographic development and its legal status. A further index of these German origins can be found in the economic activities of the Jews of Poland. As noted, the economic backwardness of Poland allowed for some expansion of Jewish economic activity. We have noted in the Boleslav charter reference to Jewish trade that sounded like eleventh- and twelfth-century rights granted to German Jews. At the same time, Boleslav's charter very much reflects the thirteenth-century Jewish move into moneylending of the pawnbroking variety that had become so central to Jewish economic life in Germany.

There is one last index of the German origins of Polish Jewry, derived from the realm of Jewish cultural life. During our centuries, there are recurrent references to contact between the leadership of Polish Jewry and the rabbis of Germany. To be sure, the Jews attracted to Poland were not yet successful during our period in establishing vibrant institutions and reaching heights of cultural achievement, although such accomplishments lay just beyond the end of the fifteenth century. Nonetheless, the connections with the rabbinic elite of Germany and the rootedness of Jewish religious customs and intellectual concerns in prior German Jewry serve as yet further indication of Germanic roots.

In this regard, we must note the fascinating phenomenon of the emergence of Yiddish as the Jewish language of Polish Jewry. We have noted throughout this study Jewish adoption of the local vernaculars as the language of everyday communication. In the south and the northwest of Europe, this meant a variety of Romance dialects; in the north-central areas, this meant a variety of Germanic dialects. Little evidence for these Jewish vernaculars has survived. Occasionally, writings in the vernacular formulated in Hebrew characters have allowed some insight into the Jewish language developments. Whether the Romance or Germanic dialects spoken by the Jews of medieval Europe were identifiably distinct from the languages used by their majority contemporaries is a point of some contention among linguists. What is clear, however, is that the importation of German into Poland by immigrating Jews represents a new development. In Poland, the migrating Jews did not adopt the language of their new environment. Rather, they held fast to the language and culture with which they had arrived. This linguistic tenaciousness seems to have been rooted in two factors. The first was the overall Germanic migration into Poland, which made the urban areas – within which the Jewish migrants first settled – heavily German in language and culture. Secondly, the Jewish migrants into Poland – unlike their predecessors in eleventh- and twelfth-century northern France and

Germany – seem to have viewed their new environment as distinctly backward and to have clung to their prior language as a sign of cultural superiority. In any case, the emergence of Yiddish among the Jews of Poland serves as a last index of the German origins of this developing Jewry.

As noted, the Jewish immigrants into Poland seem to have taken advantage of economic backwardness to expand the range of their activities. Trade reemerged among the Jews, alongside the moneylending that had become so central further westward. The role of the nobility in Poland opened up new economic opportunities as Jews began to manage the estates of the nobility, an occupation that would develop into a major Jewish activity subsequent to our period. Like their counterparts in Hungary, Jews also played a role as toll collectors and tax farmers, suggesting once again a governance structure that was more primitive and thus more open than was the case further westward across northern Europe.

The crises suffered by Poland during the thirteenth and fourteenth centuries seem to have strengthened, rather than weakened the position of the Jews. The Mongol invasion of the 1240s moved Polish authorities like Boleslav of Kalisch to concern over revitalization of devastated urban areas through support for the immigration of Christian and Jewish German townspeople. It was out of this concern that Boleslav adumbrated the charter that was to become the foundation privilege for Polish Jewry.

The crisis spawned by the Black Death in the mid-fourteenth century and the reaction to it on the part of the Polish authorities are yet more striking. While the Black Death resulted in the weakening of Jewish life in the more settled areas of western Christendom in which Jews still lived, in Poland the devastation once again moved the authorities to greater support for the Jews. The Black Death happened to coincide in Poland with the reign of Casimir the Great (1333–1370), the period during which the Polish monarchy reemerged into a position of significant power, limited to be sure by the role the nobility had come to play. Casimir the Great reenacted twice during his reign the favorable charter of Boleslav of Kalisch. In so doing, he was clearly making an effort to reassure the Jews of the support of the monarchy and thereby to attract additional Jewish settlers into his realm. The steadfast support of this iconic figure in the history of the Polish monarchy set, for the Jews, an invaluable precedent.

The range of Jewish economic and social activities and the energetic support of the Polish authorities before and after Casimir the
Great combined with the anxieties associated with Poland's position
at the eastern extremity of Latin Christendom to move Church leadership to express regular concern about the place of the Jews in Polish
society. Ecclesiastical leaders, ranging from the popes down through
archbishops and bishops and into the ranks of popular preachers, regularly expressed misgivings about many aspects of Jewish life, com-
plaining that the fragility of Poland and its Christian identity required
special attention to the issues presented by the Jews, who were once
more perceived to present major dangers to Christian society and
faith. Again, the backwardness of Polish society, its needs, and its
resultant openness to the Jews served as an effective counterweight
to the considerable ecclesiastical pressure regularly exerted.

The Jews immigrating into Poland brought with them a set of economic abilities, political sensitivities, and cultural achievements; they
also brought with them less savory baggage – a host of negative popular images that combined traditional Christian anti-Jewish motifs
with the set of intensified slanders that had emerged in the more
westerly areas of northern Europe during the twelfth and thirteenth
centuries. These images were quickly adopted into the storehouse
of Polish folklore concerning the Jews and occasioned the kind of
calls to violence, and sometimes actual violence, we have seen further
westward. Crusading agitation on occasion sparked anti-Jewish sentiment and outbreaks. More strikingly, the newer claims of blood libel
and host profanation began to surface in fourteenth- and fifteenth-
century Poland, galvanizing mob animosity and violence against the
Jews. By and large, the anti-Jewish violence was circumscribed, and
the authorities were fairly successful in quashing it. In a few cases,
the agitation resulted in temporary expulsion of Jews from given
municipalities. Overall, the security situation of Polish Jewry during
the latter centuries of our period was considerably better than the
situation in Germany.

As noted, Polish Jewry was organized along the lines of earlier
Ashkenazic Jewry, with the locus of power residing in the local Jewish
community. For our period, we have little evidence of this apparatus in operation. The rapid evolution of Jewish communal structure
subsequent to our period suggests that sturdy foundations were being
quietly laid during the thirteenth through fifteenth centuries. This
is true for both clarification of the power structure at the local level

and for the emergence of a more encompassing framework within which the many Jewish communities of Poland could cooperate.

The same broad observation is applicable to the institutions and achievements of Jewish cultural life as well. We have noted at an earlier point the rapidity with which cultural maturation took place further westward in northern Europe, especially in northern France, and have suggested that this rapid efflorescence was due in part to the stimulation of a dynamically developing majority society and culture. In Poland, both the majority stimulation and the Jewish creativity were absent during our period. Rather, the more normal pattern of slow communal development, with cultural achievement realized only after centuries of settlement, is what we find in Polish Jewry. Nonetheless, we can once again suggest the establishment of a stable cultural foundation upon which sixteenth- and seventeenth-century Polish Jewry was able to erect a considerable institutional framework and to achieve important cultural creativity.

Polish Jewry, alongside Hungarian Jewry, shows the pressures that moved Jews away from the more advanced centers of northern Europe and the readiness of the more peripheral areas to extend a welcome to immigrant Jews who might bring with them some of the progress achieved further westward. New sets of Jewish communities were established. These new communities enjoyed enhanced economic opportunities and governmental support; they were by no means free of the ecclesiastical pressure or the dangerous popular stereotypes that had developed further westward. Out of this mix emerged a set of Jewish communities destined to become major centers of Jewish life in the centuries following the year 1500 and to serve, at a much later date, as the reservoir from which Jewish life would be reestablished in such areas as Germany, France, and England.

6

MATERIAL CHALLENGES, SUCCESSES, AND FAILURES

·

The time has come to attempt a composite picture of the Jewish experience in medieval western Christendom, in both material and spiritual terms. The preceding surveys of the diverse Jewish communities that constituted medieval Jewry in Latin Christendom suggest that such a composite picture must necessarily blur some of the idiosyncrasies of the specific communities in favor of a more generalized portrait, but such blurring is unavoidable. On the material plane, the core of this more generalized portrait involves identification of the obstacles that threatened to obstruct – and in some instances did obstruct – successful Jewish acceptance into the European environment and delineation of the Jewish responses to those obstacles. On the spiritual plane, the core of this more generalized portrait involves the pressures brought to bear on Jewish identity and the Jewish efforts to meet and surmount these pressures.[1]

The Jewish experience upon which we have focused has been judged by some a success and by others a failure. Ultimately, however, the Jewish effort to establish a presence in medieval western Christendom while maintaining fidelity to Jewish tradition cannot be simplistically judged either a success or a failure. This Jewish effort involved both successes and failures, and the combination of achievement and shortcoming must be presented in all its complexity.

Historical experience, of course, flows unbounded. While we have isolated a period in the history of western Christendom and designated it "medieval," in fact there was unbroken continuity between 1499 and 1501, between the fourteenth century and the sixteenth century, between medieval and modern Jewish experience in Europe. Thus, Jewish successes and failures in our period can only be fully understood when seen from the perspective of developments in European life and Jewish life that postdate 1500. Indeed, to a significant extent, the history of medieval Jewry in western Christendom is still being played out and retrospective judgments still evolving.[2]

OBSTACLES AND ATTRACTIONS

The impediments to successful Jewish settlement in medieval western Christendom were considerable. In a number of ways, the Christian majority saw Jewish presence in medieval Latin Christendom as problematic, as an unnatural irritant. Central to this negative Christian view of Jewish presence was an underlying yearning for homogeneity, the generally unarticulated hope for a uniformly Christian society.[3] Medieval European Christians, at all levels of society, broadly shared an unspoken aspiration toward a society composed entirely of adherents of the one true faith, with all facets of societal life flowing from and oriented toward the Christian – or more precisely the Roman Catholic – religious vision. This mindset was essentially utopian, the yearning for an ideal state of affairs. As we have seen and shall remind ourselves shortly, the official Church view was more nuanced and more fully rooted in here-and-now realities.[4] Nonetheless, the unofficial, by and large inarticulate, and yet widespread yearning for homogeneity served as a powerful obstacle to the Jews of medieval western Christendom. While Judaism and the Jews traditionally challenged Christianity and Christians, the hopes for a monolithic Christian society in western Christendom much intensified majority resistance to the burgeoning Jewish minority, which in obvious ways detracted from the vision of an ideal Christian society.

To a considerable extent, the aspiration toward homogeneity was rooted in the Jews' Hebrew Bible, which was simultaneously part of Christian Scripture. Messianic imagery in the Hebrew Bible portrays a world in which all of humanity will accept the one true God and live by his teachings. As we shall see, medieval Jewish criticism of Jesus as Messiah emphasized heavily the lack of such religious unanimity, as well as the lack of human amity and concord supposed to flow from religious unanimity.[5] For medieval European Christians, such unanimity on the larger global scene was obviously not yet in place. The external world was rife with competing religious visions, the most potent of which was Islam. Yet, medieval Latin Christendom harbored internally no religious vision that could compete effectively with Christianity. Neither Islam nor Judaism offered serious competition within medieval western Christendom. In this circumscribed sphere, hopes for a fully christianized society might flourish and did, at least *sub rosa*. Thus, the Jews who were making their presence increasingly obvious during our period were perceived as detrimental to this broad aspiration of majority Christian society.

Here, as has frequently been the case throughout this book, the contrast with the medieval Muslim world is instructive. The medieval Muslim world was far more diversified than medieval western Christendom. While medieval Muslims might well have dreamed of a day when Islam would be totally victorious, such a vision hardly seemed achievable in the here-and-now, even within the realm of Islam, which was in fact highly variegated. For medieval western Christendom, the vision of a thoroughly christianized society – while not realistic for the Western world altogether – could seem realistic within the boundaries of Europe. That possibility transformed Jewish presence into a negative, an intrusion on Christian dreams.

The unspoken yearning for a homogeneous western Christendom was expressed at diverse levels of majority society and in diverse ways. We have noted recurrently extravagant papal rhetoric, claiming primacy in western Christendom in general and over the Jews in particular. This rhetoric reflects in part the aspiration for a religiously monolithic society. It lay at the root of the Roman Catholic Church's zealous pursuit of what it perceived to be internal deviants. The same aspiration likewise served to deepen the commitment to missionizing among the Jews, the most obvious dissident group in European society. One of the features of our period was intensified proselytizing among the Jews of western Christendom, beginning during the middle decades of the thirteenth century. While Christian responsibility to bring the message of Christianity to the Jews was proclaimed by Paul and reinforced strongly by Augustine, the medieval Church commitment to wide-ranging missionizing reflects more than pious acceptance of prior norms; it reflects the deep-seated desire to remove dissidents from the European scene, in an ecclesiastically sanctioned manner.

At the other end of the social spectrum and in modalities that were ecclesiastically illegitimate, the popular crusading bands of 1096 reflect the same intense desire to remove from the European scene all non-Christian elements. We recall the broad crusading slogan, as reported by a Jewish observer: "Behold, we take our lives in our hands in order to kill and to subjugate all those kingdoms that do not believe in the Crucified." Now, this was surely not official crusading rhetoric; however, it does reflect a more simplistic and normally unarticulated drive toward religious homogeneity. More specifically, these crusaders expressed their intentions vis-à-vis the Jews in the following terms: "Let us wipe them out as a people; Israel's name will be mentioned no more. Or else let them be like us and acknowledge the son born of menstruation [a pejorative reference to Jesus]."[6] Physical or spiritual annihilation of the Jews is the expressed objective, with the result a completely Christian European society.[7] The crusading bands and their radical thinking were vigorously repudiated by Church leadership. Nonetheless, they expressed a hope that was in fact alive within large sectors of the Christian majority and made the Jews an unattractive element in medieval western Christendom.

At the same time, there was an official Church position that guaranteed the Jews a legitimate place within Christian society, acknowledging the realities of pre-redemptive, non-utopian existence.[8] These guarantees were real and meaningful. They served, *inter alia*, to repudiate the popular crusader sloganeering and to protect Jews against forcible baptism. At the same time, the official status accorded the Jews was hardly dignified – Jewish status was necessarily secondary. In the formal Church view, much emphasized by powerful medieval popes like Innocent III, Judaism and Jews were obviously inferior to Christianity and Christians, and that inferiority was to be reflected in every aspect of Jewish life. The physical manifestations of Judaism, for example synagogues, were supposed to be more modest than neighboring churches. More broadly, Jews were to comport themselves in a subservient manner, which would make it obvious which group was descended from the freeborn son of Abraham, i.e. Christians, and which was the offspring of the servant woman, i.e. Jews. While inferiority is somewhat difficult to define and enforce, insistence on the secondary status of the Jews did in fact impact Jewish life. Like the unofficial yearning for a monolithic Christian society, insistence on Jewish inferiority took a toll on the Jews of medieval western Christendom. Majority Christians were moved by the notion of inherent limitations on Jewish existence and by perceptions that Jewish successes represented a breaching of boundaries and unacceptable achievement.

The official status of the Jews in medieval western Christendom included a second major element as well. The Jews hosted in Christian society were to live in such a way as to inflict no harm on the host society. The Jewish potential for harm was, at the outset of our period, broadly defined in two ways – as blasphemous defamation of Christian *sancta* and as deleterious impact on the beliefs and behaviors of Christian neighbors. During our period, perceptions of these two kinds of Jewish harmfulness intensified. In the middle of the thirteenth century, Jewish blasphemy against Christianity was perceived to be part of authoritative Jewish religious tradition, as during the thirteenth century the Talmud became known to medieval western Christendom for the first time. The Talmud seemed to include deprecation of Jesus and Mary and thus constituted officially sanctioned, indeed officially mandated Jewish blasphemy. By the end of the thirteenth century, allegations of desecration of the host wafer began to circulate. Here, increasing emphasis on the centrality of the host to Christian thinking and praxis and the notion of Jewish enmity and harmfulness combined to create an explosive accusation of Jewish blasphemy. With overtones of the cruel treatment of Jesus himself, the host desecration charge conjured up an image of Jewish blasphemy that was deep, intense, and depraved.

As ecclesiastical concerns over the beliefs and behaviors of European Christians intensified, especially with the spread of heterodox thinking during the twelfth century, anxiety over the Jewish potential for negatively influencing Christian neighbors deepened, and increasingly draconian steps were taken to preclude such negative influences. Jews were segregated in multiple ways. The new measures, such as the Jewish badge and separate Jewish neighborhoods, did more than merely segregate; they highlighted Jewish presence and Jewish inferiority. Thus, Christians were alerted to the dangers flowing from Jews, wide-ranging Jewish presence, and Jewish inferiority simultaneously.

As we proceed into the twelfth and thirteenth centuries, perceptions of potential Jewish harmfulness escalated, moving well beyond the concern with Jewish blasphemy and Jewish religious influence. Jewish business activities – carried out in a largely agrarian society – elicited a new sense of Jewish harmfulness, for example through the alleged purchase and sale of stolen goods. The Jewish move into moneylending introduced more ramified and more potent imagery of economic harmfulness. The money business has almost always aroused antipathy and anger. While providing capital is perceived as a worthwhile and useful activity, at the point of repayment of borrowed funds discomfort is often the rule. Since the Church was involved in a concerted effort to eradicate Christian usury from the twelfth century onward, the normal antipathy felt toward the moneylender was reinforced. While there was clearly a canonical distinction between Christians and Jews taking interest from Christian debtors, in the popular mind the lines tended to blur. If taking interest was forbidden for Christians, then there was surely something wrong with Jews taking interest as well. To the normal animosity toward the lender was added this further factor – the taint of an ecclesiastically stigmatized profession.

Finally, the image of the harmful Jew came to include, during the twelfth century, notions of Jewish hatred so intense as to bring Jews to commit murder upon weak and unsuspecting Christian neighbors, most often youngsters both guiltless and defenseless. This accusation, which began to surface at the midpoint of the twelfth century, was quickly embellished with imaginative overtones. Jews were alleged to commit murder in ritualized style or for ritual purposes – through recapitulation of their historic crime of crucifixion or as a reenactment of the biblical sacrificial system or in order to utilize Christian blood for Jewish religious practices.

These allegations are, on the one hand, a reflection of the deepening mistrust with which the Christian majority viewed the Jewish minority. At the same time, these images took on a reality all their own, convincing many in western Christendom of the profound dangers posed by the Jews and of the constant need for care and caution in dealing with these potentially dangerous people. Church repudiation of some of these calumnies, for example the blood libel, did little to sway the common folk; Church support for other charges, for example the allegation of host desecration, served to reinforce notions that were already deeply rooted and convincing.

All the foregoing views, which served as powerful obstacles to successful Jewish settlement in medieval western Christendom, were rooted in the rich complex of prior Christian teachings on Judaism and the Jews. To be sure, in many instances they reflect also developments on the medieval scene as well. Obvious examples of medieval developments that redirected and exacerbated prior teachings include the new emphasis on the host wafer and its significance, which fostered a damning new accusation of Jewish blasphemy, and the Jewish movement into moneylending, which served to deepen and alter the sense of potential Jewish harmfulness.

There was yet one more factor in the anti-Jewish imagery, a factor grounded in earlier Jewish history, rather than in Christian teachings. In large areas of Europe, specifically the northern sectors of medieval western Christendom, the Jews were utterly new and thus alien to the indigenous Christian population. Newcomers are rarely – if ever – popular with the long-standing residents of any territory, and medieval northern Europe was surely no exception. Jewish newness intensified the legacy of prior Christian teachings; prior Christian teachings predisposed the indigenous Christian population to see the Jewish newcomers as especially threatening and unwelcome.

These underlying anti-Jewish attitudes, by no means simple or homogeneous, served as potent obstacles to Jewish efforts at finding a meaningful place in medieval western Christendom. The obvious question to ask at this point is: in the face of all this opposition and resistance, what was the attraction of Latin Christendom to the Jews? Why did Jews choose to make their way into medieval western Christendom, and why did they opt to stay when faced with such wide-ranging Christian hostility and such intensely negative Christian pre-judgments? Indeed, when eventually banished from major principalities, why did Jews elect to stay within the boundaries of Latin Christendom, rather than returning to the Islamic sphere whence so many had originated?

It should be recalled of course that not all the Jews of medieval western Christendom made a decision to migrate into the area. Some Jews of the south were long-time residents of Latin Christendom; other Jews, especially on the Iberian peninsula, were caught up in the expansion of Christian power. Living in areas conquered by Christian armies, these Jews stayed in place and had their environment altered around them from Islamic culture and governance to Christian culture and governance. Of course, these new Jewish inhabitants of western Christendom did have the option of following the retreating Muslim armies and resettling further southward in territories that remained Islamic. Very few of them seem to have done so. On the other hand, prior to our period there was no significant Jewish presence in northern Europe. The Jewish communities that stretched from England in the west through Hungary and Poland in the east were the outgrowth of conscious decisions on the part of thousands of Jewish migrants, thus reinforcing our question of the grounds for choosing to migrate into a setting rife with resistance and antipathy.

The answer to this question seems to lie in two directions, one having to do with the Jewish minority and the other having to do with the Christian majority. By the year 1000, the Jews seem to have evolved into one of the medieval world's most mobile people. The one area of the economy from which they had receded was agriculture, which is by its very nature resistant to movement. Thus, few Jews were tied to the ground they tilled. Many Jews were heirs to centuries-old artisanal traditions, which tended to make such Jews relatively immobile. By and large, however, the Jews of the year 1000 seem to have been concentrated heavily in trade, which encourages mobility. Jewish traders were primed to move where business opportunity might beckon.

The economic circumstances of western Christendom during our period seem to have offered precisely the kind of business opportunities that would stimulate the movement of mobile Jewish traders. In large measure, these economic opportunities were highly localized and differed from sector to sector of medieval western Christendom. However, in a general way the various areas of Latin Christendom were surging forward rapidly, moving from a position of backwardness to a position of preeminence in the West altogether. Jews offered the potential of serving as valuable pioneers, bringing advanced expertise to this rapidly evolving area. In the course of our surveys of the diverse sets of Jewish communities across medieval western Christendom, we have seen a variety of Jewish pioneering contributions, which benefited simultaneously the host Christian majority and the immigrating Jewish minority.[9]

The first such pioneering contribution we have noted came on the Iberian peninsula, where the Jews who had long lived in Muslim Spain made the decision to throw in their lot with the conquering Christian kings of the north. Well integrated into the economy and governance of Muslim Spain, especially the small city-states that developed during the late eleventh and early twelfth centuries, the Jews had much to offer Christian rulers striving to maintain the sophisticated civilization they had conquered. The Jewish contribution to this effort was considerable, with both the Christian majority and the Jewish minority benefiting. To be sure, hackles were raised on the Christian side by some of the political authority that powerful Jewish magnates came to enjoy, in obvious contravention of ecclesiastical rules against such Jewish power. Nonetheless, the diversity of the population of newly christianized Spain precluded intense anti-Jewish hostility from developing out of Jewish economic successes.

When we turn northward, we encounter a slightly different situation. In the northern areas, the issue was not maintenance of a prior level of economy and governance; rather, the issue was moving a backward economy ahead. The task was daunting, but the successes were impressive. The northern areas of Europe, distinctly backward in the year 1000, had by the year 1500 surged to the forefront of the Western world. In a variety of ways, the Jews made a modest contribution to this surge. Hopes for such a contribution seem to have moved any number of northern-European rulers over the course of our period to foster Jewish presence. Perhaps more important yet, the perception of economic opportunity seemed to have inspired many Jews to make bold forays into areas new to them. For a number of centuries, the economic evolution of the northern sectors of medieval western Christendom presented continual opportunities for aggressive and innovative Jewish entrepreneurs. To be sure, these Jewish entrepreneurs and their efforts were by no means universally appreciated. To an extent, simply being innovative entailed resistance and animosity; in some instances, the grounds for the animosity were more complex.

During the eleventh and early twelfth centuries, the business opportunities offered to Jewish immigrants to these northern areas revolved around trade. The early northern charters we have examined all suggest immigrating Jews who were largely supporting themselves by buying and selling goods, and that impression is reinforced by the Jewish *responsa* literature as well. With regard to the Jewish movement into northern Europe, it seems fair to suggest that Jewish traders brought some of the advanced techniques of the Islamic world into the rather more backward sectors of medieval western Christendom. This trading activity may well have engendered hostility on the part of the Christian businessmen who were challenged by Jewish competitors or on the part of those resistant to change; it was not, however, the kind of activity that would arouse wide-ranging antipathy.

During the twelfth century, a new set of business opportunities emerged from the confluence of the need for an augmented flow of capital in a rapidly evolving economy and the Church's attack on what it projected as the sin of usury. The economic need and the religious pressures against fulfillment of that need combined to open up a dazzling new field for Jewish economic activity. Unaffected by the Church's anti-usury efforts – for a number of decades in any case – the Jews could devote themselves to an important economic activity they could more or less dominate, at least for a period of time. The Jewish attraction to moneylending is especially noticeable in the north, where Jewish presence was new and Jewish economic activity was thus more restricted than it was in the older Jewish communities of the south. Eventually, this new specialty provided enticing economic opportunities for Jews all across Latin Christendom. Such Jewish economic activity necessitated the constant search for new urban centers within which Jews might ply their specialization. Thus, the Jewish population tended to fan out from large urban centers into smaller and smaller outlying towns. This movement can be traced in some detail in northern France and England, but seems to have been ubiquitous.

We have noted, in the survey of the diverse sets of Jewish communities that made up medieval European Jewry, a variety of modalities of Jewish moneylending. In the more rapidly evolving business and governmental environment of northern France and England, Jewish lending took place against diverse forms of collateral, ranging from moveable goods to real estate. The latter kind of lending, which could only take place with strong governmental backing and sophisticated recording apparatus, was especially lucrative, resulting in the emergence of a small group of extremely wealthy and powerful Jewish bankers in England and northern France. Relations between these wealthy Jewish bankers and their governmental supporters were intense and productive, if short-lived. In the more backward economic and political circumstances of Germany, Jewish lending was almost exclusively of the pawnbroking variety, a style of lending that provided livelihoods but not the great wealth of the English and French Jewish bankers.

Moneylending constituted a new economic specialty that was mutually beneficial, helpful to the Christian majority that needed the flow of capital and lucrative to the Jewish minority that was well equipped to provide the necessary service. Jewish moneylending was, in many circles, appreciated, and Jewish lenders were prized for their service and – in some instances – for their human kindness, as the research of Joseph Shatzmiller has nicely shown.[10] Nonetheless, banking has never been a popular profession, and Jewish lenders were by and large feared and distrusted. As noted, the Church campaign against usury, while it initially exempted Jewish usury, served to taint the banking enterprise altogether. Moreover, with the passage of time, the ecclesiastical leadership of western Christendom reconsidered the issue of Jewish usury, attempting to establish significant protections for Christian debtors and eventually – at least in some circles – questioning the Jewish right to take interest altogether. Given the predisposition to see the Jews as hostile and dangerous, Jewish specialization in moneylending turned out to have deleterious side effects.

One more stage in Jewish economic history should be noted, and that stage involved the move into eastern Europe, where the kind of general backwardness resurfaced that had served as the initial impetus for Jewish migration into the north altogether. In these northeastern areas of Europe, there was again a strong desire to move forward and to match some of the achievements notable in the more westerly sectors of northern Europe. Once more, this opened up opportunities for a pioneering Jewish role, for Jews to bring into lagging areas business techniques and acumen developed in more sophisticated environments. The move into the eastern sectors of northern Europe shows one striking difference from the Jewish pioneering efforts noted elsewhere, and that difference involves the slow pace of economic progress in these eastern areas. On the Iberian peninsula and across the more westerly sectors of northern Europe, the pace of change was fairly rapid. The rapid pace of change was positive from the perspective of majority society; it was problematic for the Jewish minority in that it circumscribed the period of useful Jewish contribution. At the point when rapid change had taken place, the Jews as members of a minority community regularly found their place in the new economy challenged. The slower pace of progress in the east – while negative from the perspective of society at large – allowed the Jews to continue to play a useful role for many centuries. Jewish life in eastern Europe seems to have moved at a less frenetic pace than elsewhere, allowing Jews to settle in and maintain a stability that escaped them in the other sectors of medieval western Christendom.

THE GOVERNING AUTHORITIES

Jewish immigration into medieval western Christendom involved the significant and related obstacles of ecclesiastical limitation and popular hostility on the one hand, ranged against the appeal of economic opportunity in a rapidly developing sector of the West on the other. Jews were attracted by the latter and had to be deeply concerned with the former. This dyadic picture, however, does not convey the whole story. One more critical element must be introduced, and that element is the ruling class of medieval western Christendom, which controlled the balance between the negative factors of popular hostility and ecclesiastical limitation and the positive factor of economic lure. Where governmental authorities chose to be supportive, Jewish life could flourish. Where governmental authorities failed their Jewish clients or turned against them in one or another way, Jewish existence was compromised or even doomed.[11]

Given the general instability of a rapidly evolving society and – more specifically – the broad societal resistance to Jewish settlement, Jewish well-being required the support of effective governing authorities. In the diverse areas that constituted medieval western Christendom, the authorities tended initially to lend requisite support. In older sectors of Jewish settlement, in the south, rulers regularly protected the interests of the Jewish population. On the Iberian peninsula, as Christian rulers conquered more and more territory, they bent considerable effort toward convincing long-time Jewish inhabitants to remain in place and to contribute to maintaining and expanding the pre-existent economy and social structure. All across northern Europe, energetic rulers committed themselves to incorporating useful new Jews into their territories. Without such governmental support, old Jewish settlements undergoing change might have been seriously damaged, and new Jewish enclaves could not have been implanted.

What were the motivations of the protective rulers in the older and newer areas of Jewish settlement? Once again, economic issues were paramount, in a double sense. In the first place, many of the rulers of medieval western Christendom – especially the newly developing areas – were deeply committed to economic progress and were convinced that the Jews might make a useful contribution to such progress. We recall Bishop Rudiger's assertion that he was inviting Jews to settle in Speyer in order to enhance its economy. There is every reason to take that claim seriously, and Bishop Rudiger was far from alone in sensing the advantages that might accrue from Jewish immigration. As noted, Jews were capable of bringing into the developing areas of medieval western Christendom the fruits of prior progress in the more advanced areas from which they were emigrating. Rooted in both the Muslim and Christian spheres of the medieval West, the Jews were perceived by many rulers as useful in helping western Christendom move forward on the economic front.

There was regularly a second and narrower economic motivation as well. In medieval western Christendom, taxation was relatively primitive. Tax arrangements were grounded largely in prior custom. While reasonable in stable societies, such taxation arrangements did not fit the needs of rapidly evolving areas. In order to support the accelerating development that characterized western Christendom from the eleventh century on, new financial resources had to be available to the ruling authorities, resources that would enable them to undertake the innovative projects required to move their domains forward. The expedients investigated and utilized by the ruling class were many and diverse. In this relentless quest for further revenue, the Jews appeared to many rulers extremely valuable. They were deeply dependent upon their protectors and thus readily taxable. Jews could do little in the face of tax levies fair or unfair. In a real sense, the Jews allowed their rulers access to Christian wealth not directly available to them. This made the Jews appealing to their lords, but at the same time resented by those whom the Jews exploited so that they might meet the demands of their rulers.

The Jews of medieval western Christendom required from the governing authorities, first and foremost, protection from physical assault, a threat that flowed in part from the broad lawlessness of the period and in part from the specific anti-Jewish imagery and sentiment we have traced. Jews in medieval western Christendom regularly perceived themselves endangered and thus urgently felt the need for the protection of the governing authorities. Without effective protection by these authorities, Jewish life was under constant threat and thus ultimately untenable.

The modalities of governmental support for Jewish physical well-being were diverse. Most beneficial from the Jewish perspective were the efforts to forestall violence prior to its eruption. There were many instances in which anti-Jewish violence was almost predictable. Calls to crusade almost inevitably aroused anti-Jewish hostility and the threat of assault. We recall the Third Crusade memoir of Rabbi Eleazar of Worms, who reports happily the news of crusader setbacks in the Middle East and then notes immediately and anxiously the resultant call to renewed crusading, with its inevitable arousal of anti-Jewish sentiment. Rabbi Eleazar's memoir, and especially the letter from Mainz he embedded in it, illustrates the kind of effective governmental support in the face of threatened violence that Jews prized. The potent German emperor, Frederick I, announced harsh penalties for anti-Jewish actions and made it clear to his subordinates that the Jews must be protected. By investigating carefully the allegation of Jewish use of Christian blood and rejecting it vigorously, Emperor Frederick II attempted in similar fashion to forestall the violence that might eventuate from this allegation. Many of the rulers of medieval western Christendom took similar steps, and in many – although not all – cases such vigorous actions were successful.

Somewhat less beneficial – but valued nonetheless – from the Jewish perspective was intervention in the midst of anti-Jewish violence. The Third Crusade letter from Mainz mentioned just now includes reference to such intervention. Aroused crusaders invaded the Jewish neighborhood of Mainz, in which the Jews hoping to negotiate with the emperor had sequestered themselves. These crusaders were met by a determined contingent of imperial militia that put down the incipient violence. In the one successful governmental intervention in the Rhineland in 1096 reported by the Jewish chroniclers, Bishop John of Speyer had his militia engage the motley combination of crusaders and burghers bent on harming the Jews, and beat them back. Again, there are many similar examples from the diverse areas of western Christendom and from the various centuries we have discussed.

Least appealing from the Jewish perspective was intervention after the fact, that is to say punishment inflicted on the perpetrators of violence upon Jews. This is not to say that such after-the-fact intervention was utterly meaningless. Significant punishment of malefactors did serve to deter future aggression. In particular, cases in which it was clear that the governmental intervention was genuine and not simply a matter of realizing revenues for the ruling coffers were particularly beneficial from the Jewish perspective. Nonetheless, from the Jews' point of view, imposition of governmental force prior to and even during outbreaks of violence were far preferable to after-the-fact punishment.

Governmental support for the Jews involved more than protection of life and limb. Jewish business affairs also required the backing of the authorities. In some instances, governmental backing could mean no more than simply support in the face of litigation. We recall, for example, the provisions in support of Jewish pawnbroking in the charter extended by Frederick of Austria to his Jews in 1244. Jews were backed by the authorities in the face of a wide range of debtor claims. In other instances, more sophisticated rulers, like those of twelfth- and thirteenth-century England and France, were deeply involved in Jewish business affairs, regulating and protecting the documents upon which Jewish lending was based and assuring the Jewish creditors access to land put up as collateral for loans. Christian moralists regularly criticized such governmental support as equivalent to partnership with the Jewish moneylenders, in effect accusing the Christian authorities themselves of the stigma of usurious transactions.

Not infrequently, the authorities protected their Jews against the limitations imposed by the ecclesiastical authorities against the Jews. The Jewish badge, for example, which was deeply resented and feared by the Jews, occasioned recurrent Jewish complaints to the rulers of medieval western Christendom. On many occasions, these authorities responded empathetically to these Jewish complaints, deferring imposition of the badge. The same is true for Church efforts to restrict or prohibit Jewish usury. In many cases, the authorities protected their Jews against the more extreme anti-usury demands of the Church. The motivation for such protection often involved the loss of revenue that disruption of Jewish business would entail. To be sure, the demands of the Church were extremely difficult to resist over the long haul. Ecclesiastical leadership was prepared for long-term pressure and usually succeeded eventually in imposing its will with respect to the Jews.

Governing in the rapidly changing circumstances of medieval western Christendom was no easy task. The rulers of medieval western Christendom of course ran the gamut from tradition-bound, weak, and ineffective to innovative, powerful, and highly effective. During our period, many of the former were in effect swallowed up by the latter. Barons in such developing monarchies as England, France, and Spain often found themselves outmaneuvered and eventually impoverished or co-opted by increasingly puissant kings. Jews had to assess the advantages and disadvantages associated with the various kinds of authority that emerged across Europe. Powerful rulers offered advantages and disadvantages, as did weaker rulers. For the Jews, however, the choice was not terribly difficult. Given the popular resistance to Jewish presence and the ecclesiastical limitations on Jewish activity,

Jews were consistently drawn to more powerful authorities and distrusted weak rulers. The Jews of medieval western Christendom were
attracted to potent rulers, because their power translated into protection of Jewish lives, Jewish property, and Jewish business affairs. This
was true for the Iberian peninsula during the period of the Christian
reconquest of Spain; it was likewise true for the increasingly potent
monarchies of France and England. In contrast, weak rulers could not
provide requisite protection from the antipathy of the masses or from
the strictures of the Church. Regularly, weak political authorities
disappointed their Jewish clients, with devastating results. Thus, all
across western Christendom, Jews tended to gravitate toward strong
governments and to distrust the weak.

Our prior surveys have regularly indicated the liabilities associated
with governmental weakness. Early in our period, during the agitation to the First Crusade, Rhineland Jews learned painfully that
well-intentioned but weak authorities could not provide requisite
assistance. The German emperor was powerful, but remained far from
the scene of danger, and thus his warnings against anti-Jewish violence had little impact. The local authorities – the bishops of the
Rhineland – were clearly well intentioned, deeply committed for a
variety of reasons to protecting their Jews. They lacked, however, the
requisite military force to withstand the fury of the radical crusading
forces. Anti-Jewish agitation further westward in France resulted in
no significant Jewish casualties, as a result of more effective interven-
tions by the authorities. The cost of governmental weakness is especially obvious in late-thirteenth- and fourteenth-century Germany,
where waves of anti-Jewish violence recurrently decimated the Jewish
population of the German lands. Even instances of more temporary governmental weakness, such as afflicted the Iberian peninsula
during the early 1390s, could have devastating results. These examples of general or even temporary governmental weakness and its
toll illuminate the broad Jewish preference for strong governmental
authority.

Jews were fully aware that the more potent the authority, the more
effective its support might be. Thus, the Jews were generally drawn to
the more powerful rulers in medieval western Christendom. At the
same time, the Jews learned quickly enough that these more powerful rulers could both protect and grievously harm them. The more
powerful the governmental protectors of the Jews, the less recourse
Jews had in the face of governmental oppression.

Three factors moved European rulers to turn against their Jewish clients. The first was cupidity; the second was fidelity to the dictates of the Church; the third was absorption of popular fear and animosity. Unfortunately, it is often impossible to be sure of which motivation was at work in any given case, since anti-Jewish actions were regularly cloaked in pious rhetoric. In some instances, anti-Jewish actions were – rhetoric notwithstanding – patently grounded in material considerations; occasionally, European rulers were clearly moved by loyalty to the Church; less frequently, personal animosities are patent. In many cases, a complex combination of motives – no longer ascertainable – was at work.

The first element in governmental exploitation of Jewish wealth was clarification of Jewish status and regularization of Jewish dependency upon and exploitation by a given ruler. Much has been written about the so-called serfdom of the Jews in medieval Latin Christendom. Discussion of medieval Jewish serfdom has generally revolved around the grandiose imperial claims to control of the Jews of the empire. Much more meaningful, however, was the so-called Jewish serfdom that emerged further west in France, where the status had profound implications. In late-twelfth-century feudal France, which was a conglomeration of baronies, Jews found places for themselves in many of the duchies and counties. Efforts to control or exploit these Jews often resulted simply in flight from the problematic territory to another that remained – from the Jewish perspective – problem free. As the French monarchy began to gain ground, especially during the reign of Philip Augustus, the desire to tax the Jews and to be assured that exploited Jews not change venue intensified. As we have seen, non-retention treaties were signed between holders of Jews. Eventually, the monarchy took the lead in drawing up harsh legislation and ensuring that Jews not evade the new regulations by moving freely from place to place. Initially, stabilizing Jewish residence was achieved by bringing numerous barons to sign the new stipulations and to agree not to hold one another's Jews. With the passage of time, the monarchy felt strong enough simply to stipulate that barons who signed legislation and those who did not would be bound to honor the proprietary rights of each other over Jews. The fixing of Jewish residence patterns – designated in terms of serfdom – had practical implications for Jews so designated. It meant loss of freedom of movement, susceptibility to constraining new regulations, and inescapable taxation.

We have noted that the interest of the ruling authorities of medieval western Christendom in fostering Jewish presence was in part the desire to stimulate the economy in general and in part the yen for tax revenues. We have also noted that the dependency of the Jews on their lords meant little recourse from onerous taxation. This availability to taxation, including extremely heavy taxation, presented for the rulers of medieval western Christendom an ongoing temptation. Given the crushing need for revenues, the limits on the right to tax in general, and the availability of easily accessible revenue from the Jews, the temptation to tax and tax again was – for many rulers – nearly irresistible. The ever-pressing fiscal burdens of medieval government and the total dependence of the Jews on their royal and baronial protectors combined to move many medieval rulers to exploit Jewish wealth to the maximum, often impoverishing their Jewish clients in the process.

Indeed, the better organized the machinery of assistance to Jewish business and thus the fuller the information on Jewish economic activity, the more effective governmental exploitation might be. In England and – to a slightly lesser extent – northern France, the sophisticated apparatus established to protect Jewish lending could be readily turned into an effective mechanism for ascertaining Jewish financial resources and exploiting mercilessly those resources. We have had occasion to note, for example, relentless expropriation of Jewish wealth in England, during the reigns of King John and King Henry III. We also recall the papal letter of Pope Gregory IX, detailing Jewish complaints against the barons of northern France who utilized the Church's own anti-usury campaign to inflict harsh fiscal and physical suffering on their Jews.

Cupidity was not the only element at work in turning the rulers of medieval western Christendom against their Jewish clients. We have seen numerous rulers who seem to have been genuinely moved by a concern for Church directives and popular sentiment. The most striking example of this type of harmful governmental initiative comes from the reign of the pious King Louis IX of France, canonized subsequently as St. Louis. St. Louis's reign represents a turning point in medieval French-Jewish history, the point at which the positive direction of Jewish life in northern France was reversed and palpable decline began in both the material and spiritual spheres. Louis believed that his support undergirded Jewish existence in his realm and that he was thus morally and religiously responsible for the behavior of his Jews. When rebuked by some of his followers for outlawing Jewish usury, on the grounds that the pious king was in effect paving the way for resumption of Christian usury, Louis is reported to have responded that Christian usury was the concern and responsibility of the Church. He, however, was responsible for the Jews, and their sins rested on his soul. Thus, for the purity of his soul, he had to take requisite steps to rid his kingdom of the taint of Jewish usury. We recall that the papal call to investigate the Talmud, which was addressed to the major monarchs of Latin Christendom, elicited a response only from St. Louis. It was in the French kingdom alone that copies of the Talmud were collected, that the Talmud was investigated, and that the Talmud was eventually condemned, burned, and prohibited.

Louis IX also serves as an exemplar of rulers who shared popular fear and hatred of the Jews. The story told by his biographer Joinville, in which the pious king praised physical assault on Jews invited by churchmen to discuss religious issues (in all likelihood a missionizing endeavor) and prescribed a sword thrust to the belly as the appropriate response to Jewish discussion of religious truth suggests royal absorption of more than ecclesiastical teachings; Louis seems to have absorbed elemental popular hatreds as well.

Whatever the precise motivation, anti-Jewish stances on the part of the governing authorities – whether in the form of radical fiscal exploitation of Jewish wealth or support for harmful ecclesiastical initiatives – spelled disaster for the Jews of medieval western Christendom. The culminating step in the reversal of governmental support was the new expedient of expulsion, which emerged toward the end of the twelfth century, gained momentum during the thirteenth century, and reached a peak of sorts with the expulsions from the Iberian peninsula in 1492 and 1497.

To be sure, the fundamental ecclesiastical stance toward the Jews, which stipulated basic rights and important limitations provided Jews lived harmlessly within western Christendom, left open the question of Jewish harmfulness and the sanctions it might entail. On the simplest level, this question was intended to be answered in individual terms. Individual Jews who committed harmful acts were of course to suffer the appropriate punishment for their crimes, at the hands of the secular authorities.

Notions of corporate Jewish crime and corporate punishment of Jews developed fairly rapidly in medieval Latin Christendom. On the eve of the Second Crusade, Peter the Venerable suggested to the king of France that Jewish crimes of blasphemy and selling stolen goods were well known and should be punished by forcing the Jews as a group to defray some of the costs of crusading. We recall the claim that the Jews of Blois as a group were responsible for the murder of a Christian child, the trial by ordeal ordered by the count of Blois, and the burning of more than thirty Jews allegedly proven guilty by the unusual trial procedure. Corporate Jewish guilt and punishment became fairly standard thinking and praxis for medieval western Christendom.

There remained yet one further extension of the notion of corporate Jewish guilt and punishment, and that was removal altogether of Jews who seemed to be incorrigibly addicted to malfeasance. The expedient of expulsion was not invented in Europe between 1000 and 1500. There was a historic precedent from Visigothic Spain in the seventh century. Little historical information regarding that precedent has survived, however, occasioning considerable uncertainty as to motives and techniques. The precedent was known later on during the Middle Ages; precisely how much it affected the expulsions of the twelfth through fifteenth century is a matter of speculation. While there was a pre-1000 precedent, it was from the 1180s on in medieval western Christendom that expulsion of Jews from local territories, from counties and duchies, and from entire realms became a regular feature of Jewish existence.

Expulsion as a radical act involving numbers of Jews required explanation, and such explanations were generally forthcoming, both in the edicts of the rulers expelling their Jews and in the depictions of these expulsions by chroniclers of these rulers and their domains. Despite these pronouncements and portrayals, however, motivations are difficult to fathom. Religious obligation is almost always cited as the grounds for expulsion of Jews. Rulers portray themselves and are portrayed by their chroniclers as noble, devoted to their Church and faith, and concerned with the well-being of their subjects. Nonetheless, it is obvious that many of the expulsions of our period also resulted in heavy profit for the expelling authorities, that considerable effort was invested in maximizing these profits, and that ecclesiastical and popular approbation was assiduously cultivated through these expulsions.

Local expulsions took place all across medieval western Christendom. Most local expulsions were grounded in allegations

Jasgow University Check out/renewal receipt

ustomer name: Swallow, Kathleen

tle: Carnal knowing : female nakedness and
religious meaning in the Christian West /
Margaret R. Miles
D: 30114010031580
ue: 24-01-13

tle: Studies in early mysticism in the / Kerma
wiler Champa
D: 30114005718781
ue: 24-01-13

tle: The Jewel of Medieval Western
hristendom, 1000-1500 /Robert Chazan.
D: 30114012822247
ue: 24-01-13

otal items: 3
7/01/2013 13:21

h s 24hr loan items cannot be renewed.
lease return short loan items on time to avoid
ines.

of Jewish misdeeds. We recall, for example, the spate of local banishments stimulated across the baronies of northern France by the anti-
usury preaching of Fulk of Neuilly. During the disastrous period of
the fourteenth century, numerous localities expelled their Jews, out
of concern with perceived Jewish hostility and anti-Christian activity.

The first of the broader expulsions of our period was decreed
by King Philip Augustus of France in 1182. The edict of expulsion
has not survived, so we lack the monarch's own formulation of his
motivation. Our fullest source is the royal biographer, Rigord of
St. Denis, who locates the king's motivation in his sense of Christian
duty. Aware of a sequence of Jewish misdeeds, according to Rigord,
Philip elected to exile them. To be sure, royal profit was substantial, as
a large ransom was paid prior to the decree, and Jewish real estate was
confiscated at the time of the decree and subsequently sold, with the
proceeds going to the royal treasury. The sums realized seem to have
been considerable. To be sure, the royal domain from which the Jews
were expelled in 1182 was extremely small, and thus the expulsion
involved a relatively small number of Jews and minimal problems of
relocation. In the middle of the thirteenth century, St. Louis ordered
those Jews unwilling to observe the new anti-usury legislation to leave
the much larger kingdom over which he by then presided. In the case
of St. Louis, we can be relatively confident that the motivation was
distinctly religious.

The end of the thirteenth century saw a spate of expulsions from
territories in northwestern France. The edict of expulsion from the
counties of Anjou and Maine is revealing. The order opens with a
sequence of Jewish crimes.

In many locales of that land [the counties of Maine and Anjou], numerous Jews,
enemies of the life-giving Cross and of all Christianity, dwelling randomly
and publicly among Christians and deviating from the way of truth, subvert
perfidiously many of both sexes who are considered adherents of the Christian
faith. They seem to subvert all whom they can. They despoil these Christians
of their movable and immovable goods by their devious conceits and by the
endless abyss of usury, and thus they wickedly force these Christians to beg
for alms. What is most horrible to consider, they evilly cohabit with many
Christian maidens.

This bill of indictment is rich and impressive. What is more, the ostensibly pious count ordered a parallel expulsion of Christian usurers.
Purging the realm of sin is portrayed as paramount. Minor provisions

for confiscation of goods are made, but they are not front-and-center. Indeed, Count Charles indicates overtly that he will suffer financial loss as a result of the expulsion and that he is fully prepared for this loss. "Although we enjoy much temporal profit from the aforesaid Jews, we prefer to provide the peace of our subjects, than to fill our coffers with the mammon of iniquity, especially since by the loss of temporal good spiritual gains are achieved."[12]

This is not to say that there was no profit from the expulsion from Anjou and Maine. The edict indicates that "it has been conceded to us freely and without duress that we ought to receive from each hearth three shillings once only and from each wage earner six pence once only, as some recompense for the profit we lose through the aforesaid expulsions." The residents of Maine and Anjou were in effect taxed for the expulsion of the Jews and Christian usurers from their county. The proceeds from this taxation were unlikely to have equaled the sums realized by Philip Augustus in his late-twelfth-century expulsion or by the kings of England and France in the expulsions that followed fairly close after the expulsion from Maine and Anjou, but they were not inconsiderable.

The expulsion decreed by King Edward I of England broke new ground. While Philip Augustus had banished the Jews from royal France in 1182, the royal domain at that early point in time was – as noted – quite restricted. St. Louis's expulsion was partial only. The expulsion of 1290 represented a new phenomenon – the total banishment of Jews from a major kingdom. While the number of Jews thus dislocated may not have been all that large, the impact of such a banishment as a precedent was significant. To be sure, the Jewish stay in England was – relatively speaking – brief. They had come in the wake of 1066 and departed only a little more than two centuries later. Looking at matters this way highlights some of the danger in a survey like the present one. From the overall perspective of this book in its entirety, two centuries may seem a short period of time; from the perspective of individuals and families, two centuries is in fact a very long time. Indeed, English Jewry in all likelihood saw itself as rooted in England in precisely the same way as the royal family. In terms of both precedent and human impact, 1290 constituted a noteworthy event.

The expulsion of 1306 went well beyond 1290 in both significance and impact. Much larger numbers of Jews were uprooted in 1306, and a far more influential precedent was established. By virtue of its successes in adding southern-French territory to the royal domain, the French monarchy in 1306 was in the position of banishing Jewish communities that could trace their roots back more than a millennium. If I have argued that two centuries created a sense of Jewish belonging in England, then the sense of Jewish belonging and associated disruption was obviously far more profound in France.

The expulsions from Spain in 1492 and from Portugal in 1497 were, in a sense, merely the last of the major expulsions of the Middle Ages. There was, by the end of the fifteenth century, nothing unprecedented in banishment of Jews locally or even banishment from a major kingdom in its entirety. Nonetheless, these two culminating expulsions generated astonishment and deep despair in the Jewish world. The Jews of the Iberian peninsula were, as we have amply seen, among the oldest Jewish elements in medieval western Christendom. The period of Muslim domination on the peninsula had served to create a Jewish community that was larger, more economically diversified, more politically potent, and more culturally integrated than Jewish communities elsewhere in Europe. This was the community that would have seemed to be immune to the spate of expulsions, yet it too suffered banishment. Jewish distress was profound.

Thus, the tension between the allure of medieval western Christendom and the popular and ecclesiastical obstacles to Jewish presence therein was ultimately resolved by the various governing authorities. Where these authorities exhibited the will and the capacity to support their Jewish clients, Jews were able to live, to contribute to their environment, and to explore and enrich their own religious and cultural tradition. Where the authorities lacked the will or the capacity to support their Jews, Jewish life was either extremely difficult or impossible. Weak political authorities regularly failed to protect their Jews adequately and to support their business effectively. Strong political authorities – generally preferred by the Jews themselves – could and did support Jewish business and protect Jewish life and property. Unfortunately for the medieval Jews, there was no one to protect them from their protectors. When these strong rulers decided to exploit their Jewish clients, the exploitation could often be ruinous. When these strong rulers decided to eliminate the Jews from their domains, Jewish life came to an end.

SUCCESSES

The Jews of medieval western Christendom achieved much during the five hundred years between 1000 and 1500. Their most striking achievement was demographic. During this period, the center of gravity in world Jewish population began to shift from the East to the West, from the realm of Islam to Latin Christendom. We created at the outset of this book a hypothetical Jewish observer looking out over the Jewish world in the year 1000 and suggested that such an observer might well have neglected to note the Jews of western Christendom at all, so minuscule and insignificant was that set of Jewish communities. No observer in the year 1500 could possibly have made such an omission. As a result of developments during the intervening five hundred years, European Jewry – for all its tribulations – had begun to surpass the older Jewries of the more easterly territories. The center of Jewish life has been transferred into the realm of Christianity.

In the process of this historic shift in Jewish population, old areas of Jewish habitation were reinforced, and entirely new territories were settled by the Jews. Across much of southern Europe, where Jews had already found a place in Roman times, Jewish population expanded through the twelfth and thirteenth centuries. While the Jewish population of the Italian peninsula remained fairly stable, the Jewish communities of southern France and the Iberian peninsula grew significantly. To be sure, the growth did not continue throughout our period. The expulsion of the Jews from all of royal France in 1306 by then included the Jews of much of the south as well as those of the north. The important Jewish communities of Spain and Portugal continued almost all the way through the fifteenth century, succumbing to the sequence of expulsions only in 1492 and 1497.

Far more dramatic was the growth and development of northern-European Jewry, an entirely new branch of the Jewish people. From modest beginnings in France and Germany during the late tenth and eleventh centuries, Jewish settlement grew and expanded rapidly during the twelfth and thirteenth centuries. The vigorous Jewish community of northern France threw off a satellite community in England that flourished for more than two centuries, prior to expulsion in 1290. A short time later, in 1306, the mother Jewry of northern France was similarly exiled. Thus, over a period of three hundred years, a new set of Jewish settlements in northwestern Europe was founded, matured, and disappeared. To be sure, the descendants of these English and French Jews made their way eastward and contributed to the further growth of northern-European Jewry, and the material and spiritual achievements of these Jews was added to the legacy of Ashkenazic – and indeed world – Jewry.

The early history of Jewish settlement in north-central and north-eastern Europe exhibited a different dynamic. Here too Jewish settlements were first founded during the eleventh and twelfth centuries, and here too satellite communities were thrown off as well. The dynamic of development in these areas diverged markedly from what took place further westward. The Jewish communities of the German and northeastern lands never enjoyed the rapid growth and development of those in France and England. At the same time, they did not suffer the rapid decline that afflicted the latter Jewish communities. The flatter curve of Jewish experience in north-central and northeastern Europe seems to reflect the flatter curve of general development in these areas. Both economic and political maturation proceeded at a far slower pace. There was no business efflorescence like that of northern France and England, and correspondingly there was no political centralization such as that engineered by the French and English monarchies. The economic lag in the German lands served to encourage Jewish presence and Jewish activity; the weakness of the ruling authorities exposed the Jews of these areas to a high level of violence and insecurity. The combination of economic lag and relatively effective governance in northeastern Europe made these areas a special refuge for northern-European Jews who had suffered expulsion from England and France and had been badly battered by the insecurity of the German lands. By the end of our period, the Jewish communities of northeastern Europe were on their way to becoming the largest of the Jewries of western Christendom. In the subsequent centuries, they were fated to become the demographic centers of world Jewry altogether.

In the sphere of economic activity, the Jews of medieval western Christendom left an important legacy as well, although this legacy has been criticized in many quarters of modern Jewish life. This legacy might well be designated an economy of niches. In their earliest periods, the Jews of Palestine, Mesopotamia, and the Roman Empire seem to have involved themselves in a broad spectrum of economic activities. There is no real sense of economic specialization. This breadth of economic activity is manifest in the Jewish communities of the medieval Muslim world as well, as indicated in the brilliant research of S. D. Goitein and his students.[13] Such breadth of activity may well have characterized Jewish life early on in the older areas of southern Europe, although data are lacking for full treatment of those communities prior to the thirteenth century. The new Jewish settlements of northern Europe show a strikingly different economic profile. Jews made their way northward to fill certain lacunae in the burgeoning economies of northern Europe. The broad popular hostility to them made it impossible for these Jews to settle in a normally diversified pattern of economic activity. Rather, they tended to regularly explore and exploit new niches in a maturing economy. Thus, for example, the Jews of northern Europe moved from trade to moneylending, as new needs arose.

Evaluation of this kind of niche economy is difficult. There is of course a general societal ideal of economic diversification. Diversified economies are viewed as healthy economies, and thus to many observers the economic specialization that came to characterize the Jewish communities of medieval western Christendom was essentially distorted and unhealthy. Such an evaluation is somewhat oversimplified, however. In the first place, the Jewish choice was not between a diversified economy or a niche economy; the Jewish choice was between remaining in the Muslim world with a diversified but stagnating Jewish economy or transferring into the rapidly developing Christian orbit with a limited but burgeoning economy. Viewed in this way, the Jewish choice to make the move and sacrifice economic diversity seems defensible and reasonable.

Furthermore, while the negatives associated with a niche economy are well known, attention should also be paid to the advantages of such a niche economy. The major disadvantage of a niche economy is the threat of change that might entail loss of economic strength altogether. It is likely that something along these lines in fact happened to the Jews of medieval western Christendom during the thirteenth century. We recall the report of objections to St. Louis's effort to eliminate Jewish usury. Some of his supporters are reported to have argued that usury is an abiding necessity in all societies and that, as a result of stamping out Jewish usury, the king would in effect be causing a revival of Christian usury. Now, as Jewish usury was in fact eliminated in England and northern France, it seems highly likely that a factor in this elimination was some kind of revival of Christian lending that made the Jews dispensable.

This danger notwithstanding, it has been suggested throughout this book that the Jewish contributions to the economic development of medieval western Christendom were considerable, whether in the earlier period of specialization in trade or in the later period of specialization in moneylending or in the yet later period of multiple contributions to the lagging economy of the northeastern areas of Europe. At the same time, these limited economic specializations enabled the Jews to implant themselves successfully in the most exciting areas of the Western world at that time. Developing the adaptability to explore and exploit new niches in an ever-changing economy is no mean achievement. Thus, the tendency to dismiss Jewish economic prowess in medieval western Christendom simply on the grounds of a lack of diversification misses the mark.

Yet another area of Jewish achievement lay in the sphere of political organization and activity. Here again, there has been a facile tendency to dismiss the Jews of medieval western Christendom as hopelessly maladroit in their political insight and skill. They were, after all, ultimately unable to sustain themselves in the more advanced areas of medieval western Christendom. Once again, however, such a conclusion seems simplistic. The challenges to successful Jewish life were, as we have seen, enormous. The Jews of medieval western Christendom exhibited considerable sensitivity to the structures and forces impacting them and considerable organizational and negotiating skill.

The Jews whose history we have been reconstructing were hardly unaware of the complex circumstances within which they found themselves. They were exquisitely attuned to the negative forces of ecclesiastical pressure and popular opinion; they were likewise aware of the potential for governmental oppression. These Jews understood the complex network of authority – both lay and ecclesiastical – in medieval western Christendom and knew which authority to address under diverse circumstances. Church leadership could be appealed to in some instances; in other situations, it was the lay leadership to which Jewish concerns had to be brought. In some cases, especially in the south, small numbers of Jews actually had access to the secular courts and thus were in a direct position to know the complexities of power; in other areas, Jewish knowledge was circumscribed, but meaningful nonetheless.

Besides comprehending the complexities of power on the medieval scene, the Jews also had to be able to mobilize themselves for productive negotiation with the outside environment and for effective control of internal Jewish affairs, and this too seems to have been by and large achieved. As noted, the Jews of medieval western Christendom lacked the traditional local structures of the older Jewish communities of the Muslim sphere and – even more strikingly – the centralized authorities that had developed in both Palestine and Mesopotamia.

Nonetheless, the Jews of medieval western Christendom were successful in fashioning their own local and eventually more extended
internal communal authorities.[14]

At the local level, effective agencies and procedures were developed, although this development cannot be traced in requisite detail.
There was considerable drive in the direction of shared community authority, with all members of the community contributing and
participating. At the same time, there was also a tendency toward oli-
garchy, with the wealthiest members of the community contributing
most heavily and therefore accorded fullest power. Yet another power
element in the community was the Jewish religious leadership, which
bore potent authority. With the passage of time, the local Jewish
communities began to develop a sense of the importance of banding
together in the face of the accelerating tendency to larger governmental units in such areas as Spain, northern France, England, and Poland.
More wide-ranging Jewish organizational structures were needed to
meet the parallel tendencies toward centralization in majority society.

The first responsibility of the Jewish communal agencies was to
negotiate with the non-Jewish authorities both lay and ecclesiastical
on behalf of the Jews. The Jews of medieval western Christendom
were treated by the secular authorities as a collective, and as a collective they regularly made necessary overtures to these secular authorities. Efforts had to be made to arouse the ruling class to its responsibility for Jewish safety and security. We have noted a fascinating instance
of Jewish leadership endangering itself by remaining in Mainz during the onset of the Third Crusade in order to carry on negotiations
with the secular and ecclesiastical leadership of German society and
have seen that, in this instance, the Jewish efforts were successful.
The Jewish communal leadership also had to negotiate the tax bur-
den borne by the community, which was in many ways the key to
governmental support for Jewish life.

In addition to negotiating with the non-Jewish world, the Jewish
self-governing apparatus had the further responsibility of directing
and ordering internal Jewish affairs. This responsibility was multi-
faceted. Perhaps the first element in this internal control was erection of an effective system for assessing and collecting taxes. As
noted recurrently, Jewish taxes constituted a key element in the all-
important relationship between the Jews and their rulers. For the
purposes of taxation, as for so much else, the Jews were treated as
a collective. The external authorities anticipated revenue assessed by

the Jews upon themselves and collected through internal mechanisms. To be sure, the funds realized through this internal system of assessment and collection were in large measure delivered to the external authorities; in part, however, they provided the fuel with which the internal mechanisms of Jewish life were powered.

Yet another vital element in the system of Jewish self-rule was an independent Jewish judicial system. Such a system was of great significance to the Jews of medieval western Christendom, in part for practical reasons and in part for religious reasons. In practical terms, Jews were deeply fearful of the treatment that might be meted out by ecclesiastical and municipal courts. In religious terms, the Jewish court system constituted a critical element in the totality of the system of talmudic law under which they sought to live. Thus, Jewish courts were a desideratum, and we have noted recurrently governmental charters that promised such judicial independence to the Jews. These promises of judicial independence are especially notable in charters that attempted to attract Jewish settlers to a given territory or town.

Beyond taxation and justice, the Jewish community was responsible for providing its members with all requisite social, educational, and religious resources. Medieval western Christendom, organized around the Christian vision, saw the provision of social and educational services – as well as religious services – as vested in the Church. There were no neutral social or educational structures. Thus, the Jewish communal organization, which obviously was responsible for providing requisite religious services, was equally responsible for social and educational services as well. Indeed, the Jewish communities of medieval western Christendom took great pride in the effectiveness of their social and educational systems. In their polemical engagement with the Christian environment, Jewish authors recurrently contrast the excellence of Jewish social and educational services with the alleged lack of such well-organized and well-delivered services in the surrounding Christian majority environment.[15]

Faced with this daunting range of responsibilities, the Jewish communities of medieval western Christendom created a structure that rested on a number of different foundations. In large measure, these foundations lay in Jewish tradition. For these medieval Jews, determined to live their lives in accordance with Jewish law, acceptance of communal authority was as much a part of that law as any other religious obligation. Flaunting the authoritative dictates of the communal leadership constituted a major breach of Jewish law and deserved religious condemnation. At the same time, there was a strong sense of the need for internal unity in the face of a hostile environment. In social terms, the Jewish community could ill afford a breach in solidarity, and the need for solidarity was often cited when communal leaders encountered contentious issues. Finally, Jewish unity was a desideratum for the secular authorities of medieval western Christendom as well. The smooth functioning of the Jewish community meant maximum tranquility and maximum advantage from the Jews; internal frictions could only disrupt. Thus, the secular authorities generally stood fully behind the leadership of the Jewish community for their own advantage. A system rooted in religious obligation, social need, and the support of the ruling authorities was a powerfully grounded system.

These foundations for communal solidarity brought two major Jewish groupings to the fore within the Jewish communities of medieval Latin Christendom. The religious roots of community life projected the rabbis into positions of leadership. Given that acceptance of communal authority was a requirement of Jewish law, the religious leadership within the community had to occupy a place of prominence. The need for social solidarity and the support of the Christian ruling class brought a different group to the fore, the elite of wealth and influence. The elite of wealth exercised power within the Jewish community because of the economic and social influence that wealth conveyed. At the same time, it was precisely the same elite of wealth that was most likely to enjoy real contact with the non-Jewish courts. Generally, the two elites – those of religious learning and of wealth and power – cooperated effectively. Sometimes, they were identical; sometimes, they were bound by familial or marriage ties. On occasion, disagreements could and did develop.

As governance in medieval western Christendom developed, the Jews had to become aware of accelerating tendencies toward centralization and of the need to create agencies that would unite a number of communities for more effective negotiation with the outside world and for more effective exercise of internal Jewish authority. In some instances, such as the Iberian peninsula, this move to more centralized Jewish authority was fostered by the non-Jewish authorities. Rulers began to appoint chief rabbis who could serve as intermediaries between the royal courts and the Jewish communities of Aragon and Castile. In the north, the tendency was in the direction of internal Jewish recognition of the need for centralization and internal

Jewish structuring of agencies that would promote such centralized effort.

Thus, the Jews of medieval western Christendom, lacking powerful traditions of internal authority, created effective agencies and theories of self-government. This capacity to organize capably to meet the ramified needs of the Jewish minority was yet another major success of our period. Again, these agencies of Jewish self-government were not strong enough to preclude the deterioration that afflicted Jewish life during the latter centuries of our period; they did, however, much enhance the quality of Jewish life during the medieval centuries and constituted an important legacy left by the Jews of medieval Latin Christendom to their successors.

THE DYNAMICS OF DETERIORATION

Jewish achievements in finding a place in western Christendom were real and impressive. The first two centuries of our period show rich creativity on the part of the Jews and their royal and baronial sponsors in making this transfer in Jewish life possible. At the same time, it is clear from the foregoing surveys that this period of creativity was limited and was succeeded in the more advanced areas of western Christendom by serious deterioration of Jewish circumstances. As noted recurrently, by the year 1500 the more advanced western areas of Latin Christendom had removed their Jews entirely. Jewish life was shunted off to sectors of Italy in the south and to Germany and eastern Europe in the north, areas in which economic need made the Jews still highly useful.

The closing question to be raised in this chapter concerns the dynamics of this deterioration. In addressing this question, we shall utilize the framework already established, which posited three critical elements in majority society: the Roman Catholic Church, the populace at large, and the ruling authorities. These three elements constituted complex realities and cannot be simply defined or analyzed. In the first place, each one was hardly monolithic. Church leadership was exercised at many levels, ranging from the papacy at the top of the pyramid to the parish priest and popular preacher at the bottom. The populace was likewise multi-dimensional, ranging from wealthy townsmen to impoverished rural serfs. The same was true for the ruling class, with its emperors, kings, dukes, counts, and petty nobles. In all three cases, there was considerable local variability as well. Moreover, there was substantial interplay among the three elements. The populace and the ruling class were deeply influenced by the teachings of the ecclesiastical leadership; churchmen and rulers shared the aspirations and fears of the populace; the drive of the rulers of medieval western Christendom generally derived considerable support from both the Church and the people at large. Nonetheless, despite these caveats, tracking these three elements in relation to the Jews will facilitate our understanding of the process of deterioration.

The deterioration of Jewish circumstances has long been recognized among historians of medieval western Christendom in general and historians of medieval Jewry in western Christendom in particular.[16] There is a broad consensus that the roots of the process of deterioration can be traced to the twelfth century, with the process itself then stretching out through the ensuing centuries. More precisely, the deterioration is initially obvious in northwestern Europe in the thirteenth century, beginning with the downturn palpable in northern France and England and culminating in the expulsions of 1290 and 1306. Deterioration in the German lands began to be felt in the rampant violence of the late thirteenth and fourteenth centuries. Deterioration in the southern sectors of Europe is less easy to specify. In southern France, it was simply part and parcel of the broader developments that affected all of France, but were centered out of Paris. Italy felt, throughout the Middle Ages, a complex combination of influences. On the Iberian peninsula, the wide-ranging violence of 1391 signaled the onset of serious deterioration, although considerable reconstruction can be charted between 1391 and 1492.

A number of explanations for the deterioration have been suggested, including changing ecclesiastical perceptions of Judaism and the Jews, the accelerating rationalism stressed by western Christendom's intelligentsia, and the intensifying religious doubt felt by many in Latin Christendom combined with the Jewish role in feeding such doubt.[17] There is considerable truth in all of these explanations, but I would like to suggest a variant approach that – to an extent – incorporates them all. This approach highlights popular and ecclesiastical attitudes, which I would suggest were often closely linked; more specifically, this approach focuses upon ecclesiastical and popular fears and anxieties. In turn, these fears and anxieties were sometimes shared by the ruling class and sometimes merely exploited by those in power.[18]

Perhaps the most striking characteristic of vitalized western Christendom was its aggressiveness. From the eleventh century onward, Latin Christendom committed itself to a push outward against those it perceived to be its enemies. This aggressiveness cut across all elements of society and resulted in significant conquests at the expense of the major rival blocs – the Islamic world and Byzantium. Before too long, the aggressiveness was turned inward as well, with concern developing especially in the Church over signs of heterodoxy. Scholars have recently debated the reality of heresy in medieval western Christendom and have concluded that the pursuit of heresy tells us as much about the orthodox majority as about the allegedly heterodox minority; in fact, it may tell us more about the former than about the latter.[19] In any case, both the Church and the populace at large became deeply concerned with enemies outside western Christendom and inside it as well.

The concern with external and internal enemies posed serious dangers to the Jewish minority. Defined traditionally as enemies of Jesus and the faith he founded, the Jews were in a position to be stigmatized as enemies *par excellence*, and that in fact did happen. The Church began to identify the many dangers that allegedly emanated from the Jewish enemies and to take requisite steps to combat these dangers. Ecclesiastical policies grounded in perceptions of Jewish threat began to proliferate. On another level and in alternative ways, the folk took over these notions and expanded upon them. During the assaults accompanying the First Crusade, the enmity of the Jews was projected in historic terms, that is to say in their rejection of Jesus and responsibility for his death. Very quickly, however, this perception of historic enmity was transposed into more damaging twelfth-century perceptions of here-and-now hostility on the part of the Jews and the omnipresent dangers they presented. The combination of the sense of historic Jewish enmity and a European environment focused on enmities and their impact was lethal. Ecclesiastical leadership fostered this imagery; the populace embellished it; many in the ruling class shared it; others in the ruling class exploited it.

The direct result of this imagery was wide-ranging fear and hatred of the Jews, eventuating in recurrent violence. Our surveys revealed wide-ranging violence from the eleventh century onward, rooted in the perceptions of the Jews as dangerous enemies of Christian society and the Christian populace. To be sure, this violence reflected a low level of governance as well. Effective governments were capable of protecting their Jews and maintaining law and order. We have noted areas of Europe in which governance was generally weak, and in those areas anti-Jewish violence was a recurring feature of Jewish life almost throughout our period.

In areas of western Christendom where governance was effective, the impact of the anti-Jewish imagery was more complex. There were a number of negative possibilities in such areas. First of all, to the extent that rulers came to share the anti-Jewish imagery in either its ecclesiastical or popular format, Jewish fate was sealed. Jews would be limited in accord with stringent ecclesiastical demands or would be subject to removal altogether, on the grounds that they were unwilling to live by the rules governing their behavior in Christian society. Such seems to have been the situation of the Jews of France under St. Louis, for example.

There remained yet more complicated outcomes of anti-Jewish perceptions. One was the exploitation of Jews increasingly dependent upon their protectors. This exploitation could and did lead to a bankrupting of the Jews, thus rendering them useless to their rulers. This seems to have been the fate of the Jews of England under Henry III, leading ultimately to the banishment of the Jews from England. Yet another outcome involved the decision to curry ecclesiastical and popular favor through anti-Jewish actions. Many of the expulsions of the latter centuries of our period seem to have been rooted in the desire of rulers to win the plaudits of the Church and their followers by ridding their domains of "the Jewish enemy."[20]

The deterioration of Jewish circumstances was hardly simple. At work was a fusion of traditional imagery, an aggressive and anxious society, a powerful and concerned Church, a frightened populace, and a ruling class with multiple motivations. The deterioration of Jewish circumstances, especially in the most advanced areas of medieval Latin Christendom, was conditioned by these complex realities. The fact of this deterioration was to affect Jewish life well beyond the confines of our period.

SPIRITUAL CHALLENGES, SUCCESSES, AND FAILURES

•

The Jews in medieval western Christendom have often been portrayed as having lived comfortably (or sometimes uncomfortably) isolated lives, having maintained their ancestral faith effortlessly, and having pursued their traditional culture with a high level of equanimity and unanimity. While it is acknowledged that Jews living in the medieval Muslim sphere were fully conversant with the culture surrounding them and were deeply influenced by that culture, the Jews of western Christendom have often been projected as removed from the broad majority ambience, unchallenged in their Jewishness, and sustained solely by their own cultural heritage.[1] In fact, this beguiling picture is highly inaccurate. The Jews of medieval western Christendom were very much a part of the social and cultural ambience in which they lived, encountered a creative majority milieu seething with new ideas and ideals, and were profoundly challenged by their dynamic environment.[2]

While both majority and minority religious leadership attempted to limit Christian–Jewish social contact, three factors militated against truly effective isolation of the Jews in medieval western Christendom – demography, economics, and language. The towns of medieval western Christendom were very small by modern standards, and the Jewish communities housed in these small towns were minuscule. We recall Benjamin's portrayal of a few hundred Jews at most in the urban enclaves of northern Spain and southern France that he visited. In such small towns with their tiny Jewish communities, there could be no true isolation of the Jews as desired by both the

Church hierarchy and the Jewish leadership. Moreover, the economic circumstances of the Jews reinforced the tendency toward considerable Christian–Jewish contact. As noted, the Jewish economy was anything but variegated; Jews tended to cluster in a limited number of economic specializations. Such specialization meant that Jews served the needs of the non-Jewish population and in turn required a wide range of goods and services from the Christian majority. Such reciprocal needs obviated a high level of isolation.[3]

Finally, the linguistic factor reinforced the tendency toward integration of the Jews. Jews regularly spoke the language of the majority environment.[4] To be sure, in medieval western Christendom – unlike the Islamic sphere – the spoken language differed from the written language, and the Jews did not use Latin, the written majority language, for their cultural pursuits. Nonetheless, mastery of the local spoken idiom is obvious. Jacob ben Reuben portrays himself as exiled from his home community and befriended by a learned Christian, with no sense of any difficulty in establishing such cordial ties and discussing complex issues of religious truth. The Barcelona disputation of 1263, involving the formerly Jewish Friar Paul and the rabbi of Gerona, Moses ben Nahman, took place in the presence of a multitude of Christians and Jews, with the two protagonists understanding each other readily and both elements of the audience following the proceedings with no difficulty. Full Jewish mastery of the majority spoken language meant ready familiarity with the cultural changes taking place within majority society.

One more possibility with respect to Jewish engagement within medieval western Christian society should be raised, and that involves the oft-noted distinction between the areas of the south, where Jews had long lived and had established deep roots, and the rapidly developing areas of the north, where Jewish presence was new and has often been portrayed as isolated. One of the gauges of greater Jewish distance from majority culture often adduced is the militant Jewish rejection of conversion in the face of the crusader assaults of 1096.[5] In fact, however, the Jews of the north settled rather quickly into their new environment and adopted for themselves the language of the majority. The early intellectual giant of the new northern Jewry, the eleventh-century Solomon ben Isaac of Troyes, author of monumental commentaries on the Hebrew Bible and the Babylonian Talmud, regularly explains difficult terminology in both commentaries by citing the Old French equivalents for problematic Hebrew or Aramaic expressions. The militant Jewish rejection of crusader calls to baptism by no means proves the distancing of these northern Jews from their environment. To the contrary, it shows these Jews very much caught up in the religious exhilaration of their environment.[6] Both the older Jewish communities of the south and the younger Jewish communities of the north were deeply embedded in their milieus. To be sure, the Jews of the south were more deeply ensconced in their majority environment, as will be reflected recurrently in this chapter. However, neither the Jews of the south nor the Jews of the north were truly distanced from their Christian surroundings.[7]

The Jewish polemicists whom we shall shortly discuss attempted to portray the Christian society in which they found themselves as intellectually and morally inferior. As a polemical ploy, this tactic is entirely understandable; it should not, however, be taken as historically accurate. We well know that medieval western Christendom, from the eleventh century on, embarked on rapid and impressive change in every sphere, from the technological and economic through the intellectual and spiritual. Integrated into this dynamic environment, the Jews of western Christendom were deeply challenged by developments around them.

The first and most overt challenge involved maintaining Jewish faith. Again, while the medieval Jewish polemicists we shall encounter attempted to create for their Jewish readers the sense that Christianity as a religious alternative was contemptible and unthinkable, in fact the lure of Christendom and Christianity was considerable. It was, after all, the vigor and vitality of western Christendom that drew Jews to immigrate; this vigor and vitality extended beyond the realm of the economic and political. Jews had to be impressed with the achievements of Christian society and thus by extension of Christianity as well, although denigration of at least some of those achievements was important – as we shall see – for maintenance of Jewish identity. More directly and more tellingly, the Jews of western Christendom were subjected to powerful conversionist pressures, aimed at separating them from their ancestral community and faith. New techniques for confronting Jews with Christian truth claims were introduced, and new lines of argumentation were essayed. Given the fundamental appeal of a dynamic majority society and the organized missionizing campaign of the Roman Catholic Church, maintenance of Jewish identity was hardly simple. Jewish leaders had to formulate for their followers persuasive arguments for maintaining Jewish identity;

perhaps more important, the institutions of the Jewish community and the Jewish family had to reinforce Jewish identity and belongingness creatively.

There was a second, and subtler challenge faced by the Jews of western Christendom, a challenge that again flowed from the rapid development of majority civilization in medieval western Christendom. As noted, the period between 1000 and 1500 saw remarkable advances in every facet of European culture. Jews could hardly remain oblivious to the cultural evolution taking place around them. This cultural evolution challenged the Jews of western Christendom to evaluate and adapt their own cultural and religious traditions to the new developments taking place in their milieu. Faced with an exciting majority culture, the Jews of Europe could ill afford to allow their own cultural legacy to lag. They had to exercise their creativity to reassure themselves of the ultimate superiority of their own tradition. Of course, the pressure for such Jewish creativity was a function of the level of majority achievement. In those areas in which Christian cultural creativity was prominent, such as southern and northwestern Europe, the goad to Jewish cultural innovation and creativity was strongest; where Christian creativity was less prominent, such as north-central and northeastern Europe, the pressures for Jewish cultural innovation and achievement were considerably weaker.

The rapid cultural and spiritual evolution of western Christendom and the profound challenge it posed eventuated in a fundamental reshaping of Jewish culture and religion. New understandings of Christianity – in fact of religion in the broadest sense – emerged in medieval western Christendom, often culminating in intense dispute over truth and falsehood, over acceptable and prohibited views, over orthodoxy and heresy. While much of this rethinking took place within the institutional framework of the Roman Catholic Church, the Jewish minority was nonetheless deeply affected by the vigorous new spiritual currents palpable in majority society. Just as the majority was reshaping Christianity in a variety of directions, so too was the Jewish minority challenged to undertake its own search for new forms of Jewish culture and the deeper meanings of Jewish faith.

The missionizing campaign mounted by the Church was external and obvious. Jews could readily recognize this externally imposed threat and were forced to mobilize their resources to combat it. While there was some disagreement as to the tactics that would prove most effective, the level of consensus engendered by an obvious external danger was considerable. The subtler challenge – the challenge of majority cultural creativity and thus the challenge to reshape the essentials of Jewish culture and faith – was less overtly threatening, and thus more difficult to engage; it entailed significant changes on the internal scene and thus occasioned far more discord than did the externally imposed proselytizing onslaught. The Jews of western Christendom were deeply divided in their reactions to the broad cultural challenge they faced. Some Jews felt that internal reform had to be undertaken in order to rebuff the challenges posed by their dynamic Christian environment; others felt that embracing the innovative weakened Jews as they sought to mobilize themselves against the dangerous external pressures. When large-scale conversion did take place, in Spain in the late thirteenth and fourteenth centuries, proponents of internal change called for intensification of their efforts, while more traditional voices argued that acceptance of the new had paved the way for massive defection. In sum, the period we are studying was hardly one of tranquility and unanimity. The pressures were diverse and intense; the Jewish reactions had to be creative and multi-faceted; inevitably, the Jewish communities of western Christendom were factionalized by differences of opinion as to how best they might respond to the spiritual challenges posed by their dynamic environment.

The successes depicted in the preceding chapter resulted from the cooperative efforts of the Christian majority – or at least parts of it – and the Jewish minority to foster Jewish life in medieval western Christendom. The challenges to be analyzed in this chapter had to be met by the Jews alone. In combating these challenges, the Jews were very much on their own. The majority could not be an ally; it was in fact the adversary. The spiritual challenges were every bit as profound as the material challenges already discussed. As was true in the material sphere, so too culturally and spiritually the record is mixed, involving a combination of successes and failures. Once again, no simple reckoning will do justice to the complexities of Jewish life in medieval western Christendom.

PROSELYTIZING, CONVERSION, AND RESISTANCE

As noted earlier, Christianity was from its beginnings a missionizing faith, indeed a missionizing faith with a history of remarkable

successes. Effective proselytizing led to the christianization of the
Roman Empire; effective proselytizing transformed all of medieval
Europe, both the southern and the northern tiers, into a Christian
society. The issue of missionizing among the Jews was, for the
Church, by no means simple. The record of proselytizing success
among the Jews was quite unimpressive, suggesting that the effort
was hardly worth pursuing. At the same time, there remained potent
reasons for continued outreach to the Jews. In part, the record of
failure itself spurred the desire to try yet once more – successful missionizing among the Jews, with their lengthy history of recalcitrance,
would constitute a signal achievement; in part, the dangers seemingly
posed by unconverted Jews warranted the effort; in part, proselytizing among the Jews reflected deep yearnings for homogeneity within
western Christendom.

Since there was no significant Jewish presence in western
Christendom prior to the end of the first Christian millennium,
no major proselytizing efforts are recorded from that early period.
As Jewish presence in western Christendom increased, it was almost
inevitable that missionizing activity would begin, at first informally
and then more formally. From the 1160s and 1170s we have our first
Jewish sources that suggest informal but significant Christian religious
pressures being exerted upon the Jews of western Christendom. The
earliest of these Jewish anti-Christian polemical works, the *Sefer ha-
Berit* of Joseph Kimhi of Narbonne, presents itself as a response to
a student's request for guidance. The tone of the work suggests that
the pressures that sparked the compilation of anti-Christian arguments were quite serious.[8]

The slightly later *Milḥamot ha-Shem* of the unknown Jacob ben
Reuben, probably written in northern Spain, sets itself in a somewhat more exotic framework. As noted, Jacob claims to have been
exiled from his home Jewish community and to have been befriended
in his place of refuge by a prominent and learned Christian. The
two seem to have studied together amicably enough. At some point,
the learned and friendly Christian challenged his Jewish associate
with a simple and direct argument. The Christian claimed that the
contrasting circumstances of Christians and Jews, with the former
increasingly powerful and the latter sinking into ever-deeper degradation, suggest convincingly that God has favored the Christians
and abandoned the Jews. This claim galvanized Jacob to undertake
an extensive examination of the Christian–Jewish debate.[9] It is not

at all surprising that these first two Jewish anti-Christian polemical works should have been composed in southern France and northern Spain, the scene of intense and successful efforts to push back the forces of Islam and likewise home to considerable Jewish and Muslim minorities that recommended themselves as proselytizing targets.

Christian missionizing efforts quickly proceeded from the informal to the formal. By the middle decades of the thirteenth century, casual argumentation had given way to a well-organized campaign to win over Jews. The first major element in this new program was considerable ecclesiastical investment in language training. On occasion, learned Jews who converted brought with them knowledge of Hebrew and access to the treasures of the Jewish tradition. At the same time, an increasingly militant Church invested in Hebrew and Arabic language training for missionizing personnel. A second element in the new campaign involved the development of avenues for confronting Jews and Muslims with proselytizing arguments. Jews and Muslims living within western Christendom and under Christian rule were forced to make themselves available for missionizing sermons and debates. To be sure, this aspect to the campaign required government backing. Those authorities under whose jurisdiction Jews and Muslims lived were asked to force attendance at these sermons and debates, and some of them did. Jewish spokesmen complained bitterly of this innovation, arguing that it contravened the basic rights of Jews to live as Jews, so long guaranteed by the Church. To this, the Church leadership replied that forced attendance at sermons and debates did not constitute a violation of Jewish rights, since no coercion on religious faith was being exerted. Jews were merely being forced to hear Christian teachings; they were not being forced to accept those teachings. The choice of religious identity remained with the Jewish auditors, despite their forced attendance. Finally, new methods of argumentation were developed, with a special focus on utilization of rabbinic literature to prove to Jews that their own spiritual leaders had – knowingly or unknowingly – acknowledged Christian truth.

What were the major lines of Christian argumentation, conducted on either the informal or formal level? The most common Christian argument involved the claim that the Hebrew Bible, when read simply and properly, attests in very obvious ways to the truth of Christianity. Especially marked is the emphasis on Jesus' fulfillment of messianic prophecies. This argument can be traced back into the very earliest strata of Christian literature, the epistles of Paul and the Gospels; with the passage of time, it was expanded and embellished considerably. From earliest days, the assertion that Jesus' mission was foretold by the prophets of Israel was an important element in Christian truth claims directed at a variety of audiences. We recall that, for Augustine, Jewish attestation to the truth of the Hebrew Bible was so important as to constitute one of the prime reasons for maintaining Jews within Christian society. For debating with Jews, these claims rooted in the Hebrew Bible were key. Christians felt that Jews, who treasured the Hebrew Bible and knew it well, should have been particularly responsive to this line of argumentation.

While claims rooted in the Hebrew Bible are the most obvious element in Christian missionizing claims, other lines of argumentation were cultivated as well. Fairly early on, Christianity made its peace with Greco-Roman philosophy and contended that philosophic principles – alongside biblical proof-texts – incontrovertibly prove Christian truth. To be sure, the philosophic temper waxed and waned in Christendom of late antiquity and the early Middle Ages. By the twelfth century, however, philosophic inclinations reasserted themselves in western Christendom, and it became important to show that Christian truth and philosophic truth were one and the same. Thus, philosophic considerations began to find their place in the Christian–Jewish debate.

There was a third line of argumentation – again old but rejuvenated in medieval western Christendom – that was especially distressing to the Jews. This was the argument from observable realities, meaning specifically the successes of Christendom and the downtrodden state of the Jews. As noted, this is the argument that purportedly launched the early *Milḥamot ha-Shem* of Jacob ben Reuben. Almost all medieval Jewish polemical works accord a central role to this line of empirical argumentation.[10] What was especially problematic in this line of argumentation was its psychological impact. Jews could by no means deny the reality of Jewish degradation and at least some measure of Christian success. What they had to do was to challenge the interpretation of this contrast. However, the contrast in and of itself was distressing to Jews, and embedding it at the heart of the Christian–Jewish debate meant introducing this distress into the give-and-take of polemical exchange. This was, from the Jewish perspective, an especially problematic line of Christian argumentation.

The formalized missionizing campaign that began in the middle decades of the thirteenth century continued to pursue these pre-existent lines of argumentation; at the same time, it developed a new approach as well. This innovation seems to have been the contribution of a fairly learned convert from Judaism to Christianity, named Saul as a Jew and Paul as a Christian. Subsequent to conversion, Paul joined the Dominican Order, which was committed to purging Christian society of heresy and to expanding the ranks of Christians through missionizing activity. Friar Paul won the support of his Dominican confreres and began his preaching to the Jews in southern France, the area in which he was born and grew up. In 1263, he engineered, with broad Dominican support and the backing of King James I of Aragon, a public missionizing engagement in Barcelona with the distinguished rabbi of Gerona, Moses ben Nahman. Subsequently, Friar Paul made his way northward and, again with Dominican support, won the backing of King Louis IX of France for a similar engagement in Paris with a number of northern-French rabbis.[11]

Friar Paul, as both a former Jew and a convert to Christianity, recognized the centrality of the Hebrew Bible to the Christian–Jewish debate. He also knew, from his Jewish experience, that Christian argumentation from biblical verses encountered a powerful tradition of Jewish counter-exegesis. Jews had long been inured to Christian exegetical claims and had a rich exegetical tradition of their own. This led Friar Paul to propose that a close look at rabbinic understanding of the Hebrew Bible would show that the rabbis of old, wittingly or unwittingly, supported Christian claims. This approach – the argument that traditional Jewish exegesis or indeed free-standing rabbinic dicta support Christian truth claims – stands at the core of Friar Paul's argumentation in both Barcelona and Paris.

This line of Christian argumentation had at least three benefits. First, newness itself was an advantage. In a debate that had gone on for more than a millennium, an innovative line of argumentation was in and of itself an achievement. Secondly, attempting to prove Christianity from rabbinic sources in effect removed the truth of Christianity from dispute. The very worst outcome of confrontations with rabbis might be that Christian truth could not be proven from Jewish sources. Such an outcome would of course have no impact on Christians and would represent no discredit to the Christian faith. Finally, it was surely dispiriting for Jews to have rabbinic sources cited by a knowledgeable Dominican preacher.

Using this innovative argumentation, Friar Paul set out to argue in Barcelona that: (1) the Messiah predicted in Hebrew Scriptures had already arrived; (2) that Messiah was predicted to be both human and divine; (3) that Messiah was predicted to suffer and die; (4) with the arrival of the promised Messiah, Jewish law was intended to lose its validity. While the style of argumentation was new, the contentions to be proven were utterly traditional.

We hear of no conversionist successes associated with the preaching and disputing of Friar Paul. This did not lead the Dominican Order to repudiate his new initiative, however. Another Dominican (this time not Jewish by birth), Friar Raymond Martin, expanded and refined the innovative tack taken by Friar Paul in a monumental missionizing guide called the *Pugio fidei*. The *Pugio fidei* addresses the broadest possible range of theological issues and presents thousands of rabbinic sources to show purported rabbinic espousal of Christian doctrine. Friar Raymond presents the rabbinic texts in their original language and then offers scrupulously accurate translations into Latin. These texts and the arguments derived from them were intended to be utilized by Dominican preachers in their sermons to Jews.

The early fifteenth century saw yet another major forced disputation, this time held in Tortosa. Once more, it was a learned convert who led the Christian initiative. The Tortosa disputation differed from the earlier Barcelona and Paris disputations in a number of ways. Perhaps most important was the mood of the Jews assembled to hear the argumentation. The Tortosa disputation took place in the wake of the devastating attacks of 1391, at a point when Jewish morale on the Iberian peninsula had reached its nadir. In addition, the Tortosa disputation was far more focused. Over a two-year period, it addressed one issue only – the traditional Christian claim that the Messiah has already come. To be sure, this focused issue had a number of important corollaries – especially the role of Jesus himself as Messiah and the implication that, since the Messiah has already appeared, Jewish circumstances had become utterly hopeless. Finally, whereas there is no evidence of Jewish conversion in the wake of the Barcelona and Paris disputations, the Tortosa disputation was accompanied by significant bursts of conversion.

What were the major lines of Jewish rebuttal of the Christian claims, both traditional and innovative?[12] Since argumentation from biblical verses was central to the Christian case, let us begin with that claim and its Jewish rejection. Jews simply contested each and every verse adduced by Christians. At the same time, there were some general emphases regularly introduced. The first involved appeal to the Hebrew text of the Bible. Jews were deeply cognizant of Christian reliance on the Latin translation of Jerome and attacked that translation regularly. Secondly, Jews emphasized the importance of context, arguing that many of the Christian readings took key verses out of their immediate setting. Finally, Jewish polemicists disputed Christian emphasis on figurative reading of the Hebrew Bible, insisting instead on the literal sense of the biblical passages.

As noted, the innovative argumentation that appeared toward the middle of the thirteenth century built on the older reliance on biblical verses. Fully cognizant of the rich Jewish tradition of biblical exegesis, Friar Paul and those who followed him urged that rabbinic interpretation of biblical verses reveals Jewish acknowledgement of Christian truths. Again, the Jewish response was to contest each and every citation of a rabbinic text, with the argument that the rabbinic text was misquoted or misinterpreted. In a real sense, the new Christian argumentation elicited the same kind of dogged Jewish rejection as the older claims made directly from biblical verses.

The second line of Christian argumentation involved invocation of reason. Fairly standard cases were made that specific human needs required the incarnation of the divine or that the doctrine of a triune God was in fact not a contradiction of reason. Here Jewish polemicists both defended the traditional Jewish positions and went on the offensive against Christianity. Jews felt that the doctrines of Incarnation and Trinity were rationally indefensible. Jews were aware that Christians themselves had grave difficulties with these doctrines. Whereas for Christians these difficulties translated into massive endeavors to make the doctrines intelligible, for Jews the difficulties were utterly insurmountable, could not be explained away, and constituted irrefutable evidence of the irrationality of Christianity. For many Jewish polemicists, the doctrine of the Trinity was so absurd as to be laughable. The doctrine of Incarnation – much more important to the Jewish polemical enterprise – was not made the butt of humor; rather, for many Jewish polemicists this doctrine involved a blasphemous attack on the majesty of the Almighty.[13]

The Christian argument that Jews often found most troubling involved the contrast between Christian ascendancy and Jewish decline, understood to reflect divine embrace of Christianity and Christians and divine rejection of Judaism and the Jews. This argument had psychological impact, troubling Jews by pointing in painful directions. On the intellectual level, Jews responded by appealing, first of all, to their broad sense of the past. Jews had, over the ages, encountered great and successful empires, for example the Babylonians, the Persians, and the Greeks. Christians acknowledged that, in all these cases, worldly success did not imply theological truth. For Jews, the same was the case for Christianity as well. Christian material successes by no means implied religious truth.

This general appeal to history elided into a serious and focused attack on the achievements of Christianity, which addressed both the intellectual element and some of the psychological distress. This attack involved, at one level, consideration of the achievements of Jesus himself as purported Messiah. Contending that all biblical prophecy envisaged a redeemer who would wield remarkable earthly power, Jewish polemicists contended that Jesus showed no such worldly power; they argued that Jesus' career had involved recurrent instances of weakness and trepidation, culminating in ignominious death rather than far-reaching victories. While the spread of the religion founded by Jesus was impressive to an extent, Jewish polemicists argued that it did not reach the world-wide proportions predicted by the biblical prophets for messianic redemption. During the late twelfth and thirteenth centuries, as setbacks to crusading in the Holy Land became increasingly obvious, Jewish polemicists began to invoke Muslim power and achievement and the specific turbulence in the Holy Land to further argue the failures of Christianity.[14]

To be sure, all this questioning of Christian achievement still left the difficult issue of Jewish suffering. Diverse traditional views were invoked by Jewish authors. Most significantly, Jewish suffering was projected as a test of commitment, along the lines of divine testing of Abraham. Jewish steadfastness in the face of difficulties and suffering – that is to say maintenance of the legacy of Abraham and his son Isaac – would serve as indication to God of unshakeable loyalty and would eventually result in splendid reward.[15] Yet another biblical image appropriated by Jewish polemicists was that of Isaiah's Suffering Servant. Like that figure, the Jews too were – it was argued – exposed to groundless hatred and abuse, but theirs would be the rich reward promised by the prophet. Invocation of the figures of Abraham, Isaac, and Isaiah's Suffering Servant are doubly interesting in that they reflect a Jewish challenge to Christian claims on these biblical images. For Christians, God himself sacrificed his beloved son, as had Abraham; for Jews, it was the Jewish people who recurrently emulated Abraham's sacrifice of those nearest and dearest. For Christians, Jesus was the figure groundlessly despised and persecuted; for Jews, that figure was the people descended from the prophet Isaiah, the Jewish people.

Defense against Christian philosophical argumentation often elided into attacks on Christianity; defense against Christian claims rooted in Christian successes and Jewish failures likewise often evolved into assaults on the reality of Christian achievement. The line between defensive and offensive argumentation was necessarily porous. In some instances, Jewish polemicists went directly onto the offensive. Such thoroughly offensive thrusts are particularly noteworthy in two areas. The first involved Jewish knowledge and criticism of the New Testament. As a minority group, Jews were familiar with the central symbols of their majority neighbors. Translations of the New Testament emerged in the medieval Jewish world, largely as a vehicle for criticizing vigorously the ruling faith. Contradictions within the Gospels were noted and highlighted; Jesus' behaviors and teaching were subjected to scathing critique.[16]

The second major area of direct Jewish offensive against Christianity involved appeal to spiritual achievement, with sharp contrasts drawn between a small but highly moral Jewish minority, committed to living out the demands of the divine–human covenant, and a larger Christian majority, allegedly awash in moral failure. Among the elements in purported Christian failure were Christian bellicosity (warfare both secular and sacred was projected by Jews as a staple of Christian life at this point), Christian sexual mores or – more precisely – the allegedly debased level of Christian sexual mores, and the social abuses rampant in Christian society.[17] Ultimately, Jewish polemicists – ever sensitive to Jewish minority status and its degradations – presented their co-religionists with the choice between joining a powerful majority that was both irrational and immoral or remaining in a weak minority committed to a life of reason and ethical dignity.

Finally, we must ask about the successes of the Christian pressures and the successes of the Jewish resistance. Reliable statistics on conversions out of Judaism during our period are not available. In the absence of such statistics, we must confine ourselves to some qualitative observations. Jewish departure from the fold was hardly an unknown phenomenon. Evidence from all over western

Christendom and from all the sub-periods between the years 1000 and 1500 show at least occasional Jewish defections. Indeed, it is hard to imagine that things might have been otherwise.

In discussing conversion out of the Jewish fold, it is important to remember that such conversion was hardly a monolithic phenomenon. The Jews who converted came from many different strata of the Jewish community and left it for diverse reasons, ranging from the most mundane to the truly spiritual. Perhaps most important for our purposes is medieval Christian and Jewish awareness of the distinction among the various strata of Jewish life from which the converts might come. Following is a remark that a medieval Jewish polemicist, Rabbi Meir bar Simon, puts in the mouth of a thirteenth-century archbishop of Narbonne, suggesting that Jews should *en masse* consider conversion.

> For there are, among your sages, men both wealthy and learned who have left your faith and entered ours, as a result of having their eyes opened. In the past, when only the retrograde left you, I would not have been concerned with them. Now, however, when learned men convert, you can understand that they have found the fruit and desire to cast off the rind, eating what is within. Thus, it behooves you to learn from them.[18]

This citation suggests that, for both Christians and Jews, conversion of those on the peripheries of the Jewish community – the poor and the unlettered – meant little. By contrast, conversion of those at the center of Jewish life – the wealthy and the learned – was evidence for Christians of great success and for Jews of deep danger. We have noted the extent to which learned converts themselves became active missionizers. The Barcelona disputation of 1263 and the Tortosa disputation of 1413–1414 were led, from the Christian side, by former Jews become zealous Christian missionizers.

At times, departure from the Jewish fold reached epidemic proportions. The best-known instance of massive conversion took place, as we have seen, on the Iberian peninsula in the late fourteenth and on into the fifteenth century.[19] The wave of conversions was sparked initially by wide-ranging anti-Jewish violence in 1391. Many Jews converted under the mistaken assumption that conversions illegitimately forced upon them would be quickly underdone when life on the peninsula returned to normalcy. Such was not the case. The successes achieved through force, however, were followed by intensified missionizing activity, more successful than it had been heretofore.

Thus, loss of Jewish identity could and did take place in medieval western Christendom. To an extent, this loss of identity was the simple result of mundane considerations and aspirations. Conversion to the majority faith generally paved the way for higher social status and enlarged economic horizons, although these aspirations were often thwarted. To an extent, the dynamic growth and development of majority society worked not on Jews' immediate social and economic aspirations, but rather on a more spiritual level. Jews were often impressed with the achievements of Christian society and depressed by the secondary status and degradation of their own Jewish community. There is a perfectly human sense that some kind of truth rests with a majority; unremitting Jewish minority status and its attendant inferiority took its toll on sensitive souls.[20] Finally, the role of the Church's unremitting proselytizing campaign cannot be gainsaid. The constant pressure brought to bear by Christian preachers surely took a toll of its own.

At the same time, we must not lose sight of the achievements of the Jewish community in maintaining Jewish identity. Jews were keenly aware of the threats to their identity, and Jewish leaders fulfilled their obligations by marshaling relevant argumentation against Christianity and on behalf of the dignity and truth of the Jewish tradition. Beyond the arsenal of intellectual argumentation, the Jewish community created an educational system and a network of social relations we can no longer fully reconstruct. The steady small numerical losses and the occasional instances of large-scale conversion do not obscure the broadly successful preservation of Jewish identity. A fairly weak minority community did maintain itself under adverse circumstances. As noted at the outset, in the year 1000 the Jewish communities of western Christendom were a negligible factor on the world Jewish scene; by the year 1500 they were rising to a position of dominance. This could not have been achieved without successful preservation of Jewish identity.

STRENGTHENING TRADITIONAL LINES OF JEWISH CULTURAL CREATIVITY

We have seen that a major thrust of Christian missionizing argumentation highlighted the contrast between Christian successes and Jewish degradation. Jews did not challenge the basic reality of such a contrast; they could hardly do so. Christians thoroughly outnumbered

Jews during this period, and Christianity was a religion of power and authority while Judaism was not. Jews did challenge the quality of Christian power and authority in their absolute terms, arguing that they did not reach the level of messianic achievement. Jews also developed explanations for Jewish suffering and degradation. All this involved material considerations. What the Jews of medieval western Christendom could never allow themselves to consider was a contrast in spiritual creativity. These Jews had to make certain that their community created at a high level, so that they could remain secure in a sense of spiritual superiority. Given the dynamism of medieval western Christian society, Jews were profoundly challenged to create at a high level in both traditional and innovative cultural spheres, and they in fact did so.

Jewish cultural creativity in the Middle Ages (and in modern times as well) was anchored in the classics of Jewish religious literature – the Hebrew Bible and the Babylonian Talmud, which Jews regularly designated as their Written Torah and their Oral Torah respectively. These two classics served simultaneously as wellsprings of Jewish intellectual and spiritual activity and guidebooks for the management of everyday Jewish affairs. Understanding these two great works and their teachings was hardly a simple matter. In the first place, they are both sprawling and dense collections of material, rife with internal inconsistency. These inconsistencies of emphasis and detail necessitated ongoing study and investigation. Moreover, as the Middle Ages progressed and new intellectual styles evolved, examination of these two classics was inevitably affected. For example, as study of language and grammar progressed, the advances in linguistics affected study of both the Bible and the Talmud; likewise, growing Jewish immersion in philosophy resulted in the emergence of philosophically oriented commentaries on the Bible and at least the aggadic portions of the Talmud; similarly, the expansion in Jewish mystical thinking stimulated yet another tendency in explication of the Bible and of rabbinic tradition. Finally, first the Bible and then subsequently the Talmud were contested by Christianity. This contestation had significant impact on the way in which Jews read their classic works. Thus, understanding of the biblical and talmudic texts was by no means static; ongoing reexamination of these core works was required and was regularly undertaken. Such reexamination constituted the core of Jewish spiritual creativity throughout medieval western Christendom.

The Hebrew Bible was the very first item of study in the medieval Jewish curriculum; it was embedded at the core of the Jewish worship service and thus was encountered and pondered by Jews of all ages on a regular basis. The Hebrew Bible directed all aspects of Jewish living and thinking. It formulated for medieval Jews their sense of self and community, served as a guide to past, present, and future, and projected the ideals of reasonable and decent living. In the Christian environment, the Hebrew Bible was a profoundly controversial work. For Christians, as for Jews, it was sacred, the written record of divine revelation. To be sure, Christians read the Hebrew Bible in a different – Latin – version and from a different theological perspective. As a result, Jews had to be constantly aware of the alternative Christian understandings of the biblical text and to fend off such understandings. Reading the Hebrew Bible became, to a considerable extent, a polemical undertaking.[21]

The first line of biblical study among the Jews of western Christendom was popular and took place in the synagogue as part of the worship service. Interestingly, in western Christendom there was no effort to make the biblical text available in an alternative language format, as had happened in the Islamic sphere. In the Muslim world, major Jewish leaders, preeminently the tenth-century Saadia Gaon, had bent their efforts toward creating a biblical text in Judeo-Arabic, which clearly functioned as both the spoken and written language of the Jews. By contrast, in western Christendom, there was no such effort. This is a reflection of the language situation already noted. While Jews used the language of their surroundings for oral communication, they did not use the accepted written language – Latin – for their intellectual life. Whereas the majority combination was spoken vernacular and written Latin, for Jews the combination was spoken vernacular and written Hebrew. The emphasis on Hebrew also flowed from the polemical considerations already noted. It was very helpful in combating Christian readings of the Hebrew Bible for Jews to be in a position to regularly insist that they were basing their views on the biblical text in the divinely revealed original, rather than in what Jews perceived as a humanly crafted translation.

Teaching the biblical text in the synagogue context was achieved through the sermon. While few sermons from the early centuries of our period have survived, from the later centuries there is a considerable corpus available.[22] From this body of material, it is clear that sermons served as a first line of biblical study and Jewish education

or, to put the matter differently, that the Bible served as the prism
through which the preacher and his listeners sought to make sense of
an increasingly complex world. Biblical heroes were projected as role
models; ideals for living were extracted from biblical stories and from
prophetic exhortations; the sense of Jewish past, present, and future
was elicited; Jewish perceptions of self and self-worth were derived.
In the process, there was inevitably a running argument with the
Christian environment as to its reading or misreading of the biblical
corpus and message. Clearly, the Bible as engaged in the synagogue
served as the major educational vehicle for inculcating Jewish values
and for reinforcing Jewish identity.[23]

To be sure, biblical study proceeded beyond the synagogue and
moved onto more advanced levels. One of the major genres of
medieval Jewish intellectual creativity was the Bible commentary.
The most popular of the biblical commentaries composed in medieval
western Christendom was that of Solomon ben Isaac of Troyes, Rashi.
Indeed, Rashi's biblical commentary has been – over the ages – one of
the most popular works in the Jewish library. Rashi was committed to
a commentary that would make the Hebrew Bible accessible from a
number of points of view. His first concern was straightforward clarification of a sometimes difficult text. As noted, he often explained
difficult terms through an Old French translation. Beyond translation,
paraphrase was also used by Rashi to make opaque passages understandable. While hardly highlighting the grammatical work that had
been done in the Muslim sphere, Rashi did introduce some of those
findings into his biblical commentary, again with the aim of penetrating into the direct and unadorned meaning of the biblical text.
At the same time, Rashi was highly sympathetic to rabbinic views.
Indeed, he recurrently introduces traditional rabbinic exegesis into
his biblical commentary, as a way of linking what he and the Jewish
world saw as the interconnected Written and Oral Torahs. Rashi's
commentary regularly provides an effective sense of the interrela-
tionship of the two Torahs. Finally, Rashi was also aware of Christian
readings and sought to combat them. Rashi's commentary became
a vehicle for diffusing Jewish anti-Christian exegesis throughout the
medieval Jewish world.[24]

While Rashi's commentary seems to have been addressed to a
broad Jewish audience, there were a number of more specialized foci
to Jewish biblical commentary in medieval western Christendom.
In fact, every major intellectual tendency in medieval European

Jewry – the scientific, the philosophical, the mystical, and the polemical – found expression in biblical commentary. Given the centrality of the Hebrew Bible to medieval Jewish life and thought, the expression of all these approaches in biblical exegesis is hardly surprising. The Bible influenced every new development in Jewish thinking; each of these developments had to be squared with the biblical source of Jewish religious authority.

One such focus involved a scientific effort at eliciting the straightforward meaning of the biblical text. In the southern sectors of western Christendom, many of the immigrant Jews came from the Muslim environment that had nurtured such exegetes as Saadia Gaon and brought with them the commitment to scientific language study that was intended to get at the strict meaning of biblical words and verses. Comparative linguistic insight was utilized to pinpoint the meaning of difficult – and in some instances ostensibly well-known – Hebrew terms; increasingly acute understanding of Hebrew grammar assisted in laying bare the syntax of difficult phrases and sentences. We have earlier noted David Kimhi of Narbonne, whose widely used commentaries excel in their linguistic acuity.[25] A curious figure – slightly earlier than David Kimhi – was Abraham ibn Ezra, a wanderer set adrift by the turbulence on the Iberian peninsula during the middle decades of the twelfth century. Abraham ibn Ezra trekked across much of medieval western Christendom, writing commentaries on the various books of the Hebrew Bible and determined at all times to elicit the scrupulously scientific meaning of the text. Rabbi Moses ben Nahman of Gerona, mentioned in a number of connections and like David Kimhi and Abraham ibn Ezra heir to the rich traditions of the Muslim world, attempted as well to penetrate the literary truths of the biblical text.[26]

Across northern Europe, particularly in northern France in the wake of Rashi, a school of Jewish biblical commentators arose that was committed to straightforward contextual exegesis of the biblical text. Indeed, there was more than intellectual connection between Rashi and these exegetes. One of the most important early figures in this new school, Samuel ben Meir of Ramerupt, was a grandson of the sage of Troyes. It seems likely that this new tendency among the northern-European Jews was related in some measure to parallel proclivities in Christian biblical exegesis at the time. It is known that some of the Christian exegetes turned to Jewish scholars for assistance in their effort to plumb the straightforward meaning of the Hebrew text.[27] The encounter with Christian exegetes and exegesis may have furnished more than simply a model; the Jewish commentators may well have concluded – as Jewish polemicists had long insisted – that straightforward reading of the biblical text served as a most effective way of disproving Christian truth claims.

Jewish Bible commentary also was addressed quite directly to polemical purposes. Argumentation from biblical verses is prominent in the very earliest of the Jewish polemical works composed in medieval western Christendom, the *Sefer ha-Berit* of Joseph Kimhi and the *Milḥamot ha-Shem* of Jacob ben Reuben. Striking in the commentaries of Joseph Kimhi's son David is the commitment to engaging overtly and at some length the claims of Christian exegesis. Particularly in his commentary on the Book of Psalms, David Kimhi – after explaining the psalm in its entirety in what he saw as an objective manner – adduces and dismisses Christian readings. The Kimhi commentary on Psalms became a major vehicle for diffusion of anti-Christian argumentation among Jews all throughout the medieval period and on into modernity.

Across northern Europe, a genre of biblical commentary developed that was entirely devoted to citation of biblical verses, Christian interpretation of those verses, and Jewish rebuttal. The *Sefer Niẓaḥon Yashan* and the *Sefer Yosef ha-Mekane* – both thirteenth-century works from northern Europe – proceed through the books of the Hebrew Bible, identify verses utilized by Christian polemicists, specify the Christian thrust, and then rebut that thrust. Such collections indicate precisely how central the Hebrew Bible was to the inter-faith polemical enterprise.[28]

As philosophic speculation made its way into the Jewish world, this new-style thinking had to make its peace with prior Jewish tradition, and that meant, above all, squaring the new thought with the Bible. Already in the Muslim sphere, pre-1000 thinkers like Saadia Gaon had begun the effort to show the compatibility of philosophic speculation and biblical truth. To be sure, this meant, in some instances, reinterpreting the biblical text in order to establish this compatibility. As noted previously, reinterpretation was grounded in the sense that the biblical text had to be addressed to an earlier and less mature stage of human development, a view that raised hackles in many sectors of the Jewish community.

In the southern areas of medieval western Christendom, as philosophic speculation entrenched itself in the Jewish community, the biblical text was regularly studied from a philosophic perspective. Not surprisingly, many of the commentators engrossed in the scientific study of the Bible were deeply committed to the philosophic as well. This is, for example, very much the case with David Kimhi, noted already for both his scientific and polemical commitments. David Kimhi's commentaries regularly address philosophic issues and advance understandings of the biblical text that are consonant with philosophic truths as Kimhi understood them. We have noted previously the philosophic speculations of Levi ben Gerson in fourteenth-century southern France. Levi ben Gerson was also a biblical exegete of note. His wide-ranging commentaries represent an effort on his part to convey his philosophic insights to a broader Jewish audience, through the medium of a biblical commentary.

Finally, the powerful new Jewish mystical impulses were regularly centered on the biblical text. Once again, the mystics were in effect committed to an effort to proceed beyond the surface meaning of everyday life, the Written Torah, and the Oral Torah to a deeper understanding of all three. Thus, the biblical text served, on the one hand, as the goad and source of much mystical insight; at the same time, once more it was critical for innovative Jewish thinkers to convince themselves and others that their new insights were compatible with the record of divine revelation.

Mystical tracts that are in effect commentaries on the books of the Hebrew Bible abound from our period. One of the earliest of the southern-French mystical treatises, of uncertain authorship, is in effect a running mystical commentary on the first two chapters of the Book of Genesis.[29] Much of the central classic of medieval Jewish mysticism, the *Zohar*, is presented as a lengthy and diffuse commentary on the first five books of the Hebrew Bible. While much of this commentary simply utilizes the biblical verses as points of entry into rambling mystical discourses, setting these discourses in the context of the biblical text expresses the insistence on the biblical roots of the mystical insights and on the absolute conformity of these insights with divine revelation.[30]

For the Jews of medieval western Christendom, God had revealed his truth through the Written Torah and through its complementary Oral Torah as well. These Jews were very much committed to ordering their communal and personal lives by the dictates of both the Bible and Talmud, with a sense that the latter represented in fact an effort to make the biblical injunctions meaningful in the context of everyday life. Just as the dynamic environment of medieval western Christendom challenged the Jewish minority to new creativity in its approaches to the Written Torah, so too did it stimulate creative thinking in the realm of Oral Torah also.[31]

By the year 1000, a number of modalities for engaging Oral Torah had developed. The first of these was the rabbinic *responsum*. Normally, uncertainties as to the requirements of Jewish law – how to square observed and encountered realities with the dictates of the Talmud – were dealt with orally and locally. The local elder or rabbi could readily be consulted. When this local figure was unable to provide requisite guidance, because of the newness or complexity of the problem, the matter then passed onto a larger stage and into written format. Questions were addressed to authoritative institutions or individuals. The responses of these institutions or individuals then became part of rabbinic tradition.

In the Muslim world, centralized rabbinic institutions had emerged in late antiquity, indeed with the crystallization of the Babylonian Talmud itself. These institutions – preeminently the venerable academies of Sura and Pumbaditha, relocated in the great city of Baghdad – became the central addresses for the questions that puzzled local rabbis and teachers all across the Islamic world and into the Christian sphere as well. The rulings of the academies became an important element in rabbinic law. In western Christendom, by contrast, no such centralized institutions developed. Individuals known for mastery of Jewish law and for acuity of mind became the addressees for the difficult questions that local Jewish leaders could not answer. Such figures emerged both in the older Jewish communities of the south and in the newer Jewish communities of the north. Despite the lack of institutional sanction, the responses of these respected individuals quickly took their place of honor within the ever-expanding corpus of Jewish legal tradition.

There was a second modality for the ongoing development and expansion of Jewish law, rooted in a direct confrontation with the talmudic text, rather than in engagement with everyday realities. Study of the talmudic text was a staple of the Jewish educational system, at least at its more advanced levels. Once again, in western Christendom there were no venerable institutions of academic distinction, such as existed in the Muslim world. At least in the early stages of the development of medieval European Jewry, schools coalesced around dominant figures, again revered for mastery of Jewish

law and for penetrating intelligence. When the renown and importance of a teacher reached a very high level, the teacher himself or
his students committed to writing valuable insights as to the meaning
of the talmudic text.

Such commentaries were composed in both the older communities
of the south, where they were much influenced by the earlier study
carried out in the Muslim sphere, and in the newer communities of
the north. Curiously, it was in the latter setting that the first dominant
talmudic commentary emerged, followed by the evolution of a new
school of talmudic exegesis. The dominant commentary was that of
Solomon ben Isaac of Troyes, whom we have already encountered
as the most popular of biblical exegetes. Rashi's commentary on the
Talmud set for itself a number of objectives. The first was clarification of textual readings. In many instances, Rashi's observations begin
with the phrase: "This is the [proper] reading," indicating that the
manuscripts in his possession were diverse and uncertain. His clarification of the proper reading has by and large become normative for
subsequent talmudic study, so that we only infrequently know what
the rejected alternatives were. A second objective of the Rashi commentary was simple explication of difficult terms. As noted, he often
resorted to Old French terms in order to clarify uncertain words in
Hebrew and Aramaic. Finally and perhaps most importantly, Rashi
set out to provide a running account that would guide the reader
through the flow of the intricate talmudic argument. Indeed, he was
so successful that, throughout the subsequent Jewish world, printed
editions of the Talmud feature the commentary of Rashi, and study
of the Talmud has regularly meant study of the text with Rashi's
guidance.

Out of Rashi's pioneering efforts emerged, during the middle years
of the twelfth century, an entirely new school of talmudic exegesis,
the school of the Tosafists (the Hebrew term *Tosafot* literally means
additions and suggests the veneration accorded the exegesis of Rashi,
to which the new work was seen as supplementary). In fact, the key
early figures in this new school of exegesis were again biologically
descended from Rashi – they were his grandchildren. The goal of
the Tosafist enterprise was quite different from that of Rashi; indeed,
their goal built upon that of Rashi. Now no longer required to
clarify the proper reading and simple explication of the talmudic
text, the Tosafists were concerned with treating the sprawling talmudic text as a coherent unit. Seemingly contradictory passages were

carefully scrutinized by the Tosafists, with new explanations advanced that would resolve the ostensible contradictions. Interestingly, the Tosafists saw in the consensus behavior of their community evidence of talmudic teaching as well, so that seeming contradictions between the talmudic text and Jewish behavior resulted in careful scrutiny and proposals for resolving the ostensible discrepancies. Like the commentary of Rashi, that of the Tosafists became an accepted feature of the later printed talmudic text. Reserved for somewhat advanced students, the commentaries of the Tosafists became core to subsequent talmudic study. The Tosafist enterprise lasted about a century at its creative best, from the middle of the twelfth to the middle of the thirteenth century.[32] It has often been noted that this creative period corresponded to the emergence of a growing majority exploitation of the tools of dialectic for resolving seeming inconsistencies within the legacy of Christian canon law rulings and within the corpus of Christian theological teachings. This suggests once again Jewish immersion in majority culture and the fruitful stimulation provided by that majority culture.

There was yet a third modality of Jewish engagement with talmudic tradition, alongside the *responsum* and the commentary. As new issues were raised and clarified and as new understandings of the Talmud text proliferated, the need for manageable manuals of Jewish law became increasingly obvious. Saadia Gaon in the tenth-century Islamic sphere was an important innovator in this regard, composing a number of guides to specific areas of Jewish law. The dominant figure in codification of Jewish law in the Muslim world was Moses ben Maimon. One of the most striking Jewish intellectual figures of all times, Maimonides made numerous contributions to the field of Jewish law. Unquestionably the most important of these contributions was his massive compendium entitled the *Mishneh-Torah*. This work, in fourteen books, was remarkable in several respects. In the first place, Maimonides' mastery of prior Jewish law was unparalleled. At the same time, he was determined to present the diverse elements of Jewish law in a compilation that would be topically organized, so that a reader could peruse the table of contents and know precisely where to turn for the information sought. In addition, Maimonides, who composed most of the rest of his *oeuvre* in Judeo–Arabic, wrote his *Mishneh-Torah* in a flowing Hebrew, a Hebrew that was (and is) instantly clear and understandable. This made the *Mishneh-Torah* a work that could circulate easily throughout the entire Jewish world, which it in fact did. Finally – and most controversially, Maimonides saw the philosophic underpinnings of Jewish belief as a part of the totality of Jewish law. The opening sections of the *Mishneh-Torah's* fourteen books is devoted to identifying these philosophic under-pinnings, in a way that was often unacceptable to more traditional Jewish intellectual leaders.

Outstanding Jewish scholars throughout western Christendom made their contributions in this area as well. The most significant compendium of Jewish law was the *Arb'ah Turim (The Four Pillars)*, composed by Rabbi Jacob ben Asher in fourteenth-century Spain. It is somewhat misleading to label this work Spanish, since its author was a German Jewish scholar transplanted from the north to Christian Spain. Rabbi Jacob ben Asher enjoyed the fruits of the talmudic learn-ing of both the north and the south and bequeathed his synthesis to the subsequent Jewish world. His *Arb'ah Turim* became yet another classic created by the Jews of medieval western Christendom, studied from then until now in the academies of talmudic learning. Perhaps even more important, the framework he organized for his code, con-sisting of four major divisions of Jewish law (*Orah Hayyim*, devoted to laws of prayer, Sabbath, and festivals; *Yoreh De'ah*, devoted to rit-ual law; *Even ha'Ezer*, devoted to laws affecting women; and *Hoshen Mishpat*, devoted to civil law), became the normative framework for all such manuals of Jewish law from then until now, thoroughly dis-placing the prior organizational scheme of Maimonides.

We have noted earlier the thirteenth-century Church attack on the Talmud, centered in royal France, with all its complications. In some areas, the Talmud was prohibited entirely; in other areas, censorship of the Talmud was instituted; in yet other places, Talmud study was relatively unaffected. Despite these external pressures, talmudic study remained at the core of Jewish intellectual life, with the commentaries of Rashi and the Tosafists and the code of Rabbi Jacob ben Asher gaining increasing currency throughout all of western Christendom and indeed beyond.

INNOVATIVE LINES OF CULTURAL CREATIVITY

While Bible and Talmud study were central to the popular and more advanced curricula of Jewish study, other lines of intellectual activity were pursued as well. These alternative lines of intellectual activity never gained the kind of consensus support enjoyed by immersion in the Bible and Talmud. In some cases, such as the translation effort to be discussed immediately, the alternative lines of intellectual activity were transitory, intended to meet immediate needs; in other instances, such as philosophic inquiry, they in fact became highly polarizing within the Jewish communities of medieval western Christendom. As noted, many Jews were enthused by innovation and felt it critical to Jewish survival; others were quite leery of the new and different, seeing it as threatening to Jewish solidarity and survival.

We have noted recurrently that much of Jewish intellectual and spiritual life in medieval western Christendom was rooted in the creativity of the Jews in the Muslim sphere; we have also noted the regular use of Judeo-Arabic by the Jews living in the realm of Islam for most of their intellectual *oeuvre*. Thus, one of the first important cultural activities of the Jews in medieval western Christendom involved translation from Judeo-Arabic and Arabic into Hebrew, so that the important output of their predecessors in the Islamic sphere and the riches of the Muslim world in general not be lost. To be sure, Jews were not alone in concern for absorbing the creativity of the Muslim world through translation. Christian society also was becoming aware of the riches available in Arabic and was likewise committed to a translation effort. Not surprisingly, Jewish translators were regularly drafted into the more general enterprise as well.

Obviously, those Jews who had lived in the Muslim world, especially on the Iberian peninsula, and had been forced to emigrate into Christian territories were particularly committed to the translation enterprise and especially adapted to it. Joseph Kimhi, already mentioned, was one such migrating Jew who lent his skills to the translation effort. The dominant figure, however, was a fellow-southern-French Jew, Judah ibn Tibbon of Lunel. The range of Judah's translations is most impressive. He rendered into Hebrew many of the major authors of the tenth through twelfth centuries in the Islamic world, including the oft-mentioned Saadia Gaon, Bahya ibn Paquda, Solomon ibn Gabirol, and Judah ha-Levi. Judah ibn Tibbon's translations involved commitment to a firm method, with an emphasis on literal rendition of the original. Judah also penned lengthy prefaces to many of his translations, explaining their importance and clarifying issues of genre. He clearly believed that a translator was hardly a technician. For Judah ibn Tibbon, the translator must know languages well – both the language from which the translation is made and the language into which the translation is made – and must also be expert in the subject matter.

Beyond his own achievements, Judah ibn Tibbon also attended to the raising and educating of a remarkable son and continuator in the translation enterprise. We know a good deal more of the education of Samuel ibn Tibbon than we do of almost any other medieval Jew, as a result of an unusual testament penned by father for son. In this document, Judah ibn Tibbon spells out a *paideia* of sorts, indicating the essentials of genuine education as conceived in the Jewish communities of Muslim Spain. This model includes study of Bible, Talmud, Arabic language, Hebrew grammar, literary style, and the major sciences. The model is rigorous and demanding; it reflects a Jewry very much integrated into and affected by the intellectual milieu of the majority.

Samuel ibn Tibbon, although occasionally criticized by his father, seems in fact to have fulfilled the vision of this demanding model and became a key figure in the ongoing translation of Andalusian Jewish culture into western Christendom. Samuel ibn Tibbon translated a number of lesser works by Maimonides, as well as works of Aristotle and Averroes. It was, however, his translation of Maimonides' *Guide of the Perplexed* that won him greatest renown. In this important under-taking, Samuel followed his father's insistence on literal translation, seemingly in defiance of Maimonides' own suggestions. The translation took a number of years, with an edition presented in 1204 and a revised version with glossary completed nine years later. Ibn Tibbon's translation paved the way for the flourishing of a new Jewish philosophic temperament in western Christendom, with attendant intellectual and spiritual dislocation as well.

Samuel ibn Tibbon's son-in-law, Jacob Anatoli, rounds out our picture of the family and its place in the Jewish translation enterprise. Jacob studied with Samuel in Marseilles, where the latter relocated from his ancestral home in Lunel. Jacob eventually left Marseilles and his father-in-law in response to an invitation to join the cir-cle of Christian translators at the imperial court in Naples. There, Jacob participated in the Latin translations of Averroes sponsored by Emperor Fredrick II. At the same time, he continued the family com-mitment to the translation of works of Greek and Arabic philosophy into Hebrew, reinforcing the effort already noted to transplant the culture of the Islamic world into the new Jewish home in western Christendom.

The rich Jewish culture fashioned by the Jews in the medieval Muslim world involved study of the classical literature of the Jews, the Bible and the Talmud; it also included immersion in Arabic science, philosophy, and *belles lettres*. Beyond these diverse fields of study, the Jews in the Muslim sphere committed themselves to two major new avenues of Jewish cultural creativity, the first of which was Hebrew poetry. Whereas Arabic was regularly used in all other spheres of Jewish cultural activity, in poetry – a highly prized cultural outlet in the Muslim realm – the Jews utilized Hebrew exclusively, in both sacred and secular compositions. It has regularly been suggested that the use of Hebrew in poetry reflects a sense of competition with Arabic, an effort to show that the language of the Jewish minority was as beautiful and could be used as impressively as the language of the Muslim majority. Again, many of the immigrants into areas of southern Europe brought with them interest in poetry and the capacity to write it well. The legacy of poetic creativity was nurtured by these southern-European Jewish immigrants. One major and somewhat different southern-European Jewish poet was Immanuel of Rome, whose poetry shows signs of considerable influence from the Christian environment of Italy in which he lived and created. This southern-European Jewish poetry was – like that of the Muslim world – often polarizing among the Jews. Some of the motifs and imagery of this poetry raised deep objections in more traditional sectors of the Jewish community.

The newer Jews of northern Europe absorbed little of the poetic legacy of the Jewish communities of the Muslim sphere or of their Christian environment. To the extent that they were at all involved in poetic creativity, it was along the lines of earlier synagogal poetry. Hebrew poetry of this more traditional type became a major vehicle through which the Jews of the north expressed their reactions to the difficulties they encountered and reinforced their ideals and aspirations. Jewish historical consciousness was regularly expressed through the medium of such poetry.[33] This northern poetry, sacred and far less immediately accessible than the secular poetry of the Muslim sphere and southern Europe, was sufficiently valued and sufficiently obscure as to require an exegetical literature, which the Jews of northern Europe provided.

The second arena of innovative Jewish creativity in the Muslim sphere was philosophy, which had a far greater propensity than poetry for arousing anxiety and anger and for creating dissent. Jewish life in antiquity had produced little in the way of philosophic speculation. The giant figure of Philo of Alexandria was in effect absorbed by Christianity and lost to the Jewish world. Once again, the integration of the Jews into the Muslim world and their comfort with the Arabic language and its literature made philosophic speculation a possibility for the Jews in this area. In fact, for many Jews, philosophic speculation became a necessity. The growing sophistication of Muslim thinkers could not go unchallenged. Some Jews at least were unwilling to see their tradition as any less rational and any less philosophically profound than that of their neighbors.

Like their Muslim peers, Jews were attracted to philosophical speculation and were challenged by it as well. Particularly problematic was the seeming disparity between the teachings of the philosophers and the doctrines bequeathed to Muslims and Jews by their religious traditions. For the Jews, this meant a perceived gulf between the abstractions of philosophic thought and the often anthropomorphic imagery of both the Bible and the Talmud. For philosophically inclined Jews, the gulf was deeply distressing and had to be bridged, often by reinterpretation of the Jewish classics. For those Jews disinclined to philosophic speculation, the end result was unwarranted tampering with the sacred legacy of the past.[34]

The towering figure of Jewish philosophy in the Muslim world was Moses ben Maimon, who was – as we have seen – a remarkably gifted and productive intellectual giant. Maimonides could not be written off as untutored in the classical literature of the Jews or as a peripheral member of Jewish society. As noted, he was a respected communal leader and an acknowledged master of the talmudic corpus. For philosophic concerns to thus penetrate into the heart of rabbinic Judaism was, for the adherents of Jewish philosophy, an enormous boon; for those suspicious of Jewish philosophizing or hostile to it, the activities of Maimonides were disconcerting in the extreme.

Maimonides himself was obviously concerned with the social implications of his philosophic speculation. His philosophic *magnum opus*, the *Guide of the Perplexed*, was deliberately couched in an obscure format. The gifted teacher who was capable of formulating his findings in rabbinic law so transparently did not compose his dense and opaque philosophic treatise out of an inability to write clearly. The obfuscation was surely deliberate, intended to ward off those unsuited for deep philosophic inquiry and its wide-ranging and potentially dangerous ramifications.

As we have seen repeatedly, the Jews immigrating into southern Europe brought with them veneration for the rich Jewish culture of the Muslim world they were leaving, with commitment to the philosophic enterprise looming large as part of this veneration. Samuel ibn Tibbon's translation of the *Guide of the Perplexed* opened the way for the Jews of western Christendom – or at least its southern sectors – to study firsthand the most important work of medieval Jewish philosophy. This translation was critical to the emergence of a broad following for Maimonides and his speculation. This diverse following covered a considerable spectrum of opinions, ranging from those mildly influenced as to content and committed to maintaining discrete limitations on philosophic speculation to those more profoundly committed to Maimonidean teachings and their dissemination. These Maimonidean partisans included many scholars revered for their talmudic knowledge and thus above reproach; they also included others more peripheral to the Jewish community and highly suspect.

Among the more important of those fully devoted to the cause of philosophy was Samuel ibn Tibbon himself. Beyond his important translation of the *Guide*, Samuel composed two important works of his own – a commentary on the book of Ecclesiastes and a discussion of Genesis 1:9.[35] In both cases, philosophy and exegesis are intricately intertwined. Samuel was utterly committed to the resolution of the seeming distance between biblical and philosophic truth. He quoted liberally from the biblical corpus and, at the same time, from the philosophers. His master in all this was Maimonides, whom he cites extensively. For Samuel, as one of the more radical Maimonideans, philosophic inquiry was crucial to Jewish survival and had to be undertaken widely and openly. Samuel was clearly aware of the divisiveness of the enterprise to which he was devoted, but saw it as a necessity.

During the early years of the thirteenth century, controversy erupted – initially in Languedoc – over philosophic speculation.[36] In part, the objections to the philosophic camp flowed simply from change, the disruption of prior thinking patterns; in part, the objections were far deeper and more focused. The essential issue confronted by the philosophic camp involved the seeming disparity between the abstract conclusions of the philosophers and the concrete imagery of the biblical corpus. For many, this meant a simple choice – either philosophic abstraction or biblical anthropomorphism. In all three monotheistic camps, however, there was considerable unwillingness to choose between the two tendencies, a conviction that beneath the seeming discord lay essential harmony. How to achieve such harmony was the heart of the medieval philosophic dilemma.

For most Jewish philosophers, as for their Muslim and Christian counterparts, the solution lay in the invocation of a special kind of reading of the biblical text. Jewish philosophers like Maimonides could readily appeal to a venerable Jewish tradition suggesting that revealed truth, while stemming from the omniscient divine source and thus immutable, had to be couched in terms understandable to the specific human audience to which it was addressed. Thus, biblical anthropomorphisms represent, in this view, essentially an accommodation to the level of understanding of the biblical Israelites. This means of course that the anthropomorphisms are not to be taken in their simple and literal sense, for they were never intended to be taken that way. This view of accommodation to the level of Israelite society has implications for the realm of religious praxis as well. The sacrificial system, for example – so central to the core biblical narrative and to Jewish religious life through much of antiquity – was likewise cast as an accommodation to the developmental level of Israelite society, not intended by God to represent an eternal formula for worshipping the divine.

For the anti-philosophic camp, this solution was fraught with problems – it was in fact profoundly threatening. The first problem was simply the element of change itself, which is always disruptive. The sheer newness of the approach distressed many medieval Jews, as parallel views in the other two monotheistic communities distressed many medieval Muslims and Christians. The discomfort with change went deeper. A key element in traditional Jewish historical thinking was veneration for past hero figures and a sense of historical diminution, with the leaders and common folk of the present far inferior to their predecessors. The philosophic view of revelation reversed that traditional evaluation, making prior generations inferior in their capacity for religious understanding and valorizing the present generation, with its ability to see beneath the biblical rhetoric and to recognize truths unacknowledged by their ancestors. This reversal of historical valence was profoundly disquieting to the anti-philosophic camp.

There was a yet more upsetting concern. The new reading of the biblical text involved relativization of the divinity and the praxis of relating to it, acknowledgement of the legitimacy of changing views

of God and of religious obligation. Relativizing biblical injunction
entailed two serious liabilities. The first was recognition that this was
precisely the path already taken by Pauline Christianity in its efforts to
dissociate itself from the practical injunctions of Jewish religious life.
Finding themselves moving in such Christian pathways was deeply
distressing to many medieval Jews. Moreover, the relativization of
religious praxis constituted a slippery slope. While the sacrificial system could be dismissed, since it was no longer in actual practice,
what of much of the rest of Jewish ritual? Was it likewise simply an
accommodation to prior and less mature religious sensibilities? Was
it too dispensable, like the sacrificial system?

The controversy over philosophy first erupted during the early
decades of the thirteenth century in the town of Montpellier. There,
a conservative talmudic scholar named Solomon ben Abraham leveled
a series of charges against Maimonides and his followers. Every phase
of this controversy is difficult to reconstruct, because of the polemical distortions introduced by the adherents of both camps, the anti-
Maimonideans and the pro-Maimonideans. The difficulties begin
with the initiating figure of Solomon ben Abraham of Montpellier,
who is portrayed in one camp as a thoughtful and moderate defender
of Jewish tradition and in the other as radical and obscurantist. It does
seem that each camp enrolled upstanding and respected Jewish leaders to its cause. It is likewise difficult to identify the specific charges
leveled against the philosophers and their writing, because – once
again – there is a high level of exaggeration in the writings of both
sides. Clearly, the central author involved is Maimonides, venerated
as a student of the Talmud, but feared by some as a philosophic innovator. Precisely how the figure of Maimonides was manipulated by
various elements in the controversy is again hazy. It is also clear that
the central issue for the anti-Maimonideans was innovative reading
of the biblical text and religious praxis, with the perceived threat that
such reading could occasion the disintegration of the entire structure
of Jewish religious life. Once more, however, the diverse positions
are difficult to reconstruct. The controversy spilled over into adjacent
Spain and up into northern Europe. Rumor was spread that the anti-
Maimonideans denounced Maimonides' *Guide* to the inquisitorial
courts active in southern France, a claim that cannot be definitively
refuted, but that seems highly unlikely.

Despite the ongoing controversy, a galaxy of Jewish intellectuals
all across southern Europe maintained the philosophic enterprise

all through the thirteenth through fifteenth centuries – for example Levi ben Gerson, Isaac Pollegar, Joseph ibn Kaspi, and Moses Narboni during the fourteenth century, and Profiat Duran, Hasdai Crescas, Joseph Albo, Isaac Bibago, and Isaac Abravanel during the fifteenth. Each of these and many others continued to immerse themselves in the broad philosophic corpus and to compose works in which they strove to accommodate the teachings of the philosophers and the dictates of Jewish tradition. What is especially impressive in this effort was its commitment to spreading these philosophic under-standings throughout the Jewish community. No longer was philos-ophy viewed as the preserve of a small and narrow stratum of Jewish society; rather, it was increasingly viewed as an enterprise central to Jewish life and spiritual survival.[37] As noted, this conviction led to deep disquiet among the opponents of the philosophic enterprise. Since philosophic speculation was no longer the privilege of a nar-row elite, but was now intended to affect Jewish life more broadly, its potential impact loomed increasingly large and – for its opponents – was increasingly dangerous. We have noted earlier the struggle to ban philosophic speculation or at least to limit it significantly. These efforts – like the philosophic inquiry itself – were a constant of Jew-ish life across southern Europe throughout the latter centuries of our period. Interestingly, the pursuit of philosophic truth – so central to Jewish life in the south – made no significant inroads among the Jews of northern Europe, who were never deeply influenced by the riches of Jewish creativity in the Islamic realm.

Alongside philosophic inquiry, there developed also – in both southern and northern Europe – an intense commitment to mys-tical speculation. Medieval Jewish mystical speculation is extremely difficult to study. In contrast to the poetry and philosophic inquiry just now discussed, medieval Jewish mysticism conveys little sense of sharp innovation; rather, it has a timeless quality to it. Students of Jewish mysticism have traced many of the medieval mystical themes well back into antiquity; students of early Christianity have noted striking parallels between medieval Jewish mystical speculation and the imaginative ruminations of Christian thinkers of the second and third centuries. Indeed, the mystics themselves regularly fostered a sense of age-old verities being recovered, rather than new insights. The language of the mystics was often a talmudic combination of Hebrew and Aramaic; the attribution of mystical writings to much earlier figures was common. What can be safely said is that, in twelfth- and thirteenth-century western Christendom, there was remarkable efflorescence of Jewish mystical writings, culminating in the composition of the classical work of the genre, the *Zohar*.[38]

Among the Jewish mystics, the legacy of Jewish life in the Muslim sphere seems to have been less telling. While there was mystical speculation among these earlier Jews, there is no sense of a legacy translated and carried over into Christendom, as was the case in so many other cultural domains. In a broad sense, the underlying issue in most of the mystical writings involves bridging the gap between a transcendent deity and humanity. Since Christianity had proceeded further along this path – as a result of its doctrine of Incarnation – than either Islam or Judaism, the Jewish mystics of medieval western Christendom may well have been stimulated to a considerable extent by their new environment. Especially in the areas of southern France, where creative and innovative rethinking of Christian symbols and beliefs was rife during the latter decades of the twelfth century, there was considerable stimulation to Jewish mystical speculation from the majority milieu. Efforts to pinpoint the influences on the new mysticism have turned in many directions and have generally been inconclusive. Suggestions include the impact of Jewish thinking long transmitted orally, a positive role for philosophy in fostering certain issues and motifs, a negative role for philosophy in requiring counter-thinking, the impact of the religious ferment in majority Christian society.

The emergence of the *Zohar* as the authoritative text of medieval Jewish mysticism has tended to consign much of the evolving mystical literature of the late twelfth and early thirteenth century to obscurity. Scholarly labors of the past century have recovered this literature and have revealed dynamic and fluid mystical speculation all across southern France and northern Spain from the middle decades of the twelfth century onward. Many of the figures whose work has been unearthed were previously unknown; at the same time, it is clear that mystical speculation – like philosophic inquiry – penetrated the ranks of leading scholars in the more traditional domains of Jewish creativity. Rabbi Moses ben Nahman of Gerona, encountered already as a crucial voice in combating the burgeoning Christian missionizing efforts and in both biblical and talmudic exegesis, lent his considerable prestige to the new mystical proclivities; his role in and support for the new mystical speculation lent it the kind of legitimacy that Rabbi Moses ben Maimon lent to philosophic inquiry.

As noted, during the second half of the thirteenth century the new mystical speculation eventuated in the composition of the classic of medieval Jewish mysticism, the *Zohar*. Purporting to be the writing of the second-century Rabbi Simon bar Yohai, the *Zohar* is a complex work that recent scholars attribute – at least in its main lines – to the late-thirteenth-century Castilian Moses de Leon. Cast largely in the format of free-wheeling biblical commentary, the *Zohar* addresses the widest possible range of theological and spiritual issues. Perhaps its central theme – or at least its most influential theme – is the shaping and explication of a complex vision of the supernal world, whose ten *sefirot* are engaged in constant and dynamic interaction. It is the role of humanity – especially the centrally located Jewish element in humanity – to affect in positive terms these ongoing interactions. Indeed, Jewish behaviors take on cosmic significance through their impact on the interaction of the *sefirot*.[39]

The new mystical speculation was by no means limited to the southern sectors of western Christendom only. In the north, new lines of mystical speculation developed as well. Once again, identifying the innovative and explaining it have proven difficult or impossible. What distinguishes the northern from the southern mystical speculation is especially the linkage of such speculation in the north to a powerful pietism, with heavy emphasis on the imperatives of the divine will and the importance of human response to those demands. This German pietism seems to have been restricted to rather limited groups, but its broad ideals were purveyed to larger segments of northern-European Jewry through the pietistic writings of some of its leading figures, drawn from the ranks of the leading rabbis of the German lands. The relationship of this northern stream of Jewish mystical speculation and that of the south has not been fully clarified.

Historical narrative had never been a mainstay of Jewish intellectual life. During the early centuries of the Middle Ages and within the Muslim sphere, Jews composed little in the way of history. The Jews in the Christian world showed considerably more interest in the Jewish past. The Jews of the south, long settled along the northern shores of the Mediterranean, were – not surprisingly – concerned with Rome and the earlier phases of Jewish history. At a fairly early point in time, probably during the tenth century, Italian Jewry produced a major historical work, the *Book of Josippon*. While purporting to be a Hebrew translation of Josephus's account of the war between the Jews and the Romans, there is much in the book that reflects subsequent rendering of the Greek original into Latin and much that seems to reflect authorial embellishment. The end result is a lengthy and elegant account of Jewish life in antiquity, couched in a flowing Hebrew. The book was widely disseminated and interpolated during the Middle Ages and was regularly cited as authoritative by Jewish exegetes and thinkers. For Jews living in the Christian world, *Josippon* seems to have provided a Jewish view of the history of the Roman civilization so prized by the Latin West and of the Jewish place in that civilization.

The same kind of broad historical interest is reflected in the work of yet one more talented Jew displaced from his Andalusian origins during the middle decades of the twelfth century. Abraham ibn Daud was both philosopher and historian. Like Moses ben Maimon, Joseph Kimhi, and Judah ibn Tibbon, he left Muslim Spain. In Abraham's case, the move was a mild one, at least in geographical terms, as he relocated to Christian Toledo. There, perhaps influenced by the same sense of Roman history that moved the author of *Josippon*, Abraham ibn Daud composed a brief history of the Roman emperors and a lengthier history of the Jews under Greek and Roman rule.

Abraham ibn Daud's historical *magnum opus* moved in a different direction. His *Sefer ha-Kabbalah* left the Greco-Roman sphere and focused on the history of Jewish law. Ibn Daud, stung by internal Jewish critiques of the chain of Jewish tradition, set out to construct that chain in a manner that would brook no opposition or dissent. Beginning with Sinai, he traces the history of Jewish teachings, moving from generation to generation and teacher to student. While by no means unprecedented, ibn Daud's work became the widely quoted standard for this genre.

At the same time, ibn Daud undertook in his *Sefer ha-Kabbalah* a second task, a rather more poignant one. In his closing chapter, intended ostensibly to bring the chain of Jewish tradition down to his own day, he in fact did much more. He composed, as it were, a paean of praise to the Spanish Jewry of which he had been a part and which he thought he saw disintegrating before his very eyes. He described the greatness of this Spanish Jewry, with its courtiers, grandees, rabbis, and scholars, and sketched its downfall. He ended with the firm conviction that the demise of medieval Spanish Jewry, as tragic as it might be, by no means spelled the end of the saga of the Jews. According to ibn Daud, the God who controls history had already established new centers of Jewish life, which ibn Daud projected as lying in the Christian sphere, both in southern Europe and in the north.[40]

The Jews in the northern sectors of western Christendom did not immerse themselves in the long-range history of their people, satisfied to cite the fragmentary data in the Talmud and the more extensive details in *Josippon* when such information was required. They also exhibit no wide-ranging sense of their own past, such as found in ibn Daud's reconstruction of the history of the Jews in Muslim Spain. The Jews of the northern sector did, however, manifest an alternative sense of history, highly innovative in its own way and very much influenced by the dynamic and militant environment in which these Jews found themselves. From early on, these northern Jews composed accounts of contemporary events, generally centered on crisis moments. In some instances, the crisis was resolved happily; more often the crisis eventuated in tragedy, which had to be memorialized and explained.

The most famous of these historical memoirs were the three Hebrew narratives that depict the crusader assaults of 1096 on the great Jewish communities of the Rhineland. These three narratives were written at varying times, ranging from quite close to 1096 down through the later decades of the twelfth century.[41] The most interesting of the narratives is – not surprisingly – the earliest, the so-called *Mainz Anonymous*. Written fairly soon after the events themselves, this narrative, which portrays only the attacks on the three great Rhineland settlements of Speyer, Worms, and Mainz, was intended – first of all – to alert Jewish readers to the constellation of forces at work in majority society in 1096: the crusaders, the authorities, and the burghers. All three groups are portrayed in all their complexity. The crusaders are portrayed as a diverse group, some willing to spare the Jews in return for funding and some implacably committed to destroying Jewish life. The authorities are depicted as uniformly committed to protection of their Jewish clients, but often incapable of so doing. The burghers are the most diversified group of all – some in league with the murderous crusaders, some opposed to them, and some wavering in their commitments. The author also portrays the Jewish reactions in all their complexity – the efforts to elicit protection from the authorities, the attempts to negotiate with the crusaders themselves, acceptance of baptism under duress, and – most important of all to the author – the widespread Jewish readiness for martyrdom.

Providing information to Jewish readers was clearly important to the *Mainz Anonymous*, but that was not its only objective. Since

Christian onlookers – often quite friendly to their endangered Jewish neighbors – regularly argued that the massacres themselves proved abandonment by God and the need to convert, the *Mainz Anonymous* had to provide as well an explanation for the sanguinary events of 1096. How could a community of Jews known for its commitment to God's covenant have been subjected to such murderous persecution? We have seen that Jewish suffering constituted a major Christian argument in the missionizing efforts of the twelfth and thirteenth centuries. It is reported as a Christian argument already in 1096, with the suggestion that the Jewish losses reflected the sinfulness of the Jews and God's abandonment of them. The *Mainz Anonymous* offered a remarkably audacious alternative to his Jewish readers. In his view, the Rhineland Jews were in fact exemplary in their prior allegiance to God. Since God had determined to test his people, he had to choose the strongest of Jews, not the weakest – hence the test was imposed on the pious Jews of the Rhineland. In the event, these pious Jews came through the test brilliantly. They resisted almost all blandishments, choosing overwhelmingly to die at the hands of the crusaders or at their own hands rather than submit to baptism. Such heroism would eventually win great rewards for the Jewish people as a whole; the martyrs themselves were immediately rewarded with passage into the highest realms of paradise.

In the process of making this case, the *Mainz Anonymous* composed a truly remarkable historical narrative, peopled with unforgettable characters drawn from every sector of the Jewish community. Women in particular – so often unrepresented in the writings of medieval Jews – play a central role. The narrative breathes an air of certitude and militancy; indeed, it is as militant as the corresponding Latin crusade narratives. To a considerable extent, the Jewish author in fact composed a counter-crusade narrative. He argues that the vast Christian undertaking, which after all seemed highly successful, was in fact meaningless. It was conducted in terrestrial terms only and achieved only transitory terrestrial objectives. The profoundly significant achievements associated with the First Crusade were the Jewish martyrdoms. It was the Jewish victims of crusader fury – not the crusaders themselves – who were the heroes of the campaign. The *Mainz Anonymous* in effect rewrote the story of the First Crusade, transforming victors into ciphers and victims into heroes. In the process, he added a new element into the limited repertoire of Jewish historical writing.

A new genre of cultural creativity that emerged out of the Jewish experience in western Christendom was polemical literature.[42] In this area, the prior legacy was skimpy. The Jews in the medieval Muslim world had produced very little polemical writing. The pressures already noted in western Christendom necessitated the development of a fairly ramified polemical literature. The earliest exemplars of this literature emerged in southern Europe, where the missionizing pressures were first felt intensely. Eventually, this literature was composed in the north as well, although with a slightly different flavor. Polemical materials were composed in a number of literary genres – for example biblical commentaries, treatises, and dialogues. The most popular of these genres was the dialogue, which allowed for the creation of dynamic give-and-take and the creation of appealing (Jewish) and unappealing (Christian) characters. As we proceed into the fourteenth and fifteenth century, many of the polemical writings become increasingly technical and less accessible.[43]

Let us focus briefly on one example of the polemical dialogue, penned by one of the great intellectual figures of medieval Jewry, Rabbi Moses ben Nahman of Gerona. As noted, Rabbi Moses was forced to meet the new missionizing argumentation developed by the former Jew, Friar Paul of the Dominican Order, in a public disputation in Barcelona. The ground rules of the disputation specified that only rabbinic sources could be discussed, with the friar attempting to show their Christological content and the rabbi limited to rebutting that Christological content. In the wake of the encounter, Rabbi Moses – a gifted writer in many genres – composed a narrative account of the proceedings that is exceedingly rich and colorful. He depicts a scene of great danger to himself and his fellow-Jews: a Christian opponent who is aggressive, but ill-informed and foolish; a royal patron who is decent and supportive, albeit misguided in his theology; and a Jewish spokesman (Rabbi Moses himself), who is learned and clever and consistently carries the day. In the course of this narrative, Rabbi Moses suggests that he was able to completely rebut the new argumentation of Friar Paul and, in addition, to show that older lines of Christian argumentation were deficient as well. Whatever the historical accuracy of this account, its detail, color, pace, and drama made it widely read by Jews all through the Middle Ages and on into modernity.[44]

In addition to the more traditional study of Talmud and Bible, the Jews of western Christendom branched out into alternative cultural

directions as well. To an extent, they were influenced by their predecessors in the Muslim sphere; to an extent, they were affected by the
rich creativity of the Christian majority. In any case, the end result
was a vibrant Jewish culture, aimed ultimately at responding to both
the direct and indirect challenges of medieval western Christendom.
Creative Jewish thinkers sought, in a variety of genres, to arm their
fellow-Jews against the informal and formal missionizing thrusts of
majority Christian society. At the same time, through their creativity
they showed that the Jewish minority, despite its small numbers and
political weakness, was capable of maintaining a superior intellectual
and spiritual profile within a dynamic majority cultural ambience.

NEW AND CREATIVE JEWISH CULTURES

At the outset of this study, we established a number of geographic
distinctions, the most significant of which distinguished the Jewish
communities of the south, with their deep roots along the northern shores of the Mediterranean and their profound connections to
the rich cultural legacy created by the Jews of the Muslim sphere,
from the Jewish communities of northern Europe, so new in their
communal history and identity. In effect, this chapter has suggested
that two disparate Jewish cultures evolved across Europe during the
period between the years 1000 and 1500. Southern-European Jewish
culture was deeply influenced by the legacy of Jewish creativity in
the Muslim world and by extensive contact with the contemporary
Christian environment; it was inclusive in its parameters, ranging
from traditional concerns with Bible and Talmud into innovative
domains, especially philosophy and mysticism; it was wracked by
internal tensions and debates. In contrast, the newer Jewish communities of northern Europe – more distanced, but by no means isolated
from surrounding culture – fashioned a culture that was more limited in its parameters and more cohesive, spared much of the turmoil
generated in southern-European Jewish culture.

Subsequent to our period, Jews have recurrently attempted to
assert the superiority of one or the other of these contrasting cultures. Especially with the onset of modernity and the new challenges posed by intensified contact with a vibrant majority society,
the southern-European Jewish experience has often been introduced
as a valuable precedent and has been valorized as authentic Jewish
cultural creativity.[45] In reaction, other voices have highlighted the

northern-European Jewish experience as quintessentially Jewish and have criticized the southern-European Jews for their absorption of non-Jewish forms and values. No valorization has been essayed in this study. For our purposes, it suffices to note that two separate cultural stances and two distinct patterns of cultural creativity emerged in medieval western Christendom. Each was destined for a lengthy history and for profound impact on subsequent Jewish life.

While so different in their patterns of cultural expression, the Jewries of southern and northern Europe were united in fundamental ways. Both found themselves living as minority communities in a dynamically developing majority, and both were profoundly challenged by their environment. As noted recurrently in this chapter, the challenges were both explicit – in the extensive missionizing endeavor on the part of the Christian majority – and implicit – in the high level of majority creativity that required a commensurately high level of Jewish cultural creativity as well. Despite the differing cultural directions taken by the two sets of Jewries, both proved capable of achieving the kind of creativity that enabled their members to take pride in the Jewish minority of which they were a part.

EPILOGUE

―――――――――― • ――――――――――

As noted early on, the Jewish experience in medieval western Christendom left negative recollections in the memory of both the Christian majority and the Jewish minority. For the Christian majority, the Jews of medieval Europe have been recollected as a hostile, disruptive, and harmful minority community. For subsequent Jewish memory, the medieval European experience has been recalled as an unending cycle of persecutions and expulsions.[1]

Hopefully, the present account has served to complicate these folk memories. While it is true that the Jews of medieval western Christendom were widely perceived by their Christian contemporaries as disruptive and harmful, the realities were far more complex. The Jews were welcomed by elements in the Christian population for the contribution they might make, and warm human contact between Jews and their Christian neighbors is recurrently documented. Equally important, the Jews of medieval Latin Christendom posed significant questions that have still not been resolved by European societies. The most fundamental of these questions involves openness to diversity. This question was answered by and large negatively during our period. As we have seen, the more advanced areas of western Christendom expelled their Jews, in effect opting for homogeneity as a principle of societal organization. That, however, is hardly the end of the story. Subsequent to the year 1500, Europe has continued wrestling with the issue of diversity, first as a result of the disintegration of the medieval Roman Catholic synthesis and more recently as a result of modern population movement and globalization. Thus,

the Jews performed the difficult and painful task of putting diversity
on the societal agenda and suffering the negatives associated with
raising such difficult questions. Retrospectively, voices in modern
Europe that have espoused diversity have come to reevaluate and
esteem the medieval Jewish contribution to the ideal of a heterogeneous society.[2]

Negative Jewish memories have been yet more intense. There has
been, to be sure, awareness of some of the grand cultural and spiritual achievements of the Jews of medieval western Christendom, but
that awareness has done little to efface the broader sense of persecution and expulsion, of pain and suffering. Once again, this book
has taken issue with the overarching folk memory. There has been
no effort to dismiss the reality of majority fear and animosity, negative ecclesiastical policy and imagery, governmental exploitation,
recurrent violence, and banishment. However, it has regularly been
noted that these negatives by no means constituted the whole of
the story. There were numerous achievements associated with the
effort to embed Jewish life in medieval western Christendom. These
achievements included the transition of the center of gravity in Jewish life from the Islamic world to Christendom, the development of
new economic outlets, the fashioning of effective self-governance,
and the attainment of intellectual and cultural heights in a number of
domains.

Less obviously, the Jews of medieval western Christendom developed in ways that have proven highly adaptive to modern living. First
among these new characteristics was willingness for demographic
movement and change. The movement of Jews into medieval western
Christendom was itself a sign of Jewish readiness to break through the
prior limits of Jewish settlement. First the northwestern and north-
central areas of Europe were opened to Jewish settlement, followed by
northeastern Europe as well. Moreover, the Jews whose fate we have
been tracing committed themselves more generally to wide-ranging
mobility, to preparedness for movement and change. As we have
seen, some of the movement was forced upon these Jews. They were
expelled from England, from France, from sectors of Germany and
Italy, and eventually from Spain and Portugal. Alongside this forced
movement, however, the Jews of medieval Latin Christendom show
a growing willingness to uproot themselves voluntarily in search of
opportunity. The descendants of the Jews who made the decision
to move into western Christendom and especially of the Jews who

chose to move into the hitherto uncharted north continued to show a propensity for voluntary movement; these Jews became a fairly mobile people, at a point in time when mobility was far from the norm. Jews in England, France, and Germany moved into old towns in which Jews had never previous settled; they moved into entirely new towns; they moved eastward into Hungary and Poland when these developing areas began to show promise.

Moreover, as soon as opportunities resurfaced in more western areas, the Jews of eastern Europe responded with alacrity to these new options. Jews began migrating back into German territories reopened to Jewish settlement; they exploited opportunities further westward in lands such as Holland and England, where new forms of political thinking were enabling Jewish settlement under innovative circumstances. In the most striking movement of all, these Jews began streaming westward into the New World during the nineteenth century, as word of the opportunities available there penetrated eastern Europe. In effect, the initial impulse to immigrate into medieval western Christendom and the subsequent migrations — involuntary and voluntary — to which that initial decision led transformed the Jews into one of the most mobile of human communities. In this sense, they were — despite all their imputed backwardness — very much in the vanguard of modernity. To the extent that modernity has involved the willingness to break the bonds of ancestral geographic limitation and to venture forth into new areas as opportunity beckons, the Jews of medieval western Christendom were quintessentially modern.

Much the same is true for Jewish economic activity. Once again, the hallmark of the Jews we have been studying was adaptability. They came into new areas of settlement first as traders; they moved into the field of moneylending as new opportunities beckoned; in late medieval eastern Europe, they adapted once more. It again seems reasonable to suggest that this economic adaptability, fashioned out of the constraints imposed on the Jewish experience in medieval western Christendom, came to serve the descendants of these medieval Jews well in their encounter with the Western world during the modern period. Like the capacity for mobility bequeathed by the medieval Jews to their heirs, so too their economic adroitness — once more born out of necessity — proved advantageous. Studies of all areas of the modern West have indicated the Jewish capacity for discerning evolving economic needs and exploiting the opportunities presented by these evolving needs. In foreign trade, merchandising of all kinds, development of the modern media, and formation of innovative intellectual and technological pursuits, the Jews of the modern West seem to have absorbed the lessons first learned by those ancestors whom we have been studying.[3]

Yet another success of the Jews of medieval western Christendom was maintenance of Jewish identity in the face of considerable majority pressure for conversion. Jews were able to create the internal institutions for maintenance of Jewish identity and to fashion convincing rationales for remaining Jewish. The ability to exist in a dynamic and challenging environment, to appreciate the vigor of that environment while adopting a stance of critical distance, to enjoy the stimulation of majority creativity, and yet to maintain minority identity constituted a major Jewish achievement during our period and a significant legacy to modern Jewry, which has remained committed to the stimulating European setting that had cost so much medieval Jewish grief and encouraged so much medieval Jewish creativity.

Simplistic majority and minority memories require considerable correction and nuance. Hopefully, the present study has provided some of the requisite correction and nuance for majority and minority memories of the Jewish experience in medieval western Christendom.

NOTES

—————————— · ——————————

PREFACE

1. See the important essay by Gavin I. Langmuir, "Majority History and Postbiblical Jews," *Journal of the History of Ideas* 27 (1966): 343–363, reprinted in Langmuir's *Toward a Definition of Antisemitism* (Berkeley: University of California Press, 1990), 21–41.

2. Special mention should be made of the contribution of general medievalists to the recent study of medieval Jewish history. Once the province of specialists in the history of the Jews only, reconstruction of the medieval Jewish past has benefited enormously from the work of North American medievalists like Gavin I. Langmuir, William Chester Jordan, Robert Stacey, and Mark D. Meyerson and from a host of European medievalists, especially in England, Spain, and Germany.

3. The recent overall histories of the Jews that include important sections on medieval Jewry include: Salo W. Baron, *A Social and Religious History of the Jews* (2nd ed., 18 vols.; New York: Columbia University Press, 1952–1983), vols. 3–12; Haim Hillel Ben-Sasson, *A History of the Jewish People* (Cambridge, Mass.: Harvard University Press, 1976), 385–723; Robert M. Seltzer, *Jewish People, Jewish Thought: The Jewish Experience in History* (New York: Macmillan, 1980), 323–450. The two one-volume histories are Kenneth R. Stow, *Alienated Minority: The Jews of Medieval Latin Europe* (Cambridge, Mass.; Harvard University Press, 1992), and Leonard B. Glick, *Abraham's Heirs: Jews and Christians in Medieval Europe* (Syracuse: Syracuse University Press, 1999). Also valuable are two recent essay collections from Germany – Christoph Cluse (ed.), *The Jews of Europe in the Middle Ages (Tenth to Fifteenth Centuries)* (Turnhout: Brepols, 2004), and

the museum exhibit catalog entitled *The Jews of Europe in the Middle Ages* (Ostfildern: Hatje Cantz Publishers, 2005).

4. Suggestions for further reading will be provided in the notes. A website currently being constructed by the Center for Online Judaic Studies (www.cojs.org) will include considerable material on the Jews in medieval western Christendom, ranging from digital photographs of important artifacts to major primary sources in English translation to essays of varying lengths on key topics in medieval European Jewish history.

5. Note the valuable observations along this same line in Arthur Green, *A Guide to the Zohar* (Stanford: Stanford University Press, 2004), xiii–xiv.

6. The two most comprehensive collections of source materials in English are Jacob Rader Marcus (ed. and trans.), *The Jew in the Medieval World: A Source Book: 315–1791* (rev. ed.; Cincinnati: Hebrew Union College Press, 1999), and Robert Chazan (ed. and trans.), *Church, State, and Jew in the Middle Ages* (New York: Behrman House, 1980). In the bibliography, I have separated the sources from the secondary readings in order to further encourage exploration of the primary data. Since this book is addressed to a general audience, I will not cite the sources in their original, but will indicate available English translations.

INTRODUCTION

1. Benjamin's travelogue was published in a critical edition with English translation as *The Itinerary of Benjamin of Tudela*, ed. Marcus Nathan Adler (London: Henry Frowde, 1907). There is a rather copious literature on the reliability of Benjamin's account. The contemporary consensus is that the travelogue reflects an actual trip, although some of the details – especially for the easternmost portions of Benjamin's journey – might be suspect.

2. There is considerable uncertainty as to the precise meaning of the numbers given by Benjamin.

3. Again, the precise meaning of these figures is unclear.

4. See Robert Chazan, "Then and Now: Jewish Life at the End of the First and Second Christian Millennium," *The Solomon Goldman Lectures* 8 (2003): 51–70. Both Simon Dubnow and Salo W. Baron, in their multi-volume overviews of the Jewish past, stress the importance of this transition.

5. See Robert Chazan, *Fashioning Jewish Identity in Medieval Western Christendom* (Cambridge: Cambridge University Press, 2004), chap. 3, for discussion of the pre-twelfth century Jewish engagement with Christianity or lack thereof.

6. For a valuable overview of Jewish engagement with Christianity in the Islamic sphere, see Daniel J. Lasker, "The Jewish Critique of Christianity

under Islam in the Middle Ages," *Proceedings of the American Academy for Jewish Research* 57 (1991): 121–153.

7. This was not case in the frontier areas of western Christendom, especially Spain and Hungary. See, for example, Robert I. Burns, *Muslims, Christians, and Jews in the Crusader Kingdom of Valencia* (Cambridge: Cambridge University Press, 1984); Mark D. Meyerson, *Jews in an Iberian Kingdom: Society, Economy, and Politics in Morvedre, 1248–1391* (Leiden: Brill, 2004); idem, *A Jewish Renaissance in Fifteenth-Century Spain* (Princeton: Princeton University Press, 2004); and Nora Berend, *At the Gates of Christendom: Jews, Muslims, and "Pagans" in Medieval Hungary, c. 1000–c. 1300* (Cambridge: Cambridge University Press, 2001).

8. I will occasionally use the term "Europe" instead of "western Christendom." Overall, I prefer the latter term for two reasons. In the first place, western Christendom only slowly became synonymous with Europe, because of the areas that remained well into our period outside Christian control. Secondly, the term "western Christendom" highlights the extent to which Christianity was the unifying element within this sprawling and diverse area.

9. For a striking description of this fault line, see R. W. Southern, *The Making of the Middle Ages* (New Haven: Yale University Press, 1953), 20–25.

10. Southern- and northern-European Jewries have often been equated with the Jewish designations Sephardic and Ashkenazic, although this conflation is not quite accurate. The biblical term Sepharad was applied by medieval Jews to the Iberian peninsula. Thus, the designation Sephardic was used for Iberian Jews. It was not extended to cover the rather different Jewries of southern France and Italy. The biblical term Ashkenaz was originally applied by medieval Jews to the areas of Germany. Since eventually the Jews of England were expelled eastward to France and the Jews of France eastward to Germany and many of the Jews of Gemany eastward to Hungary and Poland, the designation Ashkenazic was extended eventually to all of northern European Jewry, stretching from England in the west through Poland in the east.

11. This distinction is extensively treated in Berend, *At the Gates of Christendom*, chap. 1. Berend used terminology of core and periphery; I have preferred terminology of interior and exposed, out of concern that identifying such areas as the Iberian and Italian peninsulas as peripheral might convey a misleading impression.

12. The studies available for the Jewish communities of the diverse areas of medieval western Christendom will be cited regularly in the notes.

13. Interestingly, the year 1000 is taken as the starting point for William Chester Jordan's excellent survey *Europe in the High Middle Ages* (London: Penguin Books, 2002). The developments that moved Jordan to begin

his survey with the year 1000 constitute precisely the factors that transformed Europe into the home of an increasingly large number of Jews.

14. See, e.g., Cecil Roth, *The History of the Jews of Italy* (Philadelphia: Jewish Publication Society of America, 1946), and Robert Bonfil, *Jewish Life in Renaissance Italy*, trans. Anthony Oldcorn (Berkeley: University of California Press, 1994).

15. Throughout this book, there will be references to aspects of Jewish activity that show a high level of integration into the majority ambience. For a general statement of this integration on the cultural level, see Ivan G. Marcus, "A Jewish–Christian Symbiosis: The Culture of Early Ashkenaz," in *Cultures of the Jews: A New History*, ed. David Biale (New York: Schocken Books, 2002), 449–516. Interestingly, the recent one-volume histories of the Jews in medieval Europe and the recent collections of essays noted above, in the preface, differ in this regard, with a majority opting for "of." They are entitled: *Alienated Minority: The Jews of Medieval Latin Europe*; *Abraham's Heirs: Jews and Christians in Medieval Europe*; *The Jews of Europe in the Middle Ages (Tenth to Fifteenth Centuries)*; and *The Jews of Europe in the Middle Ages*. In the important opening essay to the volume edited by Cluse, Alfred Haverkamp makes an explicit case for the history of the Jews in medieval Europe as both Jewish and European – see Alfred Haverkamp, "The Jews of Medieval Europe in the Middle Ages: By Way of Introduction," in *The Jews of Europe in the Middle Ages (Tenth to Fifteenth Centuries)*, 1–15.

16. See the trail-blazing collection of Solomon Grayzel (ed. and trans.), *The Church and the Jews in the XIIIth Century* (2 vols.; Philadelphia and New York: Dropsie College and Jewish Theological Seminary, 1933–1989), and Shlomo Simonsohn (ed.), *The Apostolic See and the Jews: Documents* (7 vols.; Toronto: Pontifical Institute of Mediaeval Studies, 1988–1990).

17. See especially J. M. Rigg (ed.), *Select Pleas, Starrs, and Other Records from the Rolls of the Exchequer of the Jews, 1220–1284* (London: B. Quaritch, 1902); H. Loewe et al. (eds.), *Starrs and Jewish Charters in the British Museum* (Cambridge: Cambridge University Press, 1930); J. M. Rigg et al. (eds.), *Calendar of the Plea Rolls of the Exchequer of the Jews Preserved in the Public Record Office* (5 vols.; London: Macmillan, 1905–1992).

18. The pioneering collections of Jean Regne (ed.), *History of the Jews in Aragon: Regesta and Documents 1213–1327* (rev. ed., Jerusalem: Magnes Press, 1978), and Yitzhak Baer (ed.), *Die Juden im christlichen Spanien* (rev. ed., 2 vols.; Farnborough: Gregg International, 1970) – both originally published in the 1920s – remain enormously valuable.

19. Note the series of books on specific Jewish communities published in the series Hispania Judaica. The extremely important studies of Mark D. Meyerson, *Jews in an Iberian Kingdom: Society, Economy, and Politics in Morvedre, 1248–1391* and *A Jewish Renaissance in Fifteenth-Century Spain*,

have already been cited above, n. 7. All these studies are grounded in the rich Spanish archival materials.

20. This effort has been coordinated by Shlomo Simonsohn and the Diaspora Research Institute at Tel-Aviv University. Multi-volume collections have been completed for Genoa, Mantua, Milan, Piedmont, Rome, Sicily, and Umbria.

21. On the narrative sources, the classic study is Yosef Hayim Yerushalmi, *Zakhor: Jewish History and Jewish Memory* (Seattle: University of Washington Press, 1982). On the poetry, note especially the valuable study of Susan L. Einbinder, *Beautiful Death: Jewish Poetry and Martyrdom in Medieval France* (Princeton: Princeton University Press, 2002).

22. For a study of the earliest polemical composition from western Christendom, see Chazan, *Fashioning Jewish Identity in Medieval Western Christendom.*

23. It should be noted that the three broad geographic areas and their subdivisions lend themselves to a unified narrative in differing measure. In some cases, e.g. northern France and England, a unified narrative is fairly easy to achieve; in some cases, e.g. Spain, it is considerably more difficult (note the insistence in the two Meyerson volumes cited on the differences among the various regions of the Iberian peninsula); in some cases, most prominently Italy, a unified narrative is impossible.

24. This organizational scheme necessitates some measure of repetition; I make every effort to keep repetition to a minimum. More specifically, there are of necessity themes in the chapter on the Church that recur in the subsequent three chapters. I try to treat the general issue in the chapter on the Church and its more specific ramifications in the subsequent chapters. A second source of repetition involves the narrative chapters, on the one hand, and the analytic chapters on the other. With respect to the material aspects of Jewish life, I provide fullest detail in the narrative chapters; in the analytic chapter (chap. 6), I simply refer to developments described more fully previously. With respect to the cultural and spiritual aspects of Jewish life, I reverse this pattern, providing overviews in the narrative chapters and fuller discussion in the analytic chapter (chap. 7).

25. See above in the preface, n. 3, for some prominent names.

26. Some scholarly tension is inevitable. Scholars begin their work with skills and interests. Inevitably, the skills and interests of those trained in Jewish history and general medieval history diverge. It is precisely from the complementary of the two groups that so much progress has eventuated.

27. For the expression of Jewish memory through ritual and liturgy, see Yerushalmi, *Zakhor.*

28. Yerushalmi, *Zakhor*, chaps. 2–3.

1. Inscriptions are the most long-lived of the remnants of Jewish life in western Christendom prior to the year 1000. For the most up-to-date collection of these inscriptions, see David Noy (ed.), *Jewish Inscriptions of Western Europe* (2 vols.; Cambridge: Cambridge University Press, 1993–1995). For Christian literary sources reflecting Jews and Jewish life, see the valuable collection by Bernhard Blumenkranz (ed.), *Les auteurs latins chrétiens du moyen âge sur les juifs and le judaïsme* (Paris: Mouton, 1963); this collection extends into the early years of the twelfth century.

2. Two excellent overviews of Jewish experience in the medieval Muslim world are available: S. D. Goitein, *Jews and Arabs: Their Contacts through the Ages* (New York: Schocken, 1955), and Bernard Lewis, *The Jews of Islam* (Princeton: Princeton University Press, 1984). Goitein's multi-volume study of the daily life of the Jews reflected in the Cairo Genizah is a monument of recent scholarship on medieval Jewish life – *A Mediterranean Society: The Jewish Communities of the Arab World as Portrayed in the Documents of the Cairo Genizah* (6 vols.; Berkeley: University of California Press, 1967–1993).

3. For more on this, see below.

4. Indeed, this complex relationship is critical to understanding post-1500 Jewish history in the Christian world as well. For a thoughtful and well-formulated overview of this historic relationship, see James Carroll, *Constantine's Sword: The Church and the Jews* (Boston: Houghton Mifflin, 2001). For a more focused analysis of pre-medieval and medieval Church views of Judaism and the Jews, see Jeremy Cohen, *Living Letters of the Law: Ideas of the Jew in Medieval Christianity* (Berkeley: University of California Press, 1999).

5. This ambiguity and this ambivalence are highlighted throughout Cohen's valuable *Living Letters of the Law*.

6. For a fine overview of the various scholarly positions on Paul's relationship to Judaism and the Jews, see John Gager, *Reinventing Paul* (New York: Oxford University Press, 2000).

7. Cohen, *Living Letters of the Law*, emphasizes the ambiguity and ambivalence of Paul's position vis-à-vis Judaism and the Jews.

8. For a valuable recent study of the lengthy and complex process described briefly here, see Marcel Simon, *Verus Israel*, trans. H. McKeating (London: Oxford University Press, 1986); Miriam S. Taylor, *Anti-Judaism and Early Christian Identity: A Critique of the Scholarly Consensus* (Leiden: E. J. Brill, 1995); and Daniel Boyarin, *Border Lines: The Partition of Judaeo-Christianity* (Philadelphia: University of Pennsylvania Press, 2004).

9. Augustine's views of Judaism and the Jews have been studied extensively. The most penetrating treatment is that of Cohen, *Living Letters of the Law*, chap. 1.

10. For recent treatments of this critical juncture, see Shaye J. D. Cohen, *From the Maccabees to the Mishnah* (Philadelphia: Westminster Press, 1987); Lawrence H. Schiffman, *From Text to Tradition: A History of Second Temple and Rabbinic Judaism* (Hoboken: Ktav, 1991).

11. For a useful introduction to this literature, see Jacob Neusner, *Introduction to Rabbinic Literature* (New York: Doubleday, 1994).

12. See Lee I. Levine, *The Ancient Synagogue: The First Thousand Years* (New Haven: Yale University Press, 2000).

2 THE PAN-EUROPEAN ROMAN CATHOLIC CHURCH

1. The best broad introductions to the medieval Church and the Jews are Baron, *A Social and Religious History of the Jews*, 4: 5–20; 9: 3–134, and the closing volume of Simonsohn, *The Apostolic See and the Jews*. The latter is especially comprehensive. Cohen, *Living Letters of the Law*, is a superb introduction to ecclesiastical imagery of the Jews.

2. All these developments will be treated in this chapter.

3. See Jeremy Cohen, *The Friars and the Jews: The Evolution of Medieval Anti-Judaism* (Ithaca: Cornell University Press, 1982).

4. Chazan, *Church, State, and Jew*, 44–45.

5. Idem, *European Jewry and the First Crusade* (Berkeley: University of California Press, 1987), 225.

6. On Bernard's position, see below, in the section on ecclesiastical policy.

7. See below, in the section on Church imagery of Judaism and the Jews.

8. Chazan, *Church, State, and Jew*, 34.

9. Ibid.

10. Ibid., 32.

11. For further detail, see below, in the section of ecclesiastical policy and in chap. 4.

12. See chaps. 4 through 7 for discussion of the emergence of expulsion as the modality for inflicting corporate punishment on the Jews.

13. Both citations can be found in Grayzel, *The Church and the Jews in the XIIIth Century*, 1: 93–95.

14. Ibid., 1: 93.

15. Chazan, *Church, State, and Jew*, 103–104. For fuller analysis of Bernard's position, see idem, *Medieval Stereotypes and Modern Antisemitism* (Berkeley: University of California Press, 1997), 41–46.

16. See below, chap. 5.

17. Grayzel, *The Church and the Jews in the XIIIth Century*, 1: 227–231.

18. See below, in this section.
19. Grayzel, *The Church and the Jews in the XIIIth Century*, 1: 201–203.
20. See below, chap. 5.
21. Grayzel, *The Church and the Jews in the XIIIth Century*, 1: 297.
22. Ibid., 309.
23. Ibid., 241–243.
24. For these allegations, see Judah Rosenthal, "The Talmud on Trial," *Jewish Quarterly Review* 47 (1956–1957): 58–76 and 145–169.
25. Grayzel, *The Church and the Jews in the XIIIth Century*, 1: 251–253.
26. Ibid., 275–281.
27. See below, chap. 4.
28. In citing verses from the Hebrew Bible, I will generally use the new Jewish Publication Society translation. I have done so here, although with slight modification.
29. For a succinct overview of evolving ecclesiastical positions on moneylending, see John T. Noonan, Jr., *A Church that Can and Cannot Change: The Development of Catholic Moral Teaching* (Notre Dame: University of Notre Dame, 2005), 127–146.
30. For further detail on the issue of Jewish lending and crusader protection, see Chazan, *European Jewry and the First Crusade*, 179–191.
31. Grayzel, *The Church and the Jews in the XIIIth Century*, 1: 313.
32. Ibid., 307.
33. See below, chap. 4.
34. For the accelerating pressures of the twelfth century, see Chazan, *Fashioning Jewish Identity in Medieval Western Christendom*; for Jacob ben Reuben and his *Milhamot ha-Shem*, see especially 98–103.
35. Idem, *Daggers of Faith: Thirteenth Century Christian Missionizing and the Jewish Response* (Berkeley: University of California Press, 1989).
36. Idem, *Barcelona and Beyond: The Disputation of 1263 and Its Aftermath* (Berkeley: University of California Press, 1992).
37. Yitzhak Baer, *A History of the Jews in Christian Spain*, trans. Louis Schoffman et al. (2 vols.; Philadelphia: Jewish Publication Society, 1961–1966), 2: 170–243.
38. For the contrast between Bernard and Peter, see Chazan, *Medieval Stereotypes*, 41–52.
39. Grayzel, *The Church and the Jews in the XIIIth Century*, 1: 105–107.
40. Ibid., 115.
41. Ibid., 107–109: blasphemy against Jesus; 137–139: blasphemy against the host; 107, 127, and 141: usury.
42. Ibid., 109.
43. For full treatment of the host allegation, see Miri Rubin, *Gentile Tales: The Narrative Assault on Late Medieval Jews* (New Haven: Yale University Press, 1999).

44. The early and influential study on this period was Charles Homer Haskins, *The Renaissance of the Twelfth Century* (Cambridge, Mass.: Harvard University Press, 1927); for more recent treatments, see Robert L. Benson and Giles Constable (eds.), *Renaissance and Renewal in the Twelfth Century* (Cambridge, Mass.: Harvard University Press, 1982), and Giles Constable, *The Reformation of the Twelfth Century* (Cambridge: Cambridge University Press, 1996).

45. For Christian argumentation based on this Isaiah passage and Jewish responses, see Chazan, *Fashioning Jewish Identity*, chap. 7. For an extensive collection of Jewish explications of this text, see Samuel R. Driver and Adolf Neubauer (trans.), *The "Suffering Servant" of Isaiah according to the Jewish Interpreters* (Oxford: James Parker, 1877).

46. See below, chap. 7, and Chazan, *Fashioning Jewish Identity*, chaps 8–10.

47. See Beryl Smalley, *The Study of the Bible in the Middle Ages* (3rd ed.: Oxford: Blackwell, 1983).

48. For fuller discussion, see below, chap. 7.

49. Again, see below, chap. 7.

50. On this imagery of Christianity in general, see Elliot R. Wolfson, *Language, Eros, Being: Kabbalistic Hermeneutics and Poetic Imagination* (New York: Fordham University Press, 2004), especially chap. 5. For the *Zohar* in particular, see Green, *A Guide to the Zohar*, chap. 7.

51. For fuller discussion of this symbiotic invigoration, see below, chap. 7.

3 THE OLDER JEWRIES OF THE SOUTH

1. Recall the distinction established in the introduction between the Jewish communities of southern Europe and those of the north.

2. It seems likely the largest Jewish community in medieval southern Europe was that of the Iberian peninsula, which was predominantly under Muslim rule at the beginning of our period.

3. Recall the distinction established in the introduction between exposed and interior portions of medieval western Christendom.

4. The best overviews of the history of the Jews in medieval southern France are Baron, *A Social and Religious History of the Jews*, 3: 43–64 and 9: 82–91, and William Chester Jordan, *The French Monarchy and the Jews: From Philip Augustus to the Last of the Capetians* (Philadelphia: University of Pennsylvania Press, 1989), 105–127, 162–176, and 223–237.

5. See again, Noy, *Jewish Inscriptions of Western Europe*.

6. Benjamin of Tudela, *Itinerary*, 3–4.

7. For more on the translation effort, see below, chap. 7.

8. This important text is available in an English translation by Frank Talmage as *The Book of the Covenant* (Toronto: Pontifical Institute of Mediaeval Studies, 1972).

9. The same Frank Talmage produced one of the fullest biographies of a medieval Jewish leader in his *David Kimhi: The Man and the Commentaries* (Cambridge, Mass.: Harvard University Press, 1975).

10. Selections from the early southern-French kabbalists are available in *The Early Kabbalah*, ed. Joseph Dan and trans. Ronald Kiener (New York: Paulist Press, 1986). *Sefer ha-Bahir*, with all its difficulties, is available in an English translation by Arye Kaplan (Northvale: Jason Aronson, 1995).

11. For the changes in Capetian policy in the north, see below, chap. 4.

12. For discussion of the polemical writings of Rabbi Meir bar Simon, see Chazan, *Fashioning Jewish Identity*, 105–114.

13. See idem, "Anti-Usury Efforts in Thirteenth-Century Narbonne and the Jewish Response," *Proceedings of the American Academy for Jewish Research* 41–42 (1973–1974): 45–67.

14. Again, for the details of this evolving anti-usury legislation in northern France, see below, chap. 4.

15. Idem, "A Jewish Plaint to Saint Louis," *Hebrew Union College Annual* 45 (1974): 287–305.

16. For the details of this process, see Jordan, *The French Monarchy and the Jews*, 162–176.

17. Again, see below, chap. 4.

18. See the valuable essay of Daniele Iancu-Agou. "Provence: Jewish Settlement, Mobility, and Culture," in Cluse, *The Jews of Europe in the Middle Ages*, 175–189.

19. An English translation of this important work has been provided by Seymour Feldman, *The Wars of the Lord* (3 vols.; Philadelphia: Jewish Publication society, 1984–1999).

20. Medieval Spanish Jewry has been studied extensively. For broad treatments, see Baron, *A Social and Religious History of the Jews*, 4: 27–43 and 10: 118–219, and Baer, *A History of the Jews in Christian Spain*. Again, special mention should be made of Meyerson, *Jews in an Iberian Kingdom* and *A Jewish Renaissance in Fifteenth-Century Spain*.

21. See especially Bernard S. Bachrach, *Early Medieval Jewish Policy in Western Europe* (Minneapolis: University of Minnesota Press, 1977), chap. 1.

22. See Eliyahu Ashtor, *The Jews of Moslem Spain*, trans. Aaron Klein and Jenny Machlowitz Klein (3 vols.; Philadelphia: Jewish Publication Society, 1973–1984).

23. Chazan, *Church, State, and Jew*, 99–100.

24. Note parallels in the later thinking of St. Bernard during the Second Crusade – see above, chap. 2.

25. Chazan, *Church, State, and Jew*, 69–70.

26. Ibid., 71.

27. See Abraham ibn Daud, *Sefer ha-Qabbalah: The Book of Tradition*, ed. and trans. Gerson D. Cohen (Philadelphia: Jewish Publication Society, 1967).

28. On the Kimhis and ibn Tibbons, see above. For the arrival of Iberian Jews in southern Italy as well, see below.

29. Yom Tov Assis, *The Golden Age of Aragonese Jewry: Community and Society in the Crown of Aragon, 1213–1327* (London: The Littman Library of Jewish Civilization, 1997).

30. Idem, *Jewish Economy in the Medieval Crown of Aragon 1213–1327: Money and Power* (Leiden: E. J. Brill, 1997).

31. It should be emphasized that there were substantial differences among the various areas of the Iberian peninsula. These differences are regularly reflected in the overviews of Salo Baron and Yitzhak Baer and very prominently in the recent two-volume study of Mark D. Meyerson.

32. See Benjamin Z. Kedar, *Crusade and Mission: European Approaches toward the Muslims* (Princeton: Princeton University Press, 1984).

33. Unwilling to acknowledge Christianity as a viable alternative for medieval Jews, many modern historians of medieval Jewry have tended to explain fourteenth- and fifteenth-century Christian missionizing successes in terms of violence, despair, and ulterior motives. Fuller attention must be accorded the very serious Church commitment to bringing its message to Jews and the impact of that protracted effort.

34. There is some uncertainty as to the location of Jacob ben Reuben. I have been convinced by the arguments of Carlos del Valle for a Spanish locale – "Jacob ben Ruben de Huesca. Polemista. Su patria y su epoca," in *Polemica Judeo-Cristiana estudios*, ed. Johann Maier et al. (Madrid: Aben Ezra Ediciones, 1992), 59–65.

35. See above, chap. 2.

36. Baer, *A History of the Jews in Christian Spain*, 1:327–354.

37. For evaluations of the multi-faceted career of Nahmanides, see Isadore Twersky (ed.), *Rabbi Moses ben Nahman (Ramban): Explorations in His Religious and Literary Virtuosity* (Cambridge, Mass.: Harvard University Press, 1983).

38. See above, in the section on southern France.

39. David Berger, "How Did Nahmanides Propose to Resolve the Maimonidean Controversy?" in *Me'ah She'arim: Studies in Medieval Jewish Spiritual Life in Memory of Isadore Twersky*, ed. Ezra Fleischer et al. (Jerusalem: Magnes Press, 2001), 135–146.

40. See the classic studies of Gershom Scholem on this Spanish kabbalah, along with the newer works of Moshe Idel and Elliot R. Wolfson. All are cited in chap. 7.

41. Again, see above, in the section on southern France.

42. For fuller information on the *Zohar*, see below, chap. 7.

43. This view was espoused with special force by Yitzhak Baer. It is stressed in his extensive account of the crisis of 1391, in *A History of the Jews in Christian Spain*, 2:95–169.
44. See below, chap. 5.
45. Baer, *A History of the Jews in Christian Spain*, 2: 259–270, and more fully Meyerson, *A Jewish Renaissance in Fifteenth-Century Spain*.
46. Such in fact had happened in the wake of 1096 – see below, chap. 5.
47. Meyerson, *A Jewish Renaissance in Fifteenth-Century Spain*, has much interesting material on converts resuming Jewish practice and belief.
48. As a result of the special circumstances in Portugal, the story of the Portuguese New Christians is somewhat different from that of the New Christians of Spain.
49. For a number of schemes for depicting the geographic diversity of medieval Italy, see Bonfil, *Jewish Life in Renaissance Italy*, 9–11.
50. Note the prior discussion of southern France and Spain, on the one hand, and of northern European Jewry in chaps. 4 and 5 on the other.
51. Both the major recent overviews of medieval Italian Jewry – Baron, *A Social and Religious History of the Jews*, 4: 20–27 and 10: 220–296 and Roth, *The History of the Jews of Italy*, 38–152 – have great difficulty with organizational structure.
52. None of these three areas will be described in the detail found earlier for southern France and the Iberian peninsula and subsequently for northern France, England, Germany, and eastern Europe. This is lamentable, but the result of the special circumstances of the Italian peninsula.
53. Benjamin of Tudela, *Itinerary*, 5–10 and 78–79. Again, precisely what these numbers mean is not clear.
54. An English translation of this valuable text is available – see Ahimaaz ben Paltiel, *The Chronicle of Ahimaaz*, trans. Marcus Salzman (New York: Columbia University Press, 1924).
55. Noy, *Jewish Inscriptions of Western Europe*, 150–181.
56. In a number of ways, Donnolo provides interesting parallels to Hasdai ibn Shaprut, the major tenth-century figure on the Iberian peninsula.
57. On this persecution and the migration it sparked, see above in the section on Spain.
58. Note the valuable article of Shlomo Simonsohn, "Sicily: A Millennium of Convivenza (or Almost)," in Cluse, *The Jews of Europe in the Middle Ages*, 105–121.
59. Noy, *Jewish Inscriptions of Western Europe*.
60. Benjamin of Tudela, *Itinerary*, 6–7.
61. The early part of this story can be found in Chazan, *Church, State, and Jew*, 293–294.
62. Benjamin of Tudela, *Itinerary*, 5–6.
63. On the *Constitutio*, see above, chap. 2.

64. Indeed, Rome was a continuous home to a considerable Jewish community from late antiquity down to the twenty-first century.

65. Note the valuable demographic information in Michele Luzzati, "Northern and Central Italy: Assessment of Research and Further Prospects," in Cluse, *The Jews of Europe in the Middle Ages*, 191–199.

66. For details on England, northern France, and Germany, see below, chaps. 4 and 5.

67. Recall the penetration of the moneylending specialty into southern France and Spain as well.

68. Sixteenth-century creativity and the Counter-Reformation trials and tribulations of northern-Italian Jewry lie beyond the purview of this book.

69. Luzzati, "Northern and Central Italy," 194. Jewish mobility is likewise emphasized in Meyerson's study of the Jews of Valencia and Iancu-Agou's essay on the Jews of Provence. It will emerge as a central theme in the epilogue.

4 THE NEWER JEWRIES OF THE NORTH: NORTHERN FRANCE AND ENGLAND

1. See below, chap. 6, for fuller discussion of the mix of success and failure.

2. Recall these geographic distinctions, as laid out in the introduction.

3. Jordan, *The French Monarchy and the Jews*, 128–129.

4. For overviews of medieval northern-French Jewry, see Baron, *A Social and Religious History of the Jews*, 4: 43–64 and 10: 53–82; Robert Chazan, *Medieval Jewry in Northern France: A Political and Social History* (Baltimore: Johns Hopkins University Press, 1973); and Jordan, *The French Monarchy and the Jews*.

5. As noted, the first part of this source can be found in Chazan, *Church, State, and Jew*, 293–294.

6. Ibid., 103.

7. Rigord's depiction of the last of these actions – expulsion of the Jews – can be found in ibid., 311–312.

8. Recall evidence in the preceding chapter for the appearance of moneylending as a Jewish economic activity in southern France, Spain, and Italy. In these older settings, with their more variegated Jewish economy, moneylending did not assume the central importance that it did in the newer areas of the north, with their more limited Jewish economic outlets.

9. Chazan, *European Jewry and the First Crusade*, 226.

10. Ibid., 287–288.

11. See above, chap. 2.

12. For full analysis of this incident and the Jewish responses it generated, see Robert Chazan, "The Blois Incident of 1171: A Study in Jewish Intercommunal Organization," *Proceedings of the American Academy for Jewish Research* 36 (1968): 13–31.
13. Chazan, *Church, State, and Jew*, 115–116.
14. For the narrative of Ephraim of Bonn, see Shlomo Eidelberg (trans.), *The Jews and the Crusaders* (Madison: University of Wisconsin Press, 1977), 121–133, with this passage on p. 131. Note Ephraim's indication that Jewish lending in France and England was different from that in Germany, with governmental authorities deeply involved. His report of total forgiveness of Jewish loans does not seem credible.
15. Chazan, *Church, State, and Jew*, 305–306.
16. See Louis Finkelstein, *Jewish Self-Government in the Middle Ages* (New York: Jewish Theological Seminary, 1925).
17. See again Finkelstein, *Jewish Self-Government*.
18. See below, chap. 7.
19. The changes in Jewish life occasioned by the rule of the Capetians from Philip Augustus onward are carefully analyzed by Jordan in *The French Monarchy and the Jews*.
20. Ibid., 89, for the designation as erratic and for the importance of "predictability of social experience."
21. Jordan suggests that the twenty percent constituted part of the ransom.
22. Jordan suggests that concern with the Church in fact was part of the motivation for the *captio* of 1210.
23. Grayzel, *The Church and the Jews in the XIIIth Century*, 1: 107.
24. Castigation of Jews as outsiders had the ironic implication of condoning Jewish usury in principle. Recall the argument of the archbishop of Narbonne, cited above in chap. 3, that Jews and Christians were in fact brethren.
25. Chazan, *Church, State, and Jew*, 212.
26. Jordan, *The French Monarchy and the Jews*, 96.
27. Chazan, *Church, State, and Jew*, 213.
28. Ibid., 216.
29. See above, chap. 2.
30. Grayzel, *The Church and the Jews in the XIIIth Century*, 1: 275–281.
31. Haym Soloveitchik, "Catastrophe and Halakhic Creativity: Ashkenaz – 1096, 1242, 1306, and 1298," *Jewish History* 12 (1998): 71–85.
32. For a full description of this incident, see Rubin, *Gentile Tales*.
33. For details, see below.
34. Note the extensive discussion of patterns of relocation in Jordan, *The French Monarchy and the Jews*, chap. 13.
35. For the edict, see Chazan, *Church, State, and Jew*, 80–83.
36. For overviews of medieval English Jewish history, see Baron, *A Social and Religious History of the Jews*, 4: 75–86 and 10: 92–115, and Cecil Roth, *A*

History of the Jews in England (3rd ed.; Oxford: Oxford University Press, 1964), 1–131.

37. For details on these five volumes, see above, in the introduction.
38. H. G. Richardson, *The English Jewry under Angevin Kings* (London: Methuen, 1960); R. B. Dobson, *The Jews of York and the Massacre of 1190* (York: University of York, 1974); Robert C. Stacey, *Politics, Policy, and Finance under Henry III: 1216–1245* (Oxford: Oxford University Press, 1987), chap. 4; Robin Mundill, *England's Jewish Solution: Experiment and Expulsion, 1262–1290* (Cambridge: Cambridge University Press, 1998).
39. Thomas of Monmouth's narrative was edited and translated by Augustus Jessopp and Montague Rhodes James as *The Life and Miracles of St. William of Norwich* (Cambridge: Cambridge University Press, 1896).
40. Gavin I. Langmuir has argued that Thomas of Monmouth was the creator of this new allegation – see "Thomas of Monmouth: Detector of Ritual Murder," *Speculum* 59 (1984): 822–846, reprinted in idem, *Toward a Definition of Antisemitism*, 209–236. Langmuir's view has been challenged by John McCulloch, "Jewish Ritual Murder: William of Norwich, Thomas of Monmouth, and the Early Dissemination of the Myth," *Speculum* 72 (1997): 698–740. No matter who precisely first advanced the notion, the significance of the innovation in mid-twelfth-century England is indisputable.
41. The Wurzburg accusation, to be discussed in chapter 5, took place a few years later, in 1147.
42. Roth, *A History of the Jews in England*, 15.
43. For more detail, see below, chap. 5.
44. Again, see below, chap. 5.
45. Stacey, *Politics, Policy, and Finance under Henry III*, 143–144.
46. Ibid., 154.
47. For the text, see Mundill, *England's Jewish Solution*, 291–293.
48. See the discussion of these views in ibid., chap. 8.

5 THE NEWER JEWRIES OF THE NORTH: GERMANY AND EASTERN EUROPE

1. Note the parallels to Jewish circumstances in fragmented Italy, although Italian Jewry never achieved the demographic strength of German Jewry.
2. Overviews of medieval German Jewry are more difficult to compose, because of the lack of unity on the German political scene. The fullest can be found in Baron, *A Social and Religious History of the Jews*, 4: 64–75 and 9: 135–236.
3. The two complementary documents can be found in Chazan, *Church, State, and Jew*, 58–59.
4. Ibid., 60–63.

5. Ibid., 63–66.
6. See above, chap. 4.
7. Note the concern of Rabbi Solomon ben Isaac – Rashi – in his Talmud commentary with the accurate reading of talmudic passages. See below, chap. 7.
8. See above, chap. 4, for First Crusade violence in France.
9. For these various voices, see Robert Chazan, *God, Humanity, and History: The Hebrew First Crusade Narratives* (Berkeley: University of California Press; 2000), chaps. 2–6.
10. Ibid., chap. 2. A translation of the text can be found in Chazan, *European Jewry and the First Crusade*, 225–242.
11. Recall the evidence of proto-crusading animosity on the Iberian peninsula during the 1060s noted above, chap. 3. On the revenge motif, see Jonathan Riley-Smith, "The First Crusade and the Persecution of the Jews," in *Persecution and Toleration*, ed. W. J. Shiels (Oxford: Blackwell, 1984), 51–72. I have completed a study of the millenarian elements reflected in the Hebrew narratives, entitled "'Let Not a Residue nor a Remnant Escape': Millenarian Enthusiasm in the First Crusade."
12. The converts were in fact permitted to return to Jewish life; recall the altered situation in 1391 noted above, in chap. 3.
13. Chazan, *European Jewry and the First Crusade*, 230.
14. Gen. 22:16–18.
15. See above, chap. 2.
16. Again, the narrative of Ephraim of Bonn can be found in Eidelberg, *The Jews and the Crusaders*, 121–133.
17. Rabbi Eleazar's narrative can be found in Chazan, *Church, State, and Jew*, 118–122.
18. See above, chap. 4.
19. See above, chap. 4, and below, chap. 7.
20. For more on the German-Jewish Pietists, see below, chap. 7.
21. Chazan, *Church, State, and Jew*, 84–88.
22. The papal–imperial rivalry over the Jews is heavily emphasized in Baron, *A Social and Religious History of the Jews*, 9: 136–147.
23. Chazan, *Church, State, and Jew*, 124.
24. Exod. 12:13.
25. Grayzel, *The Church and the Jews in the XIIIth Century*, 269–271.
26. Chazan, *Church, State, and Jew*, 124–126.
27. See above, chap. 3.
28. Recall these distinctions in the introduction
29. For overviews, see Baron, *A Social and Religious History of the Jews*, 10: 20–31, and Berend, *At the Gates of Christendom*.
30. This diversity is emphasized by both Baron and Berend. This population diversity is reminiscent in what we have seen in Spain and southern Italy, in chap. 3.

31. On the romantic but discredited notion of Khazar origins for eastern European Jewry, see below.
32. Note the valuable map in Berend, *At the Gates of Christendom*, 59.
33. Ibid., 225.
34. For overviews, see Baron, *A Social and Religious History of the Jews*, 10: 31–51, and Bernard D. Weinryb, *The Jews of Poland: A Social and Economic History of the Jewish Community in Poland from 1100 to 1800* (Philadelphia: Jewish Publication Society, 1973), 17–103.
35. This thesis was strongly enunciated by Arthur Koestler, *The Thirteenth Tribe: The Khazar Empire and Its Heritage* (New York: Random House, 1976).
36. See Weinryb, *The Jews of Poland*, 31.
37. Chazan, *Church, State, and Jew*, 89–93.

6 MATERIAL CHALLENGES, SUCCESSES, AND FAILURES

1. As noted in the introduction, some repetition is unavoidable. I have attempted to limit such repetition to the extent possible.
2. The epilogue includes brief observations on this legacy.
3. Mark D. Meyerson, in his important two-volume study of the Jews of Morvedre, has argued cogently that the yearning for a homogeneous Christian society was considerably reduced on the Iberian peninsula, where societal heterogeneity was the reality. Nonetheless, the yearning did materialize, as did eventually the reality.
4. See above, chap. 2.
5. See below, chap. 7.
6. Chazan, *European Jewry and the First Crusade*, 225.
7. Recall my recent essay, "'Let Not a Residue nor a Remnant Escape,'" with the argument that these aspirations reflect millenarian exhilaration.
8. Again, see above, chap. 2.
9. For an overview of Jewish economic acivity during our period, see Baron, *A Social and Religious History of the Jews*, 4: 150–227, and 12: 3–197.
10. Joseph Shatzmiller, *Shylock Reconsidered: Jews, Moneylending, and Medieval Society* (Berkeley: University of California Press, 1990).
11. For an overview of Jewish relations with the governing authorities, see once again Baron, *A Social and Religious History of the Jews*, 11: 3–76.
12. Chazan, *Church, State, and Jew*, 314–317.
13. Goitein, *A Mediterranean Society*, 2.
14. The best overview of medieval Jewish communal organization remains Salo W. Baron, *The Jewish Community: Its History and Structure to the American Revolution* (3 vols.; Philadelphia: Jewish Publication Society, 1942), 1: 208–282, supplemented by idem, *A Social and Religious History of the Jews*, 5: 58–78.

15. See below, chap. 7.
16. For a review of a number of modern analyses of the process of deteri-
    oration, see Jeremy Cohen, "Recent Historiography on the Medieval
    Church and the Decline of European Jewry," in *Popes, Teachers, and
    Canon Law in the Middle Ages*, ed. James Ross Sweeney and Stanley
    Chodorow (Ithaca: Cornell University Press, 1989), 251–262.
17. For the importance of changing ecclesiastical perceptions, see Cohen,
    The Friars and the Jews; for the impact of the new rationalism, see Anna
    Sapir Abulafia, *Christians and Jews in the Twelfth Century Renaissance*
    (London: Routledge, 1995); for the role of religious doubt, see Gavin
    I. Langmuir, *History, Religion, and Antisemitism* (Berkeley: University of
    California Press, 1990).
18. Some recent analyses, e.g. those of R. I. Moore, *The Formation of a
    Persecuting Society* (Oxford: Blackwell, 1987), and John Boswell, *Chris-
    tianity, Social Tolerance, and Homosexuality: Gay People in Western Europe
    from the Beginning of the Christian Era to the Fourteenth Century* (Chicago:
    University of Chicago Press, 1980), suggest an active role on the part of
    the lay authorities in the arousal of anti-outsider sentiment. This does
    not seem to have been the case with the Jews.
19. This is suggested by Moore, *The Formation of a Persecuting Society*, and
    by Mark Gregory Pegg, *The Corruption of Angels: The Great Inquisition
    of 1245–1246* (Princeton: Princeton University Press, 2001).
20. Here, the suggestions of Moore and Boswell as to the role played by the
    lay authorities seem appropriate.

7 SPIRITUAL CHALLENGES, SUCCESSES, AND FAILURES

1. This sense of isolated and untroubled Jewish cultural and spiritual
   existence has regularly been contrasted with modern Jewish integration into the surrounding culture and the dislocation entailed by this
   integration.
2. The facile contrast between modern Jewish integration into majority society and pre-modern distancing from majority society involves,
   for most observers, modern Jewry on the one hand and pre-modern
   eastern-European Jewry on the other. However, we have noted already –
   in chap. 5 – some of the uniqueness of the late medieval Jewish experience in eastern Europe, with its enhanced distancing from a minimally
   challenging majority environment. The differences between eastern-
   European Jewish life and Jewish life across medieval western Christendom only intensified in the early modern centuries. One of the objectives of this book is to distinguish between the late medieval and early
   modern eastern-European Jewish experience and the experience of the

Jews in medieval western Christendom, which was by no means socially isolated and spiritually untroubled.

3. The economic profile of medieval Jewry in Europe and its impact on majority–minority contact and interaction has been stressed by Jacob Katz, *Exclusiveness and Tolerance: Jewish–Gentile Relations in Medieval and Modern Times* (Oxford: Oxford University Press, 1961), 24–36.

4. Note the eastern-European exception – see above, chap. 5.

5. Recall the sharp contrast drawn between this pattern of Jewish behavior and the massive conversions of 1391 on the Iberian peninsula. For criticism of this sharp distinction, see above, chap. 3.

6. Chazan, *European Jewry and the First Crusade*, 99–136.; idem, *God, Humanity, and History*, 191–210.

7. Recent anthropologically oriented studies have emphasized the embeddedness of medieval European Jews in their environment. Interestingly, two of the most important of these studies – Ivan G. Marcus, *Rituals of Childhood: Jewish Acculturation in Medieval Europe* (New Haven: Yale University Press, 1996), and Elisheva Baumgarten, *Mothers and Children: Jewish Family Life in Medieval Europe* (Princeton: Princeton University Press, 2004) – both address Jewish life in the northern sectors of medieval western Christendom and argue convincingly for the impact of the majority environment upon the Jewish minority.

8. Again, this valuable text is available in an English translation by Talmage as *The Book of the Covenant*. For observations on the book and its author, see Chazan, *Fashioning Jewish Identity*, 94–98.

9. Ibid., 98–103.

10. Ibid., 181–197.

11. Chazan, *Barcelona and Beyond*, for the Barcelona encounter; idem, *Medieval Jewry in Northern France*, 149–153, for the Paris encounter.

12. For an overview of medieval Jewish polemical thinking and literature, see Baron, *A Social and Religious History of the Jews*, 9: 97–134. For a close look at the first hundred years of these efforts, from the 1160s to the 1260s, see Chazan, *Fashioning Jewish Identity*.

13. See Daniel J. Lasker, *Jewish Philosophical Polemics against Christianity in the Middle Ages* (New York: Ktav, 1977), and Chazan, *Fashioning Jewish Identity*, chap. 12.

14. Chazan, *Fashioning Jewish Identity*, chaps. 9–10.

15. This was the position taken by the narrators of the events of 1096 – see above, chap. 5.

16. For a translation of chap. 11 of *Milḥamot ha-Shem*, in which Jacob ben Reuben quotes and attacks passages from Matthew, see Joshua L. Levy, *Sefer Milḥamot Hashem, Chapter Eleven: The Earliest Jewish Critique of the New Testament* (unpub. doct. diss.: New York University, 2004).

17. Chazan, *Fashioning Jewish Identity*, chap. 14.

18. *Milḥemet Miẓvah*, 226b–227a. Note the specification that wealthy and learned Jews were converting. This suggests of course that these new conversions were not the result of poverty or ignorance. Nicholas Donin, who led the anti-Talmud campaign that began in the 1230s, and Friar Paul Christian, who led the new missionizing effort that seems to have begun only slightly later, constitute highly visible – but by no means unique – examples of learned converts. For an overview of medieval Jewish conversion in the northern areas of Europe, see Elisheva Carlebach, *Divided Souls: Converts from Judaism in Germany, 1500–1750* (New Haven: Yale University Press, 2001), 11–32. Further study of Jewish conversion for the various areas of medieval western Christendom is a desideratum.

19. Recall also the evidence of considerable Jewish conversion in the County of Provence toward the end of our period. See above, chap. 3.

20. Recall that the conversion of Abner of Burgos in the early fourteenth century seems to have been sparked by his ruminations on the downtrodden state of the Jewish people – see above, chap. 3.

21. For an overview of Jewish biblical exegesis for at least the first half of our period, see Baron, *A Social and Religious History of the Jews*, 6: 152–168 and 235–313.

22. See Marc Saperstein (ed. and trans.), *Jewish Preaching 1200–1800: An Anthology* (New Haven: Yale University Press, 1989).

23. Recall the sermon delivered in the synagogue of Narbonne by Rabbi Meir bar Simon in the wake of a Christian missionizing address. The rabbi built his sermon around key biblical verses, utilized to show an unbreakable divine commitment to redemption of the Jewish people, to explain the tardiness of that redemption, and to indicate the bounteous rewards that unswerving Jewish devotion would entail.

24. The popularity of Rashi's commentary has resulted in widespread translation of his many biblical commentaries into a variety of languages, including English. For an English translation of Rashi's commentary on the Pentateuch, see *Chumash with Targum Onkelos, Haphtaroth and Sabbath Prayers and Rashi's Commentary* (5 vols.; London: Shapiro, Valentine & Co., 1929–1934); for his commentary on Psalms, see *Rashi's Commentary on Psalms*, trans. Mayer Gruber (Leiden: Brill, 2004).

25. See again Talmage, *David Kimhi: The Man and the Commentaries*.

26. For an English translation of Naḥmanides's influential commentary on the Pentateuch, see Moses ben Naḥman, *Commentary on the Torah*, trans. Charles B. Chavel (5 vols.; New York: Shilo, 1971–1976); for an anaylsis of his literary sensitivity, see Michelle Judi Levine, *The Poetics of Characterization in Nachmanides's Commentary to Genesis* (unpub. doct. diss.: New York University, 2000).

27. See the important work of Beryl Smalley, *The Study of the Bible in the Middle Ages* (3rd ed.; Oxford: Basil Blackwell, 1983).
28. Note the edition and English translation of the *Sefer Niẓaḥon Yashan* – see David Berger (ed. and trans.), *The Jewish–Christian Debate in the High Middle Ages* (Philadelphia: Jewish Publication Society, 1979).
29. For an English translation of this fairly brief text, see Dan and Kiener, *The Early Kabbalah*, 80–85.
30. For a detailed sense of the contents of the *Zohar* and its exegetical character, see below, n. 39.
31. There is no comprehensive account of Jewish creativity in English for this important area of Jewish creativity during our period.
32. The decline of the Tosafist school has often been associated with the deteriorating external circumstances of Jewish life in northern France, including the condemnation of the Talmud. Recently, Haym Soloveitchik has argued that the decline simply reflects the normal trajectory of intellectual and spiritual creativity – "Catastrophe and Halakhic Creativity."
33. Again, see Einbinder, *Beautiful Death*, and Yerushalmi, *Zakhor*.
34. For broad overviews of Jewish philosophy during our period, see Baron, *A Social and Religious History of the Jews*, 8: 55–137; Colette Sirat, *A History of Jewish Philosophy in the Middle Ages* (Cambridge: Cambridge University Press, 1985); and Daniel H. Frank and Oliver Leaman (eds.), *History of Jewish Philosophy* (London: Routledge, 1997; Routledge History of World Philosophies), 294–414. A valuable set of texts in English translation is available in Daniel H. Frank et al. (eds.), *The Jewish Philosophy Reader* (London: Routledge, 2000).
35. See James T. Robinson, *Samuel ibn Tibbon's Commentary on Ecclesiastes* (unpub. doct. diss.: Harvard University, 2002).
36. For a useful overview of the controversy, see Idit Dobbs-Weinstein, "The Maimonidean Controversy," in Frank and Leaman (eds.), *History of Jewish Philosophy*, 331–349.
37. This change in the status of philosophy is highlighted in two valuable essays – Marc Saperstein, "The Social and Cultural Context: Thirteenth to Fifteenth Centuries," in Frank and Leaman (eds.), *History of Jewish Philosophy*, 294–330, and Charles H. Manekin, "Hebrew Philosophy in the Fourteenth and Fifteenth Centuries: An Overview," in ibid., 350–378.
38. Medieval Jewish mysticism has attracted extensive scholarly interest over the past half century, with a focus on the creativity of our period. The classical works are those of Gershom G. Scholem – see especially his *On the Kabbalah and Its Symbolism*, trans. Ralph Manheim (New York: Schocken, 1965), and *Origins of the Kabbalah*, ed. R. J. Zwi Werblowski and trans. Allan Arkush (New York: Jewish Publication Society, 1987). More recent overviews are provided by Moshe

Idel, *Kabbalah: New Perspectives* (New Haven: Yale University Press, 1988), and Elliot R. Wolfson, *Through a Speculum that Shines: Vision and Imagination in Medieval Jewish Mysticism* (Princeton: Princeton University Press, 1994) and *Language, Eros, Being: Kabbalistic Hermeneutics and Poetic Imagination* (New York: Fordham University Press, 2004).

39. The *Zohar* is now available in a new English translation with commentary by Daniel C. Matt, (2 vols.: Stanford: Stanford University Press, 2004). For a brief introduction to the *Zohar*, see Green, *A Guide to the Zohar*; for a much fuller introduction with translated selections, see Fischel Lachower and Isaiah Tishby (eds.) and David Goldstein (trans.), *The Wisdom of the Zohar: An Anthology of Texts* (3 vols.; London: The Littman Library of Jewish Civilization, 1989).

40. See again the superb edition and translation of *Sefer ha-Kabbalah* by Gerson D. Cohen, much enriched by the important excursus on key aspects of ibn Daud's thought.

41. On these narratives, see Chazan, *God, Humanity, and History*.

42. For overviews, see above, n. 12.

43. For an important example of such later polemical works, see Hasdai Crescas, *The Refutation of the Christian Principles*, trans. Daniel J. Lasker (Albany: State University of New York Press, 1992).

44. For an English translation of the Nahmanides narrative, see Charles B. Chavel (trans.), *Ramban: Writings and Discourses* (2 vols.; New York: Shilo, 1978), 2: 656–696; for an analysis, see Chazan, *Barcelona and Beyond*, 100–141.

45. Note the interesting essay by Ismar Schorsch, "The Myth of Sephardic Supremacy," in *From Text to Context: The Turn to History in Modern Judaism* (Hanover: Brandeis University Press, 1994), 71–92. In effect, nineteenth-century Ashkenazic Jews looked to medieval Sephardic Jewry for models of synergistic interaction with a vibrant majority environment. As suggested here, medieval southern-European Jewry (by no means all Sephardic) did involve itself more deeply than the Jews of northern Europe with its majority milieu. However, this did not mean that the northern-European Jews of our period were detached from their majority environment in the ways that later became prevalent among their successors, especially in eastern Europe, and that so distressed the nineteenth-century thinkers discussed by Schorsch.

EPILOGUE

1. For the negative majority and minority recollections, see above, in the introduction.

2. In various sectors of Europe, especially Spain, Germany, and Poland, local scholars have begun – as noted – to investigate in depth the medieval Jewish experience, out of a sense that this experience forms part of the

national patrimony. This conviction reflects a new sense of the ideals of national identity in these countries.

3. For valuable observations on modern Jewish economic activity, see Derek Jonathan Penslar, *Shylock's Children: Economics and Jewish Identity in Modern Europe* (Berkeley: University of California Press, 2001). In a provocative and fascinating study, Yuri Slezkine, *The Jewish Century* (Princeton: Princeton University Press, 2004), has suggested that the Jews have been the quintessentially modern folk, the human community best prepared for the opportunities offered by modernity. To the extent that Slezkine's suggestion is correct, I would urge that it was primarily the difficult experience in medieval western Christendom that afforded modern Jews this unusual preparedness.

BIBLIOGRAPHY

———————— · ————————

PRIMARY SOURCES

Abraham ibn Daud. *Sefer ha-Qabbalah: The Book of Tradition*. Ed. and trans. Gerson D. Cohen. Philadelphia: Jewish Publication Society, 1967.

Ahimaaz ben Paltiel. *The Chronicle of Ahimaaz*. Trans. Marcus Salzman. New York: Columbia University Press, 1924.

Baer, Yitzhak (ed.). *Die Juden im christlichen Spanien*. Rev. ed. 2 vols. Farnborough: Gregg International, 1970.

Benjamin of Tudela. *The Itinerary of Benjamin of Tudela*. Ed. and trans. Marcus Nathan Adler. London: Henry Frowde, 1907.

Berger, David (ed. and trans.). *The Jewish–Christian Debate in the High Middle Ages*. Philadelphia: Jewish Publication Society, 1979.

Blumenkranz, Bernhard (ed.). *Les auteurs latins chrétiens du moyen âge sur les juifs and le judaïsme*. Paris: Mouton, 1963.

Chazan, Robert (ed. and trans.). *Church, State, and Jew in the Middle Ages*. New York: Behrman House, 1980.

Crescas, Hasdai. *The Refutation of the Christian Principles*. Trans. Daniel J. Lasker. Albany: State University of New York Press, 1992.

Dan, Joseph (ed.) and Ronald Kiener (trans.). *The Early Kabbalah*. New York: Paulist Press, 1986.

Driver, Samuel R. and Adolf Neubauer (trans.). *The "Suffering Servant" of Isaiah according to the Jewish Interpreters*. Oxford: James Parker, 1877.

Eidelberg, Shlomo (trans.). *The Jews and the Crusaders*. Madison: University of Wisconsin Press, 1977.

Frank, Daniel H. et al. (eds.). *The Jewish Philosophy Reader*. London: Routledge, 2000.

Grayzel, Solomon (ed. and trans.). *The Church and the Jews in the XIIIth Century*. 2 vols. Philadelphia and New York: Dropsie College and Jewish Theological Seminary, 1933–1989.

Kimhi, Joseph. *The Book of the Covenant*. Trans. Frank Talmage. Toronto: Pontifical Institute of Mediaeval Studies, 1972.

Lachower, Fischel and Isaiah Tishby (eds.) and David Goldstein (trans.). *The Wisdom of the Zohar: An Anthology of Texts*. 3 vols. London: The Littman Library of Jewish Civilization, 1989.

Levi ben Gershom. *The Wars of the Lord*. Trans. Seymour Feldman. 3 vols. Philadelphia: Jewish Publication Society, 1984–1999.

Loewe, H. et al. (eds.). *Starrs and Jewish Charters in the British Museum*. Cambridge: Cambridge University Press, 1930.

Marcus, Jacob Rader (ed. and trans.). *The Jew in the Medieval World: A Source Book: 315–1791*. Rev. ed. Cincinnati: Hebrew Union College Press, 1999.

Moses ben Nahman. *Commentary on the Torah*. Trans. Charles B. Chavel. 5 vols. New York: Shilo, 1971–1976.

Moses ben Nahman. "The Disputation at Barcelona." In *Ramban: Writings and Discourses*, 2: 656–696. Trans. Charles B. Chavel. 2 vols. New York: Shilo, 1978.

Noy, David (ed.). *Jewish Inscriptions of Western Europe*. 2 vols. Cambridge: Cambridge University Press, 1993–1995.

Régné, Jean (ed.). *History of the Jews in Aragon: Regesta and Documents 1213–1327*. Rev. ed. Jerusalem: Magnes Press, 1978.

Rigg, J. M. (ed.). *Select Pleas, Starrs, and Other Records from the Rolls of the Exchequer of the Jews, 1220–1284*. London: B. Quaritch, 1902.

Rigg, J. M. et al. (eds.). *Calendar of the Plea Rolls of the Exchequer of the Jews Preserved in the Public Record Office*. 5 vols. London: Macmillan, 1905–1992.

Saperstein, Marc (ed. and trans.). *Jewish Preaching 1200–1800: An Anthology*. New Haven: Yale University Press, 1989.

Sefer ha-Bahir. Trans. Arye Kaplan. Northvale: Jason Aronson, 1995.

Simonsohn, Shlomo (ed.). *The Apostolic See and the Jews: Documents*. 7 vols. Toronto: Pontifical Institute of Mediaeval Studies, 1988–1990.

Solomon ben Isaac. *Chumash with Targum Onkelos, Haphtaroth and Sabbath Prayers and Rashi's Commentary*. Trans. A. M. Silberman and M. Rosenblum. 5 vols. London: Shapiro, Valentine & Co., 1929–1934.

Solomon ben Isaac. *Rashi's Commentary on Psalms*. Trans. Mayer Gruber. Leiden: Brill, 2004.

Thomas of Monmouth. *The Life and Miracles of St. William of Norwich*. Ed. and trans. Augustus Jessopp and Montague Rhodes James. Cambridge: Cambridge University Press, 1896.

The Zohar. Trans. and comm. Daniel C. Matt. 2 vols. Stanford: Stanford University Press, 2004.

SECONDARY WORKS

Ashtor, Eliyahu. *The Jews of Moslem Spain*. Trans. Aaron Klein and Jenny Machlowitz Klein. 3 vols. Philadelphia: Jewish Publication Society, 1973–1984.

Assis, Yom Tov. *The Golden Age of Aragonese Jewry: Community and Society in the Crown of Aragon, 1213–1327*. London: The Littman Library of Jewish Civilization, 1997.

Assis, Yom Tov. *Jewish Economy in the Medieval Crown of Aragon 1213–1327: Money and Power*. Leiden: E. J. Brill, 1997.

Bachrach, Bernard S. *Early Medieval Jewish Policy in Western Europe*. Minneapolis: University of Minnesota Press, 1977.

Baer, Yitzhak. *A History of the Jews in Christian Spain*. Trans. Louis Schoffman et al. 2 vols. Philadelphia: Jewish Publication Society, 1961–1966.

Baron, Salo W. *The Jewish Community: Its History and Structure to the American Revolution*. 3 vols. Philadelphia: Jewish Publication Society, 1942.

Baron, Salo W. *A Social and Religious History of the Jews*. 2nd ed. 18 vols. New York: Columbia University Press, 1952–1983.

Baumgarten, Elisheva. *Mothers and Children: Jewish Family Life in Medieval Europe*. Princeton: Princeton University Press, 2004.

Ben-Sasson, Haim Hillel. *A History of the Jewish People*. Cambridge, Mass.: Harvard University Press, 1976.

Benson, Robert L. and Giles Constable (eds.). *Renaissance and Renewal in the Twelfth Century*. Cambridge, Mass.: Harvard University Press, 1982.

Berend, Nora. *At the Gates of Christendom: Jews, Muslims, and "Pagans" in Medieval Hungary, c. 1000–c. 1300*. Cambridge: Cambridge University Press, 2001.

Berger, David. "How Did Nahmanides Propose to Resolve the Maimonidean Controversy?" In *Me'ah She'arim: Studies in Medieval Jewish Spiritual Life in Memory of Isadore Twersky*, 135–146. Ed. Ezra Fleischer et al. Jerusalem: Magnes Press, 2001.

Bonfil, Robert. *Jewish Life in Renaissance Italy*. Trans. Anthony Oldcorn. Berkeley: University of California Press, 1994.

Boswell, John. *Christianity, Social Tolerance, and Homosexuality: Gay People in Western Europe from the Beginning of the Christian Era to the Fourteenth Century*. Chicago: University of Chicago Press, 1980.

Boyarin, Daniel. *Border Lines: The Partition of Judaeo-Christianity*. Philadelphia: University of Pennsylvania Press, 2004.

Burns, Robert I. *Muslims, Christians, and Jews in the Crusader Kingdom of Valencia*. Cambridge: Cambridge University Press, 1984.

Carlebach, Elisheva. *Divided Souls: Converts from Judaism in Germany, 1500–1750*. New Haven: Yale University Press, 2001.

Carroll, James. *Constantine's Sword: The Church and the Jews.* Boston: Houghton Mifflin, 2001.

Chazan, Robert. "Anti-Usury Efforts in Thirteenth-Century Narbonne and the Jewish Response." *Proceedings of the American Academy for Jewish Research* 41–42 (1973–1974): 45–67.

Chazan, Robert. *Barcelona and Beyond: The Disputation of 1263 and Its Aftermath.* Berkeley: University of California Press, 1992.

Chazan, Robert. "The Blois Incident of 1171: A Study in Jewish Intercommunal Organization." *Proceedings of the American Academy for Jewish Research* 36 (1968): 13–31.

Chazan, Robert. *Daggers of Faith: Thirteenth Century Christian Missionizing and the Jewish Response.* Berkeley: University of California Press, 1989.

Chazan, Robert. *European Jewry and the First Crusade.* Berkeley: University of California Press, 1987.

Chazan, Robert. *Fashioning Jewish Identity in Medieval Western Christendom.* Cambridge: Cambridge University Press, 2004.

Chazan, Robert. "A Jewish Plaint to Saint Louis." *Hebrew Union College Annual* 45 (1974): 287–305.

Chazan, Robert. *Medieval Jewry in Northern France: A Political and Social History.* Baltimore: Johns Hopkins University Press, 1973.

Chazan, Robert. *Medieval Stereotypes and Modern Antisemitism.* Berkeley: University of California Press, 1997.

Chazan, Robert. "Then and Now: Jewish Life at the End of the First and Second Christian Millenium." *The Solomon Goldman Lectures* 8 (2003): 51–70.

Cluse, Christoph (ed.). *The Jews of Europe in the Middle Ages (Tenth to Fifteenth Centuries).* Turnhout: Brepols, 2004.

Cohen, Jeremy. *The Friars and the Jews: The Evolution of Medieval Anti-Judaism.* Ithaca: Cornell University Press, 1982.

Cohen, Jeremy. *Living Letters of the Law: Ideas of the Jew in Medieval Christianity.* Berkeley: University of California Press, 1999.

Cohen, Jeremy. "Recent Historiography on the Medieval Church and the Decline of European Jewry." In *Popes, Teachers, and Canon Law in the Middle Ages*, 251–262. Ed. James Ross Sweeney and Stanley Chodorow. Ithaca: Cornell University Press, 1989.

Cohen, Shaye J. D. *From the Maccabees to the Mishnah.* Philadelphia: Westminster Press, 1987.

Constable, Giles. *The Reformation of the Twelfth Century.* Cambridge: Cambridge University Press, 1996.

del Valle, Carlos. "Jacob ben Ruben de Huesca. Polemista. Su patria y su época." In *Polemica Judeo-Cristiana estudios*, 59–65. Ed. Johann Maier *et al.* Madrid: Aben Ezra Ediciones, 1992.

Dobbs-Weinstein, Idit. "The Maimonidean Controversy." In *History of Jewish Philosophy*, 331–349. Ed. Daniel H. Frank and Oliver Leaman. London: Routledge, 1997. Routledge History of World Philosophies.

Dobson, R. B. *The Jews of York and the Massacre of 1190.* York: University of York, 1974.

Einbinder, Susan L. *Beautiful Death: Jewish Poetry and Martyrdom in Medieval France.* Princeton: Princeton University Press, 2002.

Finkelstein, Louis. *Jewish Self-Government in the Middle Ages.* New York: Jewish Theological Seminary, 1925.

Frank, Daniel H. and Oliver Leaman (eds.). *History of Jewish Philosophy.* London: Routledge, 1997. Routledge History of World Philosophies.

Gager, John. *Reinventing Paul.* New York: Oxford University Press, 2000.

Glick, Leonard B. *Abraham's Heirs: Jews and Christians in Medieval Europe.* Syracuse: Syracuse University Press, 1999.

Goitein, S. D. *Jews and Arabs: Their Contacts through the Ages.* New York: Schocken, 1955.

Goitein, S. D. *A Mediterranean Society: The Jewish Communities of the Arab World as Portrayed in the Documents of the Cairo Genizah.* 6 vols. Berkeley: University of California Press, 1967–1993.

Green, Arthur. *A Guide to the Zohar.* Stanford: Stanford University Press, 2004.

Haskins, Charles Homer. *The Renaissance of the Twelfth Century.* Cambridge, Mass.: Harvard University Press, 1927.

Haverkamp, Alfred. "The Jews of Medieval Europe in the Middle Ages: By Way of Introduction." In *The Jews of Europe in the Middle Ages (Tenth to Fifteenth Centuries)*, 1–15. Ed. Christoph Cluse. Turnhout: Brepols, 2004.

Iancu-Agou, Danièle. "Provence: Jewish Settlement, Mobility, and Culture." In *The Jews of Europe in the Middle Ages (Tenth to Fifteenth Centuries)*, 175–189. Ed. Christoph Cluse. Turnhout: Brepols, 2004.

Idel, Moshe. *Kabbalah: New Perspectives.* New Haven: Yale University Press, 1988.

The Jews of Europe in the Middle Ages. Ostfildern: Hatje Cantz Publishers, 2005.

Jordan, William Chester. *Europe in the High Middle Ages.* London: Penguin Books, 2002.

Jordan, William Chester. *The French Monarchy and the Jews: From Philip Augustus to the Last of the Capetians.* Philadelphia: University of Pennsylvania Press, 1989.

Katz, Jacob. *Exclusiveness and Tolerance: Jewish–Gentile Relations in Medieval and Modern Times.* Oxford: Oxford University Press, 1961.

Kedar, Benjamin Z. *Crusade and Mission: European Approaches toward the Muslims.* Princeton: Princeton University Press, 1984.

Bibliography

Koestler, Arthur. *The Thirteenth Tribe: The Khazar Empire and Its Heritage.* New York: Random House, 1976.

Langmuir, Gavin I. *History, Religion, and Antisemitism.* Berkeley: University of California Press, 1990.

Langmuir, Gavin I. "Majority History and Postbiblical Jews." *Journal of the History of Ideas* 27 (1966): 343–363.

Langmuir, Gavin I. "Thomas of Monmouth: Detector of Ritual Murder." *Speculum* 59 (1984): 822–846.

Langmuir, Gavin I. *Toward a Definition of Antisemitism.* Berkeley: University of California Press, 1990.

Lasker, Daniel J. "The Jewish Critique of Christianity under Islam in the Middle Ages." *Proceedings of the American Academy for Jewish Research* 57 (1991): 121–153.

Lasker, Daniel J. *Jewish Philosophical Polemics against Christianity in the Middle Ages.* New York: Ktav, 1977.

Levine, Michelle Judi. *The Poetics of Characterization in Nachmanides's Commentary to Genesis.* Unpub. doct. diss.: New York University, 2000.

Levy, Joshua L. *Sefer Milḥamot Hashem, Chapter Eleven: The Earliest Jewish Critique of the New Testament.* Unpub. doct. diss.: New York University, 2004.

Lewis, Bernard. *The Jews of Islam.* Princeton: Princeton University Press, 1984.

Luzzati, Michele. "Northern and Central Italy: Assessment of Research and Further Prospects." In *The Jews of Europe in the Middle Ages (Tenth to Fifteenth Centuries),* 191–199. Ed. Christoph Cluse. Turnhout: Brepols, 2004.

Manekin, Charles H. "Hebrew Philosophy in the Fourteenth and Fifteenth Centuries: An Overview." In *History of World Philosophy,* 350–378. Ed. Daniel H. Frank and Oliver Leaman. London: Routledge, 1997. Routledge History of World Philosophies.

Marcus, Ivan G. "A Jewish–Christian Symbiosis: The Culture of Early Ashkenaz." In *Cultures of the Jews: A New History,* 449–516. Ed. David Biale. New York: Schocken Books, 2002.

Marcus, Ivan G. *Rituals of Childhood: Jewish Acculturation in Medieval Europe.* New Haven: Yale University Press, 1996.

McCulloch, John. "Jewish Ritual Murder: William of Norwich, Thomas of Monmouth, and the Early Dissemination of the Myth." *Speculum* 72 (1997): 698–740.

Meyerson, Mark D. *A Jewish Renaissance in Fifteenth-Century Spain.* Princeton: Princeton University Press, 2004.

Meyerson, Mark D. *Jews in an Iberian Kingdom: Society, Economy, and Politics in Morvedre, 1248–1391.* Leiden: Brill, 2004.

Moore, R. I. *The Formation of a Persecuting Society.* Oxford: Blackwell, 1987.

Mundill, Robin. *England's Jewish Solution: Experiment and Expulsion, 1262–1290*. Cambridge: Cambridge University Press, 1998.

Neusner, Jacob. *Introduction to Rabbinic Literature*. New York: Doubleday, 1994.

Noonan, John T., Jr. *A Church that Can and Cannot Change: The Development of Catholic Moral Teaching*. Notre Dame: University of Notre Dame, 2005.

Pegg, Mark Gregory. *The Corruption of Angels: The Great Inquisition of 1245–1246*. Princeton: Princeton University Press, 2001.

Penslar, Derek Jonathan. *Shylock's Children: Economics and Jewish Identity in Modern Europe*. Berkeley: University of California Press, 2001.

Richardson, H. G. *The English Jewry under Angevin Kings*. London: Methuen, 1960.

Riley-Smith, Jonathan. "The First Crusade and the Persecution of the Jews." In *Persecution and Toleration*, 51–72. Ed. W. J. Shiels. Oxford: Blackwell, 1984.

Robinson, James T. *Samuel ibn Tibbon's Commentary on Ecclesiastes*. Unpub. doct. diss.: Harvard University, 2002.

Rosenthal, Judah. "The Talmud on Trial." *Jewish Quarterly Review* 47 (1956–1957): 58–76 and 145–169.

Roth, Cecil. *A History of the Jews in England*. 3rd ed. Oxford: Oxford University Press, 1964.

Roth, Cecil. *The History of the Jews of Italy*. Philadelphia: Jewish Publication Society of America, 1946.

Rubin, Miri. *Gentile Tales: The Narrative Assault on Late Medieval Jews*. New Haven: Yale University Press, 1999.

Saperstein, Marc. "The Social and Cultural Context: Thirteenth to Fifteenth Centuries." In *History of Jewish Philosophy*, 294–330. Ed. Daniel H. Frank and Oliver Leaman. London: Routledge, 1997. Routledge History of World Philosophies.

Sapir Abulafia, Anna. *Christians and Jews in the Twelfth Century Renaissance*. London: Routledge, 1995.

Schiffman, Lawrence H. *From Text to Tradition: A History of Second Temple and Rabbinic Judaism*. Hoboken: Ktav, 1991.

Scholem, Gershom G. *On the Kabbalah and Its Symbolism*. Trans. Ralph Manheim. New York: Schocken, 1965.

Scholem, Gershom G. *Origins of the Kabbalah*. Ed. R. J. Zwi Werblowski and trans. Allan Arkush. Philadelphia: Jewish Publication Society, 1987.

Schorsch, Ismar. "The Myth of Sephardic Supremacy." In *From Text to Context: The Turn to History in Modern Judaism*, 71–92. Hanover: Brandeis University Press, 1994.

Seltzer, Robert M. *Jewish People, Jewish Thought: The Jewish Experience in History*. New York: Macmillan, 1980.

Shatzmiller, Joseph. *Shylock Reconsidered: Jews, Moneylending, and Medieval Society*. Berkeley: University of California Press, 1990.

Simon, Marcel. *Verus Israel*. Trans. H. McKeating. London: Oxford University Press, 1986.

Simonsohn, Shlomo. "Sicily: A Millennium of Convivenza (or Almost)." In *The Jews of Europe in the Middle Ages (Tenth through Fifteenth Centuries)*, 105–121. Ed. Christoph Cluse. Turnhout: Brepols, 2004.

Sirat, Colette. *A History of Jewish Philosophy in the Middle Ages*. Cambridge: Cambridge University Press, 1985.

Slezkine, Yuri. *The Jewish Century*. Princeton: Princeton University Press, 2004.

Smalley, Beryl. *The Study of the Bible in the Middle Ages*. 3rd ed. Oxford: Blackwell, 1983.

Soloveitchik, Haym. "Catastrophe and Halakhic Creativity: Ashkenaz – 1096, 1242, 1306, and 1298." *Jewish History* 12 (1998): 71–85.

Southern, R. W. *The Making of the Middle Ages*. New Haven: Yale University Press, 1953.

Stacey, Robert C. *Politics, Policy, and Finance under Henry III: 1216–1245*. Oxford: Oxford University Press, 1987.

Stow, Kenneth R. *Alienated Minority: The Jews of Medieval Latin Europe*. Cambridge, Mass.: Harvard University Press, 1992.

Talmage, Frank. *David Kimhi: The Man and the Commentaries*. Cambridge, Mass.: Harvard University Press, 1975.

Taylor, Miriam S. *Anti-Judaism and Early Christian Identity: A Critique of the Scholarly Consensus*. Leiden: E. J. Brill, 1995.

Twersky, Isadore (ed.). *Rabbi Moses ben Nahman (Ramban): Explorations in His Religious and Literary Virtuosity*. Cambridge, Mass.: Harvard University Press, 1983.

Weinryb, Bernard D. *The Jews of Poland: A Social and Economic History of the Jewish Community in Poland from 1100 to 1800*. Philadelphia: Jewish Publication Society, 1973.

Wolfson, Elliot R. *Language, Eros, Being: Kabbalistic Hermeneutics and Poetic Imagination*. New York: Fordham University Press, 2004.

Wolfson, Elliot R. *Through a Speculum that Shines: Vision and Imagination in Medieval Jewish Mysticism*. Princeton: Princeton University Press, 1994.

Yerushalmi, Yosef Hayim. *Zakhor: Jewish History and Jewish Memory*. Seattle: University of Washington Press, 1982.

INDEX

·

A short note on names
The development of surnames in medieval Europe varied considerably from place to place, occurring earlier in Islamic areas and southern Europe. The following rules should help the reader locate persons listed by name in this index. Persons given descriptive titles will be found under their first name: Peter the Hermit is under P. Persons with a geographic identification are listed under their first names: Alexander of Hales is in the A's. Persons very commonly referred to by a title or geographic identification are listed under it: Jean de Joinville, for instance, is always known as Joinville. Persons with commonly known nicknames are listed under the nickname: Moses ben Maimon is under Maimonides. Cross-references or double-postings are provided at the full name. Persons with the appellation of ben – will be found under their first name: Abraham ben Isaac of Lunel is under A. Persons with the appellation of ibn – are listed under that element: ibn Tibbon family of Lunel is under I. Persons with a sobriquet beginning ha- or he- are listed under that element: Judah ha-Levi will be found under H. Titled nobility are listed under their first names: Theobald, count of Blois, is under T. Persons with genuine surnames are listed under those surnames: Nicholas Donin is under D, David Kimhi under K.

Aaron of Lincoln, 159
Abner of Burgos/Alfonso of Valladolid,
    101–102, 308
Abraham and Isaac, biblical story of
    Jewish polemical literature's use of, 254
    Meshullam ben R. Isaac of Worms and
        other Rhineland, martyrdoms,
        179–180
Abraham ben David of Posquières (rabbi),
    80
Abraham ben Isaac of Lunel (rabbi), 80
Abulafia, Abraham, 120
aggressiveness
    Jewish polemical literature criticizing
        Christian tendency toward, 255

as primary quality of Western European
    Christendom, 241
Ahimaaz ben Paltiel, 117
Alexander II (pope), 93–94
Alexander III (pope), 50, 55
Alexander of Hales, 45–50, 51
Alfonso I (king of Aragon), 56
Alfonso of Valladolid/Abner of Burgos,
    101–102, 308
Almohades and Almoravides, 95, 105, 118
Angevin rule in southern Italy and Sicily,
    118
Anjou and Maine, expulsion of Jews from,
    229
Aragon. *See* Spain, Jewish communities of

Arba'ah Turim (*The Four Pillars*) of Rabbi
  Jacob ben Asher, 267
Aristotle, Jewish translations of, 269
Armleder assaults, 195
Ashkenazic Jews, 89, 232, 282–283, 291,
  310
Augustinian synthesis
  Alexander II's letter on Jews of Spain
    reminiscent of, 94
  formulation of, 36–38
  on Jewish attestation to biblical truth,
    250
  later elaboration of, 44–51
  missionizing encouraged by, 211
  negative imagery and perception of
    harmfulness in, 67
Averroes, Jewish translations of, 269

Babylonian Talmud, dominance of, 26, 39,
  40, 41, 264. *See also* Talmud and
  talmudic studies
badges. *See* clothing restrictions and
  requirements
Baer, Yitzhak, 102
Baghdad, Jewish community of, 3
Baldwin, count of Flanders, 132, 154
banking. *See* moneylending by Jews
Barcelona disputation, 63–65, 101,
  102–105, 244, 251, 252, 256, 281
Bela IV (king of Hungary), 200, 201, 203
bellicosity. *See* aggressiveness
Benedict of Norwich, 158
Benjamin of Tudela, 2–5
  demographics of Jewish communities
    described by, 243
  on Italian Jewish communities, 116, 121,
    123
  Muslim legacy and, 25
  on southern-French Jewish
    communities, 78, 79–81
  Spanish origins of, 94
Bernard of Clairvaux, 47, 53, 68, 133, 137,
  298
Bet ha-Beḥirah of Menahem ben Solomon
  Meiri, 89
biblical study and exegesis, 259–263
  alternative language formats for Bible,
    259
  Christian canonization of Scripture,
    33–34
  Christian development of, 71, 72–73,
    259, 261

Christian yearning for homogeneous
    culture partly derived from
    scriptural warrant, 210
  commentaries, 260–263
  contextual exegesis, 261
  Isaiah (biblical book)
    used as Christian proof-text, 37, 72,
      73–74
    used in Jewish polemical literature, 254
  Jerome's Latin Bible, Jewish polemical
    criticism of, 253
  Jewish development of, 74, 259–263
  Jewish emphasis on use of original
    Hebrew, 259
  Jewish knowledge and criticism of New
    Testament, 255
  Jewish polemical counter-exegesis, 251,
    252, 259, 262
  language study and, 74, 259, 261
  missionizing use of, 249
  mysticism influencing, 263
  in northern France, 140–141
  philosophical study and, 262–263,
    272–274
  popular presentation in the synagogue,
    259–260
  in Rome and papal states, 123
  in sermons, 259
  in southern Italy and Sicily, 119
  in Spain, 103
biology, racist emphasis on, in Spain, 109
Black Death. *See* plague
blasphemy of Jews, beliefs regarding
  Alexander of Hales's concerns regarding,
    45–50
  ecclesiastical policy regarding, 56–58
  ecclesiastical views as to, 69, 70, 213
  Innocent III's accusations regarding, 69
  in northern France, 136
  Spain, ecclesial concerns in, 98
  Talmud perceived as blasphemy, 56–58,
    70, 98, 147–148, 225–231, 267
blood libel and ritual murder, beliefs
    regarding, 214
  crucifixion of Jesus, as recapitulation of,
    192, 214
  in England, 157–158, 159, 160, 164
  Frederick II's investigation and
    repudiation of, 192–193
  in Germany, 184–185, 191–194, 197
  Innocent III's accusations regarding, 70
  in northern France, 136–137, 150–151

origins of, 160
papal investigation and repudiation of, 70
Passover and, 185–192
in Poland, 204, 207
Boleslav of Kalisch, 203–204, 206
Boleslav the Brave (king of Poland), 201
Boleslav the Great (king of Poland), 202
Book of Brilliance, The (Sefer ha-Bahir), 83, 84
Book of Josippon (Sefer Yosippon), 117, 277, 279
Book of the Wars of the Lord, The (Sefer Milḥamot Adonai) of Gersonides, 89
Book of Tradition, The (Sefer ha-Kabbalah) of Abraham ibn Daud, 96, 278
Brun of London, 158
burials. *See* cemeteries
Byzantium, 2, 116, 118, 199

Calixtus II (pope), 50
canon law study, talmudic study paralleling innovations in, 74, 266
Capetian conquest of southern France, 86–87
Capetian consolidation in northern France. *See under* northern France, Jewish communities of
captio. See confiscation of Jewish goods
Casimir the Great (ruler of Poland), 206
Castile. *See* Spain, Jewish communities of
Catholic Church. *See* Roman Catholic Church
cemeteries
confiscation in northern France, 142, 153
in Hungary, 201
inscriptions as evidence of Jewish life in Western Europe, 78, 117, 121, 294
Speyer Jewry, charter of, 203
census of English Jews, 165
challenges, successes, and failures, 209–210
attraction of Western Europe for Jews, 215–219
in cultural, intellectual, and spiritual life (*See* cultural, intellectual, and spiritual life)
demographic successes achieved, 232–233
dynamics of deterioration in European Jewish communities, 239–242
in economic life (*See* economic challenges, successes, and failures)

homogeneity, Christian yearning for, 210–212, 248, 285
negative imagery (*See* negative imagery and perception of harmfulness)
organization (*See* organization of Jewish communities)
political authority, relationship with, 219–231 (*See also* politics, government, and Jews)
settlement of Jews in Western Europe generally, 210–219
utter newness of Jews and Judaism to large areas of Europe, 215
Charles, count of Anjou and Maine, 230
Christian bellicosity and aggressiveness. *See* aggressiveness
Christian culture, Jewish engagement with, 243–247, 282
biblical contextual exegesis, 261
canon law study, talmudic study paralleling innovations in, 74, 266
inevitability of, 6–7
isolationism, myth of, 243, 306
mysticism, 105, 275, 276
in northern France, 140
northern vs. southern areas of Europe, 244
pietism, 186
poetry of Immanuel of Rome influenced by Christian tradition, 124, 270
translations, Jewish involvement in, 118, 268, 269
vibrancy of medieval renaissance, consequences of, 70–75
Christian legacy prior to 1000, 27–38
accession of faith to power, compared to Islam, 27–28
ambivalence at heart of, 29
Augustinian synthesis, 36–38
crucifixion, Jews blamed for, 33
differentiation of Christianity from Judaism, necessity of, 32
ecclesiastical organization, beginnings of, 34
establishment of Christianity as dominant religion in Roman Empire, 35–36
gentile dominance of early Church, 32–33
historical Jesus and his followers, 30–31
history, Christian sense of, 37
missionizing, proselytization, and conversion, 38

Christian legacy prior to 1000 (*cont.*)
negative imagery of and positive
restrictions on Jews within
Christendom, 34–36, 67
Paul's influence on, 31–32, 44, 57
presence of Jews in Western Europe
before 1000, 23, 40, 44, 294
recognition of Jewish rights within
Christian society, 36–38
rejection of Christianity by majority of
Jews, 33
relationship between Judaism and
Christianity as faiths, 28–29
Scripture, Christian canonization of,
33–34
Christian yearning for homogeneity,
210–212, 248, 285
Christians working for Jews
ecclesiastical ban on, 55
Speyer Jewry charter allowing, 174
Church. *See* Roman Catholic Church
circumcision
English charges of Jewish circumcision of
Christian boy, 164
slaves of Jews not to be circumcised,
Constantine's edict regarding, 35
Clement VI (pope), 196
clothing restrictions and requirements, 213
England's requirement of distinctive garb,
163
Fourth Lateran Council's imposition of,
56, 163, 223
governmental resistance to ecclesiastical
imposition of, 223
northern France, badge requirements
after return of 1315, 152
coin-clipping, English Jews accused of,
166
coin-minting by Jews in Hungary, 200
confiscation or *captio* of Jewish goods
in England, 164
in northern France, 142, 144, 146, 151,
153
Constantine the Great (emperor), 35–36
Constantinople, Jewish community of, 2
Constitutio pro Judeis, 50–51, 52, 68, 123
conversion and converts. *See* missionizing,
proselytization, and conversion
corporate Jewish crime and punishment,
notions of, 227
Councils of the Church
Elvira, Council of, 34, 35

Fourth Lateran Council, 48, 56, 61, 145,
163, 189
Third Lateran Council, 55, 163
crucifixion, Jews blamed for
blood libel murder viewed as
recapitulation of, 192, 214
crusades and revenge motif, 178,
304
in Gospel accounts, 33, 67
by Innocent III, 68, 69
in northern France, 136
crusades and crusading
ecclesiastical protection of Jews with
regard to, 52–54
economic contributions by Jews to,
135–136, 178
in England, 160
in Germany (*See* Germany, Jewish
communities of)
against heresy in southern France,
85
Jewish narratives of, 279
moneylending by Jews and, 60–61,
138
negative imagery and perception of
harmfulness and, 67–68
in northern France, 135–136, 137–138,
148
revenge motif and anti-Jewish actions
and sentiments, 178, 304
theological position on Jews and, 46–47,
50
cultural, intellectual, and spiritual life,
243–247
biblical study (*See* biblical study and
exegesis)
Christian culture (*See* Christian culture,
Jewish engagement with)
divine favor, cultural vitality regarded as
sign of, 72, 73–74
English Jewry's lack of cultural legacy,
154
general creativity of medieval Christian
renaissance
Jewish culture challenged by, 246–247
missionizing, proselytization, and
conversion efforts spurred by,
71–73, 246
in Germany, 175, 181, 185–187, 198
historical writing, 277–280
in Hungary, 201
innovative forms of, 267–282

Islam and
   Jewish culture evolved in, 25, 26
   Jewish engagement with Islamic
      culture, 25
   Muslim Spain, 92–93
   isolationism, myth of, 243, 306
   in Italy
      Rome and papal states, 123–124
      southern Italy and Sicily, 117–120
   language (*See* language study; languages
      used by European Jews)
   missionizing by Christians (*See*
      missionizing, proselytization, and
      conversion)
   mysticism (*See* mysticism)
   northern and southern Jewish cultures
      compared, 282–283
   in northern France, 139–141, 147–148,
      152
   philosophy (*See* philosophy)
   pietism, German, 183, 186–187, 277
   poetry, 124, 140, 270
   in Poland, 205, 208
   rabbinic literature and culture (*See*
      rabbinic literature and culture)
   southern Europe, linguistic and cultural
      unity of, 78
   in southern France, 80–85, 88–89
   in Spain, 92–93, 102–105
   superiority, Jewish sense of
      general creativity of medieval
         Christian renaissance challenging,
         246–247
      Jewish polemical literature
         encouraging, 245, 255
      persecutions of Rhineland Jews in
         1096 and, 73
   talmudic study (*See* Talmud and talmudic
      studies)
   translation of texts, 268–269

Dante, 124
David of Melun (rabbi), 57
Dead Sea Scrolls/Qumran community, 31,
   33
death of Jesus. *See* crucifixion, Jews blamed
   for
Decretales, 46, 47, 56
Decretum of Gratian, 47
demographics of Jews
   changes of 13th century, 124–125
   distribution circa 1000, 1–9

engagement with majority culture and,
   243
Islam, Jews living under
   demographic distribution circa 1000,
      2, 3, 24
   demographic distribution circa
      1250–1500, 5
   mobility as characteristic of, 127, 132,
      216, 286–287
   northern Europe, later but eventually
      dominant Jewish communities of,
      129–131
   shift of population into western
      Christendom after 1000, 3–6
   success of settlement patterns in Western
      Europe, 232–233
diaspora communities of Jews
   eastern European Jews, German origins
      of, 170, 198, 200, 203
   English Jews' migration from
      northwestern France, 154
   from Muslim Spain, 95–97, 118
   prominence in ancient and early
      medieval world, 39
   southern-French Jews, disappearance of,
      89–90
   Turkish Empire, Spanish exiles moving
      to, 114
disputations between Jews and Christians.
   See under missionizing,
   proselytization, and conversion
diversity, Christian fear of, 210–212, 248,
   285
diversity of Muslim world compared to
   Latin Christendom, 211
divine favor, cultural vitality regarded as
   sign of, 72, 73–74
Dobson, R. B., 156
Dominicans
   Barcelona disputation, 63–65, 101,
      251–252
   England, missionizing in, 163
   heresy in southern France, formed to
      combat, 85
   missionizing work of, 101, 251–252
   seized Jewish books entrusted to, 57, 148
Domus conversorum, 163
Donin, Nicholas, 48, 56, 57, 147, 307
Donnolo, Shabbetai, 117
dress, distinctive. *See* clothing restrictions
   and requirements
dualism in southern France, 81

eastern Europe, Jewish communities of, 170, 198–199
economic challenges, successes, and failures related to, 219
German origins, 170, 198, 200, 203
Hungary, 199–201 (*See also entry at* Hungary)
Poland, 201–208 (*See also entry at* Poland)
source materials for, 15
ecclesiastical authority. *See* Roman Catholic Church
economic challenges, successes, and failures, 216–219. *See also* moneylending by Jews
contributions of Jews to development of medieval western Christendom, 234, 287
eastern Europe, move into, 219
engagement with majority culture, 244
in England (*See under* England, Jewish communities of)
in Germany, 172, 174, 181–182, 187, 188, 189–190, 197
governing authorities
exploitation of Jewish communities by, 225–226, 242 (*See also under* England, Jewish communities of)
support for Jewish communities, economic reasons behind, 220–221
in Hungary, 200
in Italy
northern Italy, 125–127
southern Italy and Sicily, 117
leadership role of Jewish elite, 238
mobility of Jews and, 216
negative imagery, business activities of Jews contributing to, 213
niche economy, Jewish legacy of, 233–235
in northern Europe generally, 217
in northern France, 132–135, 152
in Poland, 203, 204, 206
in southern France, 79
in Spain, 92, 97–98, 216
taxation (*See* taxation of Jews)
Edward I (king of England), 87, 165–167, 230
Egyptian Jews, 2, 3
Eleazar of Worms (rabbi), 183–184, 185, 186, 221

elite of Jewish community, leadership role of, 238
Elvira, Council of, 34, 35
emanationism, 84
Emicho of Flonheim, 177, 178, 194
England, Jewish communities of, 154–156
William I, the Conqueror, movement of Jews from Normandy under, 154
under Henry I, 156
under Stephen, 157
under Henry II, 158–160
under Richard I, the Lionheart, 160–161
under John, 161–162
under Henry III, 162–165
final expulsion by Edward I, 165–167
blood libel and ritual murder, accusations of, 157–158, 159, 160, 164
captio or confiscation of goods of, 164
census of, 165
crusades, effects of, 160
cultural legacy, lack of, 154
economic life and royal exploitation of finances
under Henry I, 156
under Henry II, 158–160
under Richard the Lionheart, 161
under John, 162
under Henry III, 162, 164–165
Edward I's abolition of moneylending, 166
coin-clipping accusations, 166
ecclesiastical efforts to limit Jewish business, resistance to, 163
Exchequer of the Jews, 155, 161
expansion of settlements under Henry II, 158–160
expulsion of 1290, 87, 125, 156, 166–167, 230
historiography, 155
immigrant status of, 154, 156
missionizing, proselytization, and conversion
Domus conversorum, establishment of, 163
expulsion of 1290, conversion in face of, 166
York riots, attempts at accepting conversion in, 161
negative imagery and perception of harmfulness in, 156–158, 159–160, 163–164, 166

northwestern France, migration from,
154
rioting against, 160–161, 164
royal control of, 154
source materials for, richness of, 14, 155,
156
tallages or taxation of, 159, 162, 164–165
Ephraim of Bonn, 53, 60, 138, 182–183,
184–185
Eugenius III (pope), 50, 60
expulsions of Jews, 227–231
corporate Jewish crime and punishment,
as extension of notion of, 228
from England, 87, 125, 156, 166–167,
230
German absorption of French refugees,
194
from Germany, 196, 197–198
from Hungary, 201
localized, 228
moneylending leading to, 62
from northern France (*See under*
northern France, Jewish
communities of)
Polish immigration resulting from, 203
from Portugal, 114, 227, 231
prior to 1000, 228
Sephardic Jewry's transcendence of, 89,
114
from southern France, 79, 87–88
from southern Italy and Sicily, 120
from Spain, 89, 113–115, 227, 228, 231
tensions of Jewish presence within
Christendom resolved by, 231

Ferdinand of Aragon, 113
forced conversion. *See under* missionizing,
proselytization, and conversion
Four Pillars, The (Arbaʿah Turim) of Rabbi
Jacob ben Asher, 267
Fourth Lateran Council, 48, 56, 61, 145,
163, 189
France, Jewish communities of, source
materials for, 14. *See also* northern
France, Jewish communities of;
southern France, Jewish
communities of
Franciscans
England, missionizing in, 163
moneylending, Observantine objections
to, 126
seized Jewish books entrusted to, 57, 148

Frederick, duke of Austria, 188–190, 191,
203, 223
Frederick I Barbarossa (emperor), 174, 184,
222
Frederick II (emperor), 118, 119, 190, 191,
192–193, 222, 269
Fulda blood libel incident, 192–193
Fulk of Neuilly, 133, 134, 145

Germany, Jewish communities of, 169–170
Armleder assaults, 195
baronial vs. imperial power struggles,
effects of, 190–191, 197
blood libel and ritual murder, accusations
of, 182–185, 191–194, 197
crusades and crusading
donations and food given by
Rhineland Jews for, 135–136, 178
First Crusade persecutions (*See subhead*
persecutions of Rhineland Jews in
1096, *this entry*)
Second Crusade, repercussions of,
182–183
Third Crusade, repercussions of,
183–184
cultural, intellectual, and spiritual life,
175, 181, 185–187, 198
eastern European Jews migrating from,
170, 198, 200, 203
economic life, 172, 174, 181–182, 187,
188, 189–190, 197
expulsions
French refugees, German absorption
of, 194
from German towns, 197–198
plague-related, 196
governmental support and exploitation,
general lack of, 181–182, 187–194,
197
Italian Jews compared, 169–170
missionizing, proselytization, and
conversion
blood libel accusations, forced
conversions incident to, 185
blood libel accusations, Frederick II's
use of converts to investigate,
192
persecutions of 1096, baptisms
undertaken to avoid, 178, 179
persecutions of 1096, Jewish rejection
of conversion and martyrdom in
response to, 178–181, 244

Germany, Jewish communities of (*cont.*)
   Speyer charter safeguards regarding, 174
  negative imagery and perception of harmfulness, 173, 184–185, 187, 191–198
  origins of, 170
  papal vs. imperial power, effects of conflict between, 187, 190
  persecutions of Rhineland Jews in 1096, 175–181
    Bernard of Clairvaux's attempts to forestall repetition of, 53, 182
    bishops' attempts to forestall, 177
    burghers, actions of, 177–178
    Christian vs. Jewish view of meaning of, 180
    crusader mentality contributing to, 47, 52
    crusading armies vs. popular non-military bands, 178
    Jewish actions and martyrdoms in response to, 178–181, 244
    Mainz Anonymous on, 176–181, 279–280
    narrative accounts of, 176
    New Christians of Spain compared, 107
    spiritual and cultural superiority, Jewish sense of, 73
  pietism, 183, 186–187, 277
  plague, effects of, 194, 195–196
  rights and protections, charters and grants providing, 172–174, 179, 184, 188–190
  Rindfleisch massacres, 194
  self-government by, 173, 188
  source materials for, 15
  Speyer Jewry
    founding of, 171–174
    persecution of 1096 (*See subhead* persecutions of Rhineland Jews in 1096, *this entry*)
  Worms, charter of Jews of, 174
Gershom of Mainz (rabbi), 175
Gersonides (Levi ben Gerson of Orange), 89, 263
ghettoization and segregation, ecclesiastical policy regarding, 55, 213
Goitein, S. D., 233
government. *See* politics, government, and Jews

Graetz, Heinrich, 19–21
Granada. *See* Spain, Jewish communities of
Gratian, 47
graves and graveyards. *See* cemeteries
Greco-Roman legacy
  crucifixion as, 33
  of early Christians, 30
  establishment of Christianity as dominant faith, 35–36
  Islam's preservation of, 26
  of Jews, 30, 39
  philosophical principles of, 250 (*See also* philosophy)
Gregory I the Great (pope), 51
Gregory IX (pope), 53, 54, 56, 58, 148, 226
Guide of the Perplexed of Maimonides, 82, 271, 272
Guillaume de Broue, 86

ha-Cohen, Rabbi Zerahiah ben Isaac, 80
ha-Darshan, Moses, 79
ha-Levi, Judah, 96, 268
ha-Lorki, Joshua (Hieronymus of Sancta Fide), 108
harmfulness of Jews, perceptions of. *See* negative imagery and perception of harmfulness
he-Hasid, Judah (rabbi), 186
Hebrew Bible. *See* biblical study and exegesis
Hebrew poetry, Jewish tradition of, 124, 140, 270
Henry, count of Champagne, 137
Henry I (king of England), 156
Henry II (king of England), 158–160
Henry III (king of England), 156, 162–165, 226, 242
Henry IV (emperor), 173, 174, 178, 188
heresy. *See also* inquisition
  Christian concern with, symptomatic of fear of internal enemies, 241
  mysticism as, 83
  southern France associated with, 81, 85
  in Spain
    Ferdinand and Isabella, activities of, 114
    New Christians and, 110–113
Hieronymus of Sancta Fide (Joshua ha-Lorki), 108
Hillel ben Samuel, 120

historical writing, Jewish practice of, 277–280

historiography
of English Jewry, 155
Spain, missionizing of Jews in, 299

history, Christian sense of, 37

Hohenstaufen rule in southern Italy and Sicily, 118–119

homes of Jews or Muslims, Christians forbidden from working or living in, 55

homogeneity, Christian yearning for, 210–212, 248, 285

host desecration by Jews, beliefs regarding, 213
French incident of 1290, 150–151
in Germany, 193, 194, 197
papal recognition of claims of, 70
in Poland, 207

Hugh of Lincoln, 164

Hungary, Jewish communities of, 199–201. *See also* eastern Europe, Jewish communities of
cultural, intellectual, and spiritual life, 201
diversity of populations in, 200
ecclesiastical pressure to impose limitations on, 200
economic life of, 200
expulsion of 1360, reversal of, 201
German origins, 200
Mongol invasions, 199, 201
political positions held by Jews in Hungary, 200–201

Huozmann, Rudiger, bishop of Speyer, 171–173, 178, 188, 220

Iberian peninsula, Jews of
Portugal, 114, 227, 231
Spain (*See* Spain, Jewish communities of)

ibn Daud, Abraham, 96, 117, 278
ibn Ezra, Abraham, 261
ibn Gabirol, Solomon, 268
ibn Nagrela, Samuel, 93
ibn Paquda, Bahya, 268
ibn Shaprut, Hasdai, 93, 300
ibn Tibbon family of Lunel, 81–82, 96
ibn Tibbon, Judah, 81–82, 268–269
ibn Tibbon, Samuel, 82, 269, 272
ibn Verga, Solomon, 114

imagery of Jews. *See* negative imagery and perception of harmfulness

Immanuel of Rome, poetry of, 124, 140, 270

Incarnation, Jewish polemical literature's attacks on doctrine of, 253

Innocent III (pope)
ecclesiastical policy and the Jews, 56, 60
heresy, attacks on, 85
negative imagery and perception of harmfulness used by, 68–69
Philip Augustus ordered to restrict usury of Jews by, 145
on secondary status of Jews in Christendom, 212
theological doctrine on the Jews, 48, 51

Innocent IV (pope), 57, 58, 70, 148, 192

inquisition
Ferdinand and Isabella's fervor for, 114
New Christians of Spain and, 110–113
southern France, emergence in, 85

inscriptions as evidence of Jewish life in Western Europe, 78, 117, 121, 294

intellectual life. *See* cultural, intellectual, and spiritual life

Isaac of London, 158

Isaac, son of Meshullam ben R. Isaac of Worms, 179–180

Isabella of Castile, 113

Isaiah (biblical book)
used as Christian proof-text, 37, 72, 73–74
used in Jewish polemical literature, 254

Islam, Jews living under, 24–27
accession of faith to power, compared to Christianity, 27–28
cultural, intellectual, and spiritual life
evolution of Jewish culture within Islam, 25, 26
Jewish engagement with Islamic culture, 25
in Muslim Spain, 92–93
demographic distribution circa 1000, 2, 3, 24
demographic distribution circa 1250–1500, 5
diaspora from Muslim Spain to parts of Islamic world, 95–97
diversity of Muslim world compared to Latin Christendom, 211
institutional framework of Jewish life, 25
less singular minority status compared to western Christendom, 25

Islam, Jews living under (*cont.*)
    missionizing, proselytization, and
        conversion to Islam, 26, 28, 98
    mysticism, Islam's lack of influence on,
        276
    origins of most Jews in western
        Christendom in, 24
    philosophical study emerging from
        Islam, 74
    poetry tradition and, 124, 270
    relationship between Judaism and Islam
        as faiths, 28–29
    in southern Italy and Sicily, 116, 118
    in Spain (*See under* Spain, Jewish
        communities of)
    taxation and other restrictions on Jews
        and Christians, 24–25
    translation of Judeo-Arabic and Arabic
        texts, 118, 268–269
    Turkish Empire, Spanish exiles moving
        to, 114
Islamic culture, Jewish engagement with, 25
isolationism of pre-modern Jews, myth of,
    243, 306
Italy, Jewish communities of, 115–116, 127
    Benjamin of Tudela on, 116, 121, 123
    demographics, 13th century changes in,
        124–125
    diversity and fragmentation of, 115–116
    German Jews compared, 303
    longevity of, 127
    northern Italy, 124–127
        economic opportunities in, 125–127
        mobility of Jews of, 127
        movement of Jews into, 124–125
    prior to 1000, 115
    Roman history, Italian Jewish interest in,
        and *Book of Josippon*, 277
    Rome and papal states, 120–124
        cultural, intellectual, and spiritual life,
            123–124
        intercessory role, 122–123
        prior to 1000, 120–121
        stability of Roman Jewish community,
            123
    source materials for, 15
    southern Italy and Sicily, 116–120
        Angevin rule in, 118
        Aragonese rule in, 118, 120
        Byzantine rule in, 116, 118
        cultural, intellectual, and spiritual life,
            117–120

economic life of, 117
expulsions of 1492, 120
Hohenstaufen rule in, 118–119
Muslim rule in, 116, 118
Norman rule in, 118
Spain compared, 90

Jacob Anatoli, 82, 269
Jacob ben Asher (rabbi), 267
Jacob ben Meir (rabbi) of Ramerupt, 138,
    139
Jacob ben Reuben, 63, 100–101, 244, 248,
    250, 262
Jacob ben Yekutiel, 122, 132, 154
James I the Conqueror (king of Aragon),
    63, 98, 150, 251
Jerome's Latin Bible, Jewish polemical
    criticism of, 253
Jewish faith and identity, maintenance of,
    245–246, 257, 288
Jewish historical writing, 277–280
Jewish isolation/integration, myth of, 243,
    306
Jewish legacy prior to 1000, 38–42
    diaspora communities, prominence of,
        39
    Greco-Roman civilization, influence of,
        30, 39
    religious life, structure of, 40–41
    subject status, evolution of culture to
        deal with, 39–40
Jewish polemical literature, 15, 281
    argumentation used in, 252–255
    biblical counter-exegesis of, 251, 252,
        259, 262
    on Christian mysticism and popular
        religious belief, 105
    dialogue format, 281
    earliest examples of, 248
    first appearance of, 63, 100
    of German pietists, 186
    Jewish suffering, counter-arguments
        based on, 254
    of Meir bar Simon, 86
    observable reality of Christian vs. Jewish
        circumstances, arguments based on,
        250, 253–255
    offensive vs. defensive attacks, 253,
        255
    rabbinical counter-interpretation, 253,
        258
    reason and philosophy, use of, 253, 255

relativization of divinity and religious praxis, fears regarding Jewish philosophy and, 274
  sense of Jewish superiority encouraged by, 245, 255
  in southern France, 63, 100
  in Spain, 100–101
  specific Christian doctrines of Incarnation and Trinity attacked in, 253
Jewish sense of superiority
  general creativity of medieval Christian renaissance challenging, 246–247
  Jewish polemical literature encouraging, 245, 255
  persecutions of Rhineland Jews in 1096 and, 73
Jewish source material, 15–16
Jewish suffering and martyrdom
  Armleder assaults, 195
  in England, 160–161, 164
  Jewish polemical literature's counter-arguments based on, 254
  Mainz Anonymous on, 176–181, 280
  New Christians of Spain compared to Rhineland Jews, 107
  of Rhineland Jews in persecutions of 1096, 178–181, 244
  Rindfleisch massacres, 194
Jews in Europe prior to 1000, 23, 40, 294
  expulsions, 228
  Germany, no early indications of Jews in, 170
  Hungary, 200
  Iberian peninsula, 91–92
  Italy and Sicily, 115, 120–121
  northern Europe, 130, 131
  Poland, 202
  Roman Catholic Church and, 44
  southern France, 78
  Visigothic Spain, 91–92, 228
Jews of medieval Europe
  academic interest in, ix–x, 7, 17–18, 19–21
  ambivalence associated with, xii, 29, 38
  broad scope of study of, x–xii
  challenges, successes, and failures of (*See* challenges, successes, and failures)
  as chief minority presence in western Christendom, 7

Church and (*See* Roman Catholic Church)
  cultural, intellectual, and spiritual life of (*See* cultural, intellectual, and spiritual life)
  demographics (*See* demographics of Jews)
  engagement with Christian culture (*See* Christian culture, Jewish engagement with)
  geographic boundaries, 9–11
  Jewish perspective on, 21
  maintenance of faith and identity by, 245–246, 257, 288
  narrative structure, current work's use of, 16–18
  negative and stereotypical approach to study of, need to expand, 18–22
  negative folk memories stemming from experiences of, 286
  positive contributions of, 285–288
  prior legacies of, 25 (*See* prior legacies)
  role of Jews in wider community, 7, 12–13
  singular status of Jews as minority compared to Islam, 25
  source materials for, 13–16
  southern Europe, older Jewish communities of, 77–78 (*See also* Italy, Jewish communities of; southern France, Jewish communities of; Spain, Jewish communities of)
  temporal boundaries, 11–12
John, bishop of Speyer, 177, 222
John (king of England), 161–162, 226
Joinville, Jean de, 149, 227
Jonathan of Lunel (rabbi), 80
Jordan, William Chester, 130, 141, 146, 194, 195
Josephus, 31, 117
Josippon, Book of (Sefer Yosippon), 117, 277, 279
judaizing, New Christians of Spain accused of, 112
Jurnet of Norwich, 158
Justin Martyr, 72

kabbalah
  in southern France, 84
  in Spain, 105
Kalonymide family's transfer from Italy to Rhineland, 170

Khazar kingdom, origins of Polish Jewry
    in, 202
killing of Christians by Jews, beliefs
    regarding. *See* blood libel and ritual
    murder, beliefs regarding
Kimhi, David, 82, 89, 261, 262, 263
Kimhi family of Narbonne, 81, 82–83, 96
Kimhi, Joseph, 82, 248, 262, 268
Kimhi, Moses, 82

landed property, lending against, 133, 189,
    218
language study
    biblical exegesis and, 259, 261
    missionizing, Christian language training
        for purposes of, 249
    rabbinic literature and culture affected
        by, 258
languages used by European Jews, 6
    biblical texts available in, 259
    engagement with majority culture and,
        13, 244
    Latin not used by Jews, 259
    Maimonides' use of Judeo-Arabic and
        Hebrew, 266
    in Muslim countries, 25
    in northern France, 140
    numerous languages, Jewish facility in,
        117, 118
    printing houses established by Jews in
        northern Italy and, 127
    in southern France, 78
    in Spain, 92, 102
    Yiddish, Polish Jews' use of, 205–206
Languedoc. *See* southern France, Jewish
    communities of
Lateran Council III, 55, 163
Lateran Council IV, 48, 56, 61, 145, 163,
    189
Latin not used by Jews, 259
law
    canon law study, talmudic study
        paralleling innovations in, 74, 266
    Maimonides' recognition of
        philosophical underpinnings of, 267
    manuals of Jewish law, 266–267
    Sefer ha-Kabbalah (The Book of Tradition)
        of Abraham ibn Daud, 96, 278
Levi ben Gerson of Orange (Gersonides),
    89, 263
limitations on Jews. *See* rights of and
    restrictions on Jews

Louis VII (king of France), 137, 151
Louis VIII (king of France), 146
Louis IX (king of France/St. Louis)
    ecclesiastical views of Jews and, 49, 62,
        65, 242
    Edward I's policy resembling, 165
    missionizing, proselytization, and
        conversion, 251
    niche economy established by Jews,
        threat to, 234
    northern-French Jews and, 147,
        148–150
    politics, government, and Jews, 226–227,
        230
    reign as turning point in French Jewish
        history, 125
    southern-French Jews and, 87
Louis X (king of France), 152–153
Luzzati, Michele, 127

Magna Carta, 162
*Maḥberet ha-Tofet ve-ha'Eden (The Maqama of
    Hell and Heaven)* of Immanuel of
    Rome, 124
Maimonides (Moses ben Maimon)
    Christian culture, Jewish engagement
        with, 75
    Guide of the Perplexed, 82, 271, 272
    Jacob ben Asher's legal schematic
        replacing work of, 267
    law manual of, 266
    Mishneh-Torah, 266
    Muslim Spain, transfer of family to
        Egypt from, 96
    philosophical speculation, Jewish
        tradition of, 267, 271–273, 274
    southern-French Jews and, 82, 83, 84,
        86
    southern-Italian and Sicilian Jews and,
        119
    Spanish Jews and, 104
    translations by Samuel ibn Tibbon, 269,
        272
Mainz Anonymous, 176–181, 279–280
*Maqama of Hell and Heaven, The (Maḥberet
    ha-Tofet ve-ha'Eden)* of Immanuel of
    Rome, 124
Martinez, Ferrand, 106
martyrdom, Jewish. *See* Jewish suffering
    and martyrdom
Mary, mother of Jesus, and Jewish religious
    sensibilities, 105

Mathilda (empress and putative ruler of
England), 157
medicine and science, Jewish involvement
in
Muslim Spain, 92
southern Italy and Sicily, 117, 119
Mediterranean Europe, older Jewish
communities of, 77–78. *See also*
Italy; southern France; Spain
Megillat Ahima'az of Ahimaaz ben Paltiel,
117
Meir bar Simon of Narbonne (rabbi),
86–87, 256, 308
Menahem ben Solomon Meiri of
Perpignan (rabbi), or the Meiri, 88
Meshullam ben R. Isaac of Worms,
179–180
Mesopotamian Jews, 1
Milhamot ha-Shem of Jacob ben Reuben,
63, 100–101, 248, 250, 262
Milhemet Mizvah (*The Obligatory War*) of
Rabbi Meir bar Simon, 86
milk of Christian wet nurses to Jewish
children, 48
millenarian expectations and anti-Jewish
sentiment, 178, 304
Mishnah, 40, 41
Mishneh-Torah of Maimonides,
266
missionizing, proselytization, and
conversion, 247–257
Barcelona disputation, 63–65, 101,
102–105, 244, 251, 252, 256,
281
biblical exegesis, use of, 249
Christian emphasis on, 28, 38
disputation as means of
Barcelona disputation, 63–65, 101,
102–105, 244, 251, 252, 256, 281
ecclesiastical policies regarding, 63–65,
66
forced attendance of Jews at, 249
in northern France, 149, 152
Paris disputation, 149, 251, 252
in Spain, 101 (*See also under* Spain,
Jewish communities of)
Tortosa disputation, 66, 108, 252,
256
ecclesiastical policy on, 62–66
in England
Domus conversorum, establishment of,
163

expulsion of 1290, conversion in face
of, 165
York riots, attempts at accepting
conversion in, 161
forced attendance of Jews at debates and
sermons, 249
forced conversion
Church policy against, 52, 212
Constitutio pro Judeis forbidding, 52
in Germany (*See subhead* missionizing,
proselytization, and conversion,
under Germany, Jewish communities
of)
in Muslim Spain, 98
New Christians of Spain, problems
raised by, 109
formal campaign of, 249, 251
general creativity of medieval Christian
renaissance tending to spur, 71–73,
246
in Germany (*See* Germany, Jewish
communities of)
homogeneity, reflecting Christian desire
for, 211, 248
Islam
forced conversions in Muslim Spain,
98
Jewish conversion to, 26, 28
Jews restricted as to, 35
language training for, 249
maintenance of Jewish faith and identity
in face of, 245–246, 257
New Christians of Spain (*See* New
Christians of Spain)
in northern France, 149 (*See also subhead*
Paris disputation, *this entry*)
northern- vs. southern-European Jewish
engagement with Christian culture
and, 244
observable reality of Christian vs. Jewish
circumstances, arguments based on,
71–73, 248, 250
Paris disputation, 149, 251,
252
philosophical principles/reason, use of,
250
Provençal Jews, conversion rather than
expulsion chosen by, 88, 308
rabbinic literature, utilization of, 249,
251–252, 258
rebuttals by Jews (*See* Jewish polemical
literature)

missionizing, proselytization, and
conversion (*cont.*)
richer Christian knowledge of Jewish
and Muslim thought gained by, 101
in Spain (*See under* Spain, Jewish
communities of)
successes in, 255–257
New Christians of Spain (*See* New
Christians of Spain)
Provençal Jews, conversion rather than
expulsion chosen by, 88, 308
reasons for, 257
Rhineland persecutions of 1096,
baptisms undertaken to avoid, 178,
179
Tortosa disputation, 66, 108, 252
wealthy and learned converts,
significance attached to, 256, 307
Tortosa disputation, 66, 108, 252, 256
use of Jewish converts
blood libel, Frederick II's use of
converts to investigate, 192
as evidence of Christian success and
danger to Jewish identity, 256, 307
knowledge of and access to Jewish
tradition via, 249
mobility as characteristic of Jews, 127, 132,
216, 286–287
moneylending by Jews, 217–219
abolition of
in England, 166
in northern France, 148–149, 152–153
crusaders, 60–61, 138
ecclesiastical objections to, 58–62, 126,
134, 144–146, 223
ecclesiastical protection of, 54–55
England, royal exploitation of Jewish
finances in (*See under* England,
Jewish communities of)
expulsions resulting from, 62
in Germany, 172, 187, 188, 189–190
greater significance in northern vs.
southern areas, 301
in Hungary, 200
landed property, lending against, 133,
189, 218
negative imagery and perception of
harmfulness, contributing to, 213
niche economy, Jewish legacy of,
233–235
in northern France (*See under* northern
France, Jewish communities of)

in northern Italy, 125–126
pawnbroking (*See* pawnbroking by Jews)
in Poland, 203, 205, 206
political backing for, 222
ecclesiastical restrictions, government
resistance to, 223
German lack of, 181–182
governmental protections used for
exploitative purposes, 226
in northern France, 133–134, 147
revival of lending practices by Christians
possibly leading to expendability of,
221
sacred objects used as collateral, 59
in southern France, 80
in Spain, 98
usury
Christians restricted from, 56
Fourth Lateran Council's definition of
excessive Jewish usury, 145
Mongol invasions, 199, 201, 203, 206
Moses ben Maimon. *See* Maimonides
Moses ben Nahman. *See* Nahmanides
Moses de Leon, 277
Moses of Bristol, 158
Mundill, Robin, 156
murder of Christians. *See* blood libel and
ritual murder, beliefs regarding
Muslim cultures. *See* Islam, Jews living
under
mysticism, 275–277
biblical study and exegesis influenced by,
263
Christian mysticism as influence on
Jewish mysticism, 105, 275, 276
as developed by Jewish and Christian
cultures, 75
German pietism and, 183, 186–187,
277
in Germany, 187
Islam's lack of influence on, 276
kabbalah
in southern France, 84
in Spain, 105
rabbinic literature and culture affected
by, 258
in southern-French Jewish communities,
83–84, 276
in southern Italy and Sicily, 118, 120
in Spain, 104–105
transmission from southern to northern
Europe, 170

Zohar (*The Book of Illumination*), 75, 105, 263, 276, 277

Nahmanides (Moses ben Nahman)
  Barcelona disputation, 63–65, 101, 102–105, 244, 251, 281
  as mystic, 276
  as philosopher, 101–102
  as talmudic and biblical scholar, 103, 261
Nathan ben Yehiel of Rome, 123
negative imagery and perception of harmfulness, 213–215. *See also* blasphemy of Jews, beliefs regarding; blood libel and ritual murder, beliefs regarding; crucifixion, Jews blamed for; host desecration by Jews, beliefs regarding
  Alexander of Hales on, 47–48, 50
  corporate Jewish crime and punishment, notions of, 227
  dynamics of deterioration in European Jewish communities and, 239–242
  ecclesiastical policy regarding, 55–62
  ecclesiastical projections of, 66–70
  economic activities of Jews contributing to, 213
  in England, 156–158, 159–160, 163–164, 166
  folk memory vs. reality of Jewish contributions, 285–288
  in Germany, 173, 184–185, 187, 191–198
  in northern France, 134–136, 150–151
  in Poland, 207
  prior to 1000, 34–36, 67
  in Spain, 98
  Talmud, 70, 225–231
negative Jewish folk memories of European experience, 286
New Christians of Spain
  anti-Jewish violence, 1370s–1391, 106
  Christianity challenged by, 109
  conversions of 1391, 106–111, 256
  heresy and inquisition, 110–113
  increased missionizing in wake of conversions, 107–108
  philosophy blamed for conversions of, 107
  racist emphasis on biology and, 109
  Rhineland Jews' response to persecution compared, 107
New Testament, Jewish knowledge and criticism of, 255

newness of Jews and Judaism to large areas of Europe, 215
Norman rule in southern Italy and Sicily, 118
northern Europe, Jewish communities of, 129–131. *See also entries at* eastern Europe, England, Germany, northern France
  contemporary narratives composed in, 279
  economic opportunities in, 217
  engagement with majority culture, depth of, 244
  southern-European Jewish culture compared, 282–283
  utter newness of Jews and Judaism, 215
northern France, Jewish communities of, 131–132
  baronial and royal protections of 11th–12th centuries, 132, 134, 137–138
  blood libel and ritual murder, accusations of, 136, 150–151
  Capetian consolidations and movements against Jews, 141
    stages of, 146
    under Philip Augustus, 141–146
    under Louis VIII and early reign of Louis IX, 142
    mature reign of Louis XI and Philip III, 148–150
    under Philip the Fair, 150–152
    enhanced royal control of Jews, 143–144, 152
  captio or confiscation of Jewish goods, 142, 144, 146, 151, 153
  crusades and crusading, effects of, 135–136, 137–138, 148
  cultural, intellectual, and spiritual life, 139–141, 147–148, 152
  disputations between Jews and Christians, 149, 152
  economic life of, 132–135, 152
  English Jewry originating in, 154
  expulsions of Jews from
    baronial expulsions of 1190s, 141, 143
    Philip Augustus's expulsion of Jews from royal domain in 1182, 142, 143, 151, 229, 230
    readmission of Jews to royal domain in 1198, 143

northern France, Jewish communities of
(*cont.*)
Louis IX's expulsion of Jews unwilling
to observe anti-usury legislation,
229, 230
local expulsions at end of 13th
century, 229
Philip the Fair's expulsion of 1306,
141, 151–152, 230
readmission of Jews to royal domain in
1315, 152–153
final expulsion of 1394, 153
German absorption of refugees, 194
immigrant status of, 154
languages used by, 140
missionizing, proselytization, and
conversion efforts against, 149 (*See
also subhead* Paris disputation, *this
entry*)
moneylending by Jews, 132–135
abolition of usury under Louis IX and
Philip III, 148–149
ecclesiastical objections to, 134,
144–146
erosion of system under Louis VIII
and Louis IX, 146–147
forbidding of usury under Louis X,
152–153
governmental backing of, 133–134,
147
readmission of Jews to royal domain in
1198, reasons for, 143
remission of debts owed to Jews in,
103, 138, 142, 146
restrictions and rules established by
Philip Augustus, 143, 145
negative imagery and perception of
harmfulness in, 134–136,
150–151
organization and inter-communal
cooperation of, 138–139
Paris disputation, 149, 251, 252
source materials for, 14, 131,
132
southern France, Capetian conquest of,
86–87
synagogues, confiscation of, 142, 153
Talmud, confiscation and burning of,
147–148, 267
northern Italy. *See under* Italy, Jewish
communities of
Norwich blood libel incident, 157–158

Obligatory War, The (*Milḥemet Miẓvah*) of
Rabbi Meir bar Simon, 86
observable reality of Christian vs. Jewish
circumstances
Christian missionizing arguments based
on, 71–73, 248, 250
Jewish polemical literature's
counter-arguments to, 250, 253–255
Observantine Franciscans' objections to
moneylending, 126
Oral Torah. *See* Talmud and talmudic study
organization of Jewish communities, 222
German Jews, self-government rights of,
173, 188
inter-community relationships,
development of, 138–139, 238
in northern France, 138–139
in Poland, 207

Palestinian Jews, 1
Palestinian Talmud, 41
papacy. *See also* Roman Catholic Church,
and particular popes
Jews of papal states (*See under* Italy,
Jewish communities of)
source materials for Jewish history and,
14
Paris disputation, 149, 251, 252
Passover ritual and blood libel, 185–192
Paul (apostle), 31–32, 44, 67, 211, 274
Paul Christian (friar)
Barcelona disputation, 63–65, 101,
102–105, 108, 244, 251–252, 281
Paris disputation, 149, 251–252
pawnbroking by Jews, 218. *See also*
moneylending by Jews
in Germany, 182, 189–190, 197
governmental backing of, 223
in Poland, 205
perceptions of Jews. *See* negative imagery
and perception of harmfulness
Peter the Hermit, 136, 178
Peter the Venerable of Cluny, 48, 68, 136,
228
Petrus Alfonsi, 48
Philip Augustus (king of France), 133, 138,
141–146, 151, 225, 229, 230
Philip III (king of France), 149
Philip IV the Fair (king of France), 87, 88,
141, 150–152
Philo of Alexandria, 271
philosophy, 270–275

biblical study and exegesis influenced by, 262–263, 272–274
as central to Jewish life and spirituality, 275
Christian development of, 72
controversy over, 272–274
Jewish development of, 74
Jewish law, Maimonides' recognition of philosophical underpinnings of, 267
Jewish polemical literature's use of, 253, 255
Maimonides and, 267, 271–273, 274
missionizing use of, 250
mysticism as alternative to, 84
rabbinic literature and culture affected by, 258
relativization of divinity and religious praxis, fears regarding, 273
in southern France, 82, 84
in southern Italy and Sicily, 119–120
in Spain, 103–104, 107
physicians, Jews as
    Muslim Spain, 92
    southern Italy and Sicily, 117, 119
Piast dynasty of Poland, 201
pietism, German, 183, 186–187, 277
plague
    in Germany, 194, 195–196
    in Hungary, 201
    in northern Italy, 125
    papal attempts to protect Jews during, 196
    in Poland, 206
    in Spain, 105–106
poetry, Jewish tradition of, 124, 140, 270
Poland, Jewish communities of, 201–208.
    See also eastern Europe, Jewish communities of
    blood libel and ritual murder, accusations of, 204, 207
    Casimir the Great, reign of, 206
    charter of Boleslav of Kalisch (1264), 203–204, 206
    communal structure of, 207
    cultural, intellectual, and spiritual life, 205, 208
    ecclesiastical pressure to restrict, 207
    economic life of, 203, 204, 206
    expulsions from rest of Europe leading to immigration to, 203

immigrant urban dwellers, Polish encouragement of, 200
Mongol invasions, 203, 206
negative imagery and perception of harmfulness, 207
origins of, 202–203
plague in, 206
relationship between monarchy and nobility, repercussions of, 201–202
Yiddish, persistence of, 205–206
polemics, Jewish. *See* Jewish polemical literature
politics, government, and Jews, 219–231.
    See also organization of Jewish communities
    anti-Jewish actions by ruling authorities, 225–231
    dynamics of deterioration in European Jewish communities and, 239–242
    ecclesiastical restrictions, resistance to, 223
    economic exploitation of Jews, 225–226, 242 (*See also under* England, Jewish communities of)
    economic motivations for supporting Jews, 220–221
    Germany, ramifications of lack of governmental power in, 181–182, 187–194, 197
    in Hungary, 200–201
    moneylending, backing for (*See under* moneylending by Jews)
    northern France
        Capetian consolidations in (*See under* northern France, Jewish communities of)
        governmental backing of moneylending by Jews in, 133–134, 147
    physical protection of Jews by ruling authorities, 221–222
    religion-based motivations of authorities, 226–227
    serfdom of Jews, 225
        German imperial support and exploitation, general lack of, 181–182, 187–194
        northern France, enhanced royal control of Jews in, 143–144, 152
    in Spain, 97, 98
    strong vs. weak rulers, advantages and disadvantages of, 223–224

politics, government, and Jews (*cont.*)
  success of Jews at negotiating medieval
    power structures, 222
  taxation (*See* taxation of Jews)
polygamy, Rabbi Gershom of Mainz's
  forbidding of, 175
polytheists, Muslim treatment of, 24
Portugal, 114, 227, 231
preaching. *See* sermons
printing houses established by Jews in
    northern Italy, 127
prior legacies, 23
  Christian legacy, 27–38 (*See also*
    Christian legacy prior to 1000)
  Greco-Roman (*See* Greco–Roman
    legacy)
  Islam, 24–27 (*See also* Islam, Jews living
    under)
  Jewish legacy, 38–42 (*See also* Jewish
    legacy prior to 1000; Jews in
    Europe prior to 1000)
proselytization. *See* missionizing,
    proselytization, and conversion
protection of Jews. *See* rights of and
    restrictions on Jews
Provençal Jews. *See also* southern France,
    Jewish communities of
  conversion rather than expulsion chosen
    by, 88, 308
Pugio fidei of Raymond Martin, 65, 101,
    252

Qumran community/Dead Sea Scrolls, 31,
    33

rabbinic literature and culture, 257–267. *See
    also* biblical study and exegesis;
    Talmud and talmudic studies
  in Germany, 175, 185, 198
  Jewish polemics making use of, 253,
    258
  language and grammar studies affecting,
    258
  missionizing leading to richer Christian
    knowledge of, 101
  missionizing use of, 249, 251–252, 258
  mysticism affecting, 258
  in northern France, 140–141
  philosophy affecting, 258
  Rashi's sympathy for, 260
  in Rome and papal states, 123
  in southern France, 80–81

in southern Italy and Sicily, 119
  Spain, ecclesiastical concerns in, 98
rabbinic *responsum*, 264
rabbis, leadership role of, 222
racist emphasis on biology in Spain, 109
Ralph (Cistercian monk), 53
Rashi (Rabbi Solomon ben Isaac of
    Troyes), 140–141, 175, 244, 260,
    261, 265, 267
Raymond Berenguer IV, count of
    Barcelona, 95
Raymond Martin (friar), 65, 101, 252
Raymond Penaforte, 47
restrictions on Jews. *See* rights of and
    restrictions on Jews
Rewards of the Soul, The (*Tagmulei ha-Nefesh*)
    of Hillel ben Samuel, 120
Rhineland Jews. *See* Germany, Jewish
    communities of
Richard I the Lionheart (king of England),
    160–161
Richardson, H. G., 156
rights of and restrictions on Jews
  accelerating emphasis on limitation over
    protection, 52
  Alexander of Hales on, 45–50
  Augustinian synthesis of, 36–38
  Constitutio pro Judeis, 50–51, 52
  ecclesiastical policy regarding, 51–66
  German charters and grants, 172–174,
    179, 184, 188–190
  Hungary, ecclesiastic pressure to impose
    limitations on Jews of, 200
  intercessory role of Jews in Rome and
    papal states, 122–123
  under Islam, 24–25
  northern France
    enhanced royal controls under Philip
      Augustus, 143–144
    protection of Jews by royal and
      baronial patrons in 11th and 12th
      century, 132, 134, 137–138
  in Poland, 203–204, 207
  protection of Jews by Church
    authorities, 52–55, 70, 196, 212
  protection of Jews by governing
    authorities, 221–222
  Roman Empire, 36
  ruling authorities, role of (*See* politics,
    government, and Jews)
  secondary status of Jews (*See* secondary
    status of Jews within Christendom)

theological position of Roman Catholic Church regarding, 44–51

Rigord of St. Denis, 133, 142, 143, 229

Rindfleisch massacres, 194

ritualized murder by Jews, beliefs regarding. *See* blood libel and ritual murder, beliefs regarding

Roman Catholic Church, 43–44

  beginnings of ecclesiastical organization, 34

  Councils

    Elvira, Council of, 34, 35

    Fourth Lateran Council, 48, 56, 61, 145, 163, 189

    Third Lateran Council, 55, 163

  cultural and spiritual creativity of medieval renaissance, effects of, 70–75

  diversity and unity of medieval Western Europe typified by, 43–44, 75–76

  dynamics of deterioration in European Jewish communities and, 239–242

  German imperial rivalry with papacy, effects on Jews of, 187, 190

  governmental resistance to restrictions of, 223

  moneylending by Jews

    ecclesiastical objections to, 58–62, 126, 134, 144–146, 223

    ecclesiastical protection of, 54–55

  negative imagery and perception of harmfulness projected by, 66–70

  papal rhetoric reflecting general Christian desire for homogeneity, 211

  policies of, 51–66

  protection of Jews by, 52–55, 70, 196, 212

  Spain, Jewish communities of, 98

  theological doctrine of (*See* theological doctrine on Jews and Judaism)

Roman Empire. *See* Christian legacy prior to 1000; Greco–Roman legacy

Roman history, Italian Jewish interest in, and *Book of Josippon*, 277

Rome, Jews of. *See under* Italy, Jewish communities of

Roth, Cecil, 159

Rudiger (Huozmann), bishop of Speyer, 171–173, 178, 188, 220

ruling authorities. *See* politics, government, and Jews

Saadia Gaon, 259, 261, 262, 266, 268

sacrifice of son of Meshullam ben R. Isaac of Worms, 179–180

Samuel ben Meir (rabbi) of Ramerupt, 139, 261

Scaccarium Aaronis, 159

science and medicine, Jewish involvement in

  Muslim Spain, 92

  southern Italy and Sicily, 117, 119

Scripture. *See* biblical study and exegesis

secondary status of Jews within Christendom, 39–40, 212

  observable reality of Christian vs. Jewish circumstances

    Christian missionizing arguments based on, 71–73, 248, 250

    Jewish polemical literature's counter-arguments to, 250, 253–255

  sense of Jewish superiority despite general creativity of medieval Christian renaissance challenging, 246–247

    Jewish polemical literature encouraging, 245, 255

    persecutions of Rhineland Jews in 1096 and, 73

Sefer ha-Bahir (*The Book of Brilliance*), 83, 84

Sefer ha-Berit of Joseph Kimhi, 248, 262

Sefer ha-Kabbalah (*The Book of Tradition*) of Abraham ibn Daud, 96, 278

Sefer Hasidim, 186

Sefer Milḥamot Adonai (*The Book of the Wars of the Lord*) of Gersonides, 89

Sefer Nizzaḥon Yashan, 262

Sefer Yezirah, 118

Sefer Yosef ha-Mekane, 262

Sefer Yosippon (*Book of Josippon*), 117, 277, 279

segregation and ghettoization, ecclesiastical policy regarding, 55, 213

Sephardic Jews, 89, 91, 114, 282–283, 291, 310

serfdom of Jews, 225

  German imperial support and exploitation, general lack of, 181–182, 187–194

serfdom of Jews (*cont.*)
  northern France, enhanced royal control
    of Jews in, 143–144, 152
sermons
  counter–missionizing sermon of Rabbi
    Meir bar Simon of Narbonne, 308
  forced attendance of Jews at missionizing
    sermons and debates, 249
  popular biblical study and exegesis in,
    259
sexual mores of Christians, Jewish criticism
  of, 255
Shatzmiller, Joseph, 218
Sicily. *See under* Italy, Jewish communities of
Simon bar Yohai, 277
slave-owners, Jews as, 34, 35, 174
social abuses in Christian society, Jewish
  criticism of, 255
Solomon ben Abraham, 274
Solomon ben Isaac of Troyes (rabbi) or
    Rashi, 140–141, 175, 244, 260, 261,
    265, 267
southern Europe, Jewish communities of,
    77–78. *See also* Italy, southern
    France, *and* Spain
  engagement with majority culture, depth
    of, 244
  linguistic and cultural unity of, 78
  northern-European Jewish culture
    compared, 282–283
southern France, Jewish communities of, 78
  Capetian conquest of, 86–87
  cultural, intellectual, and spiritual life of,
    80–85, 88–89, 276
  disappearance of, 89–90
  economic activities, 79
  expulsions of 1306, 79, 87–88
  heresy, association of area with, 81, 85
  language of, 78
  philosophy practiced in, 82, 84
  prior to 1000, 78
  rabbinic culture, 80–81
  source materials for, 14
southern Italy and Sicily. *See under* Italy,
    Jewish communities of
Spain, Jewish communities of, 90–91
  Barcelona disputation, 63–65, 101,
    102–105, 244, 251, 252, 256, 281
  baronial resentment of, 98
  Christian reconquest
    11th–12th centuries, 93–97
    13th century, 97

15th century, 114
    anti-Muslim sentiment extended to
      Jews, 93–94
    positive relationship of Jews to
      Christian reconquerors, 93–95,
      97–98
  cultural, intellectual, and spiritual life,
    92–93, 102–105
  economic life of, 92, 97–98, 216
  expulsion of, 89, 113–115, 227, 228,
    231
  heresy and inquisition in
    Ferdinand and Isabella's fervor for, 114
    New Christians, 110–113
  ibn Daud's memorial to, in *Sefer
    ha-Kabbalah*, 278
  Italy compared, 90
  languages of, 92
  Languedoc, Aragon's attempt to
    conquer, 86
  marriage of Ferdinand and Isabella and
    uniting of Aragon and Castile, 113
  medicine, Jewish involvement in, 92
  missionizing, proselytization, and
    conversion
    Barcelona disputation, 63–65, 101,
      102–105, 244, 251, 252, 256, 281
    Christian efforts, 98
    conversions of 1391, 106–111 (*See also*
      New Christians of Spain)
    formal disputations, 101
    increased missionizing following 1391
      conversions, 107–108
    modern historiography of, 299
    Muslim Spain, forced conversions in,
      98
    Tortosa disputation, 66, 108, 252, 256
  moneylending activities, 98
  Muslim Spain
    conquest by Muslims, 91
    cultural, intellectual, and spiritual life,
      92–93
    diaspora of Jews from, 95–97, 118
    interlude of Muslim rule, 92–93
    persecution of Jews in, 98, 118
    profound effect of, 90–91
  New Christians (*See* New Christians of
    Spain)
  plague in, 105–106
  political power of, 97, 98
  prior to 1000, 91–92
  regional differences, 299

Roman Catholic Church and, 98
Sephardic Jews, 89, 91, 291
source materials for, 14
southern Italy and Sicily, Aragonese rule
    in, 118, 120
Tortosa disputation, 66, 108, 252, 256
Visigothic Spain, 91–92, 228
Speyer Jewry
    founding of, 171–174
    persecution of 1096 (*See under* Germany,
        Jewish communities of)
spiritual life. *See* cultural, intellectual, and
    spiritual life
Stacey, Robert, 156, 164–165
Stephen (king of England), 157
subject status of Jews within Christendom.
    See secondary status of Jews within
    Christendom
suffering, Jewish. *See* Jewish suffering and
    martyrdom
Summa theologica of Alexander of Hales,
    45–50
superiority, Jewish sense of
    general creativity of medieval Christian
        renaissance challenging, 246–247
    Jewish polemical literature encouraging,
        245, 255
    persecutions of Rhineland Jews in 1096
        and, 73
synagogues
    confiscation in northern France, 142,
        153
    in Hungary, 201
    poetry of, 270
    popular biblical exegesis in, 259–260
    prior to 1000, 41
    sermons, 259
Syrian Jews, 2, 3

Tagmulei ha-Nefesh (*The Rewards of the Soul*)
    of Hillel ben Samuel, 120
Talmud and talmudic studies, 41, 263–267
    Alexander of Hales on, 46, 48–49, 50
    Babylonian Talmud, dominance of, 26,
        39, 40, 41, 264
    blasphemy, Talmud perceived as, 56–58,
        70, 98, 147–148, 225–231, 267
    blood libel investigations and, 193
    canon law study paralleling innovations
        in study of, 74, 266
    centralized institutions for, lack of, 264
    commentaries, 264–266

confiscation and burning of Talmud in
    northern France, 147–148, 267
    ecclesiastical policy regarding, 56–58,
        98
    in Germany, 175, 185, 198
    manuals of Jewish law, 266–267
    negative imagery and perception of
        harmfulness and, 70, 225–231
    in northern France, 139–141, 147–148,
        152
    Palestinian Talmud, 41
    rabbinic *responsum*, 264
    Rashi (Rabbi Solomon ben Isaac of
        Troyes), 140–141, 175, 244, 260,
        261, 265, 267
    in Rome and papal states, 123
    in southern France, 80–81
    in southern Italy and Sicily, 117
    in Spain, 98, 103
    Tosafists, 265–266, 267, 309
taxation of Christians for local expulsion of
    Jews from Anjou and Maine, 230
taxation of Jews
    in England, 159, 162, 164–165
    under Islam, 24–25
    Polish and Hungarian Jews as tax
        farmers, 206
    ruling authorities' support/exploitation
        of Jews and, 221, 225–226
Theobald, count of Blois, 137, 138, 151
theological doctrine on Jews and Judaism
    Augustinian synthesis, formulation of,
        36–38
    Constitutio pro Judeis, 50–51
    development of Church views as to,
        44–51
    Summa theologica of Alexander of Hales,
        45–50
Third Lateran Council, 55, 163
Thomas Aquinas, 72
Thomas of Monmouth, 150, 157–158,
    303
Tortosa disputation, 66, 108, 252, 256
Tosafists, 265–266, 267, 309
Tovey, Blossier de, 155
translations of texts
    Christian practice and use of, 72, 268
    Christian translations, Jewish
        involvement in, 118, 268, 269
    in Italy, 118
    Jewish polemical criticism of Jerome's
        Latin Bible, 253

translations of texts (*cont.*)
  Jewish translation of Judeo-Arabic and
    Arabic texts into Hebrew, 118,
    268–269
Trinity, Jewish polemical literature's attacks
  on doctrine of, 253
Turkish Empire, Spanish exiles moving to,
  114

Urban II (pope), 46, 52, 135
usury. *See also* moneylending by Jews
  Christians restricted from, 56
  Fourth Lateran Council's definition of
    excessive Jewish usury, 145

Visigothic Spain, Jews of, 91–92, 228
Vives of Cambridge, 158

wet nurses to Jewish children, Christian
  women as, 48

William I the Conqueror (king of
    England), 154, 171–174
William of Norwich, 157–158
Written Torah. *See* biblical study and
    exegesis
Wurzburg blood libel incident, 184

Yehiel of Paris (rabbi), 57
Yerushalmi, Yosef Hayim, 18
Yiddish, Polish Jews' use of,
    205–206
York, attacks on Jews at, 160
Yosippon, 117, 277,
    279

Zimberlin, John, 195
Zipporah, wife of Meshullam ben R. Isaac
    of Worms, 179–180
Zohar (*The Book of Illumination*), 75, 105,
    263, 276, 277

Cambridge Medieval Textbooks

Already published

Germany in the High Middle Ages *c.* 1050–1200
HORST FUHRMANN

The Hundred Years War
England and France at War *c.* 1300–*c.* 1450
CHRISTOPHER ALLMAND

Standards of Living in the Later Middle Ages
Social Change in England, *c.* 1200–1520
CHRISTOPHER DYER

Magic in the Middle Ages
RICHARD KIECKHEFER

The Papacy 1073–1198: Continuity and Innovation
I. S. ROBINSON

Medieval Wales
DAVID WALKER

England in the Reign of Edward III
SCOTT L. WAUGH

The Norman Kingdom of Sicily
DONALD MATTHEW

Political Thought in Europe 1250–1450
ANTONY BLACK

The Church in Western Europe from the Tenth to the Early
Twelfth Century
GERD TELLENBACH
Translated by Timothy Reuter

The Medieval Spains
BERNARD F. REILLY

England in the Thirteenth Century
ALAN HARDING

Monastic and Religious Orders in Britain 1000–1300
JANET BURTON

Religion and Devotion in Europe *c.* 1215–*c.* 1515
R. N. SWANSON

Medieval Russia, 980–1584
JANET MARTIN

The Wars of the Roses: Politics and the Constitution in England,
c. 1437–1509
CHRISTINE CARPENTER

The Waldensian Dissent: Persecution and Survival, *c.* 1170–*c.* 1570
GABRIEL AUDISIO
Translated by Claire Davison

The Crusades, *c.* 1071–*c.* 1291
JEAN RICHARD
Translated by Jean Birrell

A History of Business in Medieval Europe, 1200–1550
EDWIN S. HUNT, JAMES MURRAY

Medieval Economic Thought
DIANA WOOD

Medieval Scotland
A. D. M. BARRELL

Roger II of Sicily
A Ruler between East and West
HUBERT HOUBEN
Translated by Graham A. Loud, Diane Milburn

The Carolingian Economy
ADRIAAN VERHULST

Women in Early Medieval Europe, 400–1100
LISA M. BITEL

Southeastern Europe in the Middle Ages, 500–1250
FLORIN CURTA